The Turn
of the Mind

Constituting Consciousness
in Henry James

Adré Marshall

Madison • Teaneck
Fairleigh Dickinson University Press
London: Associated University Presses

828
J27xmrs

Associated University Presses
440 Forsgate Drive
Cranbury, NJ 08512

Associated University Presses
16 Barter Street
London WC1A 2AH, England

Associated University Presses
P.O. Box 338, Port Credit
Mississauga, Ontario
Canada L5G 4L8

The paper used in this publication meets the requirements of the American National Standard for Permanence of Paper for Printed Library Materials Z39.48–1984.

Library of Congress Cataloging-in-Publication Data

Marshall, Adré, 1942–
    The turn of the mind : constituting consciousness in Henry James / Adré Marshall.
        p.   cm.
    Incudes bibliographical references and index.
    ISBN 0-8386-3695-0 (alk. paper)
    1. James, Henry, 1843–1916—Knowledge—Psychology.
    2. Psychological fiction, American—History and criticism.
    3. James, Henry, 1843–1916—Technique.   4. Consciousness in literature.   5. Narration (Rhetoric)   I. Title.
    PS2127.P8M37   1998
    813'.4—dc21   97-18972
                                                                             CIP

PRINTED IN THE UNITED STATES OF AMERICA

AEJ-5366

The Turn
of the Mind

Contents

For my family

Abbreviations

The following abbreviations are used:

AN   *The Art of the Novel*
Amb   *The Ambassadors*
GB   *The Golden Bowl*
NYE   New York Edition
PL   *The Portrait of a Lady*
RH   *Roderick Hudson*
WW   *Watch and Ward*

Acknowledgments

I am grateful to many friends and colleagues who helped directly or indirectly to bring this project to completion. Special thanks go to Gail Fincham, who has supported and guided this study since its inception, and has been most generous with her time and her perceptive appraisals. Her constructive criticism contributed greatly to the clarification of my ideas. I appreciate too the interest and encouragement of Peter Knox-Shaw and the good-humored efficiency with which Sue Buchanan coped with practical matters such as the complicated transatlantic exchanges.

I am indebted also to others further afield, such as Kenneth Graham, for his interest and useful suggestions, and Mary Paterson, who initially stimulated my enthusiasm for James.

My thanks go especially to my family, for their constant sympathetic support, ability to handle a recalcitrant computer, and assistance with proof-reading.

Acknowledgement is made to Princeton University Press for permission to reprint copyrighted material from the following publication: Cohn Dorrit, *Transparent Minds: Narrative Modes for Presenting Consciousness in Fiction.* Copyright 1978 by PUP. Reprinted by permission of Princeton University Press.

Where possible, the edition used has been the New York Edition of *The Novels and Tales of Henry James.* Reference to the novels and longer tales such as "The Beast in the Jungle" are usually from this edition. For some of the shorter tales, I have used *The Collected Tales of Henry James,* edited and introduced by Leon Edel. For novels that are not included in the New York Edition, I have generally used the Penguin Edition.

The Turn
of the Mind

1

Introduction

> The novel is of all pictures the most comprehensive and the
> most elastic. It will stretch anywhere—it will take in absolutely
> anything. All it needs is a subject and a painter. But for its
> subject, magnificently, it has the whole human consciousness.
> Henry James, "The Future of the Novel"

YET another book on Henry James—is it possible that after more than
a hundred and fifty years and considerably more than that number of
books on the Master there is still anything new to discuss? James has
probably generated more critical comment than any author after Shakespeare, yet it seems that *Ex James semper aliquid novi*—that there are,
indeed, still discoveries to be made, still unexamined figures in that vener-
able well-trodden carpet.

This study represents yet another turn on, and of, that pictorial carpet,
to examine the intricacies of its composition in a new light; it focuses on
various facets of the kaleidoscopic representation of consciousness in
James—hence "the turn of the mind."

As the quotation cited above indicates, James held that the novel's
primary focus is the presentation of consciousness: "for its subject, magnificently, [the novel] has the whole human consciousness." Indeed, in the
course of his novelistic career, his works reveal an increasing emphasis on
the representation of consciousness as his fictional world becomes ever
more consistently filtered through the consciousness of one or more "reflectors." Yet the complex repertoire of formal devices James deployed
in his portrayal of consciousness (and the implications of these procedures) have not as yet been examined systematically. This, then, is the
central concern of the present study: for its subject, ambitiously, it has
"[the whole] human consciousness" as depicted in the novels of Henry
James.

Given James's conception of the novel's subject and his emphasis on
its "comprehensiveness" and "elasticity," any critical approach to his own

oeuvre should ideally be equipped with a comparable capacity to "stretch anywhere" in its attempt to elucidate the subtleties and complexities of his presentation of consciousness. Many commentators, including James himself, have provided comments on his narrative strategies, but none elucidates adequately the techniques he deployed in this portrayal. In this analysis, then, I make use of relevant findings of earlier commentators while simultaneously indicating the necessity for creating new critical categories when the existing taxonomy does not stretch far enough to cover previously unidentified facets of James's technique. Throughout, I attempt to adopt an approach with sufficient comprehensiveness and elasticity to encompass all the salient features of James's strategies for depicting fictional consciousness.

In this exploration of James's "art to find the mind's construction"[1] the notion of "constituting consciousness in Henry James" has a manifold reference. It refers primarily to the multifaceted process through which James represented the consciousness of his characters in his works. This was achieved through an act of imaginative possession or assimilation, of "getting into the skin of the creature"[2]—an ability which James found supremely manifested in the works of the French novelist Balzac. What James says about Balzac is clearly equally applicable to himself:

> he . . . loved the sense of another explored, assumed, assimilated identity—
> enjoyed it as the hand enjoys the glove when the glove ideally fits. . . . What
> he liked was absolutely to get into the constituted consciousness . . . of the
> . . . articulated form of life that he desired to present.[3]

Surprisingly, although James's ability to "get into the constituted consciousness" of his characters is often acknowledged, if only implicitly, little attention has been paid not only to the range of techniques adopted in doing so but also the progressive modulation in the stylistic means whereby consciousness is constituted. This, then, is my major focus.

The notion of constituting consciousness also encompasses the process whereby the reader of James's texts attains understanding both of the consciousness of the characters and, ideally, the methods deployed in their portrayal. In the process, one hopes, readers themselves undergo an extension of consciousness. Through immersion in the novel, readers are enabled to participate vicariously in an alternative "reality"; as James says,

> The great thing to say for them [novelists] is surely that at any given moment
> they offer us [readers] another world, another consciousness, an experience
> that, as effective as the dentist's ether, muffles the ache of the actual.[4]

James highlights the analogy between the activity of consciousness in the reader, the author, and the central characters undergoing (albeit in different ways) a "process of vision." In the preface to *The American*, for example, James asserts that "the interest of everything is all that it is *his* [the 'reflector's'] vision, *his* conception, *his* interpretation: at the window of his wide . . . consciousness we are seated, from that admirable position we 'assist'" (*AN* 37).

Readers, of course, "assist" (in the French sense of being present at, rather than actively participating as suggested by the English use of "assist," which is synonymous with "help") in widely differing ways. James distinguishes between the reader who responds to "the appeal to wonder and terror and curiosity and pity and to the delight of fine recognitions" (*AN* 253) and the even more sought-after reader, that rara avis who is prepared to accord the novel the close examination it demands. He deplores "our so marked collective mistrust of anything like close or analytical appreciation," and laments the fact that the "idea of the 'technical', that question of the way a thing is done, [is] so abhorrent, as a call upon attention, in whatever art, to the wondrous Anglo-Saxon mind."[5] In lauding the "extraordinary technical wealth" of Flaubert's *Madame Bovary*, he points out that "It may be read ever so attentively, ever so freely, without a suspicion of how it is written, to say nothing of put together."[6]

In accordance with James's own emphases, my reading of representative texts endeavors to do justice to the "extraordinary technical wealth" displayed specifically in the portrayal of the inner world of the characters. Thus, in considering the way consciousness is constituted in the novels, I simultaneously pay attention to the whole spectrum of theoretical categories used by various commentators in their endeavors to categorize or classify diverse techniques used in the depiction of fictional consciousness in the novel. I then justify the selection of Dorrit Cohn's model as set out in the seminal study, *Transparent Minds*, as providing the taxonomy best suited to this enterprise (with certain modifications).[7]

Another dimension is the way in which the experiential worlds of the characters themselves are constituted by the action of their respective consciousnesses. James is consistently concerned with the way in which consciousness shapes experience and imposes form and meaning on data received through the senses. Some characters, like Strether in *The Ambassadors*, seem preternaturally well-equipped for this enterprise; these quintessential Jamesian "supersubtle fry" are endowed with a superabundance of imagination and a lively cognitive faculty. Others, like Maisie in *What Maisie Knew*, are limited by either immaturity or, initially at least, by ignorance and naiveté (for example, Isabel Archer). The activity of the constituting consciousness of the characters themselves is foregrounded here; related to the latter is the way in which not only the perceptual and conceptual "world" but also the very identity of each character is constructed or constituted by the activity of consciousness.

Primarily, of course, it is the identity of the character him- or herself which is established in this way, but in *The Golden Bowl* it has a wider range of reference, subsuming also the process whereby Maggie, struggling to attain understanding both of herself and others, and most particularly of her aberrant stepmother, resorts to a form of creative (re-)construction of the consciousness of others. Maggie is shown attributing to Charlotte, for example, thoughts and feelings to which she could not conceivably have access.

This ability to "put herself into Charlotte's skin" is analogous to the activity referred to above—that of the author or narrator "getting into the constituted consciousness of the creature." This is rendered in part through the linguistic device of free indirect discourse (style indirect libre), which modulates into a new phenomenon I have called "imputed monologue." (This device is discussed more fully in context later.)

James's concern with the activity of consciousness and its capacity to construct a world is consistent with the development of phenomenology and the concomitant insight into the crucial role of the observer or perceiver; James's novels reflect the notion that the world "in itself" is inaccessible to human understanding and all knowledge is relative to a particular observer or perceiving consciousness. It has been observed that this accords with Husserl's redefinition of the Descartes "cogito" "so that the very sense of an ontology is shown to depend on an 'egology', on the mind's constitution of the objective world."[8] Clearly James's conception of the novel as a "personal, a direct impression of life"[9] does not imply an attempt to transcribe or replicate a reality "out there," a reality in itself, as no direct access to such a "reality" is possible. The reality of the inner world of others is clearly even more inaccessible or opaque. It is because of this fundamental "opacity"—the fact that minds are not "transparent"—that writers adopt various strategies to represent them.

In this consideration of the portrayal of consciousness in James's fiction, then, I draw attention to an area which has as yet remained unexplored: that of the various strategies and narratorial stances James adopted in presenting the novel through the consciousness of his "central reflectors." Although other studies have made passing reference to this phenomenon, none has provided a systematic or in-depth analysis. (So, too, the gradual effacement of "James the old Intruder" has been noted, but not the means whereby this effacement is implemented).[10] In a recent study most promisingly entitled *Thinking in Henry James*, Sharon Cameron has approached the subject of consciousness in James, but her analysis proceeds from a completely different (and rather egregious) point of view. Cameron's main thrust is the separation of consciousness from the realm of psychology, a bold but surely rather dubious enterprise. (Further crucial differences between Cameron's reading and my own emerge in the discussion on *The Golden Bowl.*) In the present study I concentrate on the narrative strategies whereby "thinking in Henry James" is indeed depicted. These stylistic devices are examined in a selection of representative works from James's early, middle, and late periods (*Roderick Hudson, The Portrait of a Lady,* and *The Golden Bowl*). These novels, like the bulk of James's oeuvre, have already generated reams of critical comment; however, my reading differs from those of previous commentators in that I focus here on the phenomenon of consciousness and all its ramifications. My comparative study of these novels illustrates the increasing tendency to refract the action of the novel through the consciousness of one or more central reflectors, and the progressive modulation in the stylistic means whereby this shift of emphasis is depicted.

Thus, I concentrate both on exploring devices adopted in the portrayal of consciousness and on tracing the increasing subtlety and sophistication of these techniques. In examining the evolution of James's narrative strategies, I demonstrate that in *The Golden Bowl,* James's last completed novel, he uses a new technique, one that occurs in neither his own earlier novels (with the exception of the other late novel, *The Wings of the Dove*) nor, as far as I know, in the novels of any of his predecessors. As the phenomenon has not been systematically analyzed previously, no appropriate nomenclature for discussing it was available in the current critical categories. It was therefore necessary, in the interests of attaining the desired Jamesian "elasticity" and "comprehensiveness," to stretch the existing taxonomy and coin the neologism mentioned earlier to fill the gap: "imputed monologue." (This new conceptual category is discussed in context in chapter 6.)

Other previously unidentified devices, which are discussed in the context of the novels in which they occur, include quasi-figural narration, "backward speculation" (the deployment of analeptic excursions—flashbacks—through the consciousness of the reflector as opposed to the narrator), and imagistic correlative. I recognize that these terms should be used flexibly, with circumspection; thus, I attempt throughout this study to obviate the danger of fetishizing or reifying these and other terms, endeavoring instead to use them only as they facilitate clarification of hitherto unexplored aspects of James's technique.

There are other, more obvious facets of James's formal repertoire that can be seen in a new light when elucidated by this focus on the portrayal of consciousness. These include the notorious Jamesian ambiguity and his use of metaphor. It is not sufficiently appreciated that ambiguity is an inherent characteristic of the mode of figural narration that predominates in James's later works. (In figural narration, the omniscient narrator is suppressed; the narrator becomes invisible or inaudible and his or her place is taken by a figural medium or reflector character.) The character as reflector in effect assumes the narrator's function, but whereas the narrator in third-person narration is, by and large, "reliable," reflector-characters are limited by or tainted with subjectivity; their views are by their very nature partial—in all senses of the term. Indeed, it is clear that when the consciousness that registers events is located not in the narrator but in a character, or when focalization shifts from one character to another, knowledge is inescapably partial. So in James's figural novels ambiguity is not only thematic but also structural; it is woven into the very fabric rather than being merely a superimposed "figure" in—or on— "the carpet."

James himself draws a distinction between an ambiguity of "appearance" and an ambiguity of "sense" (*AN* 324). He states that he finds "a charm in any produced ambiguity of appearance," then qualifies this by claiming that this ambiguity of appearance "is not by the same stroke, and all helplessly, an ambiguity of sense" (*AN* 324). However, James does not discriminate sufficiently clearly between the two kinds of ambiguity, nor does he appear to acknowledge that ambiguity is in effect inherent in his narrative strategy. Perhaps he should have added a further distinction, that between the two kinds of ambiguity mentioned (but not sufficiently elucidated) and the further ambiguity of *presentation* exemplified in figural narration. Recognition of ambiguity as an inherent facet of figural narration would cast a different light on statements such as

> few novels resist clear analysis more stubbornly than *The Golden Bowl*. No novel in my acquaintance poses so many questions while providing so few definite answers, and none contains so many careful ambiguities of ultimate meaning. Ambiguity, indeed, could be called one of the book's major themes.[11]

Ambiguity is indeed not only a major theme but a concomitant of the technique, the "indirect and oblique view of [the] presented action."[12] This ambiguity is more pervasive in *The Golden Bowl* than in *The Portrait*, as the abdication of the adjudicating narratorial voice is more marked in the later, more consistently figural, novel and is reinforced by the absence of a reliable subsidiary commentator. (Whereas in *The Portrait* considerable insight is afforded by Ralph Touchett as supplementary "lucid reflector," no comparably reliable commentator or "touchstone" is provided in *The Golden Bowl*.)

Another striking aspect of James's narrative technique that has not been thoroughly examined is his use of metaphor, particularly in the

rendering of consciousness. In the late novels, the prevalence of the metaphoric mode in the representation of the inner world of his "central reflectors" further attests to James's interest in the constitutive powers of
consciousness and specifically of the creative imagination. Various studies on metaphor in James are extant, but none focus on the really crucial
role of the metaphoric mode in James: its cognitive function.[13] Futher-
more, although numerous critics have commented on the greater density
of imagery in James's later novels—and in his revisions of the earlier
works as reflected in the New York Edition—little attention has been paid
as yet to the location of this imagery: its concentration in the presentation
of consciousness. Comments on the function of this imagery are also
restricted in scope; insufficient attention has been given to the cognitive
function of imagery in the portrayal of consciousness.

It is also significant—and not hitherto noted—that the events of the
novel are refracted increasingly more consistently not only through the
consciousness of the central reflectors but also, specifically, through the
faculty of memory. The procedure whereby characters "revert to in
thought" (GB 1:191) or "live over inwardly" (GB 1:327) significant experiences in their lives is exemplified in, inter alia, The Portrait, The Wings
of the Dove, The Ambassadors (Strether's "backward picture" in the Luxembourg Gardens), and The Golden Bowl. Here again, a progressive
modulation can be discerned: analepses (flashbacks) refracted through
the consciousness of the characters (as opposed to those evoked by the
narratorial voice) are more frequent and more extended in the late novel,
The Golden Bowl, than in the earlier Portrait, where they are represented
primarily by Isabel's retrospective musings by the fireside. As I demonstrate in subsequent chapters, this "backward speculation" as a means
of extracting or imposing meaning acquires increasing impetus in the
later novels.

Although the focus on the portrayal of consciousness is more pronounced in James's later novels, the notion of analyzing or dramatizing
the contents or process of consciousness—and assuming access to "transparent minds"—was of central importance to James virtually from the
outset. In an early tale, "A Tragedy of Error" (1864), he observed that

> Though I have judged best hitherto, often from an exaggerated fear of trenching
> on the ground of fiction, to tell you what this poor lady said and did rather
> than what she thought, I may disclose what passed in her mind now.[14]

By the time James wrote his later work he was no longer curbed by
this "exaggerated fear": his concern was at least as much with what his
characters "thought" as with what they "said and did." He deplored the
unreality of the sharp distinction between "doing" and "feeling," stating

that "I see their doing" . . . as immensely their feeling, their feeling as their doing" (*AN* 65). Far from "trenching on the ground of fiction," James's depiction of "what passed in [the] mind" evinces an interest in the inner life, the portrayal of consciousness, which is "the subject (par excellence) that distinguished narrative fiction from non-fictional narrative to one side, from non-narrative fiction to the other—that is, from drama and film, the other genres populated by invented persons."[15]

The progressive modulation toward refracting the action of the novel through the consciousness of the central reflectors corresponds to the shift from a more "realist" mode in *Roderick Hudson* to a symbolist mode in *The Golden Bowl*. The latter represents the culmination of the process adumbrated in the other late novels of embodying "external reality" in the consciousness of the reflectors or the figural medium. Thus, *The Golden Bowl* represents the final working out of James's narrative positions: in his last completed novel James most fully implements his conception of the novel's primary focus, as indicated by the quotation above— "for its subject, magnificently, [the novel] has the whole human consciousness."

James's modifications of focus in his conception of the novel are reflected also in his critical writings. In his earlier observations, such as those expressed in "The Art of Fiction" (1884), one can discern a much greater concern with creating an "air of reality," that is, on mimetic criteria generally, than in the later prefaces, where, in assessing his own creative output, James expressed appreciation of the formal perfection of novels such as *The Portrait:*

> Such is the aspect that today "The Portrait" wears for me: a structure reared with an architectural competence . . . that makes it, to the author's own sense, the most proportioned of his productions after "The Ambassadors." (*AN* 52)

The criteria here are clearly aesthetic or formalist rather than narrowly mimetic. This movement from mimetic to more formalist/ aesthetic considerations (and this is largely a matter of emphasis) is paralleled in his movement away from the "realist" mode of his early novels to a more symbolic register in later works such as *The Golden Bowl*.

* * *

> "You see, it was really George Eliot who started it all," Lawrence was saying . . . "It was she who started putting all the action inside. Before, you know, with Fielding and the others, it had been outside. Now I wonder which is right?"[16]

Rather than enter here into a debate as to "which is right" (Lawrence himself suggested that "there ought to be a bit of both") or whether in fact "George Eliot started it all," it seems more useful to explore more fully the switch to "putting it all inside." The gradual "inward turn of the novel"[17] in the nineteenth century can indeed be fruitfully illustrated through reference to the eighteenth-century novelist, Henry Fielding, and the nineteenth/twentieth-century Henry James. An illuminating comparison can be drawn between the resolute refusal of the narrator to reveal the inner life of a character in *Tom Jones* and a contrasting readiness to do so in a comparable situation in James's *The Portrait*. In *Tom Jones,* we find "A gentle Sigh stole from Sophia at these Words, which perhaps contributed to form a Dream of no very pleasant Kind; but as she never revealed this Dream to anyone, so the Reader cannot expect to see it related here."[18] In *The Portrait,* by contrast, chapter 42 is devoted to the evocation of Isabel's thoughts—also "of no very pleasant kind"—which she never communicates to anyone. The playful assumption of the narrator of *Tom Jones* that what is not revealed to others cannot be related (an arch anticipatory exoneration from the charge of shirking his narratorial duty to keep his readers informed?) highlights "the paradox that narrative fiction attains its greatest 'air of reality' in the representation of a lone figure thinking thoughts she will never communicate to anyone."[19] Where the narrator of *Tom Jones* implies that it would be straining the bounds of credulity to pretend to communicate to the reader phenomena to which he or she can have no access, in James's novel there is no suggestion of "trenching on the ground of fiction" in revealing the contents of consciousness. This juxtaposition of Fielding and James exemplifies the "inward turn of the novel" and illustrates James's contention that the subject of the novel is not only the life of overt action—"of flood and field, of the moving accident, of battle and murder and sudden death" (*AN* 57)—but can equally be that of the "subjective adventure."

Before examining more closely James's own contribution to "the turn of the mind" and the techniques he developed for "putting it all inside," it would be useful to consider the representation of the inner life in its historical context.

In tracing the development of techniques of characterization and specifically the evocation of the inner life, one notes that the focus on representing the subjectivity of the developing character who changes inwardly is a fairly recent phenomenon in narrative. "The character whose inward development is of crucial importance is primarily a Christian element in our narrative literature."[20] In primitive narrative literature, whether Hebraic or Hellenic, the inward life is assumed but not overtly presented. Thus, although fictional consciousness is regarded as the special preserve of narrative fiction, it is a preserve that has been appropriated fairly recently. This appropriation, if not initiated by James, was certainly con-

abundance of feeling and striking paucity of intellect, is certainly of a different order from characters such as Isabel Archer, Milly Theale, or Maggie Verver; similarly Frédéric, limited by his deficiencies of moral depth, undergoes an *éducation sentimentale* (it could more accurately be deemed an *éducation sensuelle*) which is far removed from the *éducation aesthétique et morale* experienced by the quintessential man of imagination, Strether. Jamesian protagonists, unlike Flaubert's, are "finely aware and richly responsible." Thus a new direction in the portrayal of consciousness can be discerned through this comparison between Flaubert and James—a switch or progression from depicting "limited vessels" to portraying a wide spectrum of "supersubtle fry." And whereas in Flaubert we observe, with James, "the comparatively meagre human consciousness . . . struggling with the absolutely large artistic,"[47] in James the consciousness displayed is as infinitely rich, diverse, and complex as the artistic means deployed in constructing and communicating it.

The closer consonance between the narrating and the experiencing consciousness probably accounts for the more subtle manipulation of the mode of free indirect discourse in the hands of James than of his predecessor. Here the characterizing images used by Flaubert and James to suggest their respective modes of immersion in and evocation of the inner worlds of their characters seem telling. In presenting his romantically deluded protagonist, Emma Bovary, Flaubert exposes her follies and foibles with incisive, trenchant scalpel-like precision. The Flaubertian stiletto is wielded to very different effect from that of the more subtly infusing Jamesian hand wriggling into the well-fitting glove. Flaubert lays Emma's soul bare with penetrating precision, but the nature of that soul—as James says, she is a "very limited conduit"—makes a substantial ironic distance between narrator and reflector inescapable. A comparison between Emma and Isabel Archer, Maggie Verver, or Millie Theale, for instance, reveals that in James's novels, there is not the same degree of cognitive and ethical disparity between narrator and reflector.

This greater consonance between narrator and reflector makes the deployment of the mode of style indirect libre far less problematic in James. This is illustrated with particular force in the way in which the demarcation between free indirect discourse and narrator's report or "objective" narration is handled by each author. In Flaubert, "the line between the two techniques is clearly marked,"[48] whereas in James, a blurring of boundaries between the two frequently occurs, with the effect of merging the voices of narrator and reflector and creating the impression of narratorial endorsement of the reflector's thoughts. (This device, which Cohn dubs "stylistic contagion," is discussed in context later.) Because of the greater disparity between narrator and reflector in Flaubert—in terms of cognitive and psychological subtlety and complexity—a comparable

solidated and extended in his oeuvre where the centrality of the concept of inward development or a "process of vision" is so marked.

The earliest and simplest method of presenting the inward life in narration is that of "direct narrative statement."[21] This technique of direct definition of character, although less prominent in the more modern novel, is still in evidence in James's oeuvre. We find, predictably perhaps, that in his earlier novels this method is used more extensively than in later works. Even in *The Portrait* considerable insight into the protagonist's character is afforded in extensive passages of authorial comment in the first few chapters. In the later novels this direct method of characterization is rarely found.

Earlier writers, of course (notably Jane Austen, Flaubert, Stendhal, and George Eliot), abound in examples of analytical passages dealing with the inner life of their protagonists. In representing consciousness, however, the tendency was still largely to conceive of thought as simply speech minus the sound, a trend that could be traced back to Plato, who described thought as "the talk which the soul . . . has with itself about any subject which it considers."[22] This concept of thought as a kind of internal dialogue, taking the same linguistic form as oral speech, remained the prevailing (although erroneous) assumption about the nature of thought until fairly recently.[23] This is clearly an oversimplification, as it assumes too readily the complete correspondence between silent discourse and spoken thought. Speech is, by definition, always verbal, whereas thought is, by wide consensus, not necessarily so constituted: "whether thought is always verbal is to this day a matter of definition and dispute among psychologists."[24] (Consciousness is often held to include what William James called "other mind stuff," which cannot be quoted but only narrated.)

Furthermore, it has been noted that

> the distinction between speech and thought is a necessary one in view of the fact that the communication contexts of speech and thought are fundamentally different, the addresser and addressee being identical in the case of thought presentation.[25]

The prevalence of this fallacious conception of thought as unspoken speech resulted in thought in literature being represented, until fairly recently, exactly as speech would be represented. A character's unspoken thoughts were rendered in a prose very like that of his spoken discourse. Even James, in *The Portrait,* for instance, makes use of inquit phrases such as "she said" to indicate inner speech. We find, for example,

> she [Isabel] retired to rest with a sense of good fortune, with a quickened consciousness of possible felicities. "It's very nice to know two such charming

people as those," she said [to herself], meaning by "those" her cousin and her cousin's friend. (1:91)

[Ralph's] conviction [was] that if Mr Goodwood were interested in Isabel in the serious manner described by Miss Stackpole he would not care to present himself at Gardencourt at a summons from the latter lady. "On this supposition," said Ralph [to himself], "he must regard her as a thorn on the stem of his rose." (1:176)

In later novels, such as *The Ambassadors,* these phrases are replaced by more appropriate verbs such as "he reflected."

"Interior monologue," which is a more direct and dramatic device for presenting consciousness than the first method, that of "narrative analysis," was used extensively by nineteenth-century authors such as Stendhal. George Eliot, by contrast, relies heavily on "narrative analysis"; furthermore, in *Middlemarch,* for example, portrayal of the thoughts or consciousness of the characters is supplemented by extensive moral generalizations. James, on the other hand, increasingly deploys style indirect libre while suppressing authorial aphorisms and moral adjudication.

George Eliot and Flaubert illustrate the two principal ways of solving the problem of representing "the psyches of ordinary human beings, whose verbal patterns in speech and thought are inadequate in themselves to inspire the kind of interest that their authors seek on their behalf."[26] Whereas George Eliot relies on "narrative analysis," Flaubert adopts the technique of "the symbolic use of physical correlatives." In *Madame Bovary,* for instance, by using physical objects such as Emma's bridal bouquet and her dog, and varying perceptions of her garden, to symbolize his protagonist's mental states, Flaubert creates the "desired image of her psyche" without resorting to extensive or obtrusive narrative analysis.

In the case of the protagonists of James's late novels, who are by and large not "ordinary human beings" but "supersubtle fry" invested with a superabundance of intelligence and imagination, a different technique is in evidence. By contrast with George Eliot's *Middlemarch,* for example, where the narrator's rhetoric is suffused with intricate patterns of imagery, in the James novels it is in the language of the characters themselves (in the representation of both speech and thought) that a highly metaphorical mode is deployed. In *The Golden Bowl,* for instance, the crucial image of the pagoda is conjured up in the context of the protagonist's own consciousness rather than by an authorial narrator commenting on her predicament. Thus, when Maggie conceives of her situation in terms of an exotic pagoda, the device is not a physical correlative but—to coin a more accurate if inelegant neologism—an "imagistic correlative." (Whereas in the Flaubert text it is a material or "real" physical object that symbolizes mental states, in *The Golden Bowl* it is an object imaged in or generated by the protagonist's imagination—the image-making faculty—that fulfills this function.)

Although it is difficult to establish conclusively the direct influence such pioneers as Jane Austen and George Eliot had on James, in the portrayal of consciousness, it seems likely that the most significant influence in this sphere was in fact the French novelist Gustave Flaubert. James was clearly deeply impressed by the works of Flaubert and devoted several articles to a discussion of his oeuvre. Indeed, James's 1902 essay on Flaubert was written as an introduction to the first English translation of *Madame Bovary*.[27] In his appraisal of the novel, James highlights Flaubert's "extraordinary technical wealth,"[28] praising his mastery of form, structure, and rhythm, and singling out for special mention Flaubert's celebrated "impersonality." Flaubert's narratorial stance is in effect comparable to that of James himself, whose mode of presentation entails suppression of the personalized voice of the narrator. James describes this approach as essentially adopting "a certain indirect and oblique view of my presented action," which is

> not my own impersonal account of the affair in hand, but [as] my account of someone's impression of it—the terms of this person's access to it and estimate of it contributing thus by some fine little law to intensification of interest. (*AN* 327)

In *Roderick Hudson,* for example, "The centre of interest throughout 'Roderick' is Rowland Mallet's consciousness, and the drama is the drama of that consciousness"(*AN* 15–16).

Flaubert and James are generally regarded as the two prime instigators of this new trend toward what Stanzel termed "perspectivism," which implies figural presentation through a reflector-character. Of course, James did not write exclusively in the perspectival mode; novels such as *Watch and Ward, The Bostonians, Washington Square, The Europeans* and *The Awkward Age* are all "aperspectival" and deploy authorial comment in various ways. The tendency toward filtering the novel through the consciousness of his "central reflectors" is manifested ever more strongly in James's later works. (This is accompanied by a discernible shift in narratorial stance in the novels written after James's experiments with the theater in the mid-1890s. In the later novels, the narrator as historian is largely superseded by the more evanescent "hypothetical observer.")

It has been claimed that James "imbibed the notion" of adopting "the disappearance of the author" as an "aim" from Flaubert, who held that "the author should be in his work like God in the universe: everywhere present but nowhere apparent."[29] Significantly, this translation of Flaubert's statement—"L'auteur, dans son oeuvre, doit être comme Dieu dans l'univers, présent partout et visible nulle part"—differs from James's own formulation of Flaubert's position as expressed in his essay "Gustave Flaubert" (1893): "It's one of my principles that one must never write down *one's self.* The artist must be present in his work like God in Creation, invisible and almighty, everywhere *felt* but nowhere *seen*" (my emphasis).[30] His presence, then, is inevitably manifested but not always overtly "seen" or rendered audible. It is clear that James's formulation of Flaubert's stance would be consistent with his own

> on this question of the projected light of the individual strong temperament in fiction—the colour of the air with which this, that or the other painter of life . . . more or less unconsciously suffuses his picture. . . . [It is] something that proceeds from the contemplative mind itself, the very complexion of the mirror in which the material is reflected. This is the nature of the man himself—an emanation of his spirit, temper, history; it springs from his very presence, his spiritual presence, in his work.[31]

The presence of the author, then, although not audibly manifested in the form of observations dispensed by an intrusive omniscient commentator, is nevertheless all-pervasive. James's observation above is reminiscent of Flaubert's comparable claim to be exercising in his work what he called a *"faculté panthéiste."* He wrote, "C'est une délicieuse chose que d'écrire, que de n'être plus soi, mais de circuler dans toute la création dont on parle." [It's a delicious feeling to write, to be no longer oneself, but to circulate through all that one creates; literally: to circulate in all the creation one is speaking about (my translation).][32]

Ullman claims that "impersonality did not mean aloofness for Flaubert: it had as its complement a capacity for sympathetic self-identification with the protagonists of the story."[33] For Flaubert, "Style is not something external, a mere garment of thought; in Flaubert's memorable simile, it must penetrate into the thought like a stiletto."[34] Flaubert's *"faculté panthéiste"* is thus similar to James's capacity to "get into the skin of the creature," but the difference between their respective images used to describe this process is telling. Where James uses the image of a hand wriggling into a glove to suggest the process of "entering" or rendering the constituted consciousness of his characters, Flaubert's comparable yet very different image, that of the stiletto, suggests an incisive analytical penetration wielded with surgical precision—and a concomitant degree of detachment.

For both Flaubert and James, albeit in different ways, the *"faculté panthéiste"* making it possible for the author to immerse himself in the inner world of his characters and filter the novel through their perceptions led to the desired effect of effacing the intrusive narrator. But although James lauds Flaubert's narratorial stance of "impersonality," he does not proffer insight into the technical means whereby this impersonality is achieved. By the same token, he eschews comment on the devices he himself used in implementing his comparable approach. Flaubert's own terminology suggests the method and effect created by the technique of style indirect libre without specifying its stylistic or linguistic features:

> I believe that great Art is scientific and impersonal. One should, by an effort
> of the spirit, *transport oneself into the characters, not draw them to oneself.*
> That, at any rate, is my method.[35]

It is significant that translating this kinetic image into linguistic terms would yield an exact description of free indirect discourse.[36] Indeed, the deployment of this mode of presentation of consciousness is crucial here: "free indirect style is the exact equivalent, on the linguistic plane, of this withdrawal of the author from his work."[37]

Flaubert is credited with being the first novelist to make concentrated and systematic use of this construction: "It is in his hands that it first became a device of style in the proper sense of the term."[38] Ullman points out that

> The numerical data alone are significant. I have counted over 150 examples
> [in *Madame Bovary*], roughly one in every three pages; . . . . the only element
> which remains largely impervious to it is description. Even there, natural phe-
> nomena are sometimes evoked through their impact on the mind.[39]

In James's later novels, by contrast, natural phenomena are almost invari- ably evoked through the perceptions of the central characters, and even without mustering the kind of numerical data cited by Ullman, it is clear that instances of free indirect discourse are far more concentrated in the late James: they occur more frequently and in much lengthier passages. Thus, in tracing the progression from Flaubert to James one could cite these two major factors distinguishing their respective techniques: first, the infinitely greater incidence of examples of free indirect discourse in James; and second, the way in which in the later James virtually all descriptions of natural phenomena or cityscapes are registered through the consciousness of the reflector. Thus, we observe Paris through Strether's impressions and associations. (This is easier to achieve be- cause of the closer consonance between narrator and protagonist in James, where the characters are much more subtle and complex "vessels" or "conduits" of experience.)

In speculating as to the reasons why Flaubert should have been the first writer to exploit the free indirect method, Ullman contends that "his hyper-sensitive ear shrank from the accumulation of qui-s and que-s to which even the best stylists of the Classical period had remained indifferent."[40] He points out that French lacks the ease with which subordinating conjunctions and pronouns can be omitted in English. If Flaubert was indeed allergic to the piling up of repetitive "que-s" as in "il pense que" and sought to eliminate them through free indirect style, which is shorn of such tags, one could speculate as to whether James, too, was impelled by considerations of euphony in adopting the mode of free indirect discourse. His later novels were of course dictated rather than written; could James, too, have been susceptible to the grating effect of a plethora of "thats," the unlovely English equivalent of the French "que?" James did (ostensibly?) express his abhorrence of such features of English syntax; he wondered "what would have become of him [Flaubert] . . . had he been condemned to deal with a form of speech consisting, like ours, of 'that' and 'which' . . . of the blest 'it,' which an English sentence may repeat in three or four opposed sentences without in the least losing caste."[41] Is it possible that it was a desire for the euphonic that caused James to produce what some regard as the euphuistic prose of the late novels? (And is the presence of "it," "that," and "which" in that very sentence of mine so mortally offensive?) Is James in effect subjecting Flaubert's exaggerated scruples or auditory hypersensitivity to gentle ridicule? It seems highly unlikely [that] the chief consideration for either writer was to obviate being caught up in a clumsy succession of "que-s" or "thats." There are clearly far more compelling reasons for the switch to free indirect discourse, the most cogent being the desire for "impersonality," for the suppression of the intrusive narratorial voice and the exploitation of the subtle range of effects of irony and sympathy that the mode can generate.

Although Flaubert is generally credited with the successful achievement of this impersonality through the effacement of the intrusive third-person narrator, it can be observed that he did not in effect carry out this project as rigidly as one is led to believe. The Flaubertian narrator is very much there, not merely as a shadowy *éminence grise* but frequently in very vocal manifestations. The following extract illustrates this tendency. The vocal narrator comments:

He [Rodolphe] could not distinguish—for all his experience of the world—differences of feeling beneath similarities of expression. Because corrupt and lascivious lips had murmured these same expressions to him, he could not really believe that they might be genuine this time. Always be wary of hyperbolic speeches hiding undistinguished emotions, he thought to himself; as if an

> overflowing heart does not sometimes pour itself out in the emptiest of meta-
> phors, since none of us can ever express perfectly our desires or our ideas or
> our sufferings, and human speech is like a cracked cauldron on which we beat
> out tunes to make bears dance, when all the while we want to move the stars.
> (*Madame Bovary* 2.12.259)

The narratorial voice here is reminiscent of that of George Eliot in *Middlemarch,* where the reader is treated to aphorisms such as "We are all
of us born in moral stupidity, taking the world as an udder to feed our
supreme selves."[42]

Although Flaubert is widely supposed to have done away with narrative commentary and kept the author out of his fiction, what he actually
did was to refrain from placing emphasis on the personality of his narrator
in order to lend such commentary as he makes the authority of impersonality and impartiality, though in actuality it was neither impersonal nor
impartial.[43] Scholes and Kellogg contend that such manifestations of the
authorial voice are "a refined and restrained projection of the sensibility
and intellect of Gustave Flaubert"; however, in examples such as that
cited above, the rather cynical gnomic observation can surely be taken
as a *direct* expression of the authorial voice rather than merely a "restrained projection."

In James, particularly in the late novels, the elusive Flaubertian impersonality is more fully realized; the narratorial voice rarely if ever indulges
in the kind of gnomic observations cited above. Furthermore, such truisms that exist, when uttered by either the narrator or the characters
themselves, tend to be suspect and not to be taken at face value.

Another significant departure made by James is in the nature of his
protagonists. Although both Flaubert and James produced figural novels
in which events, descriptions, and impressions are transmitted through
the consciousness of their respective central reflectors (albeit to varying
degrees, and far more consistently in James), the nature of these reflectors
differs markedly. James himself observes that although Emma Bovary
"interests us by the nature of her consciousness and the play of her
mind,"[44] her fundamental deficiency as a reflector inheres in "the poverty
of her consciousness." Indeed, Flaubert's reflectors are all, according to
James, manifestations of "the comparatively meagre human consciousness." Flaubert "never approached the complicated character in man or
woman, or the really furnished, the finely civilised."[45]

Jamesian reflectors are by contrast supremely "furnished" with sensibility, intellect, and imagination. James questions why Flaubert chose,
"as special conduits of the life he proposed to depict, such inferior and
in the case of Frédéric [*L'Education Sentimentale*] such abject human
specimens?"[46] The lightweight, romantic Emma, endowed with a super-

crossing of the line between the two modes creates an effect of "narratorial usurpation"[49] of the character's perceptions and thoughts rather
than narratorial endorsement. In *Madame Bovary,* for instance, the narrator frequently feels obliged to step in and rectify the paucity of Emma's
perceptions, supplementing them with more sophisticated observations
of his own.

An example of confusion arising from injudicious shifts between the
modes of free indirect discourse and narratorial description, leading to
this "narratorial usurpation," can be seen, for instance, in Emma's visit
to the wet-nurse's cottage with Leon. The initial description of the cottage
seems to emanate from Emma's own perception, but a subsequent plethora of details suggests that the narrator is providing the kind of inventory
demanded by the tradition of the realist novel, demonstrating "a Balza-
cian concern for the social genre scene, [which] momentarily thwarts his
most characteristic purpose, the construction of the mental world of his
characters."[50]

These discrepancies between narrator and character exist not only on
the psychological level, as a perceptual and conceptual disparity, but also
on the linguistic level. At times Flaubert, while using the mode of free
indirect discourse, which allows the character to formulate her own
thoughts, adopts (albeit momentarily) a sophisticated linguistic register
which seems beyond her capacity. The following extract illustrates this
tendency:

> Yet I do love him! she said to herself.
> No matter! she was not happy, had never been happy. Where did this insuffi-
> ciency of life come from, this instantaneous decay of the things she depended
> on? . . . But, if there were somewhere a being, strong and handsome, a valiant
> nature, filled both with exaltation and refined sophistication, the heart of a
> poet in the body of an angel, a lyre with brazen cords, throbbing elegiac epitha-
> lamia up to the heavens, why then should she not chance to find him? Oh!
> What an impossibility! Anyhow, nothing was worth the trouble of searching;
> everything was a lie![51]

Although the entire passage from "she said to herself" is in free indirect
discourse—and the impression of hearing Emma's own thoughts is
strengthened by the emotionally charged exclamations and questions—
the linguistic register, in the imagery and phrases such as "elegiac epitha-
lamia," is that of the more sophisticated (and ironic) narrator rather than
Emma herself. These narratorial amplifications strike a discordant note
in view of the previously established manifest lack of such sophistication
in the reflector. Here it would perhaps be more appropriate to adopt the
mode of narrator's report of Emma's thoughts, a method George Eliot
used in such cases.

Thus, when there is too vast a gap between narrator and reflector in terms of both cognitive and ethical sophistication and linguistic register, the normally smooth transitions from one mode to the other become jarring. And when, as in Flaubert, the gap becomes a chasm, the author's strategies for bridging it can place him in a very precarious position; it becomes like balancing on a stylistic tightrope and risking periodic plunges.

These problems emanating from too gross a disparity between the psychological (including cognitive and ethical) and linguistic registers in narrator and reflector do not occur in the works of James. Without necessarily hazarding the evaluative claim that James deployed the mode of free indirect discourse more effectively than Flaubert, it is clear that the nature of the consonance between narrator and reflector in James made for smoother transitions from one mode to the other. In view of the observation that "FID is not an occasional device . . . it is a major instrument for achieving the Flaubertian type of novel"[52] one could claim that ironically, James succeeded more fully in achieving that "Flaubertian" type of novel—an approximation of the fully figural novel, where narrator is effaced while the author achieves an "imaginative self-submergence in the object . . . participation in the imagined character's experience" (143). In a case like Flaubert's where this experience—or attitude towards it—is so different from the narrator's own, can this self-submergence really be achieved? It seems that in effect a strongly marked ironic distance inevitably prevails. Dissonance, cognitive, psychological, linguistic, is unavoidable; real consonance such as that achieved by James (for example, in his depiction of Strether) is difficult to attain.

One might ask whether this observation stands up to the challenge of Flaubert's famous claim that "Madame Bovary, c'est moi." The striving after the unattainable, or dissatisfaction with the world as it is, might well be shared by Flaubert and his protagonist, but his infinitely more sophisticated perspective on these aspirations suggests that he is if anything endeavoring to expunge or exorcise from his being these Bovary-esque elements.

James then is carrying on stylistic "researches" begun by Flaubert in *Madame Bovary* in novels that are very different in temper and tone, in moral outlook and in the extent of his characters' consciousness. The lesson, the example has been thoroughly absorbed, perhaps even forgotten, but is none the less powerful and pervasive for its transubstantiation.[53]

More complex reflector-characters demand more complex modes of representation of consciousness. And a significant facet of this "transubstantiation" lies in the difference between the deployment of the metaphoric mode in the two writers. As Jamesian reflectors have more complex inner worlds, they have a much greater repertoire of cognitive devices at their disposal, and one of these is the ability to marshal all linguistic resources, especially those represented by the cognitive function of metaphor.

Thus, another significant difference between Flaubert and James is in the incidence and function of imagery—particularly that occurring in the representation of consciousness—in their respective works. (I explore James's deployment of metaphor more fully later in this introductory chapter and in the context of the novels discussed in subsequent chapters.) Flaubert's use of metaphor is one aspect of his "technical wealth" that James expressed reservations about, declaring that

> No one will care for him [Flaubert] at all who does not care for his metaphors, and those moreover who care most for these will be discreet enough to admit that even a style rich in similes is limited when it renders only the visible. The invisible Flaubert scarcely touches; his vocabulary and all his methods were unadjusted and alien to it.[54]

This view was shared by Proust, to whom metaphor was the hallmark of a great style and who found Flaubert's metaphors unimpressive: "il n'y a peut-être pas dans tout Flaubert une seule belle métaphor." [There is perhaps not a single beautiful metaphor to be found in all Flaubert's work.][55]

Some more recent commentators have similar reservations. Martin Turnell, for example, declares that "Flaubert's figures will not bear the weight of the symbolism that he tried to attach to them."[56] Scholes and Kellogg, on the other hand, contend that Flaubert's novels do have a symbolic dimension, but not necessarily rendered through imagery; as mentioned earlier, Flaubert adopts the technique of "the symbolic use of physical correlatives."

Turnell cites the following as an example of Flaubert's use of a "commonplace" image:

> Her journey to Vaubyessard had opened a yawning fissure in her life, a fissure that was like one of those great crevasses which a storm will sometimes make on a mountain-side in the course of one short night. (*Madame Bovary* 1.8.116)[57]

Turnell comments that "It is a characteristic sentence. The fact of the rift is stated with Flaubert's customary forthrightness in the first clause; the commonplace image which follows shows how he tried to force his sensibility, giving us a feeling of a vain and unrewarding hunt for the *mot juste* which always eluded him."[58]

However, consideration of the extract in context reveals that the image might well be presented in free indirect discourse, and thus be attributed to Emma rather than the narrator. In spite of the claim that "Free indirect style has the peculiarity of being very easy to recognise but rather difficult to analyse,"[59] this seems to be one of those instances where identification is not so unproblematic. The mode in which the image occurs could be interpreted as either free indirect discourse or narrator's report. If the former, this image should be attributed to Emma (who is likely to think in "commonplace" images) rather than to the narrator or more accurately here (since Flaubert is under attack for producing commonplace images), the author. Thus, in this case at least, the choice of trope would be justified. By the same token, James's intricate—if not at times somewhat baroque—tropes are appropriate to the sensibility or state of mind of the protagonist he evokes; they are adapted to the mental or imaginative capacity of their respective "vessels."

Juxtaposing comparable images from Flaubert's *Madame Bovary* and James's *The Golden Bowl* could illustrate significant differences. In Flaubert, we find, for example, "La série des memes journées recommenca. . . . L'avenir était un corridor tout noir, et qui avait au fond sa porte bien fermée" (*Madame Bovary* 1.9.123–24). [The same monotonous pattern of days started all over again. The future was a pitch-black corridor with a closed door at the end.] James, too, used the corridor image in, for example, *What Maisie Knew* and most memorably in *The Golden Bowl,* in his evocation of Maggie grappling for understanding of her situation. The greater complexity and originality of this image in James is apparent:

> her accumulations of the unanswered . . . were like a roomful of confused objects, never as yet "sorted," which for some time now she had been passing and repassing, along the corridor of her life. She passed it when she could without opening the door; then, on occasion, she turned the key to throw in a fresh contribution. (2.14)

Imagery such as this needs to be assessed in context: Maggie is, after all, an infinitely more complex character.

If one accepts the view that "Flaubert's figures will not bear the weight of symbolism," perhaps this could be regarded as one measure of the "progression" from Flaubert to James. I hope to show that, in consolidating and further extending the "technical wealth" inherited from Flaubert, James managed to forge a style that could indeed "bear the weight of symbolism," one in which the metaphoric mode is rendered immeasurably more supple and complex, capable of performing a variety of functions it had not performed previously. Preeminent among these is the cognitive function of metaphor; in James's later novels, it is through revelatory images conjured up by the imagination of the reflector as much as through balanced hypotheses or sustained sequential analysis that the protagonist attains insight.

* * *

The insight acquired in the course of the "subjective adventure" of the Jamesian protagonist invariably entails a "process of vision" experienced by the "expanding consciousness." Indeed, a "dialectic of blindness and insight"[60] animates virtually the entire Jamesian oeuvre. What James says of Strether's experience in *The Ambassadors* may be applied to all his characters, albeit to varying degrees: "he now at all events *sees,* so that the business of my tale and the march of my action, not to say the precious moral of everything, is just my demonstration of this process of vision" (*AN* 308).

One could say that the depiction of some sort of "process of vision" is a well-established novelistic convention; the novel by its very nature presents a "process of vision," a continuous, multifarious series of responses to experience—in perception and in action—during which the protagonist's inward development (usually from a state of naiveté or ignorance to a relatively enlightened state) is portrayed. In the works of James, however, the concern with this process in his protagonists is more consistently searching and more "inward" than that of his predecessors. Hence his development of techniques such as that of the "centre of consciousness," through which the events of the novel are filtered, to render this process with more subtle dramatic force. Hence, too, the greater complexity in his deployment of the techniques of rendering consciousness.

In the various "ordeal[s] of consciousness"[61] experienced in different ways by a variety of Jamesian characters, the epistemological and ethical dimensions of "the drama of consciousness" are of primary importance. Protagonists invariably find their conceptual and ethical categories thrown into disarray.

Although this study will restrict its focus to a representative selection of James's "intense perceivers" (Rowland in *RH,* Isabel in *PL,* and Maggie in *GB*) who find their "categories [taken] by surprise" (*Amb,* 1.271), a comprehensive exploration of "the range of wonderment" (*AN* 156) would include characters as diverse as the telegraphist of "In the Cage," Maisie in *What Maisie Knew,* Morgan Moreen of "The Pupil," and "portentous little Hyacinth" of *The Princess Casamassima,* who "collapses . . . overcharged with treasures of reflexion and spoils of passion" (*AN* 156). Strether, too, is charged with "treasures of imagination" at the conclusion of his adventure. Similarly, for the young lady providing the "germ" of *The Reverberator,* "her spoil . . . had been a treasure of impressions; her harvest . . . a wealth of revelations" (*AN* 184).

Jamesian protagonists are frequently depicted as "constantly staring and wondering" (*PL*, 1.45) as they are subjected to "the strain of observation and the assault of experience" (*AN* 147). Their bewilderment is the precondition for their embarking on a "process of vision"; as Paul Armstrong has noted, "Bewilderment throws into question the interpretative constructs we ordinarily take for granted as our ways of knowing the world."[62] Each of these protagonists, then, is obliged to undertake a reassessment of his or her respective "interpretative constructs."

In tracing the "process of vision" that encompasses this hermeneutic enterprise, we find that for Jamesian characters the mode of "seeing" is not fixed or static but is a dynamic process that both determines and reflects the nature of the experiences in which they are involved. Indeed, the interconnectedness of "seeing" and "being" underlies all James's fiction. "As a man is, So he Sees."[63] James would no doubt have subscribed to William Blake's aphoristic statement on the importance of "seeing," not only as an expression but also as a determinant of one's being. Just as a person's perception is governed by what [s]he essentially "is," so the mode of self-perception and the way one "sees" others and the world helps to determine one's nature. In the Jamesian world, particularly, "seeing" is consistently equated with understanding; it does not operate merely on the level of simple physical perception but involves all the faculties of observation, intuition, imagination, and rational thought. For James, Pliny's formulation would still be valid: "The mind is the real instrument of sight and observation; the eyes act as a sort of vessel receiving and transmitting the visible portion of consciousness."[64] Sight, then, is invariably associated with insight.

In rendering the process of vision, James's fiction demonstrates that he "conceived of seeing in a multiple sense, as an act of the inward even more than of the outward eye."[65] In his novels, the stimulus provided by what is perceived by the "outward" eye has far-reaching repercussions on all levels of consciousness. Seeing involves interpreting, activating what E. H. Gombrich has called the "filing systems of the mind."[66] According to Gombrich, "When we are aware of the process of filing we say we 'interpret', where we are not we say we 'see'."[67]

In many novels a character's "wealth of revelations" is precipitated by what is seen, or crystallizes around a response evoked by certain works of art such as paintings. In Strether's case, the image of a landscape painting literally and figuratively opens up startlingly new perspectives; for Milly, in *The Wings of the Dove,* the Bronzino portrait evokes a comparably revelatory insight. These images, then, can be either literal or analogical.

Similarly, revelatory disclosures can be afforded by images conjured up by the "inward eye" of the imagination. So for Maggie in *The Golden*

Bowl, an image conjured up in her imagination rather than perceived in actuality affords the greatest insight. Although the disclosure resulting from her encounter with the purveyor of the golden bowl precipitates startling recognitions comparable to those arising from Isabel's perception of the "absorbed mutual gaze" linking Osmond and Madame Merle, it is the emblematic intuition crystallized in images such as that of the pagoda and the "family coach" which have the greatest cognitive force.

This conceptualization through metaphor is a crucial facet of James's technique, thus it is surprising that no previous studies have analyzed the full import of James's deployment of the metaphoric mode in the "subjective adventure" of his characters. It is particularly noteworthy that although complex patterns of imagery are found in early works such as *Roderick,* the significance of emblematic images conjured up by the figural consciousness increases in the later novels. Thus, although imagery can serve various functions in the novel, the central emphasis here is the cognitive function of metaphors—their role of representing the world. The rhetorical function of metaphor—that of expressing the speaker's feelings or influencing the hearer—is obviously more marked in direct discourse, and as the emphasis here is on the representation of thought rather than speech, this range of functions would be less relevant here. However, it could perhaps be argued that even metaphors used in the portrayal of thought rather than speech have a subsidiary function of expressing the thinker's (rather than speaker's) feelings, or even, in the case of an inner debate or process of rationalization as seen in *The Portrait,* influencing the "hearer" or thinker herself.

The cognitive function of metaphor is obliquely indicated in James's own emphasis, in depicting the process of vision of his protagonists, on the part played by the "blest imagination . . . that . . . helped [them] to discriminate" (*AN* 316). The role of the imagination in the growth and refinement of perception and consciousness is crucial: the way one sees oneself, others, and the world, the way one "images" reality, is determined largely by the conceptions of the image-making faculty, the imagination. An analysis of any of James's novels would reveal the important part played by the imagination in the accession to sound insight or moral vision.[68]

The constructive power of the imagination is manifested in the way both the figural and the narrating consciousness use metaphor to define ideas and analyze situations and relationships in concrete terms. And the gradual appropriation of the imagistic mode by the figural as opposed to the narrating consciousness reflects the increasing capacity of the protagonist to respond imaginatively to the urgent injunction enunciated in *What Maisie Knew* and *The Golden Bowl* to "Find out for yourself." The depiction of this "finding out for oneself," as opposed to having the cognitive process managed by the narrator on the character's behalf, is re-flected in the ever-increasing capacity of the protagonist to exploit the cognitive power of metaphor. The epistemological implications are telling: as Peter Garret has observed, "To image a situation is to move toward mastery of it, to make it more firmly possessed by consciousness."[69] The recognition that a specific image arises in the consciousness of the character rather than of the narrator is crucial, as the "locus" of the image indicates who is responsible for the generation or formulation of meaning. Increasingly, it is the figural rather than the narrating consciousness that is empowered through being conceded control over the deployment of metaphor.

An important facet of James's use of metaphor is the marked incidence of iterative images, those recurring not only throughout a specific novel but running through his entire oeuvre. The increasing subtlety and sophis-tication of James's use of metaphor could be demonstrated in a compari-son between the deployment of recurrent tropes, such as that of the lock and key, in *Watch and Ward, Roderick Hudson, The Portrait,* and *The Golden Bowl.*

In *Watch and Ward,* Roger "thought of his angry vow the night before to live only for himself and turn the key on his heart. . . . Before twenty-four hours had elapsed, a child's fingers were fumbling with the key" (34). He "thought of Nora . . . as a kind of superior doll, a thing wound up with a key" (56). In a later scene, an unintended comical effect results from the verbal echo activating a conjunction of the figurative and literal "keys": Nora enters the room to demand the use of Roger's watch-key. "Roger's key proved a complete misfit, so that she had recourse to Hu-bert's. It hung from the watch-chain which depended from his waistcoat, and some rather intimate fumbling was needed to adjust it to Nora's diminutive time-piece" (*WW,* 109).

Even readers responding from a pre-Freudian perspective would surely find this conjunction of terms rather disconcerting—or ill-timed. In the later novels, this kind of naive or inept use of metaphor is replaced by a more sophisticated deployment of the metaphoric mode. In *Roderick Hudson,* the image is used mainly in dialogue, as in Roderick's "specula-tions as to the possible mischances of one's genius. 'What if the watch should run down,' he asked, 'and you should lose the key?'" (195). The image is taken up by Rowland in his letter to Cecilia where he writes, "I suppose there is some key or other to his character, but I try in vain to find it; and yet I can't believe that Providence is so cruel as to have turned the lock and thrown the key away" (237).

In *The Portrait,* the key image tends to occur more frequently in narra-tor's report (psychonarration) and style indirect libre (free indirect dis-course). We find that Isabel "took alarm at her candour: it was as if she had given to a comparative stranger [Madame Merle] the key to her cabinet of jewels" (1.267). When confronted with Osmond's declaration of love, Isabel experiences "the slipping of a fine bolt—backward, forward, she couldn't have said which" (2.18).

The ambiguity in this image (liberation or imprisonment?) is absent in its appearance in Amerigo's narrated monologue at the beginning of *The Golden Bowl:* when contemplating his imminent marriage, the prince considers that "his fate had practically been sealed . . . the moment had something of the grimness of a crunched key in the strongest lock that could be made" (1.5). The image often recurs in the delineation of Maggie's consciousness: so "the question dangled there as if it were the key to everything" (2.15), and

> her accumulations of the unanswered . . . were like a roomful of confused objects, never as yet "sorted," which for some time now she had been passing and repassing, along the corridor of her life. She passed it when she could without opening the door; then, on occasion, she turned the key to throw in a fresh contribution. (2.14)

It can thus be seen that the cognitive function of the metaphoric mode is crucial in the "process of vision" of James's characters. This is explored further in the context of the novels discussed in the latter section of this book.

*   *   *

Although a discussion of imagery is not impeded by a dearth of clear and appropriate terms to use in such an analysis, the same does not apply when we attempt to elucidate facets of James's rendering of consciousness. Here, in the plethora of theoretical concepts, one searches in vain for accurate terminology to cover phenomena such as the technique used in *The Golden Bowl* to render the process whereby one character in effect projects or construes the consciousness of another, attributing to the other thoughts to which only the narrator could conceivably have access. As Cohn has observed,

> The discourse on narrative discourse is still in Babel. Its categories are variously labeled (narrative) perspective, mode, distance, person, register, presentation, situation, point of view, aspect, focalization, field, position, voice, transmission, vision.[70]

Taxonomy proliferates but precision is lacking. Cohn's own taxonomy displays great clarity and precision, but even her model lacks the "comprehensiveness" and "elasticity" to account for the aforementioned technique encountered in *The Golden Bowl*. Before undertaking a detailed exposition of Cohn's paradigm and its application to the novels of James, I shall briefly indicate the most significant contributions of earlier commentators and elucidate concepts most pertinent to this investigation.

Among the various contending critical categories cited in Cohn's observation on the "Babel of critical discourse," the most relevant here is "focalization," which can be regarded as encompassing notions such as point of view, voice, perspective, and so on.

The most significant early commentator on point of view is, of course, James himself, who was also the first to comment fully on his own work. This concept has subsequently been modified and amplified through concepts such as those cited by Cohn: for example, perspective, voice, focalization.[71]

Although he introduced these crucial categories and expatiated on his own novels in his retrospectively conceived prefaces, James in effect throws minimal light on his narrative technique. Pronouncements on, for example, "a certain indirect and oblique view of my presented action" (*AN* 327) are not as enlightening as one would expect. Indeed, James's comments on his own management of point of view or focalization are positively misleading at times. In his preface to *The Golden Bowl,* for example, he claims that "the whole thing remains subject to the register, ever so closely kept, of the consciousness of but two of the characters" (*AN* 329); this creates expectations that the organizing principle would be that of dual focalization, whereas in effect multiple focalization is used. Furthermore, the narratorial voice still functions as focalizer at times, as in the presentation of Adam. Thus, "James the old Intruder"[72] tiptoes in and makes his narratorial presence felt even in this late novel, albeit far more stealthily.

Nevertheless, it is indisputable that overall, James, both in his novels and his critical writings, contributed to the gradual disappearance of the omniscient commentating narrator, who was superseded by the "centre of consciousness." In the course of his oeuvre, as the action of the novel is progressively filtered more consistently through the consciousness of the central reflector, the nature and function of the narrator undergoes a concomitant crucial change. The stance of biographer or historian objectively presenting "facts" about his characters is abandoned. The reader is restricted to the perspective of the characters and no longer shares the cognitive privilege of the narrator. Indeed, the frequent allusions made by the narrator of *The Golden Bowl* to a hypothetical observer serve to imply that the narrator is simply a marginally more cognitively advantaged version of the reader.

In effect, the narratorial stance in the later novels is fraught with uncertainty. Gnomic utterances, for example, are not as straightforward in *The*

Golden Bowl as in the earlier novels, and are not necessarily to be taken at face value.

One of the crucial techniques whereby the voice of the narrator is effaced and the consciousness of the character assumes prominence is that of free indirect discourse. As Roy Pascal points out,

> Free indirect style [is] one of the major devices by which narratorial report and explanation [are] supplanted; [and is] also one in which, as we shall see, the subjective perspective of the character is cunningly brought into the broader focus of the narrator's view.[73]

Another technique for suppressing the authorial voice, hence according greater prominence to the "voice" or consciousness of the reflector, is manifested in James's later novels. Here suppression of the overt authorial voice takes the form of a transmutation into other modes. Guidance is provided not by the personalized voice of the narrator but, inter alia, by a complex metaphorical mode that provides "signs" by which the reader is enjoined to participate actively in the construction of the narrative by engaging in interpretation of its complex imagistic texture. This procedure one could call, perhaps, "semiotic realism." (This technique inevitably results in increased ambiguity; in *The Golden Bowl,* for example, the reader is unsure whether the "right" interpretation is ultimately attained. The deployment of the metaphorical mode in a sense compensates for, or fills the gap left by, the virtual abolition of the audible authorial voice, thus performing a cognitive function for both reader and protagonist.)

As mentioned above, James, as first reader of (and commentator on) his own works, failed to elucidate satisfactorily his own narrative strategies. Subsequent commentators have contributed valuable insights into the representation of the inner world by further refining the concept of point of view with its attendant ambiguities; they have substituted more precise terms such as focalization, thereby laying the foundations on which Cohn's model has recently been constructed.[74]

A key concept here is, of course, that of figural narration with its heightened sense of dramatic immediacy; this is achieved through the reader being given "the illusion of following the mental processes of the central figure directly, without the obtrusive mediative presence of the narrator" or the inevitable removal to a distance necessitated by retrospective first-person narration.[75] Clearly, James's celebrated desire to "Dramatise! Dramatise!" is best served by the figural mode, where although the past tense is used, the reader experiences the action as the present. Thus one could say that it is in the figural novel, such as *The Ambassadors,* and not, paradoxically, in a "scenic" novel like *The Awk-*

ward Age, that James comes closest to achieving his ideal of the dramatic novel.[76]

Another aspect of focalization/point of view that has been neglected in critical studies until fairly recently is that of the distribution of inside views among the characters of a novel and the rhythm of their recurrence in the course of the novel.[77] Stanzel observes that the distribution of the presentation of inside views among the various characters and their relative frequency for a specific character can create a shift in the reader's sympathies to the character who is favored by the presentation of inside views.[78]

Although this claim seems to be sound, closer consideration reveals that it is of dubious general validity. For example, it can be seen that vouchsafing an inside view of Osmond, in *The Portrait,* has the effect of revealing his real intentions and dispels rather than arouses the reader's sympathy for him. So, too, in *The Golden Bowl* inner views of characters such as Charlotte, Adam, and Amerigo often tend to alienate rather than enlist the reader's sympathy. I shall demonstrate more fully in the context of the novels under discussion that although Stanzel's notion of figural narration contributed welcome clarification to this area of study, his claim that interiorization results in a kind of "subliminal wooing of the reader"[79] is an oversimplification; in the portrayal of Osmond, for example, subliminal *warning* rather than *wooing* is the effect created.[80]

An important aspect of focalization, then, that will be examined in this study is that of degree of persistence. In some cases, as in James's *Roderick Hudson* and *The Ambassadors,* focalization remains "fixed" (that is, restricted to a single character) throughout the narrative.[81] In other novels, focalization can alternate between two predominant focalizers, as in *The Golden Bowl,* where James claims that

> the whole thing remains subject to the register, ever so closely kept, of the consciousness of but two of the characters. The Prince, in the first half, virtually sees and knows and makes out, virtually represents to himself everything that concerns us

and "the function of the Princess, in the remainder, matches exactly with his; the register of *her* consciousness is as closely kept" (*AN* 329). In *The Wings of the Dove,* where five characters serve (to varying degrees) as focalizers, focalization again functions as a crucial stylistic and thematic resource.[82]

Recent studies have drawn attention to the varieties of point of view that can be achieved through deployment of the authorial voice, not primarily in its guise of "*histor,*" "bard," and "maker," but in relation to the voices of participants in the fiction. Indeed, it has been noted that

These subtle interactions between speech and thought presentation and point of view have become one of the richest and open-ended [sic] areas of interpretative significance in the novel, and thus constitute an extremely fruitful aspect of the study of style in fiction.[83]

This is indeed an area of rich and complex interpretative significance; it is also something of a minefield in which the commentator needs to tread warily, with caution and critical circumspection. Modes of representation of consciousness, in particular, are slippery constructs and notoriously difficult to pin down. In spite of the contention cited earlier that "Free indirect style has the peculiarity of being very easy to recognise but rather difficult to analyse,"[84] for instance, one finds in effect that both recognition and analysis are fraught with difficulty. The boundaries between the different modes are frequently blurred. To compound the difficulties, we find that although many commentators have produced valid observations on the narrative techniques used by various novelists in the realm of the presentation of fictional consciousness, the terminology used is often fuzzy and imprecise, if not positively misleading. We find, for example, statements such as "Flaubert comes closer, perhaps, than any of his predecessors to the intricate workings of consciousness and his method clearly points the way to the interior monologue."[85] Although few would dispute the general tenor of the statement, its formulation demands the kind of clarification afforded by more finely honed critical categories. What exactly is meant by "interior monologue" here? Does this refer only to the use of (quoted) interior monologue (in the first person and enclosed in inverted commas) or does it include what is generally known as free indirect style, of which Flaubert was indeed an early exponent?

Similarly, we find:

> Flaubert takes up a middle ground between direct authorial presentation and analysis on the one hand and a presentation entirely in term of a character's feelings, interpretations and judgements on the other. This middle ground is very much the manner of James in his novels from *The Portrait of a Lady* to *The Tragic Muse*.[86]

Such a sweeping statement fails to take account of subtleties such as the gradual modulation from authorial to figural narration in *The Portrait;* the putative "middle ground" is not a stable stance on terra firma but turns out to be a shifting stance on unstable terrain. Clearly, statements such as these need to be further clarified and the means whereby these shifts are implemented analyzed more systematically.[87]

Furthermore, comments concerning narrative strategies such as the "intermingling of the inner and the outer worlds" in *The Wings of the Dove* bristle with imprecision;[88] is this a reference to evocations of Milly's world being filtered through her own consciousness, or does it mean the intermingling of the inner world—or more accurately the inner voice—of the ("subjective") reflector and that of the ("objective") narrator, such as that exemplified in style indirect libre?

Obviously, more finely honed critical categories are needed for clarification of techniques used in the presentation of fictional consciousness. Notions like "interior monologue" need to be reassessed. Similarly, as Cohn has observed, Scholes and Kellogg's term "narrative analysis" (like "omniscient description" and "internal analysis") is unsatisfactory. Her own terminology, which is examined in the next chapter, aims at greater clarity and precision.

2

The Representation of Consciousness in Fiction: Dorrit Cohn's Model

In this chapter, I attempt to present a coherent account of central features of Cohn's paradigm as set out in *Transparent Minds: Narrative Modes for Presenting Consciousness in Fiction* while illustrating these features in representative extracts from James's novels. Although Cohn makes passing reference to several of James's novels (including *The Portrait*), the references are necessarily fairly cursory, and no mention is made of either *Roderick Hudson* or *The Golden Bowl*. In discussing these novels in the light of Cohn's model in subsequent chapters, I hope to show how new insights into the development of James's narrative strategies in the representation of consciousness can be generated through the application of this taxonomy.

In her study, Dorrit Cohn provides the most "reader-friendly" model to date for distinguishing modes of representation of fictional consciousness. Her theoretical framework was not, of course, created in a vacuum; *Transparent Minds* draws on the findings of previous theorists such as those already cited.[1] When considered in conjunction with Cohn's own work, most of these studies furnish interesting complementary material. However, Cohn's study provides the most illuminating and comprehensive account of the presentation of thought rather than speech.

Cohn's point of departure is the manifest lack of clarity and precision afforded by the current conceptual categories. According to Cohn, the concept "narrative analysis," for example, does not allow for other possibilities of presentation such as "the plainly reportorial, or the highly imagistic ways a narrator may adopt in narrating consciousness" (11). The validity of this objection is obvious when one considers the densely imagistic mode of James's presentation of consciousness in his later novels. The term Cohn has coined, "psychonarration," has the advantage of indicating more accurately "both the subject-matter and the activity it denotes." This, then, is the first (and the most indirect) of Dorrit Cohn's three designated modes of presenting consciousness in fiction in the context of third-person narration.[2]

44

For the second basic technique, Cohn proposes the term "quoted monologue" to replace the earlier "interior monologue": "since the interiority (silence) of self-address is generally assumed in modern narrative, 'interior' is a near-redundant modifier, and should . . . be replaced by 'quoted'." The two factors common to all thought-quotations, as Cohn points out, are "the reference to the thinking self in the first person, and to the narrated moment (which is also the moment of locution) in the present tense" (12).

The third technique is one that has been largely neglected in English criticism until relatively recently. As we have seen, Scholes and Kellogg identify only "two principal devices for presenting the inner life: narrative analysis and interior monologue" (193). The device omitted is in fact the technique "that probably renders the largest number of figural thoughts in the fiction of the last hundred years, that known in French as *style indirect libre* and in German as *erlebte rede*." Cohn adopts the term "narrated monologue" to replace "free indirect speech," as this implies its position "astride narration and quotation." She explains that

> Linguistically it is the most complex of the three techniques: like psycho-narration it retains the third-person reference and the tense of narration, but like the quoted monologue it reproduces verbatim the character's own mental language. (14)

Summarizing the main features of each technique, then, Cohn presents "in capsule formulation": 1. "psycho-narration: the narrator's discourse about a character's consciousness; 2. quoted monologue: a character's mental discourse; 3. narrated monologue: a character's mental discourse in the guise of the narrator's discourse" (14).[3]

PSYCHONARRATION

In exploring psychonarration, Cohn notes the avoidance of this technique in early novels. In Thackeray's *Vanity Fair,* for instance, the narrator observes that "How Miss Sharp lay awake, thinking, will he come or not tomorrow? need not be told here."[4] The narrator's lack of interest in his character's thoughts—and the concomitant avoidance of psychonarration—exemplifies a type of fiction in which "a hyperactive narrator deals with a multitude of characters and situations by rapid shifts in time and space." Prolonged inside views appeared rarely outside first-person novels; third-person novels concentrated on overt action with the inner selves of the characters revealed only indirectly through spoken language and expressive gesture. In typical nineteenth-century novels (for example, those of Dickens and Turgenev), the predominance of directly quoted conversations and the rare examples of self-communion reveal this tendency toward dramatic form.[5]

A significant factor deflecting the novels of authors such as Fielding and Thackeray from presenting inside views is the presence of a "vocal authorial narrator, unable to refrain from embedding his character's private thoughts in his own generalizations about human nature" (Cohn 22). His narrative stance commits him to explicit and often didactic evaluation. *Vanity Fair* abounds in illustrations of this phenomenon.

In this respect, Thackeray and Fielding can be seen as being at the opposite pole of a novelist like James who, in the later novels particularly, provides little authorial guidance or didactic evaluation. James himself made an apposite comment on the approach of Fielding (who, in James's book, would be categorized with Thackeray as a fellow-transgressor) claiming that *Tom Jones*'s author

> has such an amplitude of reflexion for him and round him that we see him through the mellow air of Fielding's fine old moralism, fine old humour and fine old style, which somehow really enlarge, make every one and every thing important. (*AN* 68)

In James's later novels, by contrast, there is minimal authorial "amplitude of reflexion" for or around his characters. The reader is enjoined to see them not through a specific moral perspective defined by the author but in the light of his own tentative speculations.

Cohn notes that "a typical passage of psycho-narration in a narrator-oriented novel starts with a brief sentence or two in the past, followed by several longer and more elaborate sentences in the present" (23), the gnomic present tense being used for aphoristic generic comments. Such authorial rhetoric can impede the evocation of the inner life, substituting instead either a battery (and sometimes a battering) of aphoristic utterances or else a series of mock-serious parodic injunctions (as in *Vanity Fair*)—or both.

In James's earlier novels, residual traces of this pattern can still be detected, although he rarely provides sustained exemplification of the kind of authorial narration practiced by George Eliot, where the inner life of a specific character serves primarily as "a sounding-board for general truths about human nature." In his first novel, *Watch and Ward,* we find, for example:

> He flung [the purse] on the floor, and passed his hands over his face. "Nora, Nora," he cried, "say it outright; you despise me!"
> He had become, in the brief space of a moment, the man she once had loved; but if he was no longer the rose, he stood too near it to be wantonly bruised.

Men and women alike need in some degree to respect those they have suffered
to wrong them. She stooped and picked up the *porte-monnaie,* like a beggar-
maid in a ballad. (231)

Instead of a brief sentence or two in the past, followed by several
longer and more elaborate sentences in the present, the Jamesian narrator
restricts himself to a brief excursion into the aphoristic present tense—
the generalization is short and pithy rather than protracted and wide-
ranging. This tendency is manifested throughout the novel, as indeed in
the later novels when such generalizations make a sporadic appearance.

Similarly, in this extract from *Washington Square,* the brevity of the
aphoristic generic statement is indicative of a shift away from the typical
markedly authorial mode:

if she had been told at such a moment that he would not return for a year, or
even that he would never return, she would not have complained nor rebelled,
but would have humbly accepted the decree, and sought for consolation in
thinking over the times she had already seen him, the words he had spoken,
the sound of his voice, of his tread, the expression of his face. Love demands
certain things as a right; but Catherine had no sense of her rights. (67)

James's novels, then, provide only attenuated examples of the recurrent pattern characteristic of traditional authorial narration in which the
narrator mentions an inner happening, then imposes a value judgment,
which is immediately followed by a change of tense from narrative past
to gnomic present, and a change of subject from the individual to the
species—for example, "men and women alike"—as exemplified in *Vanity
Fair* and *Middlemarch.*

In terms of the historical development of the novel, it is apparent that
as the intrusive, vocal narrator withdraws from the fictional scene a figural
consciousness of greater intellectual complexity emerges (25). It is under-
standable then, as Cohn points out, that those authors who first "insisted
on the removal of vociferous narrators from fiction—notably Flaubert and
Henry James—were also the creators of fictional minds with previously
unparalleled depth and complexity" (26).[6]

This could be illustrated through a comparison between James's
Strether and Fielding's Tom Jones, described by James as

a hero as intimately bewildered as a young man of great health and spirits may
be when he hasn't a grain of imagination: the point to be made is, at all events,
that his sense of bewilderment obtains altogether on the comic, never on the
tragic plane. He has so much "life" that it amounts, for the effect of comedy
and application of satire, almost to his having a mind, that is to his having
reactions and a full consciousness; besides which his author—*he* handsomely

possessed of a mind—has such an amplitude of reflexion for him and round him. (*AN* 68)

In the case of Tom Jones, then, all imagination, perception, and "mind" is monopolized by his creator (in the persona of narrator) who invests his protagonist only with lively animal spirits. Because of the immeasurably greater imaginative range and intellectual complexity of Strether, with his capacity for "amplitude of reflexion" in his own right, his "bewilderment" has both comic and tragic resonances.

Dorrit Cohn introduces the terms "dissonance" and "consonance" to designate the two typical narrative situations which Stanzel defines for third-person narration: authorial and figural. The term "dissonant" applies to the relationship between the narrator and the protagonist in an authorial narrative situation, and the term "consonant" to that relationship in a figural narrative situation (275).[7] Cohn cites two novels that exemplify these two types of psychonarration: *Death In Venice* by Thomas Mann and Joyce's *A Portrait of the Artist*. In the Jamesian canon, one could mention *Watch and Ward, Washington Square,* and *The Bostonians* as authorial or dissonant, with the narrator remaining distanced from the consciousness he narrates, and *The Ambassadors* as figural or consonant, in that it is "mediated by a narrator who remains [largely] effaced and who readily fuses with the consciousness he narrates" (26). (*Roderick Hudson* and *The Portrait* are more problematic as they exemplify what I have called "quasi-figural" narration.)

Cohn identifies a number of stylistic features that typify psychonarration with maximal dissonance. These include *ex cathedra* statements in the gnomic present tense, the use of "distancing appellations" (such as "poor Catherine" in *Washington Square,* and even "poor Strether" in *The Ambassadors,* "our young lady" in *The Portrait, The Wings of the Dove,* and *The Golden Bowl*), and the use of an abstract analytical vocabulary to describe the inner world. This conceptual language reveals that a dominant narrator presents the inner life in a detached way, a manner far removed from the psychic experience itself (28). These features all indicate the narrator's superior knowledge of the character's inner life and a concomitant superior ability to present it and assess it.

A comparison between the depiction of Catherine's response to her scheming suitor, Morris, and Isabel's to hers, Gilbert Osmond, could illustrate this point. In *Washington Square* (dissonant narration), the narrator informs us that "Morris Townsend was an object on which she found that her imagination could exercise itself indefinitely" (50); in *The Portrait* (comparatively consonant narration) we are *shown* the process whereby Isabel's imagination exercises itself on the subject of her ostensibly noble and self-effacing suitor, Osmond. We are given access to the workings of

Isabel's imagination, not merely told of its activity. In *Washington Square,* it is through largely dissonant psychonarration—highlighted here through the abstract analytical vocabulary, the presence of an *ex cathedra* statement in the gnomic present tense, and the distancing appellation "the poor girl"—that we learn of the nature of Catherine's passion:

> If she had been told she was in love, she would have been a great deal surprised; for she had an idea that love was an eager and exacting passion, and her own heart was filled in these days with the impulse of self-effacement and sacrifice. . . . Love demands certain things as a right; but Catherine had no sense of her rights; she had only a consciousness of immense and unexpected favors. . . . the poor girl's dumb eloquence irritated [her father]. (67–68)

In chapter 42 of *The Portrait,* by contrast, we note the absence of the aforementioned features and the way in which psychonarration modulates constantly into narrated monologue and moves away from an abstract analytical vocabulary into the more metaphorical mode associated with figural narration. Thus, instead of being told by the narrator of Isabel's ardent impulse of self-sacrifice and desire to be of service, we participate in her imaginative recreation of her earlier feelings, which are dramatized in imagery such as

> He was like a sceptical voyager strolling on the beach while he waited for the tide, looking seaward yet not putting to sea. It was in all this she had found her occasion. She would launch his boat for him; she would be his providence; it would be a good thing to love him. And she had loved him, she had so anxiously and yet so ardently given herself. (2.192)[8]

When imagery is used in *Washington Square* to depict Catherine's feeling for Morris, it is generally used by the narrator in dissonant psychonarration rather than narrated monologue (as in the extract from *The Portrait*) and, being appropriate to a conventional and somewhat limited protagonist, consists largely of bland clichés such as "she had regarded it [Morris' love], very naturally, as a priceless treasure" (79). Isabel is an infinitely more imaginative and intelligent protagonist than Catherine, and this is reflected in part in the language (speech and thought) attributed to each protagonist. A comparison between these two extracts also demonstrates that the reflector mode is better adapted to the depiction of fictional psyches of greater depth and complexity: the vocal authorial narrator is dispensable in novels such as these where the characters are eminently well endowed with the capacity for speaking—and thinking—for themselves.

A comparison between the meditative fireside vigils of the two protagonists could further elucidate differences between the dissonant authorial and (intermittently) consonant figural modes:

> Catherine sat alone by the parlor fire—sat there for more than an hour, lost in her meditations. Her aunt seemed to her aggressive and foolish; and to see it so clearly—to judge Mrs Penniman so positively—made her feel old and grave. She did not resent the imputation of weakness; it made no impression on her, for she had not the sense of weakness, and she was not hurt at not being appreciated. She had an immense respect for her father, and she felt that to displease him would be a misdemeanor analogous to an act of profanity in a great temple. (121)

In Isabel's meditative vigil, in contrast to the "abstract and analytical vocabulary" used in *Washington Square* to present the protagonist laboriously puzzling things out, we find her experiencing a "mind assailed by visions." Her attainment of understanding is presented not primarily through an abstract analytical vocabulary reflecting ratiocination but through a variety of images that at times have an almost hallucinatory quality. Her recognitions are filtered through her own consciousness and presented in a vividly metaphorical mode. This contrasts with the abstract and sophisticated vocabulary in which Catherine's thoughts are couched—"A misdemeanor analogous . . . temple"—which emphasizes that the formulation is that of the narrator rather than that of the character (thus increasing the impression of dissonance.)

According to Cohn,

> the cognitive and linguistic disparity between a narrator and his character is of particular relevance to the narration of those levels of consciousness that cannot be clearly shaped into verbal patterns by the fictional mind itself. (29)

This means that psychonarration has a greater capacity to explore the subliminal areas of the mind (hence the preponderance of psychonarration in *What Maisie Knew*). Furthermore, both explicit and implicit evaluative judgment of the figural figure by the narrator is possible through psychonarration; this accounts for the approval of critics like Booth who favor the dispensation of moral guidance for the reader of the novel.

The absence of authorial rhetoric in consonant narration (as in, for example, Joyce's *A Portrait of the Artist*) creates the impression that the narrator's knowledge of the character's psyche coincides with the character's own self-knowledge (31). In *The Ambassadors,* there are subtle disparities between Strether's knowledge and ethical norms and those of the narrator. Although *The Ambassadors* is held to typify what Cohn terms "consonant" narration, cognitive and ethical or normative discrepancies do exist between narrator and figural consciousness. Strether's blanket equation of a "virtuous attachment" with a chaste relationship, for example, would presumably not be subscribed to by the narrator, and the real nature of the relationship between Strether and Madame de Vionnet is apparent to the reader long before Strether himself is enlightened. In *What Maisie Knew,* the cognitive distance between narrator and figural consciousness is gradually narrowed toward the end of the novel. Paradoxically, a disparity of knowledge and of values between narrator and protagonist characterizes James's figural novels.

Another feature foregrounded by Cohn is what she terms "stylistic contagion"—places where psychonarration verges on the narrated monologue, marking a kind of midpoint between the two techniques where a reporting syntax is maintained, but where the idiom is strongly colored by the mental idiom of the mind it reflects (33). This phenomenon is also discussed by Leech and Short who designate as "slipping" the unobtrusive shift from one mode to another. Slipping, it is noted, can be effectively exploited in the manipulation of point of view:

> It allows an author to slip from narrative statement to interior portrayal without the reader noticing what has occurred, and as the reader has little choice but to take on trust the views of the narrator, when character and narrator are merged in this way he tends to take over the view of the character too.[9]

In the terminology used here, "narrative statement" would correspond to "psychonarration" and "interior portrayal" to "narrated monologue." The demonstrable lack of clarity in Leech and Short's terminology emerges here, as "interior portrayal" could refer to either narrator-dominated psychonarration or the merging of the two voices in narrated monologue. In "slipping" or "stylistic contagion" the ironic effect often created by narrated monologue is dissipated as the narrator moves closer to the sympathetic pole.

Chatman's discussion of this phenomenon would seem to confirm this interpretation. He states that (with reference to speech rather than thought):

> Sometimes it is not possible to decide whether the words in indirect free form are the character's or the narrator's, for example, if both speak in a highly literate manner. This is not a negative characterization, since the merging of the two voices may well be an intended aesthetic effect. The implication is "It doesn't matter who says or thinks this; it is appropriate to both character and narrator." The ambiguity may strengthen the bond between the two, make us trust still more the narrator's authority. Perhaps we should speak of "neutralization" or "unification" rather than ambiguity.[10]

An example from *Washington Square* could clarify this:

"If I don't marry before your death, I will not after," she said.
To her father, it must be admitted, this seemed only another epigram; and as obstinacy, in unaccomplished minds, does not usually select such a mode of expression, he was the more surprised at this wanton play of a fixed idea. (124)

Here the statement "obstinacy . . . expression" could be interpreted as emanating from either the narrator or Dr. Sloper, thus ostensibly creating a sense of complicity between the two voices and "neutralizing" any possible disparity between them. Later this complicity is subverted as the narrator distances himself from Sloper's mordantly ironic stance.

Scenic descriptions of Rome in both *Roderick Hudson* and *The Portrait* often exemplify stylistic contagion, as uncertainty persists as to whether the perception of the scene reflects that of the narrator or the character concerned. In *The Portrait,* for example, we find:

She had long before this taken old Rome into her confidence, for in a world of ruins the ruin of her happiness seemed a less unnatural catastrophe. . . . as she sat in a sun-warmed angle on a winter's day, or stood in a mouldy church to which no one came, she could almost smile at it and think of its smallness. Small it was, in the large Roman record, and her haunting sense of the continuity of the human lot easily carried her from the less to the greater. (2.327)

It is not clear here whether the comment that Isabel's misery was "small" in terms of the "large Roman record" should be assigned to the narrator or Isabel herself. The effect created is that of a merger of the two voices and an identification of Isabel's perception with the narrator's own.

In *Washington Square,* Dr. Sloper expresses himself in a "highly literate manner," and a witty epigrammatic style of expression characterizes both his and the narrator's discourse. Wit and irony are often used at Catherine's expense, as when the narrator's comment (stating the obvious through understatement) "But Catherine could never be sharp" is echoed three lines down by "her satiric parent" who comments sarcastically to himself, "Decidedly, my daughter is not brilliant" (58). Later the opposite effect is created when the diction of Dr. Sloper himself resonates in the narrated monologue with an almost parodic effect. Narrated monologue here is preceded by quoted monologue, but in this context the juxtaposition of the two modes does not seem to identify the formulation of the narrated monologue as that of the narrator.

"No wonder she . . . thinks me a cruel tyrant, which of course she does, though she is afraid—she hasn't the animation necessary—to admit it to herself. Poor old Catherine!" mused the Doctor; "I verily believe she is capable of defending me when Townsend abuses me!"

And the force of this reflection, for the moment, was such in making him feel the natural opposition between his point of view and that of an infatuated child, that he said to himself that he was perhaps after all taking things too hard, and crying out before he was hurt. (73)

The imitation of Sloper's own diction here emphasizes the limitations of the simplistic antithesis between his point of view (epitomizing verity or rectitude, to his mind) and that of his unfortunate daughter who is dismissed as a mere "infatuated child." The extract illustrates an incipient divergence between the voice of the narrator and that of Sloper, a divergence that is more strongly manifested as the novel progresses.

"Slipping" or stylistic contagion, then, can serve to create specific thematic and stylistic effects. Attention has also been drawn recently to a related technique, that of "switching," which can take two forms: "the first occurs when the mode of speech and/or thought of a particular character changes over time . . . a form of switching which is associated with or indicative of some degree of character or personality change," and the second type occurs when the author or narrator "consistently uses different forms of speech or thought presentation for different characters within a dialogue."[11] The first form is exemplified in *What Maisie Knew* where the gradual switch from psychonarration to narrated monologue in the latter part of the novel reflects Maisie's growing capacity to think for herself; she becomes less dependent on the narrator's formulations. The incidence and implications of these techniques will be examined more closely in the context of the selected texts.

Interestingly, although the question of ambiguity in James has been examined by various commentators (Rimmon-Kenan, Charles Samuels, and Edmund Wilson, inter alia),[12] all fail to establish a connection between this ambiguity and the aforementioned technique (stylistic contagion and "switching")—or, indeed, with the use of free indirect discourse (the term covers both free indirect speech and free indirect thought/narrated monologue). The ambiguity stemming from its use not only in association with other techniques for rendering spoken or silent discourse but even as a device in its own right, one that neutralizes the distinction between diegesis and mimesis, between the narrator's voice and that of his characters, has not been explored fully.

Another important feature distinguishing psychonarration from quoted and narrated monologues is that of temporal flexibility: the mode's capacity for "summary and expansion." In the modes of quoted monologue and narrated monologue the rendering of consciousness is "temporarily restricted to the sequential instants of silent locution, the time of narration roughly coinciding with the narrated time" (33–34). Psychonarration, by contrast, can be used to summarize an inner development over a long period of time, to render the flow of successive thoughts and feelings, or to expand and explore a specific mental instant. Chapter 42 of *The Portrait* is perhaps the most vivid illustration of the device of summary psychonarration, evoking as it does Isabel's perception of three years of married life with Osmond, which had previously been elided or to which only oblique references had been made.

Cohn draws attention to an effective device—favored by Flaubert—for "vitalizing" summary psychonarration: the striking image, which often takes the form of a "hyperbolic simile" (36). One of the examples selected from *Madame Bovary* makes an interesting comparison with a comparable image from *The Golden Bowl:* in Flaubert's text, we have "As for the memory of Rodolphe, she had buried it in the very depths of her heart; and it remained there more solemn and immobile than the mummy of a king in a subterranean tomb." In *The Golden Bowl,* Maggie conceives of her egregious situation, her relationship with her husband and his mistress, her father's wife, in terms of a fantastic structure, "some strange, tall tower of ivory, or perhaps rather some wonderfully beautiful, but outlandish pagoda" (299). Whereas in the Flaubert text, the image is rendered in the narrator's discourse, psychonarration, in *The Golden Bowl* the presentation is ambiguous, as the reader is not initially sure whether the image is conjured up by Maggie herself or by the narrator on her behalf. This uncertainty—associated, as we have seen, with "stylistic contagion"—is subsequently dispelled by the narrator's comment, "She had walked round and round it—that was what she felt" (301). In some instances, the authorial provenance of these "synoptic similes" or "imagistic distillates" is stressed and the character's own mental processes are set in the ironic context of a more enlightened perspective.

These "imagistic distillates" or analogies contrast forcibly with the kind of detailed analysis of mental processes used by earlier novelists such as Jane Austen. An apt example here would be Elizabeth's reaction to Darcy's letter in *Pride and Prejudice.* Prominent linguistic features here include the repetition of phrases suggesting cognitive activity such as "She perfectly remembered," "She was now struck with," "She saw," "She remembered that", "She remembered also, that." The narrator's analytic report is followed by quoted monologue introduced by "How despicably I have acted!" she cried," and ending with the climactic "Till this moment, I never knew myself."[13] The method of presentation here contrasts with the densely imagistic mode used in *The Portrait* to render comparable cognitive activity which also culminates in the revelation of prior self-deception and the attainment of self-knowledge. The "process of vision" in *The Portrait,* as already noted, is conveyed through a variety of images generated by the protagonist's imagination.

Cohn points out that Austen's analytical surveys are more typical of realist novels, whereas Flaubert's (and, one could add, James's) "imagistic surveys anticipate a technique frequently found in modern psychological novels, where "psycho-analogies" are used to convey a mental instant" (37). Interestingly, in Jane Austen's novels, characters using imagery in their speech are often suspect (for example, Collins in *Pride and Prejudice*): the pompous, pretentious, or duplicitous habitually indulge in imagistic language.

Summary psychonarration is found infrequently in figural novels, as this technique, with its capacity for rendering surveys covering an extended temporal span, advertizes the presence of a narrator with a distanced, bird's-eye view. In James's novels, "broader inner-time vistas" are generally achieved by being filtered through the memory of the protagonist. In *The Portrait,* for example, chapter 42 illustrates the use of this "mnemonic flashback pattern." During Isabel's retrospective vigil, the early period of her married life, to which no reference had been made up to that point, is evoked through memory. At the beginning of *The Wings,* Kate's present position is rendered through her musings rather than narratorial report. In *The Golden Bowl,* too, the Prince's situation at the inception of the novel is similarly conveyed through his own retrospective evocation, creating the impression that we have his view of it rather than the narrator's. In Isabel's vigil, in which she is depicted as "motionlessly seeing," it is through "imagistic distillates" conjured up by her imagination rather than through sustained sequential rational analysis that she attains clarity of understanding.

Whereas psychoanalogies in summary narration serve to distill the essence of mental events occurring over a long period of time, the same device in punctual narration has the opposite effect of expanding time or arresting it (41). Some authors, like Proust, use psychoanalogies in a markedly authorial manner, whereas James infuses similes more directly into the thought-stream of his characters.

At times, similes seem to induce a fusion between the narrating and the figural consciousness by blurring the line that separates them. It is difficult to tell with certainty whether a specific analogical association originates in the mind of the narrator or in the protagonist's own. In *The Ambassadors,* the image of the pail carried to the fountain could be that of Strether or of the narrator.

the time seemed already far off when he had held out his small thirsty cup to the spout of her [Maria Gostrey's] pail. Her pail was scarce touched now, and other fountains had flowed for him; she fell into her place as but one of his tributaries. (2.48).

Further on, we find that "she had shrunk to a secondary element . . . and now mainly figured for him as but part of the bristling total—though of course always as a person to whom he should never cease to be indebted" (2.49). In the first extract, the analogical association seems to emanate from the narrator (thus exonerating Strether somewhat from a charge of callous exploitation), whereas in the second the formulation suggests Strether's own expression. (The last part certainly is redolent of Strether's characteristic rather self-conscious moral fastidiousness.)

Cohn observes that "imagistic excursions" are used by Virginia Woolf to convey "moments of vision" (45). It is clear that this device is also prominent in James's novels where a central focus is invariably on "the process of vision" of the protagonist: the imagistic mode is adopted to render moments of intense illumination where the character attains sudden insight—authentic or spurious—into a specific aspect of his or her situation. In *The Portrait,* the recognition scenes (and particularly Isabel's meditative vigil), and in *The Golden Bowl,* Adam's quasi-epiphanic revelatory experience inspiring him to propose marriage to Charlotte provides instantiation of this.

It is demonstrated convincingly, then, that psychonarration, with the opportunities it affords for metaphoric representation of the inner life, is an invaluable tool for the novelist "discovering, lens in hand, the micro-structure of life"[14]—where the lens, obviously, is that of a microscope rather than telescope.

An aspect of "the micro-structure of life" that is most successfully rendered through psychonarration is that of subverbal states. Because of its "verbal independence from self-articulation," psychonarration has the capacity not only to structure and explain a character's conscious thoughts better than the character himself, but also to "effectively articulate a psychic life that remains unverbalised, penumbral, or obscure" (46). James's novel *What Maisie Knew* provides an interesting exemplification of the capacity of psychonarration to render thoughts and perceptions that the protagonist herself is unable to articulate (47).

James observes in the preface that "small children have many more perceptions than they have terms to translate them." The narrator, then, uses the mode of psychonarration to "translate" Maisie's inchoate perceptions and groping thoughts into articulate form. Maisie is the "ironic centre" of the story, whose subverbal perceptions the narrator's "own commentary constantly attends and amplifies . . . in figures that are not yet at her command" (*AN* 146). A significant aspect of *What Maisie Knew* is the increasing proportion of narrated monologue as opposed to psychonarration in the latter section of the novel, as Maisie develops the capacity to formulate her own conceptions.

Unlike Maisie, Strether has at his command a whole battery of "figures," images which function as double-edged weapons which can either clarify or obfuscate. After the revelatory encounter by the river, he conceives of his previous impossibly idealistic conception of the relationship between Chad and Madame de Vionnet as being that of someone who "had dressed the possibility in vagueness, as a little girl might have dressed her doll" (2.265). In a sense, the mature Strether too is an intermittent "ironic centre" in that, as has been noted, there is often a discrepancy between his awareness and that of the narrator; furthermore, there is a disparity between his conscious understanding of the nature of the "virtuous attachment" between Chad and Madame de Vionnet and his subliminal realization of what the attachment really entails.

Discussion of the selected novels in subsequent chapters will focus on the way in which psychonarration—particularly in the metaphoric mode—is used in conjunction with other techniques for the representation of consciousness.

Psychonarration is also eminently suited to rendering erotic experience, "an inner realm particularly in need of narrative mediation . . . with its singularly simultaneous involvement of psyche and soma" (49). Skeptics might maintain that the erotic is a realm into which James ventured rarely—or ponderously, if at all. Andre Gide, for instance, claims that James's characters "are only winged busts; all the weight of the flesh is absent, and all the shaggy, tangled undergrowth, all the wild darkness."[15] Edith Wharton echoes this criticism in an appropriately hirsute image, complaining that James "stripped his characters of all the human fringes we necessarily trail after us through life."[16] While one would willingly concede that James is at the furthest possible remove from his eponymous author in "Greville Fane," who "wrote only from the elbow down,"[17] it does not necessarily follow that he wrote only "from the neck up," as Gide's comment seems to imply, to produce mere bloodless cerebration. This idea would be promptly dispelled by even a cursory reading of the last scene between Isabel and Caspar Goodwood or the scenes of controlled—or indulged—passion between Charlotte and the Prince in *The Golden Bowl.*

It is often impossible to delimit psychonarration clearly from the narration of sensations that impinge on a character's mind, from within or from without. This is particularly true of figural narration, where the "narration of external reality is intimately related to subjective perception" and the boundary between the external and the internal is blurred. Merging of the realms of inner and outer fictional reality is facilitated when the sights characters see and the sounds they hear are introduced by perception

verbs (49). In such instances, psyche and scene are linked and it is difficult to distinguish between psychonarration and scenic description. This
phenomenon is prevalent in *The Ambassadors;* one could cite Strether's
perception of the facade of Chad's house, the scene in Gloriani's garden,
and his general perception of Paris:

> It hung before him this morning, the vast bright Babylon, like some huge
> iridescent object, a jewel brilliant and hard, in which parts were not to be
> discriminated nor differences comfortably marked. It twinkled and trembled
> and melted together, and what seemed all surface one moment seemed all
> depth the next. (1.89)

Another vivid example can be found in his perception of and response
to the French countryside in the episode where he encounters Chad and
Madame de Vionnet on the river. He sees the scene in terms of a landscape painting:

> The oblong gilt frame disposed its enclosing lines; the poplars and willows, the
> reeds and river . . . fell into a composition, full of felicity, within them; the
> sky was silver and turquoise and varnish; the village on the left was white and
> the church on the right was grey. (2.247)

Later his perception becomes more impressionistic as he sees "a village
that affected him as a thing of whiteness, blueness and crookedness, set
in coppery green, and that had the river flowing behind or before it—one
couldn't say which" (2.252).

A detailed examination of this scene would reveal that narrated perception here performs the thematic function of dramatizing the change in
Strether's mode of viewing from that associated with the Lambinet landscape he was seeking to recapture, to that of the Impressionists.[18] In the
course of the novel, Strether is initiated into a new mode of perception
in which the play of light on surfaces ("the high light of Paris, a cool full
studio-light, becoming yet treacherous") (2.76) seems to dissolve all firm
outlines and blur fixed perspectives, both visual and moral.

Purely imaginary perceptions are at times introduced by the same
phrases that signal a character's perception of the world around him; for
example, hallucinatory visions can be introduced by the phrase "he
[Adam] saw . . .", as in *The Golden Bowl.* In this instance, the technique
is used for conveying moments of spurious or suspect (as opposed to
authentic) insight.

Psychonarration is also used for the evocation of dreams in fiction
(Cohn 51). However, since James tends to restrict his focus to the more
rational, articulate areas of consciousness and avoids frequent or pro-

longed delving into the penumbral regions of the psyche, only isolated instances of dream-evocation occur.[19]

According to Leon Edel, "the unconscious cannot be expressed in its own unconscious form, since obviously this is unconscious. *We can only infer it from symbols emerging in the conscious expression of the person*" (Edel's emphasis).[20] As Cohn remarks—and Edel does not seem to perceive—"a novelist need not limit himself to symbols of the unconscious that appear in his character's consciousness as long as he uses his own language rather than his character's." Thus, psychonarration can be seen as the most direct, indeed the unique—and yet the most mediated— means of access to the subverbal strata of the mind.

In summary, we find that psychonarration is used to convey subliminal areas of experience, for the erotic, for the sphere of dreams and visions, and to render thoughts and perceptions which the protagonist herself is unable to articulate. (*The Portrait* and *The Golden Bowl* furnish examples of the evocation—through psychonarration—of the hallucinatory quality of revelatory insights experienced by Isabel, Maggie, and Adam Verver.)

It is thus clear that—contrary to the view of theorists such as Stanzel— this mode of representation, the most indirect and traditional, is eminently well-adapted to the portrayal of the least conscious strata of psychic life. The second mode, "quoted [interior] monologue," is "by definition limited to the linguistic activity of the mind, whereas the unconscious is by definition radically devoid of language" (57).

QUOTED MONOLOGUE

It was not until the middle of the nineteenth century that the quoted interior monologue became a fully established technique.[21] In earlier novels, elaborate authorial introductions preceded the infrequent monologues, which were invariably conducted in a clearly audible voice. In *Tom Jones,* for instance, we find a chapter entitled "Containing a conversation which Mr. Jones had with himself," in which the aforementioned conversation is indeed conducted *à haute voix.* Even in James's novels, particularly earlier works such as *Watch and Ward,* formulations such as Roger "said to himself" are frequently present.

In early fiction, then, characters spoke their thoughts aloud to themselves and writers used inquit phrases (phrases performing the function of identifying the speaker and sometimes indicating the mode of speaking; for example, "he cried," "she exclaimed," "they shouted"). This method of representation of silent thought is prevalent throughout pre-Realist novels.

The audibly soliloquizing voice is often associated with self-conscious posing, rationalization, or self-deceit. James makes use of this device in *Watch and Ward,* for instance, where the opportunist Fenton's self-conscious posing is revealed:

> Fenton, of course, was forced to admit that he had reckoned without his host. Roger had had the impudence not to turn out a simpleton; he was not a shepherd of the golden age; he was a dogged modern, with prosy prejudices; the wind of his favour blew as it listed. Fenton took the liberty of being extremely irritated at the other's want of ductility. "Hang the man!" he said to himself, "why can't he trust me? What is he afraid of? Why don't he take me as a friend rather than an enemy? Let him be frank, and I will be frank. I could put him up to several things. And what does he want to do with Nora, anyway?" (84)

This extract is a vivid illustration of the "rationalization and self-deceit" often attending quoted monologue, especially as the quoted monologue is embedded in authorial comment and dissonant psychonarration that highlights the contrast between Fenton's real and professed concerns. His frustration at being unable to hoodwink Roger emerges in his soliloquizing rationalization. Fenton pretends, even to himself, that his motives are above suspicion, and his solecism "Why don't he . . ." emphazises the disparities of class and education (in addition to differing ethical standards) that exist between Fenton and his host.

It is noteworthy that in *Washington Square* the character who is superlatively deficient in characteristics of "rationalization and self-deceit," Catherine Sloper, is the only important character who is not accorded access to the monologic mode of expression. Both her father and her duplicitous suitor, Morris, at times express their innermost thoughts in the form of quoted monologue. In Dr. Sloper's case, the use of quoted monologue highlights the discrepancy between his stance of parental concern for Catherine's welfare and his secret enjoyment of the game of exercising power over her and pursuing what is his prime concern—that of being proved right.

This emerges clearly in the scene where he adopts the pose of Rejected Parent disparaged by a Heartless Ingrate of a Daughter. Having informed Catherine that "If you see him, you will be an ungrateful, cruel child; you will have given your old father the greatest pain of his life" (126), he ejects her coldly and unceremoniously from his inner sanctum, refusing to respond compassionately to her sincere display of grief. His suppressed excitement at the unexpectedly interesting dimensions the game is acquiring and his cold-blooded lack of concern for his daughter's suffering is revealed in his quoted monologue: "By Jove," he said to himself, "I believe she will stick—I believe she will stick!" His callousness is highlighted by contrast with Mrs. Almond's choice of verb—"She will cling" (rather than "stick")—suggesting that she perceives Catherine's stance as a desperate need of affection rather than an obdurate refusal to give way.

Morris's quoted monologues all express his derogatory views of Mrs. Penniman and Catherine, and stress the contrast between his professed and his real feelings. For example, when Morris is in conversation with Mrs. Penniman: "'The woman's an idiot!' thought Morris; but he was obliged to say something different" (112). Mrs. Penniman asks Morris about his intentions:

"Do you mean—do you mean another marriage?"
Morris greeted this question with a reflection which was hardly the less impudent from being inaudible.
"Surely women are more crude than men!" And then he answered, audibly, "Never in the world!" (177)

When discussing Catherine's projected trip to Europe, Morris asks her,

"Should you like to see all those celebrated things over there?"
"Oh no, Morris!" said Catherine, quite deprecatingly.
"Gracious Heaven, what a dull woman!" Morris exclaimed to himself. (148)

Morris's quoted monologues—seen in conjunction with his spoken discourse and his manifest behavior—underline both his contempt for Catherine and Mrs. Penniman and his perception of women as a category of convenient beings peculiarly well adapted to the purpose of exploitation and manipulation, creatures to coerce through charm or intimidation into satisfying his needs.

"Silencing" of the monologic voice is accompanied by a change in the rhythm of quoted monologue. It is no longer confined to isolated moments set aside for inner debate (as in the chapter previously cited from *Tom Jones*) but is presented in a text that alternates between inner and outer scene, a repeated shifting back and forth between report and quotation, as is evident in the extracts cited above.

As the term "stream of consciousness" was coined by William James, it is perhaps ironical that Henry James himself made scant use of this technique. The "illogical, ungrammatical, mostly associative patterns of human thought" are not explored by Henry James. In scenes where mental activity is generated by the imaginative faculty rather than ratiocination (as in Isabel's midnight meditation), associative imagistic patterns are rendered through psychonarration and narrated monologue rather than through quoted monologue or stream of consciousness.

Although James frequently places "the centre of the subject in the [protagonist's] own consciousness" (*AN* 51), he presents that consciousness not in the state of amorphous flux that the term "stream of consciousness" suggests but in its highly organized articulate manifestations. The character's train of thought—with all the associations of the sequential, of logical organization, of moving in a specific direction, that the term inevitably implies—is rendered in somewhat stylized form, the outcome of a selection process in which "other mind stuff" has been rigorously expunged. The mental activity of James's characters is superlatively lucid and logical. As Stanzel notes of James's method of presentation in *The Ambassadors,* "he executes a cross section through Strether's consciousness at a height where the content of this consciousness already appears formulated as thoughts expressed in their traditional verbal forms."[22]

It is important to stress that the reader's evaluation of a character's quoted thoughts is determined by the perspective—which could be, for example, neutral, empathetic or ironic—in which he is placed by the narrator (66). The context of a monologue, then, is as important as its content. The varying relationship between narrator and character, the whole range of permutations between the two extremes of dissonance and consonance, distance and closeness, authorial and figural, is indicated by the following factors: the use of inquit phrases; narratorial comment; contrast between the content and the tone of psychonarration and quoted thought; indications of the narrator's omniscience and indications of temporal distance (69–70).

Cohn highlights the misconception that frequent monologizing is an indication of a unified, figural point of view; on the contrary, the aforementioned features need to be taken into account in determining the degree of consonance or dissonance. The narrator is not committed to the point of view of the character by the quotation of either spoken words or silent words.

Interior monologues are often used to reinforce the ironic distance between narrator and fictional character, as revealed in the extracts from *The Portrait* and *Washington Square.* The conjunction of interior monologues and authorial glosses heightens the disparity between the narrator's insight and his character's myopia or obtuseness.

In the following example from *Washington Square,* Dr. Sloper's monologue is set in the ironic perspective of narratorial comment on the real state of affairs:

> ". . . why doesn't she marry?" he asked himself. "Limited as her intelligence may be, she must understand perfectly well that she is made to do the usual thing." Catherine, however, became an admirable old maid. . . . From her own point of view the great facts of her career were that Morris Townsend had trifled with her affection, and that her father had broken its spring. . . . There was something dead in her life, and her duty was to try and fill the void. (203)

Doctor Sloper's tragically crass lack of understanding of his daughter is foregrounded here by the device of juxtaposing his own thoughts (rendered in quoted monologue) with the narrator's greater insight, which is rendered through psychonarration—not of Sloper's consciousness but that of Catherine.

It is clear from the examples cited that a duality of viewpoint is achieved when direct thought-quotations are combined with authorial glosses or authorially oriented psychonarration. Although James does not indulge frequently in the kind of narrator's commentary exemplified by Thackeray, who often moves from psychological characterization toward the generalizations about human nature that are typical of the authorial mode, he does achieve a distancing effect by embedding thought-quotations in ironically colored psychonarration or narrative report as in the examples from *The Portrait* and *Washington Square.*

Cohn demonstrates that psychonarration and quoted monologue, although used together with telling effect in authorial novels (in James's oeuvre, novels such as *Washington Square* and *The Bostonians*) do not blend very effectively in figural narrative situations. The creators of the greatest figural novels such as *The Ambassadors, Madame Bovary,* and *A Portrait of the Artist* use hardly any quoted monologues, but instead long stretches of narrated monologue combined with psychonarration (71).

When quoted monologues do occur, they tend to distance the figural consciousness from the narrator. The following examples from *The Ambassadors* illustrate this point:

"He thinks us sophisticated, he thinks us worldly, he thinks us wicked, he thinks us all sorts of queer things," Strether reflected; for wondrous were the vague quantities our friend had within a couple of short days acquired the habit of conveniently and conclusively lumping together. (1.42)

"If I'm going to be odiously conscious of how I may strike the fellow," he reflected, "it was so little what I came out for that I may as well stop before I begin." This sage consideration too, distinctly, seemed to leave untouched the fact that he *was* going to be conscious. He was conscious of everything but of what would have served him. (1.138)

And the consciousness of all this in her charming eyes was so clear and fine that as she thus publicly drew him into her boat she produced in him such a silent agitation as he was not to fail afterwards to denounce as pusillanimous. "Ah don't be so charming to me!—for it makes us intimate, and after all what is between us when I've been so tremendously on my guard and have seen you but half a dozen times?" (2.94)

(Here what the narrator labels Strether's "silent agitation" is articulated inwardly in quoted monologue, which takes the form of a silent address to Madame de Vionnet.)

In each of these examples (though to varying degrees), the quoted monologue is embedded in authorial comment or dissonant psychonarration (sometimes containing the distancing appellation "our friend"), ironic comment such as "sage consideration," or evaluative comment—"He was conscious of everything but of what would have served him." This device highlights Strether's lack of self-knowledge and heightens the disparity between narrator and figural consciousness. Perhaps the dubious status of *The Ambassadors* as fully figural novel is attested to by the fact that quoted monologues do indeed make a sporadic appearance.

In *The Golden Bowl* and *The Wings of the Dove* the device of the quoted monologue takes on new permutations as it modulates towards imagined speech—discourse ostensibly reflected in the consciousness of a specific character but attributed to another—or perhaps, in some contexts, attributable to the narrator. An illustration of this device is Maggie's "imagined speech" on the occasion of the prince's return from Matcham—the depiction of what she imagines him to hear her saying. Ambiguity often attends the attribution of such suppositious speeches and their designation: can they indeed be classified as quoted monologues? This mode of thought representation—to be investigated later—does not seem to be adequately catered for in Cohn's model.

The effect of quoted monologues thus depends on the context in which they occur. In authorial narrative situations, especially when they are accompanied by explicit quotation signals, monologues tend to increase the distance between a narrator and his character, "to induce ironic remove by dramatizing figural fallacies." In figural narrative situations, on the other hand,

> monologues are most effective when special devices are brought into play to insure the smooth blending of the narrating and the figural voices: omission or discreet use of inquit signals, espousal of the character's vantage point on the surrounding scene, omission of psycho-narration, syntactic ambiguity, or coloration of the narrator's language by a character's idiolect. (76)

These features are considered in context in the discussion of the relevant novels in subsequent chapters.

*   *   *

The psychological implications of quoted monologue need to be explored further. Monologues create the illusion that they reproduce what a character "really thinks" to himself, just as dialogues create the illusion that they depict what characters "really say" to each other. However, whereas fictional dialogue "imitates" real-life speech, which is readily observable, fictional monologue purports to imitate a concealed linguistic activity whose very existence cannot be established objectively (76–77).

Contrary to popular belief, interior monologue imitates neither the Freudian unconscious, nor the Bergsonian inner flux, nor William James's "stream of consciousness"; what it renders is the mental activity psychologists call inner speech or interior language. As mentioned earlier, Henry James did not attempt to render the flux of unarticulated "mind stuff" that William regarded as a vital component of the "stream of consciousness." According to William James's account, the "mind stuff" includes visual images; in Henry James's novels, indeed, visual images are an important component of mental activity and play a vital role in a character's acquisition of understanding. One could cite, for example, the revelatory nature of the images conjured up by Isabel's febrile imagination in *The Portrait*. When under stress, the imagination generates images—primarily visual—in terms of which a character can conceive of his situation. These visual images are transmuted or transcribed into verbal formulation that is rendered largely through the modes of narrated monologue and psychonarration—not quoted monologue, as the mediation of the narrator's verbal faculty is required to articulate these images. The dramatic immediacy of the image is retained by this method of "transcription," which the character herself is incapable of at that time.

Novelists who shun interior monologues do not conceive of thought primarily as verbalization. For them, thought takes shape independently of language; language is merely the vehicle of an already accomplished thought. In Isabel's midnight vigil, for example, "thought" is primarily conceived in terms of images.

Quoted monologue invariably acquires an air of sincerity when it is used against the backdrop of dialogue: "for no matter how insincere we are with ourselves, we are always more insincere with others" (82).

Cohn demonstrates that most writers prefer to tell rather than to show "those psychic happenings that their characters cannot plausibly verbalise" (88). Thus, in contradiction to Lubbock's stance lauding "showing," Cohn offers persuasive proof that "telling" can portray realms otherwise inaccessible to linguistic probing, "employing analyses, analogies and other authorial indirections to penetrate the speechless nether realm" (88).

Cohn notes further that

> Since interior monologue purports to render a real psychological process, the mimetic norms that apply to its content apply equally to its form: like the

language a character speaks to others, the language he speaks to himself will appear valid only if it is "in character." (88)

As demonstrated in the extract depicting Fenton's quoted monologue in *Watch and Ward,* James, in rendering Fenton's thoughts, scrupulously adjusts the register and vocabulary; he even incorporates grammatical errors (or provincial dialect) to reproduce a convincing simulacrum of the form as well as the content of his thoughts. This endeavor is, of course, impeded by the fact that there is no empirical basis for establishing the verisimilitude of this form of "speech" in fiction. Nevertheless, adjustments in register, vocabulary, and syntax are deployed to create an "air of reality." (This aspect is of particular importance in *What Maisie Knew* where the most radical adjustments had to be made to accommodate the immature mind of the child.)

Before proceeding to a more detailed consideration of narrated monologue, it would be useful to indicate some salient features of the three modes. As Cohn has shown, what quoted monologue gains in directness, it loses in complexity as it lacks the capacity to capture depths of thought—what transcends the verbal. Psychonarration, by contrast, gains in depth but loses in directness, while narrated monologue represents a "synthesis of antitheses." As a synthesis of showing and telling, mimesis and diegesis, it is invested with both directness and complexity, paradoxically achieving enhanced immediacy through mediacy.

NARRATED MONOLOGUE

Cohn's definition of narrated monologue as "the technique for rendering a character's thought in his own idiom while maintaining the third-person reference and the basic tense of narration" succinctly identifies the most important features of this mode of narration (100). In a sense, one could say that psychonarration and narrated monologue can explore or render the spaces between words, whereas quoted monologue is restricted to the verbal fabric, the words themselves.

Whereas quoted monologue presents thoughts formulated in the mind of a character, in narrated monologue the relationship between words and thoughts can be latent; the figural consciousness is suspended on the brink of verbalization. Ambiguity arises from this uncertainty as to whether or not the thoughts are verbalized.

Another significant feature of narrated monologue is that, in contrast to quoted monologue, it can, with its greater flexibility, be inserted with greater ease and subtlety into psychonarration. The text can weave in and out of the character's mind without perceptible transitions, fusing outer with inner reality, gestures with thoughts, facts with reflections, as illustrated in the extracts from *The Ambassadors* depicting Strether's response to Paris and the French countryside. As the same basic tense is used for the narrator's reporting language and the character's reflecting language, there is a merging of two usually distinct linguistic streams. Chapter 42 of *The Portrait* illustrates this procedure. It starts with a description of Isabel's physical position (seated in her chair in front of the fire, with the servant coming in to attend to the fire), followed by a shift into Isabel's consciousness as she considers Osmond's veiled threat that she should use her influence over Warburton to persuade him to propose to Pansy: her imagination "wandered among these ugly possibilities" until she momentarily "broke out of the labyrinth, rubbing her eyes." This is followed by Isabel's more generalized consideration of her blighted life and relationship with Osmond; her past illusions, her deception, Ralph's prophetic insight and Ralph's response to her pose of contentment. At the conclusion of the scene the focus reverts to Isabel "linger [ing] in the soundless salon" and the narrator presents concluding comments on the state of "her mind, assailed by visions" (2.204).

In examining the linguistic relationship between narrated monologue, psychonarration, and quoted monologue, Cohn identifies the distinctive grammatical features which differentiate narrated monologue from the other two modes: tense and person separate it from quoted monologue, the absence of mental verbs (the equivalent in the realm of thought, of inquit phrases in speech) such as "he thought" (and the resulting grammatical independence) separates it from psychonarration. So narrated monologue shares with quoted monologue the expression in the principal clause, with psychonarration the tense system and the third-person reference. When the thought is a question, the word order of direct discourse is maintained in the narrated monologue, thus increasing its resemblance to quoted monologue and its distinction from psychonarration (105).

In its meaning and function, as in its grammar, the narrated monologue occupies a midposition between quoted monologue and psychonarration, "rendering the content of a figural mind more obliquely than the former, more directly than the latter." Imitating the language a character uses when he talks to himself, it renders that language in the grammar a narrator uses in talking about him. Thus, in narrated monologue two voices that are kept distinct in the other two forms are superimposed.[23] Indeterminacy characterizes this mode, as it is suspended between the immediacy of quotation and the mediacy of narration, representing a synthesis of mimesis and diegesis.

Context is crucial in determining the function of narrated monologue:

> when it borders on psycho-narration, it takes on a more monologic quality and creates the impression of rendering thoughts explicitly formulated in the figural

mind; when it borders on spoken or silent discourse, it takes on a more narratorial quality and creates the impression that the narrator is formulating his character's inarticulate feelings. (106)

Thus difficulties in identifying narrated monologue—as well as determining the function—must be considered in context. Clues may be contextual, semantic, syntactic, or lexical.

To summarize, then: the narrated monologue is at once a more complex and a more flexible technique for rendering consciousness than the other techniques. "Both its dubious attribution of language to the figural mind, and its fusion of narratorial and figural language charge it with ambiguity" (107).

* * *

In placing the relatively recent mode of narrated monologue in its theoretical and historical perspective, Cohn points out that although the French and German terms "style indirect libre" and "erlebte Rede" have been the subject of intense critical discussion in France and Germany since the turn of the century, the phenomenon has been relatively neglected by English theorists until fairly recently. Significantly, since the publication of *Transparent Minds,* numerous studies of the technique of free indirect discourse have been undertaken.[24] One of the most illuminating of these is Roy Pascal's *The Dual Voice: Free Indirect Speech and its Functioning in the Nineteenth Century European Novel (1977),* which affords a comprehensive account of the origin, identification, and vicissitudes of style indirect libre. In his historical account of early investigators of the principle of narrative perspective, he points out that none discuss associated stylistic or grammatical forms. Indeed, one could add that the observations of James himself—and Percy Lubbock—could be seen in the light of these comments: for example, although James notes in the preface to *The Golden Bowl* that "the whole thing remains subject to the register . . . of the consciousness of but two of the characters" (the prince in the first half of the novel and the princess in the second), he does not expatiate on the stylistic or grammatical means whereby these subjective perspectives are embodied or dramatized. This lack of terminological precision has been remedied—with varying degrees of success—by the more recent theoretical studies cited here.

Pascal traces the early manifestations and subsequent refinement of style indirect libre (SIL; first described and analyzed by Charles Bally in 1912), which "reached full stature in Flaubert and Zola."[25] In a study that complements and extends the scope of Cohn's work, he devotes separate chapters to style indirect libre, *erlebte Rede* (literally "experienced speech") and "free indirect speech." He points out that early theorists fail to formulate "the double function of SIL, to hear it as a 'dual voice'."[26] He credits Bally with enlarging the scope of SIL beyond the reproduction of words and thoughts to include "the inarticulate vision of the characters, their sentient and nervous response to the outer world, the description, for instance, of the countryside through their eyes"[27]—what has been referred to earlier as "narrated perception."[28] The second part of Pascal's book concentrates on an examination of selected texts exemplifying free indirect speech, but unfortunately omits the novels of Henry James "in whose work it is triumphantly established" (35).

Leech and Short also offer a detailed and lucid exposition of speech and thought presentation.[29] This work highlights the complexity of the mode by demonstrating (with the aid of examples from Jane Austen, Dickens, and Nabokov) that neither the presence of the past tense and third-person pronouns nor the absence of a reporting verb are criterial in themselves for the definition of free indirect speech. "Our definition, then, is one in terms of 'family resemblance' rather than one dependent upon the presence of a particular defining feature" (329–30). Leech and Short in effect stress that contextual considerations are paramount in identifying free indirect speech, in contrast to Norman Page, for example, who "assumes that syntactic features alone determine the speech presentation category" (331).

Although English theorists have only recently recognized the significance of the device of free indirect discourse (narrated monologue), other European scholars accorded it attention much earlier.[30] Cohn declares that the initial failure of English theorists to study or even demonstrate familiarity with narrated monologue is particularly inexplicable in view of the fact that an English author, Jane Austen, was "the first extensive practitioner of the form and that it has been the preferred mode for rendering consciousness in the works of James, Lawrence, the early Joyce, Virginia Woolf" (108).[31] David Daiches, Ian Watt, Wayne Booth, and Scholes and Kellogg are cited as examples of eminent theorists who have failed to appreciate the significance of narrated monologue. (On the other hand, one could counter this criticism by pointing out that Ian Watt, at least, is not generally regarded as a "theorist.")

Cohn differentiates between the French and German terms style indirect libre and *erlebte Rede* and her own concept "narrated monologue," pointing out that the French and German terms designate not only the rendering of silent thought "but also the analogous rendering of spoken discourse, which displays identical linguistic features" (109). Cohn has chosen a term that excludes this analogous use of the technique because the problems presented by the narration of silent thoughts are different from those presented by spoken discourse. She notes that "narrated discourse," as opposed to "narrated monologue," "involves neither the ambiguity concerning the actual-potential status of language that characterizes the narrated monologue, nor the difficulties of recognizing it within its narrative context." Hence the justification for adopting a more appropriate term: "so special a phenomenon deserves a separate name" (110).[32] Cohn, then, stresses the latency of verbalization in narrated monologue, the uncertainty as to whether the thought is articulated by the character or not.

A related aspect of the difference between free indirect speech and free indirect thought is emphasized by Leech and Short:

> While FIS distances us somewhat from the characters producing the speech, FIT has the opposite effect, apparently putting us directly inside the character's mind. The reason for this is that the norm or baseline for the presentation of thought is IT, whereas the norm for speech [is] DS.[33]

This can be accounted for by the fact that the thought of others—as opposed to their speech—is not accessible to direct perception or observation, and so "a mode which only commits a writer to the content of what was thought is much more acceptable as a norm. Thoughts, in general, are not verbally formulated, and so cannot be reported verbatim" (344–45).

Thus the presentation of thought in narrated monologue is closer to empirically verifiable norms than that of quoted monologue, where the author purports to render "verbatim" what a character thinks: the reader here is enjoined to muster a greater degree of "suspension of disbelief" than is demanded by narrated monologue.

Exemplification of the distancing effect of free indirect speech as opposed to free indirect thought (narrated monologue) can be seen in *The Portrait,* where free indirect speech is often the preferred mode for rendering the speech of Madame Merle (for example, in conversation with Isabel and the Countess Gemini) and free indirect thought is frequently used to render the thoughts of Isabel and Ralph (the latter in the early part of the novel).

Cohn draws attention to the special relationship between figural narration and narrated monologue, which she describes as one of "mutual affinity and enhancement"—figural narration offers the narrated monologue its "optimal habitat." The narrated monologue, in contrast to the quoted monologue, suppresses quotation marks that would demarcate it from the narration, and

> this self-effacement can be achieved most perfectly in a milieu where the narrative presentation adheres most consistently to a figural perspective, shaping the entire fictional world as an uninterrupted "vision avec." (111)

It is important to realize, however, that the narrated monologue itself is not *vision avec,* but what Cohn dubbs *pensée avec*:

> here the coincidence of perspectives is compounded by a consonance of voices, with the language of the text momentarily resonating with the language of the figural mind. In this sense we can regard the narrated monologue as the quintessence of figural narration . . . as the moment when the thought-thread of a character is most tightly woven into the texture of third-person narration. (111)

What is achieved is thus a "special two-in-one effect" rather than merely a "dual presence," as the hiatus between the narrator and the figure is reduced to the greatest possible degree. The narrator's identification—rather than his identity—with the character's mentality is enhanced by this technique (112).

It is clear that the implications of this mode of presentation can be fruitfully explored in James's figural novels. Furthermore, as we have noted in discussing concepts such as center of consciousness, reflector, and effacement of the authorial narrator, "Henry James's own theoretical pronouncements revolve around the axis of the narrator/protagonist relationship" (114).

Before moving to a more detailed examination of the deployment of this mode of rendering consciousness in James's novels—in conjunction with quoted monologue and psychonarration—a brief indication of the various functions and effects of narrated monologue is necessary.

Among the most striking effects created by narrated monologue are those involving irony and sympathy. Because the narrated monologue is dependent on the narrative voice that "mediates and surrounds" it, it is essentially dependent on tone and context. And although the tone of the text in which narrated monologue is embedded might seem impersonal, narrated monologues tend to commit the narrator to attitudes of sympathy or irony:

> Precisely because they cast the language of a subjective mind into the grammar of objective narration, narrated monologues amplify emotional notes, but also throw into ironic relief all false notes struck by the figural mind. (117)

The ironic pole of this tonal range is most clearly in evidence when narrated monologues show up in a pronouncedly authorial milieu, framed by explicit commentary (118). This effect was apparent in the extracts from *Washington Square* and *Watch and Ward.* A character's illusions and a narrator's worldliness, romance and realism, are thrown into ironic relief through this juxtaposition. Framed by markedly dissonant psychonarration, a narrated monologue appears as though it were enclosed in tacit quotation marks, creating an effect of mock impersonation.

The empathetic pole of this technique's tonal scale can be observed in James's *The Ambassadors* and James Joyce's *A Portrait of the Artist.* One could add that in some of James's other figural novels, such as *The Wings* and *The Golden Bowl,* the empathetic attribution is not as unambiguous. The pervasive ironic mode makes it difficult to determine where one's sympathy should lie. The issues here are less clear-cut; perhaps one should distinguish between a cognitive and an emotive or empathetic scale. (This question assumes particular relevance in *The Golden Bowl* and is discussed in chapter 6 and in the conclusion.)

At times, ambiguity is heightened when the tense of the narrated monologue shifts from past to present as the protagonist formulates generalizations in her or his mind: these sound identical to the narrator's *ex cathedra* statements in the gnomic present tense. In *Roderick Hudson,* for example,

> Witnessing the rate at which he did intellectual execution on the general spectacle of European life, Rowland at moments felt vaguely uneasy for the future; the boy was living too fast, he would have said, and giving alarming pledges to ennui in his later years. But we must live as our pulses are timed, and Roderick's struck the hour very often. (106)

Here the aphoristic utterance could be that of the narrator or Rowland; the ambiguity is not really resolved, and the effect of an essential empathy between the two is created.

The narrated monologue is an ideal medium for "revealing a fictional mind suspended in an instant present, between a remembered past and an anticipated future" (126), as in chapter 42 of *The Portrait.* In such scenes, the narrated monologue adopts the temporal orientation of the figural consciousness and the past tense loses its retrospective function.

Narrated memories often refer to moments that predate the narrated time of a novel, replacing the authorial exposition of more traditional fiction (128). In *The Ambassadors,* there is the scene in the Luxembourg gardens presenting Strether's "backward picture" of his past; in *The Portrait,* chapters 4 and 6 present Isabel's childhood in the form of flashbacks. Similarly, Kate in the first scene of *The Wings,* and the prince in the opening scene of *The Golden Bowl,* relive aspects of their past through memory. (These narrated memories and narrated fantasies are examined in context in subsequent chapters.)

Cohn draws attention to the hazy region where inner and outer fictional realities are intertwined, the sphere of "narrated perception" which has been defined as "the report of a character's conscious perceptions . . . presented in such a manner that they resemble objective report," but are really "transcriptions of consciousness rather than reality" (133).[34] Exemplification of this phenomenon will be explored in *The Golden Bowl*.

The conjunction of narrated monologue with the two alternative techniques for rendering consciousness produces many interesting effects. The most recurrent sequence is the triad—psychonarration, narrated monologue, quoted monologue (134)—as seen in the following extracts from *Watch and Ward* and *The Portrait*:

> He meditated much as to whether he should frankly talk it over with her and allow her to feel that, for him as well, their relation could never become commonplace. This would be in a measure untender, but would it not be prudent? Ought he not, in the interest of his final purpose, to infuse into her soul in her sensitive youth an impression of all that she owed him, so that when his time had come, if her imagination should lead her a-wandering, gratitude would stay her steps? A dozen times over he was on the verge of making his point, of saying, "Nora, Nora, these are not vulgar alms; I expect a return." (*WW* 61–62)

Roger's crass self-interest is amusingly highlighted here; the ironic effects created by the deployment of this triad of three modes in the evocation of the "lover's" response to his protégée are less marked in the extract from *The Portrait*:

> He wondered whether he were harbouring "love" for this spontaneous young woman from Albany: but he judged that on the whole he was not. After he had known her for a week he quite made up his mind to this . . . Lord Warburton had been quite right about her; she was a really interesting little figure. . . . If his cousin was to be nothing more than an entertainment to him, Ralph was conscious that she was an entertainment of a high order. "A character like that," he said to himself—"a real little passionate force to see at play is the finest thing in nature." (*PL* 1.85–86)

Cohn points out that in such triads

> Each technique assumes its most standard function: psycho-narration summarizes diffuse feelings, needs, urges; narrated monologue shapes these inchoate reactions into virtual questions, exclamations, conjectures; quoted monologue distills moments of pointed self-address that may relate only distantly to the original emotion. (135)

This insensible shading of narrated monologue into psychonarration, or vice versa, is very frequent in figural narrative situations (137). (The narrated monologue and the quoted monologue, on the other hand, overlap only under very special circumstances.)

In summarizing the three techniques for presenting consciousness in third-person texts, Cohn recapitulates the central features of the relation between technique and narrative situation. Although the three techniques are used in varying proportions and combinations in a continuum ranging from the authorial to the figural, psychonarration tends to dominate in authorial narration, and narrated monologue in figural narration. In an authorial milieu, both quoted monologue and narrated monologue tend to take on an ironic modality. In a figural milieu, psychonarration and quoted monologue move toward each other (and toward the narrated monologue): "psycho-narration by coloration from the figural language, quoted monologue by camouflaging itself as best it can" (138). These features are examined more closely in the following chapters.[35]

3

Quasi-Figural Narration: *Roderick Hudson*

"The drama is the very drama of [Rowland's] consciousness"

In this and the following chapter I discuss an early novel, *Roderick Hudson,* and a novel from James's middle period, *The Portrait of a Lady,* as examples of quasi-figural narration or precursors of the fully figural novel.[1] In what I have called quasi-figural narration, the intrusive narrator is intermittently visible—or overtly audible—temporarily displacing the figural medium. In such instances, then, focalization is not solely through the figural consciousness. In fully figural narration, the narrator has become invisible and his or her place taken by the figural medium or reflector-character. I demonstrate in my discussion of both *Roderick* and *The Portrait* that although James uses a central reflector in these novels, his comments in the prefaces create an erroneous idea of the consistency with which this method of presentation is implemented.

In *Roderick Hudson,* much of the fictive world is filtered through the consciousness of the central reflector, Rowland Mallet, but the vocal narrator is very much in evidence, particularly in the early sections of the novel. In *The Portrait,* too, the narratorial voice constantly "attends and amplifies," and again is most prominent in the early chapters; in the course of the novel, a gradual narrowing of distance between narrator and central focalizer takes place. However, *The Portrait* differs from *Roderick Hudson* in that the presence of the vocal narrator is complemented by that of an additional focalizer and commentator, Ralph Touchett, "the most important of the heroine's satellites," who serves as a supplementary "lucid reflector."[2]

Furthermore, whereas in *Roderick* no direct access is given to the consciousness of characters other than the central reflector, in *The Portrait* the reader has access, even if only momentarily, to the consciousness of virtually every character in the novel. *Roderick* also conforms more closely to the pattern of the figural novel in that the central character is "on stage" throughout, whereas Isabel Archer is absent from a number of crucial scenes involving other characters in *The Portrait*. (In the later, more consistently figural novel, *The Ambassadors,* greater conformity to the figural mode is attained in that the narratorial presence is relatively invisible [or inaudible], the central character is not excluded from any scenes, and no access is given to the consciousness of any other characters in the novel. The subject is presented far more consistently through the consciousness of the central focalizer.)[3]

In his preface to *Roderick,* James states:

> My subject . . . defined itself—and this in spite of the title of the book—as not directly, in the least, my young sculptor's adventure. This it had been but indirectly, being all the while in essence and in final effect another man's, his friend and patron's, view and experience of him. . . . From this centre the subject has been treated. . . . The centre of interest throughout "Roderick" is in Rowland Mallet's consciousness, and the drama is the very drama of that consciousness. . . . [A]s what happened to him was above all to feel certain things happening to others, to Roderick, to Christina, to Mary Garland, to Mrs. Hudson, to the Cavaliere, to the Prince, so the beauty of the constructional game was to preserve in everything its especial value for *him*. (*AN* 15–16)

The subject of the novel, then, is "in essence and in final effect" Rowland's "view and experience" of Roderick. As previously mentioned, however, not everything is filtered through the consciousness of Rowland as the novel's single focalizer. The "view and experience" of the narrator are often overtly manifested.

Before looking more closely at examples of overt narratorial intrusion, it might be useful to consider the implications of James's comment that "It had, naturally, Rowland's consciousness, not to be *too* acute—which would have disconnected it and made it superhuman" (*AN* 16). It would seem that, paradoxically, a measure of cognitive dissonance is an inevitable concomitant of James's particular mode of figural narration. The consciousness of the narrator is inevitably more acute than that of his reflector, whose experience is to varying degrees set in the ironic—or more or less knowing—perspective of the narrator. Lubbock's observation on *The Ambassadors* is applicable to all James's figural or quasi-figural novels:

> the seeing eye is with somebody in the book, but its vision is reinforced; the picture contains more, becomes richer and fuller, because it is the author's as well as his creature's. . . . It is not all the work of the personage whose vision the author has adopted . . . some one else is looking over his shoulder—seeing things from the same angle, but seeing more, bringing another mind to bear on the scene.[4]

In fully figural narration, we recall, the narrator has become invisible and his place is taken by the figural medium or reflector-character. In quasi-figural narration, where the narrator is still intermittently visible—or audible—the "amplifying" vision of the narrator is manifested in the ways in which he transcends the parameters of the perceptual and conceptual world of the figural consciousness. Proleptic references, narratorial generalizations in the gnomic present tense, definition of and comment on the characters in the novel, remarks on novelistic procedures, and all forms of direct address to the reader are evidence of the constant attendance of the audibly intrusive narrator. And these manifestations are surprisingly ubiquitous.

Proleptic references in *Roderick* include comments such as "Mallet afterwards learned that this fair slim youth could draw indefinitely upon a fund of nervous force . . ." (64), "What he [Rowland] was really facing was a level three years of disinterestedness" (100), "long afterwards, in retrospect, he used to reflect that . . ." (251), "It was the first time Rowland had ever seen them there [tears in Roderick's eyes]; he saw them but once again" (282); and—a comment reminiscent of or anticipating Strether's refusal to name to Maria Gostrey the mysterious object manufactured at Woollet—"It was a lasting joke with Cecilia afterwards that she would never tell what Mr Whitefoot's little book had been" (96).

Some proleptic references incorporate an assumption of cultural identity with contemporary readers and ironically reflect the stance of narrator as *histor,* as in the description of the success of Roderick's statue of Adam: "He never surpassed it afterwards, and a good judge here and there has been known to pronounce it the finest piece of sculpture of our modern time" (114).

The occurrence of direct definition of or comment on characters—typifying the authorial rather than the figural mode—also contributes to the status of *Roderick* as a quasi-figural novel. The reader is informed at the outset, for example, that "Rowland Mallet had an uncomfortably sensitive conscience" and that in his sense of guilt for having neglected to visit his cousin Cecilia more frequently "Mallet's compassion was really wasted, because Cecilia was a very clever woman and a skilful counterplotter to adversity" (49). Departures from the pattern of the figural novel are also evident in that it is the "mere muffled majesty of irresponsible 'authorship'" (*AN* 328) which is responsible for producing the potted biography of Rowland in chapter 1. Justification is produced: "a rapid glance at his antecedents may help the reader to perceive" (54) and to appreciate the nature of Rowland's Puritan sensibilities and philanthropic impulses. (In a later work, such as *The Ambassadors,* this kind of information is provided through Strether's "backward picture" in the Luxembourg gardens or emerges in conversations with Maria.)

Descriptions of other characters, however, are often rendered through Rowland's perception. In the initial description of Roderick, for example, we find that after an authorial or narratorial introduction, focalization shifts to Rowland:

> Hudson was a tall slender young fellow, with a singularly mobile and intelligent face. Rowland *was struck* at first only with its responsive vivacity, but in a short time *he perceived* it was remarkably handsome. (64; my emphasis)

On the other hand, the introductory descriptions of Gloriani, Miss Blanchard, and other subsidiary characters are rendered in a mode which is predominantly authorial, although it modulates to the figural at times with objective narrator's report alternating with Rowland's subjective impression. This is illustrated in our introduction to Gloriani, a shrewdly successful sculptor who serves a foil to Roderick; Gloriani

> drove a very pretty trade in sculpture of the ornamental and fantastic sort. In his youth he had had money; but he had spent it recklessly, much of it scandalously, and at twenty-six had found himself obliged to make capital of his talent. This was quite inimitable, and fifteen years of indefatigable exercise had brought it to perfection. Rowland admitted its power, though it gave him very little pleasure; what he relished in the man was the extraordinary vivacity and frankness, not to call it the impudence, of his opinions. He had a definite, practical scheme of art, and he knew at least what he meant. In this sense he was solid and complete. (117)

Here the authorial register shifts to the figural, as the last two sentences could represent either narrator's report or Rowland's opinion. A comparable fluctuation from the authorial to the figural voice is evident in the rendering of Rowland's perception of Christina Light:

> Rowland had already been sensible of something in this young lady's tone which he would have called a want of veracity. . . . But the trait was not disagreeable, for she herself was evidently the foremost dupe of her inventions. She had a fictitious history in which she believed much more fondly than in her real one, and an infinite capacity for extemporised reminiscence adapted to the mood of the hour. She liked to idealise herself, to take interesting and picturesque attitudes to her own imagination; so that the many-coloured flowers of fiction which blossomed in her talk were not so much perversions as sympathetic exaggerations of fact. And Rowland felt that whatever she said of herself might have been under the imagined circumstances. (227)

Here psychonarration in the first sentence modulates into narrated monologue as Rowland's own perceptions of Christina are formulated in his mind. At times, however, it is difficult to establish whether the voice is that of Rowland or of the narrator; the lively wit of the phrase "infinite capacity for extemporised reminiscense adapted to the mood of the hour" seems to reflect the formulation of the narrator rather than that of Rowland. However, "And Rowland felt" could indicate that the following sentence is a continuation of what had been Rowland's formulation all along.

Descriptions of scenes or settings by the narrator—as opposed to the perception of a specific setting by a character—also reflect the perceptibility of the narrator and the temporary effacement of the figural consciousness. In many cases, however—for example, in the descriptions of Rome—it is not clear whether the description emanates from the narrator or from Rowland. When this kind of "stylistic contagion" occurs in narrated perception it highlights the fusion of the two voices, that of the narrator and the figural consciousness.

Some descriptions emanate unambiguously from the narrator:

> It was all consummately picturesque; it was the Italy that we know from the steel engravings in old keepsakes and annuals, from the vignettes on music-sheets and the drop-curtains at theatres; an Italy that we can never confess ourselves—in spite of our own changes and of Italy's—that we have ceased to believe. (347–48)

Frequently description modulates from objective narrator's report to the central character's perception. A transition from narrator-focalized to character-focalized description is illustrated in the following extract:

> it may perhaps be said that there is no other place in which one's daily temper has such a mellow serenity, and none at the same time in which acute attacks of depression are more intolerable. Rowland found, in fact, a perfect response to his prevision that to live in Rome was an education to the senses and the imagination. (159)

Generalizations about human nature, or aphoristic generic statements in the gnomic present tense, also testify to the overt presence of the narrator, but here again uncertainty frequently impedes the distinction between generalizations by the narrator and those of Rowland himself. At times the generalization is clearly proferred by the narrator, as in the following examples:

> "Gloriani, like a genuine connoisseur, cared nothing for his [Roderick's] manners; he cared only for his skill" (281)—[an evaluative comment reflecting the narrator's own values rather than Rowland's].

> "The conversation had been brief, but like many small things it furnished Rowland with food for reflection. When one is looking for symptoms one easily finds them" (368).

At other times, "stylistic contagion" reinforces the merging of the narratorial and figural voices, and the generalization could be attributed to either Rowland or the narrator—or seen as reflecting their shared assumptions: the effect created is that of consonance between the narrating and the figural consciousness:

> Witnessing the rate at which he did intellectual execution on the general spectacle of European life, Rowland at times felt vaguely uneasy for the future; the boy was living too fast, he would have said, and giving alarming pledges to ennui in his later years. But we must live as our pulses are timed, and Roderick's struck the hour very often. (106)

In the New York Edition of the novel, "the boy was living too fast, he would have said, and giving alarming pledges to ennui in his later years" is replaced by the less abstract and more colloquial "he was eating his cake all at once and might have none left for the morrow" (NYE 90), expressed in narrated monologue. This emendation seems to reflect Rowland's puritanical distrust of excess; taken in conjunction with the gnomic observation that follows, the effect is that of a corrective to the view espoused by Rowland: this generalization then becomes more unambiguously that of the narrator. A certain ironic distance between narratorial and figural consciousness is thus established here and persists throughout the revised version.[5] Citing a truism in a tone of mock-ignorance or assumed bemusement is a practice not infrequently indulged in by the narrator: "Women are said by some authorities to be cruel; I know not how true this is, but it may at least be pertinent to remark that Mrs. Hudson was intensely feminine" (336).[6] So, too, the status of generalizations occurring in a passage of psychonarration can often be ambiguous; context can be decisive in making the distinction. A comparison between two extended passages of psychonarration recording Rowland's agonizing uncertainty about Mary Garland's continuing attachment to Roderick illustrates this. In the first we read:

> There are women whose love is care-taking and patronising, and who attach themselves to those persons of the other sex in whom the manly grain is soft and submissive. It did not in the least please Rowland to believe that Mary Garland was one of these, for he held that such women were only males in petticoats, and he was convinced that this young lady's nature was typically girlish. (337)

The ascription of the first generalization is initially ambiguous, particularly as it is cast in the gnomic present tense: it could be interpreted as emanating from either the narrator or (less likely) Rowland. In the following sentence, Rowland has indisputably appropriated the opinion expressed. (On the other hand, the first sentence could be interpreted as narrated monologue and the second psychonarration, thus crediting Roland with—or holding him responsible for—both utterances. Modern readers would presumably prefer to exonerate the Jamesian narrator from implication in these sexist beliefs!)

In the later extract, the narrator at first intervenes to remind the reader of the substance of Rowland's continuing inner debate: "Rowland, in Florence, as we know, had suffered his imagination to wander in the direction of certain conjectures which the reader may deem unflattering to her constancy" (353). The narrator's voice becomes more muted as the passage continues in psychonarration:

[Rowland] did not risk the supposition that Mary had contrasted him with Roderick to his own advantage; but he had a certain consciousness of duty resolutely done which allowed itself to fancy at moments that it might not be unnaturally rewarded by the bestowal of such stray grains of enthusiasm as had crumbled away from her estimate of his companion. . . . If some day she had declared in a sudden burst of passion that she was completely disillusioned and that she gave up her recreant lover, Rowland's expectation would have gone halfway to meet her. (353)

This is followed by two transitional sentences; although the first could be seen as narrator's report, it is more likely to be narrated monologue, like the second sentence:

And certainly if her passion had taken this form no generous critic would utterly condemn her. She had been neglected, ignored, forsaken, treated with a contempt which no girl of a fine temper could endure.

A generalization then sets Mary's situation in the context of that of (other) fictional heroines:

There were girls, indeed, whose fineness, like that of Burd Helen in the ballad, lay in clinging to the man of their love through thick and thin and in bowing their head to all hard usage. This attitude had often an exquisite beauty of its own, but Rowland thought that he had solid reason to believe it never could be Mary Garland's. She was not a passive creature; she was not soft and meek and grateful for chance bounties. (353)

Here the generalization, in the past tense, ("There were girls . . .") is clearly Rowland's, as is clarified by the context: the preceding sentence (above) in narrated monologue expresses a view held by Rowland rather than by the narrator. Dramatic irony comes into play here to expose the fallaciousness of Rowland's reasoning. In grappling with the problem of

Mary's character and motivation, Rowland ironically makes no allowance for the egoism of passion and is unprepared for her later demonstration that she is ready to sacrifice everything, and even endanger Rowland's own life, for Roderick's sake. In spite of the way in which she has been treated, Roderick's interests are paramount, having a claim superior to both Rowland's and her own.

In detailing Rowland's inner debate, the narrator, anticipating a skeptical response in the reader, again intervenes with a preemptive justification: "He may perhaps be deemed too rigid a casuist, but I have repeated more than once that he was solidly burdened with a conscience" (354). Here the dramatic irony is subverted by the intrusive narrator who interferes with his own orchestration of ironic effects. In this form of quasi-figural narration the narrator, rather than relinquishing control, reverts to the didactic mechanism of direct adjudicating intervention to guide the reader's response.

Such instances of direct address to the reader—especially in the form of the first person—also reinforce the distancing effect typifying external perspective as opposed to the internal perspective of figural narration. In the following example, the first-person narratorial voice again guides the reader's judgment of Rowland: "That Mallet was without vanity I by no means intend to affirm; but there had been times when . . . you might have asked yourself what had become of his vanity" (52).

In some instances, the narrator adopts an archly speculative pose, as in:

> Just why it was that Roderick should not in consistency have been captivated [by Mary], his companion would have been at a loss to say; but I think the conviction had its roots in an unformulated comparison between himself and the accepted suitor. (161)

This speculative stance is presumably calculated to encourage a comparably speculative activity in the reader—the generation of interpretive hypotheses that must be tested against subsequent disclosures.

A similar coyness pervades the next comment that follows the "reproduction" of Mary's letter to Rowland which "was so much shorter [than Cecilia's] that we may give it entire": "It is a question whether the reader will know why, but this letter gave Rowland extraordinary pleasure" (134). Cecilia's letter, the narrator confides, was so long that "we must content ourselves with giving an extract" (133).

Commentary on the purpose and problems of novelistic presentation also abounds, at times reflecting the narrator's stance as *histor*. We are told that "it will be part of the entertainment of this narrative to exhibit [that] Rowland Mallet had an uncomfortably sensitive conscience" (49), that "this history undertakes to offer no record [of the criticisms passed upon Roderick's Adam]" (115), that "this lady's further comments upon the event are not immediately pertinent to our history" (319). Such remarks imply that the narrator-historian is carefully sifting his material before selecting that most germane to his purpose. Relevance is a prime consideration: "We shall not rehearse his [Roderick's] confession in detail; its main outline will be sufficient" (137). At times a comprehensive account is called for: "After the visit which I have related at length . . ." (169); at other times, ellipsis is practiced as "Nothing especially pertinent to our narrative had passed" (176).

Although Rowland is the single focalizer, there are other ways in which the focus becomes blurred, and insight—albeit largely indirect—is afforded into the minds of other characters. (This contrasts with the strategy adopted in *The Portrait* where direct and often extensive access is given to the consciousness of most of the characters in the novel.) At the first appearance of Christina Light, for instance, the description seems to reflect the perception of Roderick rather than Rowland. When the Light ménage advance toward them in the gardens of the Villa Ludovisi, we are told initially that "the young men, looking up, saw three persons advancing" (109). The description that follows seems to be the narrator's report, and then Rowland's speculations concerning Mrs. Light are recorded: "She had such an expansive majesty of mien that Rowland supposed she must have some proprietary right in the villa and was not just then in an hospitable mood." The subsequent description of the Cavaliere and Christina accompanied by her poodle could initially be narrative report or objective narration rather than the subjective perception of either of the two young men, but when the focus narrows to a close-up of Christina's startlingly beautiful face it appears to be Roderick's perception that is registered:

> Roderick, with his customary frankness, greeted the spectacle with a confident smile. The young girl perceived it and turned her face full upon him, with a gaze intended apparently to enforce greater deference. It was not deference, however, that her countenance provoked, but startled submissive admiration; Roderick's smile fell dead and he sat eagerly staring. A pair of extraordinary dark blue eyes, a mass of dusky hair over a low forehead, a blooming oval of perfect purity, a flexible lip just touched with disdain, the step and carriage of a tired princess—these were the general features of his vision. (109)

The impression that the view of Christina presented here is essentially Roderick's is reinforced by his exclamation immediately after this description—"Immortal powers!" cried Roderick, "what a vision!" (110) which echoes the formulation in the description itself.

On the other hand, this could well be interpreted as Rowland's impression or formulation of Roderick's vision of Christina; indeed, the perceptive observation that in spite of her splendid beauty her deportment reflected "the step and carriage of a tired princess" seems to indicate a range of intuitive sympathy in which Roderick reveals he is deficient.

Departures from the figural mode also occur when focalization seems to veer toward an inside view of Mrs. Hudson's feelings to which Rowland could not plausibly have access. (The purpose of this shifting focalization is presumably to enhance the ironic effect by giving the reader information denied to Rowland.) We are told, for instance, that "she found it infinitely comfortable to lay the burden of their common affliction upon Rowland's broad shoulders. Had he not promised to make them all rich and happy?" (326). The first sentence clearly could not reflect Rowland's own view (the phrase "Rowland's broad shoulders" if used by Rowland himself would be at variance with the narrator's repeated claim that he is incorruptibly modest) and must be the narrator's comment. However, the second sentence, in narrated monologue or free indirect speech, suggests that Mrs. Hudson functions momentarily as focalizer.

The above examples all illustrate ways in which the figural mode is imperfectly realized in *Roderick*. I shall now look more closely at the incidence and interaction of the three modes for presenting the consciousness of the central reflector in the novel.

As might be expected in a novel cast largely in the figural or quasi-figural mode, conventional quoted monologues, which tend to create an ironic distance between the narrator and the figural consciousness, are relatively infrequent. Rigorously quantitive analysis would demonstrate that not more than about ten instances of quoted monologues occur in the novel. Whereas some are relatively innocuous as in "'What is it now?' he asked himself, and invited Roderick to sit down" (369), quoted monologues in some contexts do dramatize significant discrepancies between the articulated and the unarticulated.

Quoted monologue is used in self-communing, articulating thoughts and feelings that the character does not communicate to others. In some cases it is used to formulate an opinion that a character is prevented from expressing by the conventions of social propriety. The following exchange with Mary Garland illustrates this:

"I don't know how it seems," she interrupted,—"to careless observers. But we know—we know that you have lived—a great deal for *us*."

Her voice trembled slightly, and she brought out the last words with a little jerk.

"She has had that speech on her conscience," thought Rowland; "she has been thinking she owed it to me, and it seemed to her that now was her time to make it and have done with it." (275)

Rowland's slightly cynical interpretation of Mary's utterance is rendered here in quoted monologue. Articulating these thoughts to himself might provide him with the satisfaction of feeling that he has not been "taken in"; he could hardly convey to Mary herself his suspicion that she is being insincere or at least lacking in spontaneity. Of course, the reader's interpretation might differ from his: the fact that "her voice trembled slightly," and her jerky delivery might be evidence of Mary's acutely embarrassed awareness that this expression of gratitude is one which Roderick himself should be conveying to Rowland; Roderick indeed could be classified with those "careless observers" who fail to perceive the extent to which Rowland has devoted himself to the interests of his protégé and his entourage.

Quoted monologue serves a different function in the following example, where Rowland is exclaiming to himself in wonder at the burgeoning of Mary Garland's aesthetic sense in response to Rome:

"Oh, exquisite virtue of circumstance!" cried Rowland to himself, "that takes us by the hand and leads us forth out of corners where perforce our attitudes are a trifle contracted, and beguiles us into testing unappreciated faculties!" (270)

Here Rowland's rather effusive quoted monologue, with its quaintly formal (if not archaic and self-consciously literary) wording, perhaps reflects too his incorrigible modesty; hence his attributing Mary's development to the abstract (but personified) "virtue of circumstance" when it is he himself who is the most significant feature of that "circumstance," he who by playing *cicerone* is "leading her forth." Perhaps his ever-vigilant conscience does not wish him to acknowledge, even to himself, the role he is playing in facilitating the felicitous development of his friend and protégé's fiancée.[7]

The majority of the examples of quoted monologue cited here are embedded in psychonarration, the exception being the dialogue on 275. The following extract is a rare example of a configuration conforming to the pattern of the triad described by Cohn: psychonarration, narrated monologue, quoted monologue:

He was not sure it was not a mere fancy, but it seemed to him that he had never seen her look just as she was looking then. It was a humble, touching, appealing glance, which threw into wonderful relief the nobleness of her beauty. "How many more metamorphoses," he asked himself, "am I to be treated to before we have done?" (291)

The first sentence in this extract is psychonarration, the second is probably narrated monologue, and the third indubitably quoted monologue. The quoted monologue here is used to express the mixture of fascination and exasperation Rowland experiences in his confrontations with the protean Christina. The concept of a creature subject to—or indulging in—endless metamorphoses is also applied to the vacillating Roderick: "Rowland said nothing. He was willing to wait for Roderick to complete the circle of his metamorphoses, but he had no desire to offici- ate as chorus to the play" (224).[8] The perception this time is expressed in narrated monologue rather than quoted monologue, with the verbal echo ("metamorphoses") indicating Rowland's own formulation. The ap- plication of the same image to both Christina and Roderick also empha- sizes essential similarities between them: they are both capricious, passionate, wilful, impulsive, and lacking the stability and sustained moral seriousness which characterize Rowland.

Conflicting impulses or demands in Rowland himself can be highlighted through quoted monologue, as in the evocation of his response to Rome. At the beginning of the novel we are told that

> idleness in any degree could hardly be laid at the door of a young man who took life in the serious, attentive, reasoning fashion of our friend. It often seemed to Mallet that he wholly lacked the prime requisite of a graceful *flâ- neur*—the simple, sensuous, confident relish of pleasure. (58)

After some time spent in Rome, Rowland starts succumbing to its ap- peal. His response is traced initially through psychonarration:

> He grew passionately, unreasoningly fond of all Roman sights and sensa- tions. . . . He could not have defined and explained the nature of his relish, nor have made up the sum of it by adding together his calculable pleasures. It was a large, vague, idle, half profitless emotion, of which perhaps the most pertinent thing that may be said is that it brought with it a sort of relaxed acceptance of the present, the actual, the sensuous—of life on the terms of the moment. (159)

Further on in this passage, contrasting impulses all exerting powerful influences on Rowland are dramatized in the confrontation between his more hedonistic urges and the voice of conscience; the conflict is fore- grounded through the use of quoted monologue:

> to live in Rome was an education to the senses and the imagination; but he sometimes wondered whether this were not a questionable gain in case of one's not being prepared to subside into soft dilettantism. His customary tolerance of circumstances seemed sometimes to pivot about by a mysterious inward

impulse and look his conscience in the face. "But afterwards . . . ?" it seemed to ask, with a long reverberation; and he could give no answer but a shy affirmation that there was no such thing as tomorrow and that to-day was uncommonly fine. (159–60)[9]

Here the subtle interplay of quoted monologue and psychonarration vividly evokes these contradictory impulses.

The ironic effects achieved through this subtle interplay are many and various. The following example illustrates the way in which Rowland, in consciously formulating optimistic interpretations of Roderick's temperament and conduct, suppresses recognition of less commendable features of his personality of which he has a lurking intuition. The quoted monologue is set in the ironic perspective of summary psychonarration, shifting into punctual psychonarration, which reveals subsequent developments and exposes the view expressed in the monologue to be an illusion now consigned to the past.

Rowland had found himself wondering shortly before whether possibly his brilliant young friend were without a conscience; now it dimly occurred to him that he was without a heart. Rowland as we have already intimated was a man with a moral passion, and no small part of it had gone forth into this adventure. There had been from the first no protestations of friendship on either side, but Rowland had implicitly offered everything that belongs to friendship, and Roderick had apparently as deliberately accepted it. Rowland indeed had taken an exquisite satisfaction in his companion's easy inexpressive assent to his interest in him. "Here is an uncommonly fine thing," he said to himself, "a nature unconsciously grateful, a man in whom friendship does the thing that love alone generally has the credit of—knocks the bottom out of pride!" (189–90)

This quoted monologue is analeptic in that it refers to a view formulated early on in their friendship and recalled now in a different context— embedded in a passage of summary psychonarration that traces subsequent modifications of his initial opinion of Roderick's nature.

We note too the way in which psychonarration in the first sentence is followed by the evaluative comment by the intrusive narrator reminding the reader that Rowland "was a man with a moral passion." This explicit comment on Rowland's character helps to highlight an essential difference between the two men, a difference that can be seen in the context of Rowland's suspicion that his friend lacks both a conscience and a heart, equally essential components of Rowland's own character. Rowland is beginning to discern that although Roderick is endowed with creative or aesthetic passion—which in his relations with Christina becomes interfused with erotic passion—he is radically devoid of "moral passion."

Through the interplay of quoted monologue and psychonarration, then, Rowland is depicted as grappling with these complex issues.[10]

Further on in this extract, psychonarration modulates to narrated monologue as the narrator's comment, "Rowland adhered to his conviction of the essential salubrity of genius" (190), is followed by the expression of Rowland's belief as formulated by himself: "Genius was priceless, inspired, divine; but it was also at its hours capricious, sinister, cruel; and men of genius accordingly were alternately very enviable and very helpless" (190–91); this opinion does not necessarily enjoy the endorsement of the narrator.

Rowland is not yet consciously facing the possibility that "the essential salubrity of genius" might be an illusion if a radical disjunction exists between the creative imagination and the moral imagination; moral "salubrity," then, would not necessarily be the inevitable concomitant of aesthetic endowment. In his later letter to Cecilia Rowland finally questions this concept (236).

In accordance with the predominant pattern of the novel, psychonarration and narrated monologue in this chapter alternate with extended passages of dialogue as Rowland and Roderick discuss the issues that Rowland is also grappling with internally. The narrator's voice also makes a sporadic appearance to guide the reader's judgment without imposing his own too dictatorially, as in

> It was characteristic of Rowland that he complied with his friend's summons without a moment's hesitation. His cousin Cecilia had once told him that he was the dupe of his perverse benevolence. She put the case with too little favour, or too much, as the reader chooses; it is certain at least that he had a constitutional tendency to magnanimous interpretations. (193)[11]

Cecilia's judgment of Rowland is implicitly confirmed by both his conduct and the narrator's comment; after ostensibly granting the reader the choice of accepting or rejecting Cecilia's judgment the narrator states categorically that "It is certain . . ."[12]

It is evident from the above discussion that the three modes of representing consciousness (quoted monologue, narrated monologue, and psychonarration) occur in different combinations and to varying effect in *Roderick*. The latter two modes are relatively more prevalent and almost invariably occur together; the text often weaves in and out of the mind of the figural consciousness, fusing inner and outer reality as well as "objective" narratorial report and subjective reflection. By subtle deployment of these modes of representation, insight is afforded into characters by narrating their unvoiced reflections without judging them directly. The reader is implicated in the process of identifying self-deception and distinguishing lapses in logic and clear-sightedness. I shall now examine further representative examples of the incidence and interaction of these two techniques and consider the effects achieved.

An extract near the beginning of the novel provides a useful illustration of how psychonarration, modulating into narrated monologue, can render the nuances of the reflector's state of mind. This passage is embedded in a scene of dialogue between Rowland and Cecilia; illuminating comparisons can be drawn between the voiced and the unvoiced assumptions and feelings.

> He [Rowland] had suspected from the first hour of his stay that Cecilia had a private satisfaction, and he discovered that she found it in Hudson's lounging visits and boyish chatter. Now he wondered whether judiciously viewed, her gain in the matter were not her young friend's loss. It was evident that Cecilia was not judicious, and that her good sense, habitually rigid under the demands of domestic economy, indulged itself with a certain agreeable laxity on this particular point. She liked her young friend just as he was; she humoured him, flattered him, laughed at him, caressed him—did everything but advise him. It was a flirtation without the benefits of a flirtation. She was too old to let him fall in love with her, which might have done him good. . . . It was quite conceivable that poor Cecilia should relish a pastime; but if one had philanthropically embraced the idea that something considerable might be made of Roderick, it was impossible not to see that her friendship was not what might be called tonic. So Rowland reflected, in the glow of an almost creative ardour. There was a later time when he would have been grateful if Hudson's susceptibility to the relaxing influence of lovely women might have been limited to such inexpensive tribute as he rendered the excellent Cecilia.
>
> "I only wish to remind you," she went on, "that you are likely to have your hands full." (79–80)

In the first sentence, summary psychonarration records the way in which over time Rowland's vague suspicion of Cecilia's enjoying a "private satisfaction" changes in focus to an identification of the specific source of this "satisfaction"; the company of the flamboyant Roderick Hudson. In "Now he wondered whether, judiciously viewed, her gain . . . were not her young friend's loss," a transition is made from a past to a present state of understanding; a shift then occurs from psychonarration to narrated monologue in the following sentence, where the word "judicious" recurs as indubitably Rowland's own formulation. Preceded by "It was evident," the narrated monologue here alerts the reader to the rationalization that Rowland is indulging in. An ironic discrepancy is apparent: what is "evident" to Rowland might not appear so to the narrator or the reader who, reading between the lines—or between and behind the articulated thoughts—senses that Rowland, in criticizing the "injudiciousness" of Cecilia's friendship, is emphasizing to himself that his own friendship with Roderick would be eminently prudent and salutary for the young sculptor. His use of terminology such as "philanthropically" also suggests that he is repressing any recognition that his own motives might be similarly tainted with damaging self-interest rather than adorned with glowing altruism.

The next thirteen lines in narrated monologue continue to render the substance of Roderick's thought, with the statement "So Rowland reflected" finally signaling the "re-entry" of the univocal narratorial voice (as opposed to the "dual" voice of narrated monologue) to dispel any ambiguity as to whether the above reflections might be attributed to the narrator rather than to the central reflector. (In later novels, the attribution becomes more ambiguous.)

The emphatic "It was impossible not to see," which echoes the earlier construction "It was evident," reinforces the impression that Rowland is indulging in self-justification and establishing the superiority of his friendship for Roderick over that of Cecilia, which was "not what might be called tonic." Rowland evidently feels that by providing an infusion of informed encouragement—and funds—supplemented by sporadic injections of the fortifying "advice" that Cecilia failed to provision Roderick with he will be able to guarantee the optimum opportunity for the efflorescence of Roderick's artistic talent. By failing to distinguish between the aesthetic and the ethical—or by assuming too glibly that a superabundance of creative power necessarily entails a comparable endowment of moral strength—Rowland is blind to the possible nature of the challenge enunciated further on by Cecilia: that of guaranteeing "not only the development of the artist but the security of the man." Ironically, Cecilia is far more perceptive than Rowland when it comes to understanding Roderick's frailties and susceptibilities.

Rowland's assumptions, expressed through psychonarration and narrated monologue (and in dialogue with Cecilia), are set here in the ironic context not only of Cecilia's premonitory comments but also of the narrator's proleptic reference to future developments which support Cecilia's warning: "There was a later time when. . . ."

In his conversation with his cousin, Rowland understandably does not express his reservations about her possibly deleterious effect on Roderick but instead concentrates on the positive benefits to accrue to the young sculptor from accepting his friendship and patronage. He acknowledges that apart from the altruistic desire to "start our young friend on the path to glory" he himself hopes to achieve a vicarious sense of fulfillment in that "it would give at least a reflected usefulness to my own life to offer him his opportunity" (80).

This recognition could be seen as casting an ironic light on his declared "philanthropic" pretensions, although it could be argued that there is inevitably an element of self-gratification in all ostensibly altruistic or "philanthropic" enterprises. That Rowland has pondered the question of whether one has the moral right to interfere directly with the "destiny" of another when motives are so mixed is clear from his statement to Cecilia that "I remembered there were dangers and difficulties, and asked myself whether I had a right to drag him out of his obscurity" (80). What he had not sufficiently taken cognizance of perhaps was the possibility of endangering what Cecilia calls "his moral, his sentimental security" (81).

Cecilia's warning that "circumstances, with our young man, have a great influence" (81) alerts us to the crucial issue of the influence of changed circumstances upon personal development, particularly when these changed circumstances encompass also all the ramifications of the "international theme"—the contrast between the cultures of America and Europe, which is rather simplistically viewed as a contrast between the simple and the more complex, the naive, spontaneous, and idealistic, and the more sophisticated, refined, but often morally decadent (or at least dubious).

Cecilia's (perhaps unrealistic?) demand that "you guarantee us not only the development of the artist but the security of the man" (80), taken in conjunction with Rowland's own idea of his mission as expressed here in psychonarration and narrated monologue, foregrounds an important issue in the novel: that of Rowland's accountability. Other crucial issues implicit in this extract include the whole question of the artist in society, the contrast between the creative and contemplative temperaments ("doing" and "knowing") and the related issue of the connection between the creative and the moral imagination; Rowland is to discover that the two do not necessarily coexist.

Some central issues in the novel, then, are revealed here in the interplay of psychonarration, narrated monologue, direct speech, and narratorial comment. The passage also illustrates Rowland's characteristic mind-set or ideolect: the careful, logical consideration and balancing of opposites—"her *gain*" . . . "her young friend's *loss*"—and the judgmental contrast between frivolous indulgence (emphasized by the plethora of verbs such as "flattered, laughed, caressed") on the one hand, and the restraint and sobriety of "advise" on the other. At a later stage, Rowland's distrust of the frivolous or merely pleasurable is be assailed by the captivating charms of Rome, but he does not succumb with Roderick's joyous abandon.[13]

Rowland's decision to "transplant" Roderick to Rome is given new poignancy in a later scene where Rowland, having discussed with Mrs. Hudson and Mary his vision of Roderick's prospects in Europe, is struck on his homeward walk with the beauty of the environment from which he is removing Roderick. In this passage, scenic description, psychonarration, and narrated monologue are closely interwoven as we move in and out of the figural mind.

The scenic description of "The great Northampton elms interarch[ing] far above in the darkness" (92) moves virtually imperceptibly to an evocation of the impact of the scene on the figural consciousness and is interwoven with his recollections of the scene he had just participated in:

> He had laughed and talked and braved it out in self-defence; but when he reflected that he was really meddling with the simple stillness of this little New England home, and that he had ventured to disturb so much living security in the interest of a far-away fantastic hypothesis, he paused, amazed at his temerity. (92)

Psychonarration then shifts into narrated monologue: "It was true, as Cecilia had said, that for an unofficious man it was a singular position" and back into psychonarration—"There stirred in his mind an odd feeling of annoyance with Roderick for having so peremptorily taken possession of his mind"—to suggest the charmed effect that Roderick has on him. This is followed by an evocation of his visual perception of the simple harmonious beauty of the Northampton homes:

> As he looked up and down the long vista, and saw the clear white houses glancing here and there in the broken moonshine, he could almost have believed that the happiest lot for any man was to make the most of life in some such tranquil spot as that.

The clear white houses, objects of his perception, are invested with moral significance as narrated monologue is used to clarify what they symbolize for Rowland: "Here were kindness, comfort, safety, the warning voice of duty, the perfect absence of temptation." Although the narrated monologue mode suggests that this is Rowland's own interpretation, the implicit endorsement of the narratorial voice is sensed. The "clear white houses" seem to represent the ordered, harmonious, simple beauty of Northampton life, which contrasts with the exuberant baroque splendor of Rome. Rowland is almost seduced into renouncing his scheme, but the qualification—"he could almost have believed"—indicates that he is not completely won over. The narratorial voice then links Rowland's thoughts with his perception of the outer world:

> And as Rowland looked along the arch of silvered shadow and out into the lucid air of the American night, which seemed so doubly vast, somehow, and strange and nocturnal, he felt like declaring that here was beauty too—beauty sufficient for an artist not to starve upon it. (92)

At this point we move out of the figural mind as visual and auditory perception predominates with the description of the irruption of the ebullient Roderick himself upon the scene. Rowland's momentary misgivings about his plan for Roderick are providentially dispelled by the appearance of the young sculptor himself singing a song that coincidently echoes the comment made in the preceding scene by Mary about Rowland's advent being "like something in a fairy tale" taking the form of "carrying off my cousin in a golden cloud" (91). Narrated monologue reappears here to "transcribe" Rowland's interpretation of Roderick's mood: "He was dreaming of the inspiration of foreign lands—of castled crags and historic landscapes. What a pity after all, thought Rowland, as he went his own way, that he shouldn't have a taste of it!" (93).

Any incipient oversimplification in the contrasts evoked by the "international theme" are countered here by Rowland's recognition that the American way of life as represented by Northampton is not simply a negation or absence of all Europe has to offer, limited though it is in terms of cultural richness and diversity. Although "the complete contradiction of Northampton" (107) is what Roderick later relishes in Rome, Rowland is sufficiently aware of the positive attributes of this tranquil, simpler yet potentially fulfilling way of life.

Although the use of the device of "analogous landscapes" is a well-established novelistic convention, we see here that in the figural as opposed to the authorial mode the awareness of the analogy is ascribed to the focalizer: the interpretation of the symbolic setting is undertaken by the reflector rather than the narrator. Similarly, later, in the scene in the Alps, it is Rowland rather than the narrator who registers the potentially premonitory quality of the stormy atmosphere.

A good example of how presentation can oscillate from the authorial to the figural pole is found in chapter 5, which opens three months after the departure from Northampton. Initially, the authorial mode dominates for "setting the scene" before the transition to dialogue between Rowland and Roderick and later summary psychonarration as the gap created by the ellipsis is filled by the evocation of the experience of those first three months in Europe through Rowland's recollections: "One warm still day, late in the Roman autumn, our two young men were sitting beneath one of the high-stemmed pines of the Villa Ludovisi" (103). The authorial mode is reinforced by the use of the distancing appellation "our two young men" and the subsequent "objective" description of the Ludovisi Gardens by the narrator rather than through a depiction of Rowland's impressions. After a passage of dialogue in which Roderick and Rowland discuss their experiences of the past three months, a transition is effected to summary psychonarration as Rowland "looked back on these animated weeks" (105–6). In James's own terminology, this is an example of "scene" followed by "picture"; in this case a "picture" structured by "foreshortening," as it is a condensed account of Rowland's three months' experience with the salient points foregrounded.

The predominant mode of the next three pages is psychonarration, used to depict Rowland's perception of the changes in Roderick and his own high expectations of Roderick's artistic career—intermingled with vague stirrings of premonitory concern for his future development. There are momentary shifts to narrated monologue for observations such as: "Surely youth and genius hand in hand were the most beautiful sight in the world" (107). The narratorial voice is not completely eclipsed and manifests itself in gnomic utterances such as "But we must live as our pulses are timed" (discussed earlier) and observations on Rome such as "And indeed Rome is the natural home of those spirits with which we just now claimed friendship for Roderick" (108). Another generalization here—in the past tense as opposed to the gnomic present—is clearly not sponsored by the narrator and indeed reveals Rowland's capacity for self-delusion:

> [Roderick] gave Rowland to understand that he meant to live freely and largely and be as interested as occasion demanded. Rowland saw no reason to regard this as a menace of grossness, because in the first place there was in all dissipation, refine it as one might, a vulgarity which would disqualify it for Roderick's favour; and because in the second the young sculptor was a man to regard all things in the light of his art, to hand over his passions to his genius to be dealt with, and to find that he could live largely without exceeding the circle of pure delights. (108)

The use of narrated monologue here establishes these two "truisms" as emanating from Rowland. He is to be disabused of both these illusions in the course of the novel: Roderick's Baden-Baden escapade is the first of many indications that the "vulgarity" of such dissipation is in fact no deterrent, "refine it as [Rowland] might." Roderick's ostensible capacity to "hand over his passions to his genius to be dealt with" and "transmute all his impressions into production" is proved to be illusory (108).

Rowland's blithe confidence here is set in the ironic context of the narrator's greater insight and highlighted by the dramatic irony of Roderick's subsequent irresponsible self-indulgence at Baden-Baden. Even after Baden-Baden, Rowland endeavors to convince himself that Roderick could benefit ultimately from the experience: "Rowland said at last that such experiments might pass if one felt one was really the wiser for them. "By the wiser," he added, "I mean the stronger in purpose, in will" (138). Roderick's reply seems to lend credence to Cecilia's warning about the influence of circumstances on Roderick: "Oh don't talk about the will!" Roderick answered. "Who can answer for his will? who can say beforehand that it's strong? . . . It all depends upon circumstances."[14] The protracted excursion into Rowland's consciousness afforded here by psychonarration and narrated monologue is abruptly terminated by the appearance of Mrs. Light; the narrative mode shifts into a detailed account of the ensuing scene and subsequent animated discussion of the "vision" by Roderick and Rowland.

The deployment of the imagistic mode in *Roderick* differs from that of the later novels in that it occurs more frequently in psychonarration than in narrated monologue, thus indicating the narrator's control in presenting the character's thought processes. In *The Portrait,* and particularly in the later *Golden Bowl,* conceptualization through metaphor is assigned more consistently to the reflector (the experiencing rather than the narrating consciousness) and is thus found more frequently in narrated monologue.

Conceptualization through metaphor implies a process whereby clarification of situations, relationships, experiences, ideas, and attitudes is attained through the crystallization of insights in vivid images or emblematic intuitions that can take the form of complex psychoanalogies. A related activity is that whereby the symbolic import of an event or situation is perceived; and it is often the reflector rather than the narrator in *Roderick* who registers the symbolic import of a scene.

An important scene that is invested with symbolic significance by Rowland's perception and interpretation of it is that of the artist's party where Rowland, in his emblematic position as observer on the sidelines ready to intervene if necessary (sometimes in a *deus ex machina* capacity, as in the scene at the Coliseum), is confronted with a striking tableau:

> he was struck by the group formed by the three men. They were standing before Roderick's statue of Eve. . . . Rowland stood looking on, for the group struck him with its picturesque symbolism. Roderick, bearing the lamp and glowing in its radiant circle, seemed a beautiful image of a genius which combined sincerity with power. Gloriani, with his head on one side, pulling his long moustache and looking keenly from half-closed eyes at the lighted marble, represented art with a worldly motive, skill unleavened by faith, the mere base maximum of cleverness. Poor little Singleton, on the other side, with his hands behind him, his head thrown back and his eyes following devoutly the course of Roderick's explanations, might pass for an embodiment of aspiring candour afflicted with feebleness of wing. (127–28)

The composition of the tableau is such that the special lighting effect focuses all attention on the central figure of Roderick. At this stage of his career the reader endorses Rowland's interpretation of his symbolic status: he does indeed seem to be the epitome of the romantic creative genius bearing the lamp to guide the lesser luminaries clustered around him. Roderick is often associated with the symbolism of light; there are various references to his possessing "the sacred fire" (for example, 70, 215) and ironically, when his powers start declining, he refers in a conversation with Rowland to "poor fellows whose candles burnt out in a night" (196).

Another significant network of imagery is introduced here in Rowland's interpretation of Singleton as representing "aspiring candour afflicted with feebleness of wing." At this stage Roderick seems to be the one about to soar above lesser mortals; indeed, in a later scene we find Rowland reflecting "It was reassuring to hear that Roderick in his own view was but 'just beginning' to spread his wings" (161). However, the image complex takes a new twist when Roderick, in justifying his conduct with Christina and refusing to accept the curbs Rowland attempts to impose, claims that "If you want a bird to sing, you must not cover its cage" (192). Rowland applies the same image in reflecting upon Christina's valiant effort to thwart her mother's mercenary ambitions and renounce plans for marrying her off to Prince Casamassima. Here the image occurs in narrated monologue:

> Rowland thought with horror of the sinister compulsion to which the young girl was apparently still to be subjected. In this ethereal flight of her moral nature there was a certain painful effort and tension of wing; but it was none the less piteous to imagine her being rudely jerked down to the base earth. (311)

A week after the triumphant party, when Roderick, in despair, tells Rowland "I have struck a shallow! I have been sailing bravely, but for the last day or two my keel has been grinding the bottom" (129), the imagistic mode again permeates Rowland's reflections, which are rendered in psychonarration. His observation that "He might have fancied that the fatal hour foretold by Gloriani had struck" links with the recurrent imagery of the inexorable ticking of a timepiece that is applied with such different effect to the diligent labors of Singleton; near the end of the novel, Roderick observes to Singleton that "You remind me of a watch that never runs down. If one listens hard one hears you always—tic-tic, tic-tic" (361). In grappling with the problem of loss of creative inspiration, he asks Rowland "What if the watch should run down . . . and you should lose the key?" (195). Imagery such as this, which occurs in psychonarration as well as in direct speech, differs from that used in the authorial mode (as represented by George Eliot, for example) in that it is used in the presentation of the thought or speech of a character rather than that of the narratorial voice.

The network of imagery connected with a voyage is also used in various modes—in psychonarration, narrated monologue, and direct speech. When Roderick speaks of having struck a shallow we recall that Rowland had spoken of his enterprise as "launching Roderick": "I have launched you, as I may say . . . and I feel as if I ought to see you into port" (78). The contrast between Roderick and Singleton's mode of production is indicated by Rowland's observation to the painter that "You sail nearer the shore, but you sail in smoother waters" (171), unlike "so many of the aesthetic fraternity who were floundering in unknown seas" (117).

Although this pattern of imagery is often found in direct speech, it is also incorporated into Rowland's reflections. In *Roderick,* however, imagery is less pervasive in the modes of psychonarration and narrated monologue than in spoken discourse. (In later novels, imagery becomes a more pervasive integral component of thought representation as the reflectors acquire the capacity to "think for themselves" and exploit the cognitive force of metaphor.) In the passage of psychonarration embedded in the dialogue between Roderick and Rowland here the sea image reappears in conjunction with other significant recurrent images:

> Rowland was perplexed. He was in a situation of a man who has been riding a blood-horse at a steady elastic gallop, and of a sudden feels him stumble and balk. As yet he reflected, he had seen nothing but the sunshine of genius; he had forgotten that it has its storms. Of course it has! And he felt a flood of comradeship rise in his heart which would float them both safely through the worst weather. (129)

Here psychonarration modulates to narrated monologue—"Of course it has!"—to suggest that Rowland is trying to convince himself that Roderick's being "grounded" or immobilized is temporary and simply part of a predictable pattern. "Sunshine" must inevitably alternate with "storms." This image is proleptic in that it foreshadows the scene of Roderick's death in the storm in the Alps; we recall, too, that Rowland "enjoyed Roderick's serene efflorescence as he would have done a beautiful summer sunrise" (108)—an essentially evanescent phenomenon.

The contrast between Rowland's generous comradeship and Roderick's egotistical self-absorption is hinted at by the use of a similar image at the artist's party, prior to this exchange, where we find "[Roderick] was floating on the tide of his deep self-confidence" (128). Rowland's "flood of comradeship" is less efficacious than he realizes as a relaunching or buoyancy-promoting medium for someone who is essentially self-contained. The image recurs with poignant force near the end of the novel when, in an anguished passage of psychonarration interwoven with narrated monologue, a transformation in Rowland's seemingly imperturbable benevolence is evoked: "He felt conscious of a sudden collapse in his moral energy; a current that had been flowing for two years with liquid strength seemed at last to pause and stagnate" (369).

Another image of note in this extract is that drawing an analogy between Rowland and a man riding a high-spirited horse that suddenly stumbles and stalls. The sentence following "Rowland was perplexed" is of uncertain designation in this context as it could be either the narrator's comment on Rowland's position or Rowland's own imagistic conception of his experience rendered in narrated monologue.

Ironically, the image recurs in one of Roderick's outbursts on the precarious nature of creative genius where he states to Rowland that "Nothing is more common than for an artist who has set out on his journey on a high-stepping horse to find himself all of a sudden dismounted and invited to go his way on foot" (196).

In association, the two variations on the image are significant in that in each case the person formulating the image sees himself as the rider in control of a spirited but sometimes recalcitrant mount. The image dramatizes Rowland's conception of his role as being one of both spurring on and applying salutary curbs when deemed necessary, and could be linked with the implications of his name, "Mallet," in bringing to the fore his attempt to mould Roderick according to his own conception of the true artist.

Just as narrated monologue is the mode used here to foreground the way Rowland clings with relief to a neat if implausible explanation of Roderick's behavior as a phenomenon characterizing all men of genius, so at the end of this chapter it is a rhetorical question in narrated monologue which highlights Rowland's naive faith that Roderick's moral values are after all in accord with his own: "And then—and then—was it not in itself a guarantee against folly to be engaged to Mary Garland?" (131).

The interaction of psychonarration, narrated monologue, and narratorial comment is exploited to evoke Rowland's state of mental turmoil in a passage that culminates in the dramatic imagistic portrayal of his "temptation." His mood of bitter disillusionment is rendered in psychonarration:

> He was sore at heart, and as the days went past the soreness deepened rather than healed. He felt as if he had a complaint against fortune; good-natured as he was, his good nature this time quite declined to let it pass. (249)

With a shift into narrated monologue we are given a more detailed rendering of his actual thoughts:

> He had tried to be wise, he had tried to be kind, he had engaged in an admirable enterprise; but his wisdom, his kindness, his energy, had been thrown back in his face. (249)

Representation of his thoughts later modulates back into psychonarration to focus on his state of mind:

> He felt, in a word, like a man who has been cruelly defrauded and who wishes to have his revenge. Life owed him, he thought, a compensation, and he should be restless and resentful until he found it. He knew—or he seemed to know—where he should find it; but he hardly told himself, and thought of the thing under protest, as a man in want of money may think of certain funds that he holds in trust . . . the idea of concrete compensation in a word—shaped itself sooner or later into the image of Mary Garland. (250)

The monetary image used here is significant; the very fact that his notion of "compensation" in the form of Mary Garland is couched in monetary terms suggests a fundamental flaw in his reasoning, as human emotion can hardly be reduced to or calculated in terms of mercenary notions such as profit and loss, defrauding and compensation. (The intercalated "He knew—or he seemed to know—" indicates the narrator's ironic stance here.)

Although monetary images often occur in the novel, they are most frequently used with reference to Roderick's artistic talent, and usually in dialogue as opposed to psychonarration or narrated monologue. After Baden-Baden, for example, Rowland advises Roderick, "If you have got facility, revere it, respect it, adore it, hoard it—don't speculate on it" (138). Later, when he feels his inspiration is running out, Roderick asks "Who shall assure me that my credit is for an unlimited sum?" (196) and after completing the bust of his mother, "Well, I have paid the filial debt handsomely" (277). An earlier example of monetary imagery occurring in psychonarration is where

> He [Rowland] wondered gloomily at any rate whether for men of his companion's large easy power there was not a larger moral law than for narrow mediocrities like himself, who, yielding Nature a meagre interest on her investment (such as it was), had no reason to expect from her this affectionate laxity as to their accounts. (170)

In the extract under discussion the image acquires new configurations as Rowland conceives of his disappointment in terms of being "defrauded" and needing a compensatory award in the shape of Mary.

At this point the vocal narrator, anticipating a skeptical response in the reader, intervenes to dissipate possible misinterpretation:

> Very odd, you may say, that at this time of day Rowland should still be brooding over a girl of no brilliancy, of whom he had had but the lightest of glimpses two years before; very odd that so deep an impression should have been made

by so lightly pressed an instrument. We must admit the oddity, and remark simply in explanation that his sentiment apparently belonged to that species of emotion of which by the testimony of the poets the very name and essence are oddity. (250)

This form of direct address to the reader in which the narrator discusses the character behind his back, as it were, or more specifically, discusses the plausibility of his reactions or conduct (and thus, obliquely, his own narrative technique) is rarely found in such overt form in the later novels. The comments of the narrator here echo those of the empirical author in his preface where similar misgivings are expressed:

> though there was no reason on earth . . . why Rowland should *not,* at Northampton, have conceived a passion, or as near an approach to one as he was capable of for a remarkable young woman there suddenly dawning on his sight, a particular fundamental care was required for the vivification of that possibility. The care, unfortunately, has not been skilfully enough taken, in spite of the later patching-up of the girl's figure. We fail to accept it, on actual showing, as that of a young person irresistible at any moment, and above all irresistible at a moment of the liveliest other preoccupation, as that of the weaver of . . . [the] spell that the narrative imputes to her. The spell of attraction is cast upon young men by young women in all sorts of ways, and the novel has no more constant office than to remind us of that. But Mary Garland's way doesn't, indubitably, convince us; any more than we are truly convinced, I think, that Rowland's destiny, or say his nature, would have made him accessible at the same hour to two quite distinct commotions, each a very deep one, of his whole personal economy. (*AN* 17)

The reader, of course, may feel that this preemptive action on the part of the narrator—and retrospective recuperative stance, incorporating the skepticism of hindsight, on the part of the author—are quite uncalled-for, and that indeed there is no violation of plausibility in Rowland's falling in love with a girl so eminently suited to his temperament. The narrator's attempt to achieve a "suspension of disbelief" in the reader through an invocation of appropriately eminent literary precedents—the effusions of lyric poets on the subject of romantic love—might strike one as unnecessarily arch.[15]

The fusion of inner and outer reality, with psychonarration alternating with narrative report to create the effect of weaving in and out of the figural mind—incorporating portrayal of ambient atmosphere with evocation of Rowland's mental state—is vividly illustrated in the continuation of the extract cited above:

> One night he slept but half an hour; he found his thoughts taking a turn which excited him portentously. He walked up and down his room half the night. It

looked out on the Arno; the noise of the river came in at the open window; he felt like dressing and going down into the streets. Towards morning he flung himself into a chair; though he was wide awake he was less excited. It seemed to him that he saw his idea from the outside, that he judged it and condemned it; yet it stood there before him, very distinct, and in a certain way imperious. (250)

The metaphorical presentation of the temptation embodied in Rowland's "idea" takes on different configurations: "His idea persisted; it clung to him like a sturdy beggar" (251). The expulsion of this importunate presence is finally achieved in the scene in the monastery garden where Rowland, in conversation with a monk, identifies it as "the Devil," which has been successfully "conquered" (252–53).

Psychonarration, as Dorrit Cohn points out, is the mode best suited to the portrayal of visions or hallucinatory dimensions of experience; this is exemplified in the following section where the evocation of the temptation to which Roderick is exposed is vividly achieved through psychonarration modulating into narrated monologue for the ostensibly rhetorical self-justificatory question "but if death were decreed, why should not the agony be brief?"

> The sense of the matter, roughly expressed, was this. If Roderick were really going, as he himself had phrased it, to "fizzle out," one might help him on the way—one might smooth the *descensus Averni*. For forty-eight hours there swam before Rowland's eyes a vision of Roderick, graceful and beautiful as he passed, plunging like a diver into a misty gulf. The gulf was destruction, annihilation, death; but if death were decreed, why should not the agony be brief? (251)

After an introductory statement in the narratorial voice, the imagistic mode predominates. The proleptic image of Roderick "plunging like a diver into a misty gulf" foreshadows his death plunge in the Alps later, where we find that "He had fallen from a great height . . . and his clothes and his hair were as wet as if the billows of the ocean had flung him upon the strand" (386). The recurrence of the image reanimates the question of Rowland's accountability: although in this temptation scene he does successfully resist the impulse to hasten Roderick's "*descensus Averni*"— even making the suggestion later that Roderick send for Mrs. Hudson and Mary in an attempt to revive the relationship and "save" him—we are alerted to the possibility of his indirectly precipitating Roderick's fall by exposing him in their last confrontation to the full revelation of his heartless egoism. (At the conclusion of their last interview Roderick declares "I am fit only to be alone. I am damned!" [379] before setting off on his walk.)

The fusion of the literal and the metaphorical in the image of Rowland's "fall" is also foreshadowed in an earlier warning given to Roderick by Rowland after observing the effect on him of the news of Christina's engagement to Prince Casamassima: "You are standing on the edge of a gulf. If you suffer this accident to put you out, you take the plunge" and in Roderick's declaration to Rowland that "If I hadn't come to Rome I wouldn't have risen, and if I hadn't risen I wouldn't have fallen" (244, 329).

Rowland's rationalization, rendered in narrated monologue, "but if death were decreed, why should not the agony be brief?" is particularly ironic in view of his own previously expressed confidence in the power of the will and rejection of the notion of "destiny" operating independently of human action or volition. His formulation "if death were decreed" has overtones of predestination—an appeal to the notion of which would be a diabolically devious method of self-exculpation.

It has been claimed that Rowland is in fact the direct cause of Roderick's death: "Roderick's fall from the cliff appears the outcome of wish-fulfillment," Rowland's vision of his friend's *descensus Averni* "proleptically and *coercively* figures Roderick's fall [my emphasis]," and this demonstrates that "Rowland's status as reflective center . . . affords him considerable narrative power as 'agent of Providence'."[16] It is clear that the critic here fails to observe the vital distinction between the reflector and the narrator—the figural and the narrating consciousness.

Another interpretation has it that Roderick's fall is the direct result of the loss of his "fixed ideal," Christina: "Christina's inescapable marriage to the Prince Casamassima finally shatters Roderick's image and drives him to an apparently suicidal fall from a cliff."[17] Even in this early novel, then, there is a measure of ambiguity.

At the end of the novel, it is Rowland as figural consciousness who again seems to register the symbolic import of the storm-laden alpine atmosphere on behalf of the narrator. The temporal deictic "to-day" in "the air was oppressively heavy. . . . Today . . . the white summits were invisible; their heads were muffled in sullen clouds and the valleys beneath them curtained in dun-coloured mist" (368) reinforces the impression that it is the central reflector rather than the narrator through whom the scene is focalized. (In a sense the term "pathetic fallacy" takes on new connotations here as it is the central reflector and not the narrator who registers the analogy between the landscape and the emotions at play in this scene.)

As in *The Portrait* and *The Golden Bowl,* moments of intense revelatory insight are conveyed through dramatic, often hallucinatory images. In all these novels light imagery, suggesting sudden illumination, predominates, but whereas in the later novels narrated monologue is the predominant mode for this range of cognitive imagery, in *Roderick,* these images tend to occur more frequently in psychonarration. Thus we find, when Mary Garland asks Rowland to endanger his own life by setting out to search for Roderick, "The question seemed to him a flash intenser than the lightning that was raking in the sky before them. It shattered his dream that he weighed in the scale!" (382). His illusions about Mary's possibly rewarding him for his devotion are finally shattered.[18]

At the conclusion of *Roderick Hudson,* Rowland is depicted as undergoing a process of bitter soul-searching as he watches over his friend's body in a seven-hour vigil. In trying to understand the disastrous end of his enterprise he is portrayed as weighing up a series of anguished hypotheses, trying to reason it all out. In a sense his vigil adumbrates and forms a significant comparison with Isabel's more famous midnight vigil where, in a process of "motionlessly seeing," she attempts to understand her situation. In Isabel's more extended introspective vigil the imagistic mode predominates; she is depicted not as puzzling things out through ratiocination but through being "assailed" by vivid and dramatic images.

As indicated in the comments comparing the original and the revised versions of *Roderick,* the later New York Edition is characterized by a greater infusion of imagery. The tendency to move away from the abstract to the more metaphorical is exemplified throughout James's later work, but what is most germane to this study is the increasing predominance of the metaphoric mode in the representation of consciousness. Just as James's novels trace, in different ways and with varying degrees of intensity, the "milestones on the road of so much inward or apprehensive life" for their respective protagonists, so each novel in itself marks a significant "milestone" in the author's *representation* of "so much inward . . . life."[19]

In moving from *Roderick* to *The Portrait,* then, we note the increasing tendency to refract the action of the novel through the consciousness of the central reflector, and, concomitantly, the way the metaphoric mode becomes progressively more closely interfused with the modes for representing consciousness. We have seen that in *Roderick* imagery is most concentrated in narratorial comment and dialogue; in subsequent novels the imagery becomes more predominant in psychonarration (in *The Portrait*) and narrated monologue (*The Golden Bowl*). The cognitive force of metaphor is also demonstrated more fully in the later novels, where conceptualization through imagery is engaged in by the reflector rather than by the narrator. This development is traced in the following chapters.

4

From Authorial to Figural: *The Portrait of a Lady*

"Place the centre of the subject in the young woman's own consciousness"

JAMES's preface to *The Portrait* unequivocally establishes that his primary concern is depicting the developing consciousness of his central reflector, Isabel Archer. As in *Roderick,* the emphasis is less on his protagonist's "adventures" as such than on "her sense of them, her sense *for* them" (*AN* 56). However, in spite of his declared intention to "Place the centre of the subject in the young woman's own consciousness" (*AN* 51), opinions differ as to the consistency with which he adhered to this approach. Whereas James has been considered by some to have created in Isabel Archer "a center of consciousness comparable in intensity to what he later created in Lambert Strether,"[1] others have criticized his authorial stance as being that of "the benevolent, omniscient author familiar to us from Victorian fiction."[2]

In a sense, both these claims have a certain validity. In the early sections of the novel the intrusive omniscient narrator is very much in evidence, introducing, analyzing, commenting on the characters and generally guiding the reader's response (often addressing the reader directly in the first person). Gradually, however, the preponderantly authorial mode of the early section modulates into more sustained figural narration as events are filtered more consistently through the consciousness of the central reflector, Isabel. By the end of the novel Isabel could with greater justification be described as approximating the status of "a centre of consciousness comparable in intensity" to Strether. However, this status is not consistently maintained; we note that although Strether is "on stage" throughout *The Ambassadors,* Isabel, unlike both Strether and Rowland Mallet, is excluded from many significant scenes throughout the novel and is indeed absent from the very last scene.

The movement from authorial to figural narration that Stanzel delineates in terms of the historical development of the novel can be observed in microcosm in *The Portrait,* with its gradual withdrawal of the authorial narrator—so vociferous in the early sections of the novel—and the concomitant increasing prominence of the central reflector. At the beginning of the novel we see Isabel as the narrator (and Ralph) see her; in chapter 18, the perspective changes, and we see through Isabel's eyes as she encounters first Madame Merle and then Osmond. Focalization alters, then, as Isabel moves closer to becoming a center of consciousness.

This shift is implemented gradually, however; after three years of marriage to Osmond, Isabel is revealed to the reader "framed in the doorway" by Rosier's focalizing vision. This view of her is then juxtaposed with the far more penetrating observation of Ralph before we are given access to Isabel's own consciousness in chapter 40, preparatory to more intensive immersion in chapter 42. Isabel's perspective then prevails for the latter section of the novel.

In the early sections Isabel's perception is often supplemented or rectified by that of the narrator: her view of Caspar, for example, is placed in perspective by the narrator's own "portrait" which is prefaced by the comment that "the reader has a right to a nearer and a clearer view" (1.163). Similarly, Isabel's limited understanding of Ralph is indicated by the narrator's observation that "The reader already knows more about him than Isabel was ever to know" (2.146). By contrast, in her last confrontation with Madame Merle (in the convent) Isabel's perception of her erst-while friend is neither directly rectified by the narrator nor indirectly qualified by irony, as in her first encounters with that lady.

Stylistically, the shift from authorial to figural narration is reflected (in Stanzel's terminology) in the displacement of "thought report" by "free indirect style" in the presentation of consciousness: whereas the psychological portrait of Isabel in the early part of the novel is characterized by direct narratorial comment, this is gradually superseded by presentation dominated by narrated monologue in which the narrator's voice is merged with that of the figural consciousness.

James's comments in the preface lead one to expect that presentation in *The Portrait* will be that of single focalization, comparable to that used in *Roderick;* however, in spite of Isabel's functioning as a center of consciousness, in the course of the novel we enter the consciousness or have access to the inner world of every major character and most of the minor characters, if only briefly. It seems, then, that the distribution of inner views between the center of consciousness and the subsidiary characters does not accord with James's own (retrospectively) stated intention.

On the other hand, from closer consideration of the context of James's pronouncement on "plac[ing] the centre of the subject in the young woman's own consciousness," it emerges that his technique of deploying subsidiary "reflectors" is indeed obliquely indicated. Using the image of a balance, James explains his design to

> put the heaviest weight into *that* scale, which will be so largely the scale of her relation to herself. . . . Place meanwhile in the other scale the lighter weight . . . press least hard . . . on the consciousness of [the] heroine's satellites, especially the male. (*AN* 51)

Although it is generally recognized that James makes use of Ralph (the most important of his heroine's "satellites") as a subsidiary "lucid reflector," little attention has been paid to the stylistic means whereby this "press[ing] least hard on the consciousness of [the] heroine's satellites" has been implemented. Identifying the various modes of presentation of consciousness can clearly contribute greater precision here: it is demonstrable that "put[ting] the heaviest weight into the scale" of Isabel's own consciousness entails giving greater access to her perceptual and conceptual world through the three modes of psychonarration, narrated monologue, and quoted monologue. A greater intermixture of these presentation techniques can therefore be discerned in the portrayal of Isabel than in that of her "satellites." Furthermore, psychonarration, with its more marked narratorial presence, is generally the mode used for portraying the inner world of subsidiary characters; the mode of narrated monologue is used less frequently for the depiction of the inner world of characters other than Isabel and, to a lesser degree, Ralph.

Although it is difficult to determine distribution of inside views with mathematical or statistical precision (and it might be of dubious desirability, were it feasible) careful reading of the text reveals that "press[ing] least hard on the consciousness of the heroine's satellites, especially the male" is stylistically reflected in proportionately meager access to the consciousness of these subsidiary characters through the three designated modes. By contrast, Ralph, as supplementary reflector, is accorded many extended passages of psychonarration, narrated monologue and—albeit to a lesser degree—quoted monologue, particularly in the first two-thirds of the novel. Indeed, examination of the "distribution of inner views and the rhythm of their occurrence"[3] reveals that in the first section of the novel (the first seventeen chapters) Ralph's perspective is as much in evidence as Isabel's, and throughout the novel we are accorded greater access to his point of view than to that of any other subsidiary character. In effect, he is "the novel's central observer and its second center of consciousness."[4]

Thus, although the growth of Isabel's consciousness is the focus of

interest, James uses Ralph as an ancilliary "intense perceiver" to complement the consciousness of the protagonist. Ralph, as subsidiary "lucid
reflector," is indeed at the outset endowed with more lucidity and insight
than Isabel herself. His function is more than that of a mere *ficelle*, like
Henrietta Stackpole; he provides valuable insight into Osmond's real
character which anticipates and throws into dramatic relief the subsequent discoveries of Isabel herself. (Ralph's surname, Touchett, suggests
a touchstone or criterion of truth in terms of which Isabel's own perceptions may be judged.)

Isabel's "subjective adventure" (*AN* 157) during which, like Maisie,
she is subjected to "the strain of observation and the assault of experience" (*AN* 147), is essentially a "process of vision." For Isabel, as for
Fleda Vetch, and indeed in varying degrees for all James's protagonists,
"the progress and march of [the] tale became . . . that of her understanding" (*AN* 128). In this process of discovery and enlightenment Isabel
overcomes her deficiencies of understanding and perception and ultimately achieves an approximation of Ralph's perspective as she shares
his "illumination of wisdom" (2.60). The process of vision here involves
a convergence of Isabel's view with that of Ralph and, to a lesser degree,
of others who were previously "in the know." This process culminates at
the point where Isabel and Ralph are finally united in "looking at the
truth together" (2.414).

Ralph's perspective, however, is not the only complementary view offered us. What Isabel perceives and understands is enmeshed in a closely
patterned network of parallels and contrasts with the perceptions of the
other subsidiary characters. Indeed, James stresses the importance of
placing "the more deeply wondering . . . the really sentient" (*AN* 62) in
combination with those less perceptive characters who lack "the finer
grain."[5] In his preface to *The Princess Casamassima* he states:

> I never see the leading human interest of any human hazard but in a conscious-
> ness (on the part of the moved and moving creature) subject to fine intensifica-
> tion and wide enlargement. It is as mirrored in that consciousness that the
> gross fools, the headlong fools, the fatal fools play their part for us—they have
> much less to show us in themselves. (*AN* 67)

Although not all subsidiary characters can be fitted into one or the
other of these categories of "fools," their role is primarily one of interaction with those capable of a continuously expanding consciousness—in
this case Isabel. The "lucid reflector," then, is seen in conjunction with
a constellation of lesser luminaries, who represent a range of percep-
tiveness varying from those who are much less perceptive than Isabel
herself to Ralph, who is endowed with the greatest acuity and insight.

The spectrum encompasses positions as diverse as Mrs. Touchett's surprisingly astute observation that "there's nothing in life to prevent her marrying Mr Osmond if she only looks at him in a certain way" (1.395) to the Countess Gemini's stupefied inability to understand her naively idealistic sister-in-law. Perceptions or opinions of Isabel held by other "satellites" such as Goodwood, Rosier, and Warburton are expressed in conversation or in brief excursions into their respective consciousnesses. (As for Henrietta, it is perhaps appropriate that for so blunt and categorical a commentator—and one whom Isabel accuses of having "no sense of privacy" (1.121)—her opinion should be expressed in direct discourse only rather than in inward rumination.)

Apart from the view cited above, which Mrs. Touchett expresses in conversation with Ralph, access to her inner world produces acerbic opinions such as

> that a young lady with whom Lord Warburton had not successfully wrestled should content herself with an obscure American dilettante, a middle-aged widower with an uncanny child and an ambiguous income, this answered to nothing in Mrs. Touchett's conception of success. (1.394)

A glimpse into the inner world of Warburton himself, when he is depicted at the opera in Rome with Isabel and Osmond, reveals his perception of a less admirable aspect of her character (the presentation modulates from psychonarration to narrated monologue):

> Poor Lord Warburton had moments of bewilderment. She had discouraged him, formally, as much as a woman could; what business had she then with such arts and such felicities, above all with such tones of reparation—preparation? . . . Why should she mark so one of his values—quite the wrong one—when she would have nothing to do with another, which was quite the right? (2.3–4)

In exerting her charm over her rejected suitor here Isabel seems to be acting in anticipatory gratification of one of her new admirer's prejudices: after the scene at the opera, it is revealed that Osmond "perceived a new attraction in the idea of taking to himself a young lady who had qualified herself to figure in his collection of choice objects by declining so noble a hand" (2.9).

Access to the inner life of Goodwood also reveals that he has more perception than Isabel seems to give him credit for. For example, far from being taken in by her assiduously cultivated pose of conjugal harmony, he intuitively grasps the real state of affairs; in spite of Osmond's charming manner he notes what Isabel had taken years to discover: "It seemed to him . . . that the man had a kind of demonic imagination" (2.313).

Rosier's initial view of Isabel after a few years of marriage is a superficial one: "framed in the gilded doorway, she struck our young man as the picture of a gracious lady" (2.105). This contrasts forcibly with Ralph's more penetrating view as he perceives the reality behind the mask. Through psychonarration and narrated monologue in the portrayal of the inner world of the "satellites" we are enabled to make comparisons between the thoughts of characters such as Rosier, Goodwood, Warburton, and Mrs. Touchett on the subject of Isabel and compare their insights with those of both Ralph and the narrator.

Isabel's process of vision is in essence her slow progress toward seeing herself as others have seen her. She gradually learns that some, like Osmond and Madame Merle, have seen her only in the light of an adjunct to their own purposes, while others, notably Ralph, have appreciated her for herself but have also been obliged to reassess her. Isabel's process of vision, then, encompasses seeing herself through "the successive windows of other people's interest in her" (AN 306).

When considering the incidence and proportional distribution of modes of presentation of consciousness, we notice that quoted monologue here, as in Roderick, occurs least frequently. Predictably, however, this mode is more prevalent in The Portrait than in Roderick as direct access is afforded to the consciousness of more than one reflector. As would be expected, Isabel is accorded the most generous proportion of quoted monologues (at least fifteen), Ralph about five (with diminishing frequency, and all in the first two-thirds of the novel), Rosier two, and Osmond one, embedded in a passage of dissonant psychonarration and narrated monologue.

This rare instance of quoted monologue in the depiction of Osmond's inner world is particularly revealing, set as it is in the ironic perspective of critical narratorial comment that highlights his hypocritical self-justification. Osmond is experiencing "the sense of success—the most agreeable emotion of the human heart" (2.11) at the imminent prospect of securing Isabel:

"Ah no, I've not been spoiled; certainly I've not been spoiled," he used inwardly to repeat. "If I do succeed before I die I shall thoroughly have earned it." He was too apt to reason as if "earning" this boon consisted above all of covertly aching for it and might be confined to that exercise. (2.11–12)

Here the flaws (both logical and ethical) in Osmond's mode of reasoning are explicitly rather than implicitly exposed through the conjunction of quoted monologue and narratorial comment.

The inner worlds of Madame Merle, Mrs. Touchett, and even the

Countess Gemini are briefly illuminated through psychonarration and narrated monologue. In spite of the claim that "Pansy is . . . the only significant character James never goes behind,"[6] even the inner world of the opaque Pansy is recorded in observations such as "But Pansy was not indiscreet even in thought; she would as little have ventured to judge her gentle stepmother as to criticise her magnificent father" (2.383). Explicit comment on Pansy is rendered here through the narratorial voice in psychonarration. This contrasts with the use of narrated monologue in conjunction with psychonarration for the evocation of Isabel's consciousness in the latter part of the novel: there the reader is obliged to read between the lines—or behind the articulated thoughts—relying on his own interpretation in the absence of direct narratorial comment.

As in his other novels, James uses thematically invested focalization here: the significance of the distribution of inside views is reflected in the pattern whereby, in the latter part of the novel, Ralph's perspective, so predominant in the early section, is no longer directly accessible and virtually everything is refracted through the consciousness of Isabel. The thematic significance of this stylistic device is evident in that the reader is restricted to Isabel's own perspective, participating (unaided now by the voice of direct narratorial guidance) in the "process of vision" whereby she develops greater insight into motivation previously unclear to her.

* * *

In the earlier sections of the novel, the reader is vouchsafed more insight than Isabel into the real nature of both Madame Merle and Osmond, so sharing the cognitive privilege of the narrator. This is accomplished not only by the reader's being a "privileged" spectator at scenes from which the heroine is by necessity excluded but also by crucial knowledge being afforded by direct narrator's report on events undisclosed to Isabel and, most significantly, through the portrayal of thoughts of the other characters (through the three modes of presentation of consciousness).

The reader, for instance, is able to "witness" the crucial scene between Madame Merle and Osmond (before his meeting with Isabel) in which vital information as to the true nature and motives of each is revealed. Osmond is depicted as cynical, world-weary, and prepared to consider making a new acquaintance only on the basis of his prime consideration— "What good will it do me?" (1.343). The reader is prepared for Isabel's later realization that she has been acquired as a choice objet d'art for Osmond's collection by being privy to the cold, calculating way in which he evaluates people. When Osmond stipulates the conditions on which he is prepared to condescend to have Isabel presented to him—that she

be "beautiful, clever, rich, splendid, universally intelligent and unprece-
dentedly virtuous" (1.344), Madame Merle assures him that Isabel "fills
all your requirements" (1.345) as though she were an inanimate object to
be sent on approval before being slotted into a predetermined place in
his "sorted, sifted, arranged world" (1.377). The reader is in a position to
pick up the verbal echo of Ralph's declaration to his father that he wishes
his bequest to make it possible for Isabel to "meet the requirements of
[her] imagination" (1.261); this foregrounds the difference in motivation
between these two admirers, a difference that Isabel is only later to
discover.

The impression conveyed in conversation with Osmond's erst-while
consort is later reinforced by the glimpses of his inner world afforded by
a few extended passages of psychonarration and narrated monologue
during his courting campaign in which his egotistical mode of viewing his
prospective spouse is further revealed. (Isabel herself, of course, has no
inkling of what is vouchsafed to the reader concerning her "lover's" real
motives at this stage.) Thereafter, the reader sees Osmond only through
Isabel's eyes (except for the dramatic scene between Osmond and Madame Merle that is presented in the form of a conjectural projection of a
conversation that Isabel would have been able to hear "If she had been
concealed behind one of the valuable curtains" [2.331]).

After their marriage, the reader has only indirect access to Osmond's
consciousness through Isabel's perception, Osmond's own direct discourse (notably in conversations with Isabel, Madame Merle, and Caspar
Goodwood), and descriptions of his facial expressions and expressive
gestures such as the contempt with which he greets Rosier at one of his
Thursday receptions:

> Osmond stood before the chimney, leaning back with his hands behind him;
> he had one foot up and was warming the sole. . . . Rosier . . . went up to
> shake hands with him. . . . Osmond put out his left hand, without changing
> his attitude. (2.103)

Similarly, restricted access only is given to the consciousness of Isabel's
other suitors, Warburton and Goodwood, in much shorter passages of
psychonarrration and narrated monologue.

The shift from authorial to figural narration in the course of the novel
inevitably imposes greater demands on the reader's interpretive activity.
For example, when Isabel first meets Madame Merle, her impressions of
her new friend are conveyed in narrated monologue with little supplementary narratorial comment to amplify or rectify her view. We find "our
speculative heroine" (1.245) interpreting her new acquaintance but, being
dazzled by her accomplishments, failing to perceive signs of a possible

discrepancy between her charming manner and appearance and her real nature. In the absence of direct narratorial comment, the reader has to be alert to subtle revelatory indications of artifice. These appear in, for example, the ambiguity inherent in the repetition, in the description of her piano playing, of "It showed skill, it showed feeling" (1.245), echoed later in the linguistic parallelism of "She knew how to think. . . . Of course, too, she knew how to feel" (1.267). Madame Merle's action in "turn[ing] quickly round, *as if* [my emphasis] but just aware of her presence" (1.245) also suggests a well-rehearsed display of spontaneity.

Isabel's perception that Madame Merle "knew how to think" is embedded in interesting generalizations colored by stylistic contagion:

> There are many amiable people in the world, and Madame Merle was far from being vulgarly good-natured and restlessly witty. She knew how to think—an accomplishment rare in women; and she had thought to very good purpose. Of course, too, she knew how to feel; Isabel couldn't have spent a week with her without being sure of that. (1.267)

Initially, the comment about "amiable people," cast in the present tense, seems to derive from the narrator, as does the ostensibly sexist—and potentially offensive—generalization concerning the imputed inability of most women to think. What emerges from the context, however—"Isabel couldn't have spent a week with her without being sure of that" indicates that the preceding sentences are in narrated monologue—is that both generalizations should be attributed to Isabel. (The first, if not originated by Isabel, is at least endorsed by her.) With her limited experience of her more sophisticated and intellectually advanced peers, she is determined not to join the ranks of those women who had not made the most of opportunities for intellectual stimulation and development.

What Isabel does not perceive, of course—but the reader can—is the moral ambiguity in "she knew how to feel," a formulation that again reinforces the impression of artfulness and lack of spontaneity created in their first encounter. The use of narrated monologue here subtly distances the narrator from Isabel's point of view and sets Isabel's thoughts in the ironic context created by the cognitive superiority of the narrator and reader. Isabel's naivety and susceptibility to a polished facade are subtly revealed with minimal narratorial nudging.

This is further reinforced through the judicious deployment of revelatory imagery, as in the garden image that highlights an essential difference between the freshness, vitality, spontaneity, and openness of Isabel's nature and the essentially self-contained and carefully cultivated artifice of Madame Merle: "our heroine . . . wandered, as by the wrong side of the wall of a private garden, round the enclosed talents, accomplishments, aptitudes of Madame Merle" (1.270). Here, as elswhere, the imagistic mode in psychonarration functions to convey to the reader implications to which the protagonist is impervious.

In the course of the novel, the narrowing of cognitive distance between the narrator and reflector is such that Isabel's perceptions are no longer supplemented by those of the more knowing narrator.

Apart from chapter 42, where virtually the whole chapter is devoted to rendering the activity of Isabel's hyperactive consciousness, the presentation of consciousness in the novel occurs in conjunction with other modes such as direct, indirect, and free indirect discourse; narrator's report or commentary; description; and so on.

In James's terminology, the predominant pattern in the novel is one where "picture" alternates with "scene" and "summary." In chapter 12, for example (depicting Warburton's proposal), after an initial half page of "scene"—description of Warburton's arrival and exchange of civilities with Isabel—dialogue gives way to nearly three pages of "picture" or psychonarration dominated by an evocation of Isabel's state of mind concerning Warburton and marriage. Through psychonarration we are also given a brief inner view of Warburton's feelings toward Isabel, which prompt him to propose. A degree of foreshortening or summary psychonarration is evident here. Six pages of dialogue are then followed by a concluding page where the extract modulates back into "picture" (presentation of Isabel's consciousness) where psychonarration and narrated monologue dramatize Isabel's state of mind. Within one dramatic unit, then—that of Warburton's proposal—we find a "scene" dominated by dialogue, with brief references to setting and gesture, modulating back to scene and finally again to "picture" in which psychonarration is interspersed more liberally now with narrated monologue rendering Isabel's own thoughts "verbatim" in interrogative form:

> Who was she, what was she, that she should hold herself superior? What view of life, what design upon fate, what conception of happiness, had she that she pretended to be larger than these large, these fabulous occasions? (1.156)

It is noteworthy that it is through psychonarration that Isabel's fundamental reasons for rejecting Warburton are revealed, reasons that contrast with the more conventionally acceptable justification for refusal that she proffers him in spoken discourse. Psychonarration reveals the more "metaphysical" dimension of her desire for personal liberty (which is as vague as it is compelling), which it is impossible for Isabel to communicate to Warburton:

> She couldn't marry Lord Warburton; the idea failed to support any enlightened prejudice in favour of the free exploration of life that she had hitherto entertained or was now capable of entertaining. (1.155)

This conclusion is reached after the implications of such a match as envisaged by Isabel are explored in an earlier passage of psychonarration:

> What she felt was that a territorial, a political, a social magnate had conceived the design of drawing her into the system in which he rather invidiously lived and moved. A certain instinct, not imperious, but persuasive, told her to resist—murmured to her that virtually she had a system and an orbit of her own. (1.144)

Later, what emerges is the poignant irony of her rejection of Warburton on the grounds of his being a potential threat to her liberty in his capacity as "a territorial, a political, a social magnate": Isabel, who shies away from the inevitable restrictions involved in being allied to "a collection of attributes and powers" (1.143), falls prey to a man who is merely a collection of conventions and poses. Osmond's reification of his wife as an item in his collection of precious objects represents a much greater desecration of her personal liberty than adjusting to Warburton's social system would have been.

Isabel's desire for personal liberty is emphasized in another proleptic image of incarceration and confinement: when Isabel listens to Warburton's proposal "though she was lost in admiration of her opportunity she managed to move back into the deepest shade of it, even as some wild, caught creature in a vast cage" (1.152–53). The similarity between the insight of Ralph and that of the narrator is emphasised by his later using the same image (which is used here by the narrator in psychonarration) in conversation with Isabel: when trying to dissuade her from accepting Osmond, Ralph warns her, in the scene in the Florentine garden, that "you're going to be put into a cage" (2.65).

*   *   *

A notable feature of the representation of consciousness through both narrated monologue and psychonarration is their densely imagistic texture. An interesting comparison with *Roderick* emerges here: in the earlier novel, as we have seen, imagery, although varied and recurring in complex patterns, tended to be restricted to the narratorial voice, the direct discourse of the characters (notably Roderick and Rowland himself), and Rowland's letters to Cecilia (a form of written direct discourse); it occurred relatively infrequently in the presentation of consciousness through narrated monologue. (When found in narrated monologue, such imagery tended to represent later revisions added in the New York Edition after completion of the later novels where imagery is most prevalent in psychonarration and particularly in narrated monologue.)

In this analysis of *The Portrait,* then, my primary focus is on the exploration of the incidence and implications of the deployment of this complex imagistic mode in the presentation of consciousness. A comparison between the narrator-dominated chapter 6 and the reflector-dominated chapter 42 could elucidate crucial differences between dissonant narration (which is abstract, analytical) and consonant narration (largely imagistic) in *The Portrait.* Although there is a constant oscillation between the two modes in the novel (with a marked swing away from the dissonant in the latter half), the authorial and figural modes are in a sense epitomized in these two chapters.

In chapter 6, where the narrator comments on and analyzes Isabel's psyche, an abstract analytical vocabulary is used for rendering her inner world of which the narrator has a clearer understanding than Isabel herself. Cognitive and linguistic disparity exists between the narrator and the reflector. In chapter 42, by comparison, the preponderance of narrated monologue indicates that the narrator espouses the syntax and images of Isabel's own consciousness; the adjudicating narratorial voice is suppressed, and in the absence of authorial rhetoric, disparities between the narrator's and the character's understanding are hinted at only obliquely.

In chapter 6, the narrator, adopting the stance of historian or "biographer" (1.68), informs us inter alia that

> Isabel Archer was a young person of many theories; her imagination was remarkably active. . . . Her thoughts were a tangle of vague outlines . . . she had an unquenchable desire to think well of herself. . . . The girl had a certain nobleness of imagination which rendered her a good many services and played her a great many tricks. She spent half her time in thinking of beauty and bravery and magnanimity; she had a fixed determination to regard the world as a place of brightness, of free expansion, of irresistible action. (1.66–68)

An indication of the ambivalence of the imagination—the image-generating faculty—is given here in the narrator's comment on Isabel's romantic idealism. Her "nobleness of imagination" affords her "services" in endowing her with a potential for vivid appreciation of the varied cultural riches of Europe and a heightened sensitivity to the possibilities of life in general. However, the comment that "she had a fixed determination to regard the world as a place of brightness" indicates that her inflexibly idealistic view of life could blind her to the darker aspects of human nature. Later, we find that it renders her incapable of seeing through a character like Gilbert Osmond as "her imagination added the human element which she was sure had not been wanting" (1.383). Reference to the "many tricks" played on her by her imagination can be seen as a premonitory pointer to the most devastating "trick" of all to be played on her when her imagination, dexterously steered by Madame Merle, leads her to choose Osmond.

The reference to Isabel's romantic imagination gives the reader an anticipatory inkling of a psychological weakness, hinted at earlier in chapter 4, which is to prove Isabel's undoing: "at important moments, when she would have been thankful to make use of her judgement alone, she paid the penalty of having given undue encouragement to the faculty of seeing without judging" (1.42).

This analytic comment is preceded by an observation couched in more imagistic form that is confided by the narrator during his account of Isabel's meditative vigil in the Albany house: "Her imagination was by habit ridiculously active; when the door was not open it jumped out of the window. She was not accustomed indeed to keep it behind bolts" (1.42).

The architectural metaphor introduced here in psychonarration recurs throughout the novel. The image of the bolted door ironically anticipates the proleptic intuition Isabel experiences in response to Osmond's proposal, the implications of which she fails to grasp at the time: she is to experience "the sharpness of the pang that suggested to her somehow the slipping of a fine bolt—backward, forward, she couldn't have said which" (2.18). Later, in Osmond's fortress-like Palazzo Roccanero, her mind is indeed to be confined "behind bolts," the potential ambiguity of the proleptic image—the "slipping of the fine bolt" suggesting either liberation or confinement—having been firmly resolved. The architectural image takes on these more sinister resonances in chapter 42, where Isabel conceives of herself as restricted to the narrow confines of Osmond's mental construction: "[Osmond's mind] appeared to have become her habitation" (2.194) as "he had led her into the mansion of his own habitation . . . the house of darkness, the house of dumbness, the house of suffocation" (2.196).

The later fusion of literal and metaphorical levels is anticipated here as the symbolism of the series of suggestive habitations Isabel is to be confronted or tempted with in the course of the novel gradually emerges. As Richard Chase has observed,

> The idea of leaving or entering a house, the contrast of different kinds of houses, the question of whether a house is a prison or the scene of liberation and fulfilment—these are the substance of the metaphors in *The Portrait of a Lady*.[7]

Architectural images occur in psychonarration, in direct discourse and in the narrator's comment. By contrast with chapter 6, where the narrator analyzes Isabel in the abstract, as it were, without reference to her physical presence or her own meditations, the architectural image in chapter 4 emerges in the context of the account of Isabel's first meditative vigil as she "passes in review" her life up to that point and is overwhelmed by "a host of images" (1.42). This scene could indeed be regarded as an adumbration of the process of "motionlessly seeing" that is rendered so vividly in the climactic midnight vigil. It thus gains in significance by being placed in the illuminating perspective of both the central fireside scene and the later episode on the train when, returning to Gardencourt, she is subject to "disconnected visions" that pass through her mind (2.390). The predominant mode for rendering these "disconnected visions" is psychonarration (modulating intermittently into narrated monologue), which, as Cohn has demonstrated, is the preeminent mode for portraying subliminal areas of experience.

In those scenes, as here, "things . . . as memory played over them, resolved themselves into a multitude of scenes and figures . . . . The result was kaleidoscopic" (1.46). The image of the kaleidoscope, suggesting a multiplicity of self-reflecting and mutually illuminating facets, aptly evokes the impression of the shifting perspectives experienced in a state of heightened awareness.

At times the narrator in these early chapters adopts a stance of disarming archness—or mock-modest speculation—as when his ostensible omniscience is undercut by comments such as "It may be affirmed without delay that Isabel was *probably* very liable to the sin of self-esteem" (1.67; my emphasis) and, in a previous chapter, "Of what Isabel then said no report has remained" (1.39).

In summarizing Isabel's most salient features, the narrator spells out to the reader the intended response to his preliminary sketch of her character:

> Altogether, with her meagre knowledge, her inflated ideals, her confidence at once innocent and dogmatic, her temper at once exacting and indulgent, her mixture of curiosity and fastidiousness . . . her desire to look very well and to be if possible any better, her determination to see, to try, to know . . . she would be an easy victim of scientific criticism if she were not intended to awaken on the reader's part an impulse more tender and more purely expectant. (1.69)

We find later, in one of several proleptic references, that those resistant readers who in spite of the narrator's ingenuous statement of intent persist in criticizing his heroine are also catered for: in a later address to his readers, the narrator advises

> Smile not, however, I venture to repeat, at this simple young woman from Albany who debated whether she should accept an English peer before he had

offered himself . . . if there was a great deal of folly in her wisdom those who judge her severely may have the satisfaction of finding that, later, she became consistently wise only at the cost of an amount of folly which will constitute almost a direct appeal to charity. (1.144–45)

Such direct or oblique references to the reader are frequently found in chapter 6, as in "you could have made her colour, any day in the year, by calling her a rank egoist" (1.72). In this paragraph, however, the abstract analytical vocabulary which continues in the following sentence—"She was always planning out her development, desiring her perfection, observing her progress"—shifts into the imagistic mode for an elaboration: "Her nature had, in her conceit, a certain garden-like quality, a suggestion of perfume and murmuring boughs, of shady bowers and lengthening vistas" (1.72). Thus, another important network of imagery is introduced in this early chapter; later, particularly in chapter 42, this cluster of imagery takes on significantly different resonances.

Other indications of the greater perceptibility of the narrator in this early chapter can be found in, for example, distancing appellations such as "our young lady" (1.73) and "our rustling, quickly-moving clear-voiced heroine" (1.75), appellations that are absent from the later chapter. Nevertheless, in spite of the generally unobtrusive nature of the narratorial presence in chapter 42, there are brief manifestations of the presence of the first-person narrator: for example, "that sense of darkness and suffocation of which I have spoken took possession of her" (1.99); "it used to come over her, as I have intimated" (1.202); and at the end of the chapter when, after the prolonged exploration of Isabel's consciousness through psychonarration and narrated monologue, the mode of presentation reverts to a more detached form of narrator's report of Isabel's physical attitude and perceptions of the world around her, "As I have said, she believed she was not defiant" (2.205).

*   *   *

The imagistic mode in the presentation of Isabel's consciousness is particularly in evidence in her perception of the other major characters. Throughout *The Portrait,* a complex of visual images dramatizes different modes of viewing others. In the portrayal of Isabel's perception of Madame Merle and Osmond, these visual images incorporate references to light and to viewing objects as diverse as pictures and landscapes. Isabel's perception of Osmond is anticipated in the way she responds to Madame Merle, in whom are adumbrated many qualities brought to perfection in Osmond. Isabel "liked her extremely, but was even more dazzled than attracted" (1.270–71); that is, being half-blinded by her brilliance, by the perfections of the consummately achieved "social animal," Isabel cannot judge Madame Merle very clearly or impartially. In a proleptic image, the narrator conveys that Isabel "wished to hold up the lamp for Madame Merle" (1.270), the better to illuminate her perfection, as she is destined to do for Osmond. The image recurs in direct discourse when Osmond expresses his appreciation of Isabel—seen in her capacity as a source of illumination—in a related image:

> "It's just as when one has been trying to spell out a book in the twilight and suddenly the lamp comes in. I had been putting out my eyes over the book of life and finding nothing to reward me for my pains; but now that I can read it properly I see it's a delightful story." (2.81)

Isabel could interpret this as meaning that she, as the "light of his life," has endowed Osmond's existence with a sense of meaning and purpose previously lacking; not being adept at reading between the lines (particularly those of his "book of life"), she little realizes that to him the "golden glow" she casts over his book means, primarily, valuable endowment of a different order. She is, in fact, to be relegated to "holding up the lamp" for Osmond, to highlight his superiority to the world, as she had wished to do—on a much more modest scale—for Madame Merle.

The "picture" Isabel constructs of Osmond after her visit to his hilltop villa is a vivid illustration of the composing powers of consciousness, or, more specifically, the constitutive capacity of the creative imagination. (Prior to the visit, Madame Merle had with consummate art sketched a preparatory portrait of her erstwhile consort, Osmond; with the canvas prepared, she could propel Isabel firmly in Osmond's direction so that the finishing touches could be applied to her masterpiece.) Isabel then constructs an interpretive hypothesis about Osmond and fails to adjust this hypothesis in the face of both subsequent intuitions and warnings from others. Her creative imagination constructs an appealing portrait: an image that embodies or makes concrete, as it were, her charmed vision. Like all artistic creations her picture relies on selective interpretation, highlighting the more picturesque aspects of his situation. Through psychonarration, modulating into narrated monologue for the tentative question Isabel asks herself halfway through the extract, the image is evoked:

> the image of a quiet, clever, sensitive, distinguished man, strolling on a moss-grown terrace above the sweet Val d'Arno and holding by the hand a little girl whose bell-like clearness gave a new grace to childhood. The picture had no flourishes, but she liked its lowness of tone and the atmosphere of summer twilight that pervaded it. It spoke of the kind of personal issue that touched her most nearly; of the choice between objects, subjects, contacts—what might she call them?—of a thin and those of a rich association; of a lonely, studious life in a lovely land . . . of a care for beauty and perfection so natural and so

cultivated together that the career appeared to stretch beneath it in the disposed vistas and with the ranges of steps and terraces and fountains of a formal Italian garden. (1.399–400)

It is noteworthy that what Isabel sees is "visible only to a sympathetic eye" (1.400) and that her picture "put on for her a particular harmony with other supposed and divined things" (1.399). What Isabel "supposes" and "divines" is in effect a specious projection of her aesthetic imagination that creates a romantic frame in which to place its idealized portrait. Being afforded access to Isabel's inner world through the interplay of the different modes of presentation of consciousness, the reader can see through Isabel's eyes and can simultaneously perceive more than she does, being devoid of her romantic illusions and equipped with inside knowledge of Osmond's real nature. So it is made clear, without the need for overt narratorial comment, how much is superimposed on the actual scene by Isabel's aesthetic imagination.

Isabel fails to perceive the sinister overtones in the picture she has conjured up. These are more strongly implicit in Osmond's development of Isabel's image as he sketches their future life together (the image is now used in direct discourse): "what a long summer afternoon awaits us. It's the latter half of an Italian day—with a golden haze, and the shadows just lengthening, and that divine delicacy in the light, the air, the landscape" (2.81). Only later does Isabel realize that the "lengthening shadows" can be regarded as premonitory of her future situation where, as she perceives during her midnight vigil—in a related image now cast in narrated monologue—"it was as if Osmond deliberately, almost malignantly, had put the lights out one by one" (2.190). In a modulation of the image, the "disposed vistas" of Isabel's own vision take on symbolic significance as she later finds "the infinite vista of a multiplied life to be a dark, narrow alley with a dead wall at the end" (2.189).

Thus the changes in Isabel's vision are dramatized by the imagery, by the shifting connotations of the same basic elements recurring in complex configurations in psychonarration, narrated monologue, and direct discourse. So, too, the metaphoric overtones of the "formal Italian garden" are activated when seen here in conjunction with the garden imagery often used to depict Isabel's nature. We recall the narrator's observation, in psychonarration, about Isabel's nature having "in her conceit, a certain garden-like quality, a suggestion of . . . shady bowers and lengthening vistas" (1.72). The "garden-like quality" evokes associations of natural growth and vitality, a soul more conducive to *jardin à l'anglaise* disposition—that is, natural growth gently directed by cultivated forms—than the rigid pattern of the formal Italian garden suggesting Osmond's inflexible forms and conventions. A later stage in Isabel's process of vision is rendered in a modulation of this image in narrated monologue when she realizes that "Her mind was to be his—attached to his own like a small garden-plot to a deer-park" (2.200): she is to be reduced in Osmond's eyes to a mere adjunct of himself.

The modulations of images such as these, then, serve to dramatize stages in the process of vision—and re-vision—and the later visions ascribed to Isabel, particularly in her midnight meditation, are examples of the convergence, at different levels of awareness, of the process of vision of protagonist, reader, and narrator.

Thus, the manner in which characters view both themselves and each other—a view that can be either static or dynamic—is vividly suggested through the imagery. Some view others primarily in terms of the roles in which they can be cast: Isabel sees herself as the leading lady in the drama of her life, unaware that she might be cast in another role by others more adept at stage management or at imposing their own scenario—polished performers who see her merely in a supporting role (in all senses of the term). Isabel, who is engaged in a quest for a fulfilling role to play in life, is tricked into accepting a ready-made subservient role, imagining that to play the supporting part to the leading man of her choice, Gilbert Osmond, will afford her fulfillment. In Madame Merle amd Osmond, by contrast, role-playing is associated with duplicity and a deliberate attempt to manipulate the view of them held by others.

Isabel's aesthetic imagination generates her highly embellished picture of Osmond. Her initial aesthetic appreciation is expressed in an appropriately pictorial image: "he was not handsome"—Isabel is not crude enough to be attracted by the conventionally handsome visage—"but he was fine, as fine as one of the drawings in the long gallery above the bridge of the Uffizi" (1.356).

An illuminating comparison could be drawn between the image in terms of which Isabel conceives of Osmond and the comparable image used by the narrator:

> he suggested, fine gold coin as he was, no stamp nor emblem of the common vintage that provides for general circulation; he was the elegant complicated medal struck off for a special occasion. (1.329)

The narrator's image succinctly captures features that Isabel does not detect, such as Osmond's cultivated air of exclusivity. The combination of art and money imaged by the coin also suggests the aesthetic facade masking his mercenary nature.

The image of the picture is taken up and developed by Osmond, in a passage giving access to his consciousness after the successful conclusion of his courting campaign. Here psychonarration seems to veer toward

narrated monologue in a mock impersonation of his own idiolect in the
latter part of the extract. Osmond imparts rather disquieting nuances to
the image, nuances colored by his egotism:

> If an anonymous drawing on a museum wall had been conscious and watchful
> it might have known this peculiar pleasure of being at last and all of a sudden
> identified—as from the hand of a great master—by the so high and so unnoticed
> fact of style. His "style" was what the girl had discovered with a little help:
> and now, besides herself enjoying it, she should publish it to the world without
> his having any of the trouble. (2.12)

The illusory nature of Isabel's belief in her own independence is dramatized here by the conceit of a work of art manipulating the response it
elicits from an unsuspecting observer. What Isabel does not perceive,
either, is that Osmond is all meretricious "style" and no substance. The
subtly sketched outlines of the "fine" and "anonymous" drawing are to be
fleshed out by Isabel's creative imagination—which "supplied the human
element she was sure had not been wanting" (1.383)—and given the stature of a fully achieved masterpiece.

In spite of her "wondrous vision of him fed through charmed senses
and oh such a stirred fancy" (2.192), Isabel does experience several apparently unaccountable premonitory intuitions about Osmond before finally succumbing. These provide qualifications of her defects of vision.
As these intuitions are largely impervious to rational formulation by the
figural consciousness, they are rendered through imagistic psychonarration. When Isabel considers Osmond's proposal, for example, it is
through a highly suggestive image that her imagination registers an intuitive sense of foreboding that she is unable to elucidate rationally:

> What had happened was something that for a week past her imagination had
> been going forward to meet; but here, when it came, she stopped—that sublime
> principle somehow broke down. . . . Her imagination . . . now hung back:
> there was a last vague space it couldn't cross—a dusky, uncertain tract which
> looked ambiguous and even slightly treacherous, like a moorland seen in the
> winter twilight. But she was to cross it yet. (2.21–22)

The narrator's proleptic comment concluding the extract emphasizes
his cognitive privilege and hence the discrepancy between the insight of
the figural consciousness and that of the narrator at this stage of the
novel. Unlike the protagonist, the narrator and the reader are in a position
to explore the link with the pervasive garden imagery and recall the
elaboration of the image in chapter 6 where attention is drawn to Isabel's
awareness that "there were a great many places that were not gardens at
all—only dusky pestiferous tracts, planted thick with ugliness and mis-

ery" (1.72). The verbal echo here emphasizes the irony that Isabel is unwittingly about to undertake the crossing of such "a dusky, uncertain" and "pestiferous" tract, an illusory "garden" in which, as she is only later to perceive, Osmond's "egotism lay hidden like a serpent in a bank of flowers" (2.196).

The ominous references to the descending dusk of "winter twilight" also contrast strongly with the glowing picture evoked earlier of the "long summer afternoon . . . await[ing] us." Isabel is as yet impervious to these recognitions, as to the full import of another premonitory intuition received when reassuring Pansy that she would be kind to her: "A vague, inconsequent vision of her coming in some odd way to need it had intervened with the effect of a chill" (2.86). These forewarnings—which parallel those experienced during her early acquaintanceship with Osmond—are, however, soon dispelled for lack of corroborating evidence to sustain them.

Although Isabel's imagination—"that sublime principle"—gives her access to these admonitory signs, the "wondrous vision" it has created of Osmond interferes with her ability fully to grasp their meaning. Her hyperactive imagination is not sufficiently controlled by her "faculty of judgement."

These extracts provide an adumbrative illustration of the cognitive function of metaphors—their role of representing the world. Through metaphor, what is abstract is rendered concrete; so Isabel's amorphous, undefined fear finds form and expression in the image of a "dusky, uncertain tract." This role of metaphor as an enabling device making possible the imaging or rendering concrete of intuitions about relationships that are not amenable to rational analysis is demonstrated more fully later in more sustained depictions of the activity of Isabel's consciousness; this occurs most notably in her midnight meditation where narrated monologue is used more extensively.

Just as Isabel's impressions of Madame Merle and Osmond are rendered largely in terms of recurrent images, so Ralph's perception of Isabel is frequently expressed in imagistic terms. Extensive access to Ralph's view of—and aspirations and fears for—Isabel is afforded, particularly in the early sections of the novel. These are frequently expressed in extended passages of imagistic psychonarration and narrated monologue interspersed with quoted monologue. One of the significant image clusters is that of the recurrent sea imagery that is deployed in the presentation of both thought and speech, animating both psychonarration and narrated monologue as well as direct and indirect discourse. Ralph perceives Isabel as embarking on a voyage of discovery in Europe; it is to facilitate her free exploration of life—and make the most of opportunities denied to himself—that he persuades his father to leave her a fortune: "I should like to put a little wind in her sails" (1.260) and "to see her going before the breeze" (2.262). He again uses the sea image in direct discourse when he confidently (but mistakenly) opines to his mother that

> "She has started on an exploring expedition, and I don't think she'll change her course, at the outset, at a signal from Gilbert Osmond. She may have slackened speed for an hour, but before we know it she'll be steaming away again." (1.396)[8]

This analogy between Isabel and a ship recurs in narrated monologue in Isabel's midnight vigil when, in her own consciousness, she recalls the initial idealistic impulse that motivated her to marry Osmond. Ironically, it is in much the same way that Ralph had sought vicarious fulfillment in generously facilitating the realization of the supposedly worthy ambitions of another. Here Ralph's image is reversed as Isabel sees herself as "launching" Osmond:

> He was like a sceptical voyager strolling on the beach while he waited for the tide, looking seaward yet not putting to sea. . . . She would launch his boat for him; she would be his providence. (2.192)

Ralph's interest in and admiration of Isabel are clearly revealed in an extended passage of psychonarration interspersed with an unusual abundance of quoted monologue. He expresses his conception of Isabel's value in terms of analogies with representative works of art:

> If his cousin were to be nothing more than an entertainment to him, Ralph was conscious that she was an entertainment of a high order. "A character like that," he said to himself—"a real little passionate force to see at play is the finest thing in nature. It's finer than the finest work of art—than a Greek bas-relief, than a great Titian, than a Gothic cathedral. . . . Suddenly I receive a Titian, by the post, to hang on my wall—a Greek bas-relief to stick over my chimney-piece. The key of a beautiful edifice is thrust into my hand, and I'm told to walk in and admire." (1.86)

The imagery here vividly illuminates the difference between Ralph and Osmond's respective ways of viewing Isabel. Both conceive of Isabel in terms of images drawn from the arts, but whereas Ralph's images, reflected in his quoted monologue (a Greek bas-relief, a Titian, a Gothic cathedral) suggest his respect for the beauty and integrity of the work of art in itself, the aesthetic, mercantile, and commercial images Osmond uses in narrated monologue (e.g., that comparing her mind to a "silver plate" capable of reflecting his thought "on a polished, elegant surface"

[2.79]) reveal his conception of Isabel's aesthetic and utilitarian function as an objet d'art fashioned for the sole purpose of reflecting the good taste of its owner.

Ralph's quoted monologue is followed by direct narrator's report indicating the limitations of his understanding of his cousin: "The sentiment of these reflections was very just; but it was not exactly true that Ralph Touchett had had a key put into his hand." The narratorial voice conveys that although Ralph recognizes that "his cousin . . . would take . . . a good deal of knowing," his fuller understanding of her nature is hampered perhaps by an incipient emotional prejudice: "his attitude with regard to her, though it was contemplative and critical, was not judicial." It emerges later, of course, that Ralph underestimates the influence of Isabel's naively idealistic views, her susceptibility to appearances, and her "faculty of seeing without judging" (1.42).

The use of quoted monologue for the formulation of Ralph's view of Isabel perhaps suggests that he is voicing what he feels it is safe to articulate—to acknowledge, even to himself—and that he is suppressing awareness of his incipient emotional attachment by formulating his conception of her in terms of these distancing analogies with works of art that serve to establish a measure of safe detachment.

The architectural image first used in Ralph's quoted monologue—"the key of a beautiful edifice"—recurs in the narrator-dominated psychonarration that reveals the limitations of his access to Isabel's mind:

> He surveyed the edifice from the outside and admired it greatly; he looked in at the windows and received an impression of proportions equally fair. But he felt that he saw it only by glimpses and that he had not yet stood under the roof. (1.87)

An interesting analogy can be discerned between the narrator's imagistic representation of Ralph's perception of Isabel here and the empirical author's image in the preface of the literary creation erected around his protagonist: he refers to

> this single small corner-stone, the conception of a certain young woman affronting her destiny, [which] had begun with being all my outfit for the large building of "The Portrait of a Lady." It came to be a square and spacious house . . . put up round my young woman. (AN 48)

The analogy highlights the convergence of perspective between the authorial voice and that of his representative "touchstone" in the novel.

Portrayal of Ralph's state of mind shifts from psychonarration to narrated monologue when the elaboration of the architectural image of the key to an edifice takes a more practical application: "What was she going to do with herself?" The ascription of the generalization that follows is initially uncertain, as it could emanate from either the narrator or the figural consciousness:

> This question was irregular, for with most women one had no occasion to ask it. Most women did with themselves nothing at all; they waited, in attitudes more or less gracefully passive, for a man to come that way and furnish them with a destiny. (1.87)

The statement that "Isabel's originality was that she gave one an impression of having intentions of her own" could also be that of the narrator, and is comparable to the observations made in the psychological portrait of Isabel in chapter 6. However, the return to quoted monologue here dispels the ambiguity and identifies the preceding observations as indubitably Ralph's: "Whenever she executes [her intentions]," said Ralph, "may I be there to see!" (1.87).

Devices such as these—blurring of the boundaries between the observations of the narrator and those of the figural consciousness (expressed in narrated monologue, as in the above extract)—have the effect of further reinforcing the close association between the perspective of the narrator and, in this context, that of Ralph. Indeed, Ralph could be regarded as "the impersonal author's concrete deputy or delegate, a convenient substitute or apologist for the creative power otherwise so veiled and disembodied" (AN 327).

Ralph, unlike Isabel, sees through Osmond from the outset. His more penetrating view of Osmond, which qualifies and rectifies Isabel's initially purblind view, and confirms his earlier impressions, is presented in a passage summarizing his impressions of the Osmond ménage after two years of marriage. The passage is a conjunction of quoted monologue, psychonarration, and narrated monologue that concludes with the direct intervention of the first-person narrator: "I give this little sketch . . . [of Ralph's view] for what it is worth" (2.145).

Unlike Rosier, who is taken in by Isabel's appearance as "a picture of a gracious lady," Ralph sees through the mask to the reality of the change wrought in Isabel:

> The free, keen girl had become quite another person; what he saw was the fine lady who was supposed to represent something. What did Isabel represent? Ralph asked himself; and he could only answer by saying that she represented Gilbert Osmond. "Good heavens, what a function!" he then woefully exclaimed. (2.143–44)

Ralph registers valid insight into Isabel's situation long before she herself has achieved this understanding.

Another exemplification of Ralph's functioning in the capacity of "concrete author's delegate" can be seen in the incidence of phrases first used by Ralph (in conversation with Isabel), which are then taken up not only by the fictional narrator but by the empirical author in his comments on the novel in his *Notebooks*. So, for instance, we have Ralph commenting to Isabel that "You wanted to look at life for yourself—but. . . . You were ground in the very mill of the conventional" (2.415), an observation that is echoed virtually verbatim by James in his *Notebooks:* "The idea of the whole thing is that the poor girl, who has dreamed of freedom and nobleness . . . finds herself in reality ground in the very mill of the conventional."[9] Here the voice of the author overlaps with that of a character (who is the "concrete author's delegate") in the novel. This merging of voices is reminiscent of—albeit of a different order from—that blurring of the demarcation between the voice of the narrator and that of the figural consciousness that can be found in "stylistic contagion." In the example cited, what one might call "lexical ventriloquism" involves crossing the boundary between the fictional and the empirical world. Stylistic contagion involves the blurring of boundaries *within* the text, between psychonarration and narrated monologue; a reporting syntax is maintained, but the idiom is strongly colored by the mental idiom of the mind it reflects.[10] One might designate the example first cited as intertextual as opposed to intratextual stylistic contagion.

The latter (more orthodox) form of stylistic contagion frequently incorporates a cluster of images that could be attributed to either narrator or character and are used elsewhere by the narrator in psychonarration or assigned to the respective characters in narrated monologue or direct discourse. The following example, which incorporates the iterative sea imagery, illustrates this procedure. It is an extract in which Isabel, having learned from Henrietta that Caspar has come to Rome, recalls her last interview with him before her marriage and ponders the nature of their relationship. In this extract, she muses that

> He [Caspar] had left her that morning with a sense of the most superfluous of shocks: it was like a collision of vessels in broad daylight. There had been no mist, no hidden current to excuse it, and she herself had only wished to steer wide. He had bumped against her prow, however, while her hand was on the tiller, and—to complete the metaphor—had given the lighter vessel a strain which still occasionally betrayed itself in a faint creaking. It had been horrid to see him, because he represented the only serious harm that (to her belief) she had ever done in the world: he was the only person with an unsatisfied claim on her. (2.279)

Here there is ambiguity as to whether the mode is psychonarration or narrated monologue, with the concomitant uncertainty concerning the provenance of the metaphoric comment. Initially, the mode appears to be narrated monologue as Isabel's own recollected perception is presented in the form of a metaphor depicting "a collision between vessels in broad daylight." However, the self-conscious phrase "to complete the metaphor" would seem to indicate that the mode is that of psychonarration, with the narrator rather than Isabel ("the lighter vessel") using the metaphor. The narrator's metaphor "faint creaking" could then be interpreted as the pangs of conscience Isabel experiences at the thought that "he represented the only serious harm that (to her belief) she had ever done in the world." Here the mode is indubitably narrated monologue as the formulation "It was horrid" indicates. The qualification "to her belief" would then be Isabel's, and not the narrator's ironic hint that she had in fact been responsible for much more. One page further on, the image recurs in slightly cryptic or modified form, the term "concussion" recalling the collision image but shifting from a nautical to a drawing-room confrontation:

> This gave his figure a kind of bareness and bleakness which made the accident of meeting it in memory or in apprehension a peculiar concussion; it was deficient in the social drapery commonly muffling, in an overcivilized age, the sharpness of human contacts. (2.280)

Here the critical or evaluative comment "an overcivilized age" should presumably be attributed to the narrator rather than to Isabel, although this too is not devoid of ambiguity—particularly since it recalls Isabel's ostensibly innocuous (but drily telling) comment to Warburton about her husband having "a genius for upholstery" (2.131).

* * *

The conjunction of psychonarration and narrated monologue is frequently exploited to foreground psychological processes such as rationalization and self-deception. The depiction of Isabel's thoughts is often suffused with this ironic dimension. Her initial obliquity of vision—or reluctance to face the truth—is displayed in her myopic view of both Osmond and Ralph, and her self-deception is highlighted through the interplay of psychonarration and narrated monologue. In a passage affording access to the consciousness of both Isabel and Ralph, at the end of chapter 30, the limitations of her insight—and Ralph's well-founded reservations—are clearly revealed. Through psychonarration we learn—and register the irony undetected by Isabel herself—that Isabel "noted afresh that life was certainly hard for some people, and she felt a delicate glow of shame as she thought how easy it now promised to become for herself." In attempting to come to terms with Ralph's disapproval of her choice, Isabel resorts to rationalization that is clearly revealed through narrated monologue:

> it would be his privilege—it would be indeed his natural line—to find fault with any step she might take toward marriage. One's cousin always pretended to hate one's husband; that was traditional, classical; it was a part of one's cousin's always pretending to adore one. (2.60–61)

Here narrated monologue highlights her suppression of the unpalatable recognition that Ralph's opposition might well stem from more than the conventional cousinly stance on such matters. The generalization, cast here in the past tense rather than the gnomic present employed by the narrator, is obviously Isabel's—a suspect truism from which the narrator would dissociate himself. Ironically, Isabel is to discover that Ralph's supposedly "traditional" adoration is indeed genuine, as opposed to the specious adoration displayed by Osmond ("if you've been hated you've also been loved. Ah but, Isabel—*adored!*" (2.417).

Another generalization in Isabel's narrated monologue—"You could criticize any marriage; it was the essence of marriage to be open to criticism"—foregrounds the irony of her subsequent thought: "How well she herself, should she only give her mind to it, might criticize this union of her own!" and demonstrates her aforementioned faculty for "seeing without judging." Ironically, this rejection of the necessity for "giving her mind to it" foreshadows her later midnight meditation when she does at last, belatedly, put her mind (and more specifically, her imagination) to it.

The cognitive privilege of the narrator at this stage is underscored by the shift out of narrated monologue for his statement that "We, who know more about poor Ralph than his cousin . . ." (2.61) and is reinforced by the use of the distancing appellations "our young woman" and "our young lady" in the following section.

Isabel's obliquity of vision—or reluctance to face the truth—is manifested in her dealings with Ralph, Osmond, Caspar, and Warburton. To suppress lingering feelings of guilt about her treatment of Caspar, she indulges in a ludicrously inept display of "logical induction." In trying to establish what motivated Caspar to visit her in Rome a few years after her marriage, Isabel concludes, conveniently (with his supposed reason given in narrated monologue) that he came because

> he wanted to see her. In other words he had come for his amusement. Isabel followed up this induction with a good deal of eagerness, and was delighted to have found a formula that would lay the ghost of this gentleman's ancient grievance. (2.291)

Psychonarration then changes back to narrated monologue for "following consciousness through its paces," miming the steps in her reasoning process with parodic effect. (The narrator's term "induction" is obviously used ironically as applied to the succession of non sequiturs Isabel takes refuge in:)

> If he had come to Rome for his amusement this was exactly what she wanted; for if he cared for amusement he had got over his heartache. If he had got over his heartache everything was as it should be and her responsibilities were at an end. (2.291–92)

Quod erat demonstrandum!

Another illustration of Isabel's increasing capacity for self-deception can be found later in her pondering the issue of the proposed match between Warburton and Pansy. Here again, insight into the workings of the protagonist's mind is afforded by the narration of her unvoiced reflections with no overt judgment by the narrator. We find that Isabel appears to be succumbing to Osmond's influence and adopting his moral values:

> She had come little by little to think well of the idea of Pansy's becoming the wife of the master of beautiful Lockleigh. . . . It would please [Osmond] greatly to see Pansy married to an English nobleman, and justly please him, since this nobleman was so sound a character. (2.173–74)

In the first part of this quotation, it is clear that Isabel, like Osmond, is thinking of Warburton as a personage rather than as a person and evaluating him in terms of his extrinsic rather than his intrinsic merits, so moving toward Madame Merle's position on the importance of the "shell" or "envelope of circumstances" (1.287) rather than qualities of "self"—a view she had so vehemently opposed before. She is obviously trying to delude herself in clinging to the notion that Osmond's pleasure would be "just" because "this nobleman was so sound a character." Osmond is more concerned with Warburton's wealth, rank, and position in society; character is a secondary consideration, as is his daughter's own preference for Rosier. Isabel is in fact in danger of aiding and abetting Osmond and Madame Merle to perpetrate against Pansy the same injustice that they had perpetrated against her: manipulating her into a mercenary marriage, a marriage of convenience—to others.

Narrated monologue takes us through Isabel's self-justificatory catalogue of reasons for complicity in this scheme, a catalogue of suspect motives concluding with "Lastly, it would be a service to Lord Warburton, who evidently pleased himself greatly with the charming girl." A convenient omission from this catalogue is the interests of Pansy herself, and it is rather chilling to discover that Isabel, like Osmond, had "care-

fully abstained" from consulting Pansy. Furthermore, her formulation—
"It was a pity, however, that Edward Rosier had crossed their path!"
(2.175) and "An impediment that was embodied in poor Rosier could not
anyhow present itself as a dangerous one; there were always means of
levelling secondary obstacles" (2.176)—is reminiscent of Osmond's own
attitude and is again a telling illustration of how Isabel's thinking has been
infected by the cynicism and opportunism of Osmond and Madame
Merle. Deployment of such impersonal abstract terms—reinforced by a
plethora of euphemisms—is calculated to stifle the knowledge that
Pansy's own preferences are being ruthlessly disregarded.

When representation shifts out of narrated monologue and the narrator
intervenes in the first person to comment that "It may seem to the reader
that Mrs. Osmond had grown of a sudden strangely cynical" (2.175), it is
perhaps appropriate that she should be referred to by that hollowly honorific title "Mrs. Osmond" rather than "Isabel," for in this extract she demonstrates to what extent she is prepared, as a dutiful wife, to espouse his
interests (literally and figuratively). As Ralph had observed, Isabel is
taking on the "function" of "representing Gilbert Osmond."

Later, when Isabel grasps the full implications of Osmond's mercenary
ambitions and the lengths to which he is prepared to go to secure his
daughter's assent—including a period of genteel incarceration in the convent—she dissociates herself from his schemes for Pansy; she establishes
the limits of her pliancy both by refusing to manipulate Warburton on his
behalf and defying his prohibition to go to Ralph on his deathbed.

Isabel's initially deluded view of both Ralph and Osmond is more fully
revealed in a significant passage at the beginning of chapter 35 in which
access is given successively to her consciousness and that of her "lover,"
Osmond (2.77–80).

* * *

The device of juxtaposing inner views of Isabel and Osmond on the
eve of their marriage vividly illuminates their respective modes of viewing
each other and their imminent union. The juxtaposition of the two passages of psychonarration and narrated monologue is revealing, exposing
as it does the fallaciousness of Isabel's conception of Osmond—and
validating Ralph's contention that "There's no more usual basis of union
than a mutual misunderstanding" (1.205).

Isabel dismisses the opposition of her family and friends to her alliance
with Osmond; she prides herself on her superior taste and discernment
in being able to recognize his generally unacknowledged merit, so demonstrating her liability to "the sin of self-esteem." She dismisses Ralph's
misgivings as unworthy of serious consideration, as

[Ralph's] talk about having great views for her was surely but a whimsical cover for a personal disappointment. Ralph apparently wished her not to marry at all—that was what it really meant—because he was amused with the spectacle of her adventures as a single woman. His disappointment made him say angry things about the man she had preferred even to him: Isabel flattered herself that she believed Ralph had been angry. (2.78)

Narrated monologue here vividly enacts the activity of Isabel's mind as she engages in a process of rationalization, suppressing any lingering misgivings afforded by her imagination. The punctuation, particularly the semicolons and dashes, performs the mimetic function of enacting the pauses in her mental activity, while the adverbs "surely" and "apparently" reinforce the impression that she is trying to reassure herself by dismissing her own unacknowledged subconscious doubts by refusing to allow them rational expression. She minimizes the significance of Ralph's distrust of Osmond as an individual by trying to persuade herself that he objects to her marrying per se, adopting the convenient view that his disapproval stems from the imminent loss of a source of entertainment— that of the "spectacle of her adventures as a single woman." Ironically, Ralph had indeed initially regarded Isabel as a source of entertainment "of a high order," but the reader is aware, as Isabel is not, that his feeling for her is based not merely on the pleasure of vicarious participation in her free exploration of life but on deep unselfish devotion.

The quality of this devotion contrasts telling with that of Osmond, which is revealed in the shift from an inner view of Isabel to Osmond's consciousness. This inner view is also significant in that it would seem to invalidate Stanzel's claim that

The more a reader learns about the innermost motives for the behaviour of a character, the more inclined he tends to feel understanding, forbearance, tolerance, and so on, in respect to the conduct of this character.[11]

This would certainly not be true of the reader's response to the revelation of Osmond's thoughts. The more the reader learns about Osmond's innermost motives for wanting to ensnare Isabel—motives that contrast so forcibly with his overtly expressed desires—the more his or her sympathy recedes or is withdrawn from Osmond.

As already mentioned, Osmond's exploitative, egotistical motives were revealed earlier in a conversation with Madame Merle before meeting Isabel. Here, through the representation of his consciousness, even more sinister dimensions of his egotism are exposed, as in chapter 35. As always, the crucial function of imagery is evident, as Osmond conceives of Isabel in terms of objects of aesthetic and utilitarian value: "a silver plate," a "gift."

The first part of the extract is in psychonarration:

> The elation of success, which surely now flamed high in Osmond, emitted meanwhile very little smoke for so brilliant a blaze. Contentment, on his part, took no vulgar form. (2.78)

The obviously authorial provenance of the image (Osmond could scarcely be conceived of as applying the image to himself) results in the character's own mental processes being set in the ironic context of a more enlightened perspective. This heightens the irony of the contrast between the emotions customarily experienced on such occasions and Osmond's own "elation of success"—rather than, say, of requited love—at the triumphant completion of his courting campaign. Overt signs of jubilation—"smoke"—are carefully suppressed so as to conceal the true source and extent of the "blaze" of his triumph. In this, as always, Osmond (for whom, according to Ralph, "the great dread of vulgarity" is "his special line"), is prompted not by ethical considerations but by observance of form: it would be "vulgar" form (apart from being inopportune and inexpedient) to display his real emotions.

For the reader, the image awakens echoes of the adage "there's no smoke without fire," recalling the misgivings expressed by Ralph about the projected match and reinforcing the realization—afforded by the presentation of Osmond's consciousness in this scene—of how misguided Isabel had been in ignoring these warning signs.

As a polished performer who, like Madame Merle, "knew how to feel," Osmond scrupulously observes all the forms appropriate to an "admirable [rather than "genuine"] lover." Far from being sincerely in love, as Dorothea Krook maintains,[12] Osmond—too fastidious to be merely mercenary—relishes his role of lover smitten with the charms (carefully catalogued) of his beloved. Osmond's egotism and lack of spontaneity (and lack of real feeling for Isabel as an individual in her own right) are emphasized by the narrator's intervention with the repetition and play on the phrase "forgot himself"; "He never forgot himself, as I say; and so he never forgot to be graceful and tender, to wear the appearance . . . of stirred senses and deep intentions" (2.79). His intentions, needless to say, are deeper than Isabel can imagine.

After the narrator's observation that "He was immensely pleased with his young lady;" the semicolon signals a shift to narrated monologue where his own thoughts are more directly conveyed: "Madame Merle had made him a present of incalculable value." This throws into ironic relief

Isabel's illusion, expressed above, that "she married to please herself";
in effect, she is marrying primarily to please Madame Merle and Osmond.

The terms in which he conceives of Madame Merle's felicitous arrangement give us insight into the coldly inhuman way in which he evaluates
her "worth,"—her monetary, aesthetic, and utilitarian value—as an object about to be accorded the honor of incorporation into his collection
of precious objets d'art: he views Isabel as "a present of incalculable
value" (the reader knows, of course, that Isabel's monetary value—well
in excess of seventy thousand pounds—had been calculated meticulously
before the deal was clinched). In the continuation of his narrated monologue, the three successive rhetorical questions dramatize his thought
processes and expose both his warped sense of values and his inadequate
understanding of Isabel's real nature:

> What could be a finer thing to live with than a high spirit attuned to softness?
> For would not the softness be all for one's self, and the strenuousness for
> society, which admired the air of superiority? What could be a happier gift in
> a companion than a quick, fanciful mind which saved one repetitions and re-
> flected one's thought on a polished, elegant surface? (2.79)

Osmond's egotistical narcissism, emanating from his aestheticism,[13] is
revealed in his appreciation of Isabel's mind primarily, if not solely, as a
merely passive reflecting medium; he applauds its supposed capacity to
"reflect one's thoughts on a polished, elegant surface." Ironically, in spite
of his complaint to Madame Merle about Isabel having "too many ideas"
(1.412)—her only fault in his eyes—he overestimates his ability to eradi-
cate them and reduce her to a creature as passive and pliant as his daughter. The hidden menace in "a high spirit attuned to softness" is
premonitory both of the subtle process of coercion to which Pansy is
later to be subjected and his comparable endeavor to coerce Isabel into
compliance with his mercenary ambitions for his daughter. (Later, Isabel
demonstrates that her "high spirit," although suffering a temporary de-
flection, will not be "attuned" to moral malleability and to accepting a
course of action inimical to her ideals of moral integrity.)

The conspiratorial alliterative sibilance in "softness for . . . self, and
strenuousness for society . . . superiority" emphasizes Osmond's hidden
agenda, intentions that are carefully concealed from Isabel and that Ralph
is the first to detect.

The concept of Isabel's mind as a decorative reflective surface is succinctly captured in the image of the "silver plate that he might heap up
with ripe fruits, to which it would give a decorative value, so that talk
might become for him a sort of served dessert." This view of Isabel as a
passive receptacle, incapable of acting independently—dependent on him

to elicit any response—is further developed in the reference to "the silver quality" Osmond finds in Isabel: "he could tap her imagination with his knuckle and make it ring." This propensity to "tap" Isabel both psychologically and financially is amply demonstrated later; even in their last interview before her departure for Gardencourt, Osmond exerts this power: "There was something in her imagination he could always appeal to against her judgement" (2.354).

The imagery used here in the presentation of Osmond's consciousness is revealing, and is given added impetus through the interplay of psychonarration and narrated monologue. The technique creates a new dimension in the revelation of Osmond's subtle egotism. (This was more overtly expressed in his exchange with Madame Merle where he crudely enquired after Isabel's credentials for presentation.)

Far from eliciting sympathetic understanding for Osmond, the portrayal of the inner life here, with the insight afforded into Osmond's fundamental duplicity, alienates the reader's sympathy. Consideration of the full import of such access to Osmond's consciousness thus disproves the traditional assumption, supported by Stanzel, that interiorization of the "villain," with the heightened understanding it affords, necessarily leads to a concomitant increased sympathy with his position.

The device of juxtaposing portrayal of Osmond's thoughts about the proposed marriage to Isabel with what he declares to her in dialogue—that is, covert thoughts and overt declarations—reveals the full extent of his hypocrisy. In a conversation immediately following this extract, he declares, proferring a glib aphorism,[14] that

"I won't pretend I'm sorry you're rich; I'm delighted. I delight in everything that's yours—whether it be money or virtue. Money's a horrid thing to follow, but a charming thing to meet. It seems to me, however, that I've sufficiently proved the limits of my itch for it: I never in my life tried to earn a penny." (2.80)

Osmond adopts a pose of disinterested appreciation of all Isabel's qualities, pretending that her wealth is an optional extra rather than the prime requisite. Isabel fails to detect the flawed logic of his claim to have proved the limits of his itch for money: she doesn't perceive that indolence is hardly a guarantee of immunity from avarice. (Osmond has already proved his avarice in courting Isabel and is to give further proof in his pursuit of the wealthy Warburton and rejection of the relatively impecunious Rosier as suitor for his daughter.) She also fails to detect the anomaly in his putting "virtue" on the same level as money as a desirable attribute.

After this chapter, no sustained access is afforded to the consciousness of Osmond. It is through the perceptions of Ralph and Isabel that the implications and consequences of the attitudes revealed in these extracts are reflected. Isabel's subsequent insight into her relationship with Osmond is dramatically crystallized in chapter 42, which depicts her midnight vigil.

This crucial fireside meditation scene differs from the earlier extensive explorations of Isabel's inner world (in chapter 6, for example) where we have the narrator imparting his knowledge of Isabel to the reader. Here Isabel herself is portrayed in the process of attaining knowledge both of herself and those around her as she grapples with certain crucial issues. Instead of the static, already-achieved insight conveyed by the narrator, the impression created here is of the process of thought being enacted *sur le vif*.

Through the skillful management of narrated monologue, the reader has the impression of participating in the process whereby the reflector attains insight rather than merely registering the received wisdom of the narrator. "The language does not express thoughts so much as the process of thinking": Michael Bell's comment, albeit made in a different context, seems an apt characterization of the method of presentation here.[15]

Isabel's "motionlessly seeing" here represents the most significant of the recognition scenes through which she attains understanding. The process of vision in *The Portrait* has many facets; it is accomplished by the protagonist both in scenes of recognition where she is either present as a witness or directly involved as a participant, and also in various scenes rendering a process of "motionlessly seeing" in solitary contemplation. (Her meditative fireside vigil is preceded by the scene in the Albany house and followed by a comparably meditative "backward picture" on the train returning to Gardencourt.) These insights are supplemented by information or revelations afforded by other characters, perceptions which range from the "illumination of wisdom" (2.60) provided by Ralph to the "new and violent light" (2.374) of sensational disclosures vouchsafed by the Countess Gemini.

Here, instead of indulging in rationalization and warding off discomforting truths, Isabel is actively engaged in elucidating her situation and attaining new insight into herself, Osmond, and her whole network of relationships. It is in response to the impact of Osmond's words and their menacing implications—reinforced by the "strange impression she had received in the afternoon of her husband's being more in direct communication with Madame Merle than she suspected" (2.188)—that Isabel, her mind "assailed by visions" (2.204), undertakes a drastic reassessment of her whole situation.

That first recognition scene, where the relative positions, the collusive air, and the "absorbed mutual gaze" of her husband and Madame Merle indicated a degree of intimacy previously undetected by Isabel, had aroused as yet unconfirmed suspicions. Isabel's perception of that tableau had later been referred to by the narrator as "an occasion commemorated in this history with an emphasis appropriate not so much to its apparent as to its real importance" (2.331). The "real" as opposed to the "apparent" importance of this and other phenomena is what Isabel is to grapple with in her midnight vigil. She is obliged to exercise, to an ever-increasing extent, "the power to guess the unseen from the seen, to trace the implication of things."[16] Through "something detected" in the relationship between Madame Merle and Osmond she was brought to realize that there is far more to their relationship than meets the eye, even though it is what *does* meet the eye that precipitates new insight.

In tracing Isabel's gradual awakening to the extent of her own self-deception, we recall her expressed conviction that "the only thing is to see our steps as we take them—to understand them as we go. That, no doubt, I shall always do" (1.270). Ironically, as we have seen, she is destined to understand not as she takes the steps leading her to Osmond's "house of darkness" but only afterwards, in retrospect. Thus, her enlightenment proceeds in accordance with Kierkegaard's conviction that "Life can only be lived forward and understood backward."[17] It is indeed through retracing those steps in imagination that, with the wisdom of hindsight, she attains true understanding.[18] A narratorial comment in *The Bostonians* is particularly pertinent to Isabel's experience here:

> these hours of backward clearness come to all men and women, once at least, when they read the past in the light of the present, with the reasons of things, like unobserved finger-posts, protruding where they never saw them before.[19]

The best example of this procedure is to be found in the most crucial of her recognition scenes, in what was described in the preface as Isabel's "extraordinary midnight vigil which was to become for her such a landmark" (*AN* 57).

The scene also illustrates how, in rendering the process of vision of his "intense perceivers," James demonstrates not only that he conceived of "seeing" as an act of the inward even more than the outward eye but also that "seeing" as an act of the outward eye can prepare for and culminate in insight as an acquisition of the inward eye.

Isabel's tendency to conceive of her situation in visual terms is vividly manifested here in her attempts to clarify and comprehend her situation. Mulling over what Osmond has said, she finds that "his words had put the situation before her and she was absorbed in looking at it" (2.186). Though superficially a static "picture," this scene, as James points out in the preface, "throws the action further forward than twenty 'incidents' might have done." He explains that "it was designed to have all the vivacity of incident and all the economy of picture" (*AN* 57).

James's comment could be taken as an alternative formulation of the conjunction of narrated monologue and psychonarration, the dramatic immediacy of narrated monologue having the "vivacity of incident" as it enacts the activity of the protagonist's consciousnesss, miming its very movements, while "the economy of picture," encompassing James's notion of foreshortening, suggests the possibilities of the more panoramic surveys of psychonarration which can summarize and condense impressions and thoughts—those arising here from three years' experience of married life with Osmond.

The terminology of both James and Cohn point to the complex shifts in time and space, the smooth sliding between the reflector's present moment, and her remembered past and projected future. Detailed imagistic depictions of Isabel's present state (or, more accurately, *process*) of understanding are embedded in evocations of other past conceptions or experiences and possible future implications: "Isabel, scanning the future with dry, fixed eyes, saw. . . ." (2.191).

Cohn points out that chapter 42, which epitomizes a completely inward scene (a drama of consciousness as opposed to drama presented in dialogue) is "a supreme illustration of the paradox that narrative fiction attains its greatest 'air of reality' in the representation of a lone figure thinking thoughts she will never communicate to anyone" (7). The scene demonstrates the truth of James's contention that the dramatization of the "subjective adventure," which is essentially an interpretive enterprise, can "make the mere still lucidity of her act as 'interesting' as the surprise of a caravan or the identification of a pirate" (*AN* 54).[20]

In this fusion of "incident" and "picture,"

> She sits up, by the dying fire, far into the night, under the spell of recognitions on which she finds the last sharpness suddenly wait. It is a representation simply of her motionlessly seeing. (*AN* 57)

Isabel passes her life in review as she had done in Albany before leaving for Europe; one experiences a similar "kaleidoscopic" succession of images that bring to mind T. S. Eliot's lines "The memory throws up high and dry / A crowd of twisted things."[21] The memory, stimulated by stress, generates or "throws up" images, impressions, and thoughts in an apparently haphazard fashion. Events are recalled not necessarily in chronological order but by a process of association; fragments are framed for scrutiny before sinking back into the matrix of memory. Certain crucial revelations are presented in the form of images. Thus Isabel's access to increased self-knowledge is attained not only through ratiocination but through images, which at times have an almost hallucinatory quality. These images rise to mind in previously undiscerned combinations, and an inchoate pattern of meaning gradually emerges to be imposed on formerly disparate elements of experience.

The process of conceptualization through metaphor is most vividly dramatized in this scene where various streams of imagery converge. The cognitive function of imagery is illustrated in the recurrence of certain key images in new configurations, demonstrating the significant role of iterative imagery in emphasizing the important stages in the development of the character's understanding.

A close examination of the imagery reveals the extent to which disclosures are conveyed by means of vivid and often recurrent images. Isabel's mind is "assailed by visions" (2.204) which are triggered partly by the same vision with which the scene closes: "Isabel stood there gazing at a remembered vision—that of her husband and Madame Merle unconsciously and familiarly associated" (2.205). That image, the import of which gradually emerges, is "like a sudden flicker of light" (2.165) that acts as a stimulus to start to life a host of submerged images that surge up to be subjected to rational analysis.

Of the many significant streams of images converging here, the most striking are those relating in some sense to vision or insight; this would include the recurrent light imagery. Although some of these images occur elsewhere in speech—as in Osmond's ominous declaration to Caspar that he and his wife are "as united . . . as the candle and the snuffers" (2.309), it is largely in psychonarration amd narrated monologue that this cluster of images makes its full impact. So we find Isabel musing, in an image that makes more explicit the implications of the "candle and snuffers," that "Osmond deliberately, almost malignantly, had put the lights out one by one" (2.190).

Thus, the contrast between Isabel's early idealistic aspiration (rendered in somewhat ironic psychonarration) to "move in a realm of light, of natural wisdom" (1.68), and her present altered vision (rendered in narrated monologue) is emphasized by her realization that Osmond was extinguishing her independent spirit.

Ironically, although Isabel perceives that Ralph has "the illumination of wisdom" (2.60), she had failed to heed his warning to "Wait . . . for a little more light" and to appreciate that he "might have struck a spark or two" (2.66) of insight to highlight Osmond's defects.

Metaphors evoking the theme of seeing or perceiving also reinforce the idea that Isabel is now seeing things differently, "in the light of deepening experience" (2.194). Just as she had learned to "view her friend [Madame Merle] with a different eye" (2.323), so she now has a modified perception of her husband. When he had originally declared his love for her, they were described as "exchanging a long look—the large, conscious look of the critical hours of life" (2.17–18). Now, Isabel's perception of the distance separating them is rendered in narrated monologue in which their alienation from each other is signalled by the metaphorical modification of this literal exchange of looks: "a gulf had opened between them over which they looked at each other with eyes that were on either side a declaration of the deception suffered" (2.189). Other complexes of iterative imagery that dramatize the succession of revelatory disclosures include those connected with the theater, architecture, and the ubiquitous garden images.

The composing power of the creative imagination is vividly exemplified in this capacity to reduce experience to images. It is also significant that most of the images are conjured up by Isabel herself, in narrated monologue, rather than by the narrator, on her behalf, in psychonarration. This is a measure of her cognitive progress; as Peter Garrett has observed, "To image a situation is to move toward mastery of it, to make it more firmly possessed by consciousness."[22]

Images can represent seminal stages in the evolution of consciousness when a character attains "an emblematic perception, a symbolised intuition."[23] Thus, as Garrett emphasizes,

> The problem . . . of determining whether a given image proceeds from the character's consciousness or from the narrator is therefore quite important; the locus of the image will indicate responsibility for the creation of meaning.[24]

Recognition of the modes used for representing consciousness can contribute greater precision here: the fact that images are located more frequently in narrated monologue than psychonarration indicates that Isabel is attaining understanding and control of her experience.

The cognitive power of metaphor, although apparent to the reader, is not necessarily understood by the reflector. Isabel does not consciously appreciate the significance of these images or of the imagination itself as an "aid to lucidity." When trying here to wrestle with the problem of Warburton's real motives for wanting to marry Pansy, Isabel, whose thoughts are traced through psychonarration modulating into narrated monologue, "broke out of the labyrinth, rubbing her eyes, and declared that her imagination surely did her little honour and that her husband's did him even less" (2.188). She rubs her eyes to dispel the nightmarish interpretation of the truth to which her imagination is giving her access; but what her imagination is projecting is in fact a valid reflection of the true state of affairs. Her reluctance to accept this is underscored by stylistic contagion as her thoughts are rendered in psychonarration veering toward narrated monologue in which her own formulation is suggested: "her imagination *surely*" (my emphasis). In effect, her imaginative faculty, which had previously been responsible for creating and sustaining illusions, becomes more rigorously disciplined in the course of her disillusionment and becomes actively engaged in the process of judging, interpreting, and elucidating. Thus, we find that "Isabel's imagination applied itself to this elusive point"; that is, it is now used to decipher mysteries such as that of the conspiratorial couple "in combination."

Cohn notes that the function of Isabel's analeptic excursion is not primarily to fill in the gap created by skipping over the first years of her married life; "her remembering psyche does not focus on the elided events themselves, but engages in a kind of retrospective self-analysis" (129). The most crucial insight attained is Isabel's recognition that in her idealistic assessment of Osmond she had been taken in by his facade: "she had imagined a world of no substance" and "had not read him right" (2.192). We recall her propensity, revealed earlier by the narrator, to be "guided in the selection [of books] chiefly by the frontispiece" (1.29–30). The recurrence of the image indicates the convergence of Isabel's understanding with that of the narrator, a convergence that is reflected more generally in the effacement of the narrator's voice and its displacement by that of the figural consciousness.

The recurrence also of terms or concepts originally used by Ralph emphasizes the part he has played in guiding Isabel's growing insight. For example, Isabel's newly acquired realization, expressed here in narrated monologue, that Osmond "took himself so seriously, it was something appalling" (2.196), recalls Ralph's asseveration to Isabel in the Florentine garden: "I think he's narrow, selfish. He takes himself so seriously" (2.70). Ralph also perceived that "under the guise of caring only for intrinsic values Osmond lived exclusively for the world. . . . He lived with his eye on it from morning till night" (2.144). Isabel, now seeing through Osmond's pose of indifference to the world, couches her discovery, which is rendered in narrated monologue, in similar terms: "this base, ignoble world, it appeared, was after all what one had to live for; one was to keep it for ever in one's eye . . . to extract from it some recognition of one's own superiority" (2.197).

Isabel's painfully acquired (but swiftly stifled) insight into Warburton's true motives—"She asked herself with some dismay whether Warburton were pretending to be in love with Pansy in order to cultivate another satisfaction and what might be called other chances"—also echoes that voiced by Ralph who had asked Warburton whether "among Miss Osmond's merits her being . . . so near her stepmother isn't a leading one?" (2.153).

Her most crucial recognitions, albeit still imperfect, concern her husband. Lunar imagery is used for the expression of her belief that

> he had not disguised himself, during the year of his courtship, any more than she. But she had seen only half his nature then, as one saw the disk of the moon when it was partly masked by the shadow of the earth. She saw the full moon now—she saw the whole man. . . . she had mistaken a part for the whole. (2.191)

The recognition that Isabel's thoughts here are rendered in narrated monologue enables the reader to regard them critically, as not necessarily having the endorsement of the narrator; thus the reader can perceive the limitations of what Isabel ironically believes to be a full understanding of "the whole man." She does not yet perceive that during his courting campaign he had deliberately suppressed or held in check the more reprehensible aspects of his nature and had artfully misled her as to the real nature of his interest in her, masking his mercenary motives behind a facade of urbane indifference to the worldly. Osmond's true motives had been partly masked by the rosy illumination (rather than "shadow") carefully cast by his accomplice, who was described by Ralph in appropriately cosmic imagery as "the great round world itself" (2.362).

Although "the whole man" is not yet in effect completely unmasked (Isabel discovers only later, for example, that "he had married her, like a vulgar adventurer, for her money" (2.330)) she does perceive that he represents a way of life that is the very antithesis of what she had imagined; far from epitomizing "the infinite vista of a multiplied life" (2.189) and "the high places of happiness" and liberty, which would guarantee Isabel "an orbit of her own" (1.144) he has attempted to relegate Isabel to the subsidiary position of satellite to what she now perceives to be an alien and hostile orb.

This perception is reinforced through a recurrence of the garden imagery. Psychonarration, through which it is conveyed that "The real offence, as she ultimately perceived, was her having a mind of her own at all," shifts into narrated monologue for transforming this observation into a deeply realized imaginative insight:

> Her mind was to be his—attached to his own like a small garden-plot to a deer-park. He would rake the soil gently and water the flowers; he would weed the beds and gather an occasional nosegay. It would be a pretty piece of property for a proprietor already far-reaching. (2.200)

Setting this image in the context of the earlier garden imagery suggesting Isabel's vitality, spontaneity, and dislike of confinement emphasizes the tragedy of this free spirit being reduced to a mere adjunct of a chauvinistic poseur.

Isabel has the magnanimity not only to "pity" Osmond for the deception suffered but to see herself as largely responsible for the deception. Here again the more enlightened perspective of the narrator and reader allow us to see that in attempting to render scrupulous justice, Isabel apportions more blame to herself than strict justice or an enlightened eye would demand. There is an important difference between deceiving "in intention," as Osmond does, and deceiving unwittingly, in good faith, as Isabel does; moreover, the motive in each case is very different. So it is difficult to agree with the contention that in this section "much of the analysis seems calculated to justify Isabel" who is "fittingly made to pay for her own deception."[25] As we have seen, Isabel is infinitely more deceived and plotted against than deceiving. A recognition of the function of narrated monologue and psychonarration in revealing what should be ascribed to the narrator and what to the figural consciousness would elucidate the specific kind of ambiguity exploited here and arguably obviate such misinterpretation.

Thus, Isabel does not yet see "the whole man" or grasp the full picture. Other ramifications have yet to be revealed in further scenes facilitating her process of vision, including the lurid revelations of the Countess Gemini and Madame Merle's disclosures at the convent.

The constitutive power of consciousness is foregrounded here in Isabel's realization that she had misconstrued Osmond partly because "she had mistaken a part for the whole" (2.191). Paul B. Armstrong has suggested that the novel supplies a paradigm of all interpretative process:

> Isabel's efforts to correct her imperfect view transform into the stuff of drama the very workings of the hermeneutic circle—the circle whereby one can understand the parts of any state of affairs only by projecting a sense of the whole, even as one can grasp the whole only by explicating its parts. . . . In portraying Isabel's wakening, James offers as an adventure in itself the ever-shifting relation between parts and wholes through which she seeks to recompose her world. James did not invent the hermeneutic circle, obviously, but he did discover that its movements could themselves form the action of a novel.[26]

Apart from dramatizing the interpretive process, this midnight meditation can also be regarded as a scene of temptation in that Isabel is shown weighing the possibility of adopting her husband's view, and specifically, of seeing in his way the projected match between Warburton and Pansy. After being confronted with Osmond's scarcely veiled threat that he would hold her responsible if the scheme failed, she is obliged to reassess her stance. The scene begins and concludes with a reference to the temptation of playing the role of dutiful wife and helping him realize his ambitions for his daughter in violation of her own wishes. Ultimately, understanding the true state of both Warburton's and Pansy's feelings, Isabel resists the temptation to propitiate or placate Osmond. At this stage, however, as the portrayal of Isabel's consciousness shifts out of narrated monologue to establish greater critical detachment, the narrator intervenes in the first person, and uses a telling image that indicates the limits of her understanding:

> As I have said, she believed she was not defiant, and what better proof of it than that she should linger there half the night, trying to persuade herself that there was no reason why Pansy shouldn't be married as you would put a letter in the post-office? (2.205)

The narrator's image here suggests a heartless readiness to dispatch Pansy almost on a COD basis and reinforces the impression that Isabel is adopting Osmond's instrumentalizing view, being prepared to view others as a means to an end. Her view of Ralph, too, is problematic, still obscured by self-delusion. A generalization in the gnomic present tense— reinforced by the ironic narratorial comment in the last sentence—serves to stress the cognitive distance between the protagonist and the narrator here:

> it seemed to her an act of devotion to conceal her misery from him. . . . It gave her plenty to do; there was passion, exaltation, religion in it. Women find their religion sometimes in strange exercises, and Isabel at present, in playing a part before her cousin, had an idea that she was doing him a kindness. It would have been a kindness perhaps if he had been for a single instant a dupe. (2.203–04)

In her self-deluded state, Isabel does not yet perceive that Ralph both recognizes the true state of affairs and would welcome her confidence. As narrated monologue foregrounds the disparity between the understanding of the reflector and the reader, the latter can see, as Isabel manifestly does not, that her policy toward Ralph is compounded both of concern for him and of pride.

The midnight meditation, then, is one of the important "milestones on the road of so much inward or apprehensive life,"[27] a milestone that indicates both the distance Isabel has traveled and the tracts she has yet to traverse.

Before Isabel's process of vision is complete, the insights achieved in various ways by Isabel herself have to be corroborated and supplemented by others. Her last crucial recognitions are derived from revelations vouchsafed by the Countess Gemini and Madame Merle. These disclosures have been prepared for not only by dramatized scenes of recognition and "motionlessly seeing" but also, less obtrusively, through the activity of her subconscious mind rendered through psychonarration. Thus, for instance, we find that "sometimes, at night, she had strange visions; she seemed to see her husband and her friend—his friend—in dim, indistinguishable combination" (2.278).

Isabel's reaction to her sister-in-law's revelations is appropriately rendered in visual terms, as a response to what she "saw": after being exposed to the countess's Pandora's box of exotic disclosures, Isabel is described as sitting "staring at her companion's story as at a bale of fantastic wares some strolling gypsy might have unpacked on the carpet at her feet" (2.368).

Similarly, in the last meeting between Isabel and Madame Merle at the convent, Isabel is depicted as seeing

> in the crude light of that revelation which had already become part of experience . . . the dry staring fact that she had been an applied handled hung-up tool, as senseless and convenient as mere shaped wood and iron. (2.379)

Here again her strongly visual imagination—and tendency to conceive of things in analogical terms—is manifested. Furthermore, in "she saw the dry staring fact" the act of attaining insight is dramatized by endowing a normally perceptual verb with strong cognitive connotations, and simultaneously giving abstract thoughts and perceptions the status of objective entities. Thus, Isabel "saw" not a visible object but a "fact," an intangible abstract entity that is invested with concrete reality (in effect, the essential process of metaphor is encapsulated here in vividly rendering concrete what is abstract). This procedure is reinforced in the way adverbs describing *how* she saw—staring dry-eyed, gazing fixedly—are transposed into adjectives describing *what* she saw: "dry, staring fact."

The phrasing also recalls the earlier important moments of recognition enacted in her midnight vigil where Isabel was depicted as "scanning the future with dry, fixed eyes" (2.191). Now, when we find in psychonarration that she "saw it all as distinctly as if it had been reflected in a large, clear glass" (2.378), what Isabel "sees" has more validity than in chapter 42 where it is through narrated monologue that her imperfect insights are conveyed, as when she thinks, mistakenly, that "she saw the whole man." Thus, the phrase "she saw (that)" could in some contexts be ambiguous, as it could indicate either objective report or subjective reflection. The status or validity of what is "seen" is affected accordingly.

It is significant that in this scene an evocation which starts as narrator's report shifts virtually imperceptibly into narrated monologue or narrated perception so that no distinction is made between the interpretation of the narrator and that of Isabel:

> She had not proceeded far before Isabel noted a sudden break in her voice, a lapse in her continuity, which was in itself a complete drama. This subtle modulation marked a momentous discovery—the perception of an entirely new attitude on the part of her listener. (2.378)

The phrase "Isabel noted" is followed by an account of Madame Merle's discovery that "the person who stood there was not the same one she had seen hitherto, but was a very different person—a person who knew her secret." This insight is ascribed to Madame Merle by Isabel; the fact that no confirmation of her interpretation is provided by the narrator indicates that her interpretations can now be regarded as consonant with the narrator's and can hence replace them. At this stage of the narrative, then, Isabel's perceptions no longer have to be qualified or supplemented by the narrator.

When Madame Merle reveals that "it was Ralph who imparted to you that extra lustre which was required to make you a brilliant match" (2.388), Isabel, described at the outset as "constantly staring and wondering" (1.45) once again, and for the last time, "stood staring" (2.388) just as other Jamesian heroines are portrayed as staring wide-eyed in wonder and disbelief as the more startling aspects of their respective worlds are revealed. This oblique indication of their state of mind supplements the more direct exposure through psychonarration and narrated monologue.

Isabel's return to the Edenic Gardencourt completes the circular movement framing the action of the novel with its concomitant growth of consciousness in the protagonist; it throws into relief the distance—spiritual, emotional, cognitive—that she has traveled since setting out on her exploration of life. Like Laura Wing in "A London Life," she now "knew almost everything. . . . The place was the same but her eyes were different: they had seen such sad, bad things in so short a time."[28]

Throughout the novel, the theme of illumination or revelation—or extension of consciousness—has been dramatized in visual metaphor or imagery associated with light. Undergoing her "process of vision," Isabel, far from radiantly "moving in a realm of light" (2.368), finds herself in a realm pervaded by the eerie chiaroscuro of surrealistic nightmare. Just as "there was a lurid light on everything" (2.303) during her midnight meditation, and subsequently, embroiled in successive bouts of recognition generated by the Countess Gemini and Madame Merle, Isabel "seemed today to live in a world illumined by lurid flashes" (2.388).

In Isabel's last scene with Caspar Goodwood, a confluence of two streams of imagery—the iterative light imagery and a cluster of sea images—vividly dramatizes their final encounter. Isabel's previous conception of Caspar as providing a possible place of refuge is in a sense put to the test here. In a passage of psychonarration modulating to narrated monologue, it is revealed that Caspar had at one stage been perceived as representing a haven rather than a threat to her liberty:

> she reflected that she herself might know the humiliation of change . . . and find rest in those very elements of his presence which struck her now as impediments to the finer respiration. It was conceivable that these impediments should some day prove a sort of blessing in disguise—a clear and quiet harbour enclosed by a brave granite breakwater. (1.323)

In their final encounter, the sea imagery again predominates, now evoking Isabel's response to Caspar's display of passion:

> The world . . . seemed . . . to take the form of a mighty sea, where she floated in fathomless waters. . . . here was help; it had come in a rushing torrent. I know not whether she believed everything he said; but she believed just then that to let him take her in his arms would be the next best thing to her dying. This belief, for a moment, was a kind of rapture, in which she felt herself sink and sink. (2.435)

A noteworthy feature of the evocation of Isabel's consciousness here is the reassertion of the presence of the intrusive narrator with the arch disclaimer of omniscience: "I know not whether she believed." Imagistic psychonarration, in which sea imagery is combined with the iterative light imagery to suggest revelatory insight, continues to be used to depict Isabel's turbulent emotional state: "the next instant she felt his arms about her and his lips on her own lips. His kiss was like white lightning, a flash that spread, and spread again." Isabel, after submitting to the "white lightning" of Caspar's kiss, resurfaces to extricate herself: "So had she heard of those wrecked and under water following a train of images before they sink. But when darkness returned she was free" (2.436).

We recall Isabel's belief early in the novel that "if a certain light should dawn she could give herself completely" (1.72). She had subsequently been deceived as to the nature of the "light" prompting her to give herself to Osmond, and when now confronted with the "white lightning" of Caspar's sexual power, this "flash of white lightning" with its Lawrentian associations of intense consuming physical passion evokes the idea of violent illumination complementing the other lurid flashes to which Isabel has been exposed. In a new flash of insight, she now sees that flight with Caspar offers no feasible alternative.

"The whole of anything is never told; you can only take what groups

together."[29] At the culmination of her "subjective adventure" or hermeneutic enterprise Isabel has attained self-knowledge and insight into her
situation. As the emphasis in this study is on the representation of consciousness, space does not permit discussion of the merits of her decision
to return to Rome. Through exploring the portrayal of her inner world,
however, insight can be gained into her state of mind and conflicting
impulses, her tendency to rationalize and the residual romanticism or
unexpunged personal pride prompting her to cling to the "ghastly form"
of her marriage.

It has been noted that in *The Portrait,* the shift from authorial to figural
narration in the course of the novel is reflected in the increasing preponderance of narrated monologue in the representation of Isabel's consciousness in the latter half of the novel. The process of conceptualization
through metaphor (in the consciousness of the reflector as opposed to
that of the narrator) which is so vividly exemplified in chapter 42, is to
be implemented with even greater complexity in James's last completed
novel, *The Golden Bowl.* Whereas *Roderick* and *The Portrait* (and later,
The Ambassadors and *Maisie*), use single focalization—with varying degrees of consistency—*The Golden Bowl,* like *The Wings of the Dove,*
exemplifies multiple focalization. This is accompanied by the virtual effacement of the intrusive first-person narrator. Once again, however, significant discrepancies exist between James's declared project as set out
in the preface and the strategies implemented in the novel itself.

5

Dual or Multiple Focalization?:
The Golden Bowl

"Baths of benevolence and the vigilance of care"

ALTHOUGH the intrusive omniscient narrator is less pervasively present in *The Golden Bowl* than in James's earlier novels, the authorial mode has not been completely eclipsed by the figural. The voice of the narrator—often, surprisingly, in its first-person manifestations—is still intermittently present. In the earlier novels the narrator sometimes emerges as a distinct personality (for instance, in *Washington Square*) and invariably guides the reader in his assessment of the characters and the action of the novel; in *The Golden Bowl,* no distinct narratorial "personality" emerges and narratorial comment is largely confined to observations on novelistic presentation punctuated by the occasional gnomic utterance.

In introducing Amerigo "at the moment we are concerned with him" (1.3), for example, the narrator refers to him as "our personage" and subsequently describes his state of mind on "the occasion of which we thus represent him" (1.10–11). Throughout the novel, phrases such as "As I have said" (1.19), and, more appropriately perhaps, "as I have hinted" (1.153), "we have seen how . . . for our young woman" (2.41), and "as we know" (2.280) recur.

Comments on novelistic procedure such as "The little crisis was of shorter duration than our account of it" (1.49) and "might I so far multiply my metaphors, I should compare her to" (2.7) are less ubiquitous than in *The Portrait,* but are often cast in similar vein. One, however, is particularly striking for its "meta-novelistic" overtones: the narrator, after an evocation of Adam Verver (past and present) in the billiard room at Fawns, returns to the present of narration and refers to his presentation of Adam "on the occasion round which we have perhaps drawn our circle too wide" (1.150–51). This comment inevitably recalls the observation made by the author (as opposed to the narrator) in the preface to *Roderick*

149

Hudson, where he speaks of novelistic technique in terms of an analogy with the geometer who must not draw his circle too wide: "Really, universally, relations stop nowhere, and the exquisite problem of the artist is eternally but to draw, by a geometry of his own, the circle within which they shall happily appear to do so" (*AN* 5).

Surprisingly, one even finds the occasional generalization in the gnomic present tense, as in: "so apt is the countenance, as with a finer consciousness than the tongue, to betray a sense of this particular lapse" (1.342), and, in an observation worthy of George Eliot, "We have each our own way of making up for our unselfishness, and Maggie. . . ." (2.101). The formulation is reminiscent of a comparable gnomic utterance in *Middlemarch:* "We are all of us born in moral stupidity, taking the world as an udder to feed our supreme selves. Dorothy. . . ."[1]

In view of the cited representative examples of narratorial intrusion, it is an oversimplification to aver, as David Seed does, that "the narrator tends, in the post-1900 novels, to be subsumed into the very texture of the prose."[2]

The Golden Bowl differs from *The Portrait* in that there is no marked shift from authorial to figural narration in the second half of the novel, as there is in the earlier work. Although there are almost twice as many instances of direct narratorial intrusion in the first half as in the second, these are in the form of isolated sentences or phrases. The progressive effacement of the narratorial voice in favor of the figural consciousness is much more consistently implemented in *The Portrait*. In *The Golden Bowl,* the modulation is more from that of multiple focalization in the first volume, where access is given to the consciousness of virtually every character, to single focalization in the second, where everything is filtered almost exclusively through Maggie's consciousness.

Although the narrator is not completely un-voiced, the function of the narratorial voice is thus more circumscribed in *The Golden Bowl*. There is no flaunting of cognitive privilege such as in *The Portrait,* where confidential asides to the reader—"We, who know more than [the protagonist] . . ."—indicate both the narrator's omniscience and the assumption of shared cognitive superiority linking narrator and reader. Whereas we are assured in *The Portrait* that "The reader has a right to a nearer and a clearer view" than that of the protagonist, and "the reader knows more about him [Ralph] than Isabel was ever to know," *The Golden Bowl* is devoid of such reassuring acknowledgment of fundamental reader's "rights." Instead, the reader is restricted to the perspective of the characters and, deprived of a narrator who, as Lubbock put it, "looks over the character's shoulder, sees what he sees and simultaneously sees more,"[3] is frequently left floundering; here one is implicitly enjoined to "do half the labour [oneself],"[4] as in response to Maggie's injunction to the prince to engage in the epistemological and moral project to "Find out for yourself!" (2.203).

In James's earlier novels, as we have seen, the narrator frequently adopts the stance of biographer or historian "objectively" presenting "facts" about his characters—particularly information concerning their past. In *The Golden Bowl,* the "facts" about a specific character's past history are largely filtered through the consciousness of other characters in the novel. In the opening section of the novel, for example, the "history" of the relationship between Amerigo and Maggie is refracted through the consciousness of the prince. Retrospective evocation of the past is supplemented by "filling in" in dialogue, as in the colloquies between Fanny and Bob Assingham in which Fanny relates Charlotte's past and her connection with both the Ververs and Amerigo. Adam seems to be a significant exception here; his past experience is presented by the narrator rather than by any of the other characters.

A feature that is more marked in *The Golden Bowl* than in earlier novels is the emergence of a hypothetical observer or suppositious spectator to whom the narrator makes frequent allusion. A new narratorial stance is thus established. As David Seed has noted, "In place of biographer, historian or lawyer, the narrator, from 1895 onwards, typically phrases his comments by reference to a hypothetical observer."[5] Seed links this development to the influence of James's experiments with the theater, pointing out that "such references also put the reader into an imaginary audience and limit the narrator's scope to explaining what might be inferred from a particular scene" (514). (It might be argued that this approach is already adumbrated in *The Portrait,* where in the first scene, for instance, the reader participates with the narrator in gradually establishing or inferring information about the characters.)

These allusions thus function as a means of establishing the contract with the reader, implying that the narrator is merely a slightly more cognitively advantaged version of the reader and that they share the same world to which the language of the novel refers. In discussing this point in a general study of the narrative stance in various fictional texts, Culler notes, with reference to the novels of Balzac, that "The hypostatized observers act as *personae* for the reader and suggest how he would have reacted to the spectacle that is being presented."[6] In *The Golden Bowl,* the intention at times seems to be to suggest how the reader *should* have (rather than would have) reacted. The following ironic comment seems to be an oblique hint as to the putative deficiencies of the "real" as opposed to the "Ideal" reader: the narrator, demonstrating how "taste in [Adam] as a touchstone" (2.345) "served him to satisfy himself both about Amerigo and the Bernardino Luini . . . [and] about Charlotte Stant and an extraordinary set of oriental tiles" (1.196–97), states blandly that "Nothing perhaps might affect us as queerer, had we time to look into it, than this application of the same measure of value to such different pieces of property as old Persian carpets, say, and new human acquisitions" (1.196).

Here, the assumption of shared cognitive superiority becomes one of complicity in superficiality as the narrator implies that neither he nor his readers have time to linger over the implications of Adam's attitude, central though this may be to developments in the novel. Perhaps the irony is directed at the *persona* of the narrator himself and his conventional contract with the reader: what is being ironized would be his traditional function of commenting fully on the action in the manner of Trollope or George Eliot. Is the contract between reader and narrator being subjected to ironic re-evaluation? Or perhaps the narrator is implying that, having been alerted to the significance of Adam's aestheticism by the narrator, the reader should explore the implications for her/himself—"do half the labour." The suppositious observer, in other words, is often guilty of superficial observation which merits chiding in the same way as does the practice of "people who read novels as an exercise in skipping."[7] On the other hand, this could be taken as a satirical or snide comment on a society made up of readers who either share Adam's materialistic approach or fail to dissociate themselves from it.

Other references to the hypothetical observer in the novel are usually less ambiguous and do not often entail the kind of narratorial nudging implicit in the above example. There are innocuous references such as "Adam Verver . . . might have been observed, had there been a spectator in the field" (1.125), "for a spectator of these passages between the pair" (2.128), counterpointed with the more ironic "the spectator of whom they would thus well have been worthy might have read meanings of his own into the intensity of their communion" (1.33) and "for a spectator sufficiently detached they might have been quite the privileged pair they were reputed" (2.354). An ironic contrast between what is seen by the characters and what is perceived by the narrator and reader is further exemplified in the last scene of the novel where Adam and Maggie observe Amerigo and Charlotte seated together:

> Their eyes moved together from piece to piece, taking in the whole nobleness. . . . The two noble persons seated in conversation and at tea, fell thus into the splendid effect and the general harmony: Mrs. Verver and the Prince fairly "placed" themselves, however unwittingly, as high expressions of the kind of human furniture required aesthetically by such a scene. The fusion of their presence with the decorative elements, their contribution to the triumph of selection, was complete and admirable; though to a lingering view, a view

more penetrating than the occasion really demanded, they also might have figured as concrete attestations of a rare power of purchase. (2.360)

The narrator's tone here is unmistakably sardonic. "A view more penetrating than the occasion really demanded" is the view the "hypostatized observer," the reader, can share with the narrator; the characters themselves cannot afford such penetrating gazes that would expose the speciousness and fragility of their painfully achieved "general harmony." Here, as Kenneth Graham has observed, "Narrative penetration . . . takes place in the very act of denying its appropriateness."[8] (Further discussion of the implications of this extract will follow later.)

* * *

The Golden Bowl represents the culmination of the process adumbrated in the other late novels of embodying outward "reality" in the consciousness of the reflector or reflectors. The comment that *The Golden Bowl* is "the novel to end all novels"[9] (an ambiguous statement, as it implies that the work could be regarded either as the apex or the deathblow of the novel as a form) is thus ironically appropriate, as *The Golden Bowl* carries to its logical conclusion the view held by Dorrit Cohn that the presentation of consciousness is the special preserve of narrative fiction.

In his preface to *The Golden Bowl*, James refers (obliquely) to his narrative strategy in his observation on "the still marked inveteracy of a certain indirect and oblique view of my presented action" (*AN* 327). This method of presentation gives the reader little interpretative guidance and can lead the unwary into an epistemological labyrinth. As Dorothy Krook avers,

> the indirect method of presentation predominates here to the almost complete exclusion of direct statement; and as one grunts and sweats one's way through this most late of Jamesian works, perpetually losing one's way amidst the qualifications and parentheses, struggling to keep a hold on the proliferating subtleties of analysis, the relentlessly sustained metaphors, the tormenting crypto-statements of the elliptical, allusive, digressive dialogues, one has reason to believe James meant what he said when, in a letter to Hugh Walpole . . . in reply to some unforgivable question Walpole had asked about *The Ambassadors,* he commented, "How can you say I do anything so foul and abject as to 'state'"?[10]

Krook's comments reflect many of the difficulties readers customarily experience in grappling with *The Golden Bowl* (albeit that the "relentlessly sustained metaphors" have a more functional purpose than Krook seems to acknowledge). Indubitably, mere "abject" "stating" or "telling" by an omniscient narrator has been virtually superseded by "showing";

"scene" and "picture" have displaced the authorial "summary." And as the consciousness that registers events is located not in the narrator but in a character, with focalization shifting from one reflector to another, knowledge is inescapably partial. (Reflector-characters are limited by subjectivity; their views are by their very nature partial—in all senses of the term.)

The ambiguity inherent in figural narration is more pervasive in *The Golden Bowl* than in *The Portrait,* as the abdication of the adjudicating narratorial voice is more marked in the later novel and is reinforced by the absence of a reliable subsidiary commentator. Whereas in *The Portrait* considerable insight is afforded by Ralph Touchett as supplementary "lucid reflector," no comparably reliable commentator or "touchstone" is provided in *The Golden Bowl.* In place of the steady "illumination of wisdom" generated by Ralph, one has erratic sparks of insight struck by Fanny Assingham, who, though often astute, is sometimes more like an *ignis fatuus* than a guiding light. (She is certainly fatuous when interpreting Charlotte's motives for her unexpected return on the eve of Maggie's marriage, determinedly seeing those motives in the best light possible— that is, in an idealistic, romantic light—and giving Charlotte credit for noble motives which she must have suspected were lamentably absent.)

In the course of the novel it emerges that as choric commentator Fanny is not only more fallible than Ralph, but has a penchant for dispensing insights of dubious viability. She is ultimately superseded by Maggie herself as "lucid reflector" invested with the most complete understanding. Even here, however, uncertainty persists as to exactly what Maggie knew.

As it is in *The Golden Bowl* more than in any previous work that James demonstrates his conception of the novel's primary focus—"for its subject, magnificently, [the novel] has the whole human consciousness"—we find his strategy of refracting virtually everything through the consciousness of the central reflectors is stylistically implemented through a greater preponderance of narrated monologue, in passages of greater length and complexity.

In his preface to *The Golden Bowl,* James creates the impression that this novel is constructed on the principle of dual rather than multiple focalization—or even of single focalization, twice:

> the whole thing remains subject to the register, ever so closely kept, of the consciousness of but two of the characters. The Prince, in the first half of the book, virtually sees and knows and makes out, virtually represents to himself everything that concerns us. . . . The function of the Princess, in the remainder, matches exactly with his; the register of her consciousness is as closely kept. (*AN* 328–29)

However, the "solicitous or even attentive" reader (*AN* 330) might notice certain apparent discrepancies: volume 1 abounds in scenes from which the ostensibly sole reflector, the prince, is excluded; indeed, access is given to the consciousness of all the central characters, thus exemplifying multiple rather than single focalization. Furthermore, although in volume 2, "The Princess," there is only one scene that takes place entirely outside Maggie's consciousness (chapter 3—a conversation between Fanny and Bob Assingham), focalization is not fixed in the rest of the volume: in the scene depicting the smashing of the golden bowl, it is Fanny rather than Maggie who functions as focalizer. Thus, as in *The Portrait,* observations in the preface create erroneous expectations: what is supposedly dual focalization is in effect multiple. Furthermore, the multiple focalization is only partly figural; instances of narratorial mediation occur throughout.[11]

In each case, then, the organization of inner views is more complex than comments in the relevant preface lead us to expect. In *The Golden Bowl,* departures from the compositional structure of dual focalization ("the register . . . of the consciousness of but two of the characters") can be clearly revealed in a schematic outline of the distribution of inner views in volume 1.

Volume 1 of *The Golden Bowl,* "The Prince," consists of three books. In Book 1, the prince is the reflector in five of the six chapters. In chapter 4, we find the first of the analytical colloquies between Fanny and Bob Assingham, and chapter 6, although dominated by the prince, also gives brief access to Charlotte's consciousness. Book 2 uses Adam Verver as the center of consciousness in its seven chapters, but in chapters 3 and 4 we find brief excursions into Maggie's inner world. Book 3 consists of eleven chapters; in the first, Charlotte functions as reflector, but not throughout, as Fanny's consciousness then becomes the focus—until the end of chapter 3. From chapters 4 to 9 the focus again reverts to the prince, although intermittent access is afforded to Charlotte's consciousness. In the last two chapters the choric commentary of the Assinghams again predominates.

The shift in focalization is signalled by the initial phrase of each of the three books of volume 1: In book 1, "The Prince had always liked his London" (1.3); book 2: "Adam Verver, at Fawns . . ." (1.125); book 3: "Charlotte, halfway up the 'monumental' staircase . . ." (1.245). Thus, in what appears to be a departure from James's declared strategy, we find that the prince is the focalizer in only eleven of the twenty-four chapters of "his" half of the novel—and a focalizer heavily mediated by the narrator at that.

The author's elaboration of his initial observation clarifies this ostensible anomaly:

the Prince, in the volume over which he nominally presides, is represented as in comprehensive cognition only of those aspects as to which Mrs. Assingham doesn't functionally . . . supersede him. This disparity in my plan is, however, but superficial; the thing abides rigidly by its law of showing Maggie Verver first through her suitor's and her husband's exhibitory vision of her, and of then showing the Prince . . . through his wife's. . . . It is the Prince who opens the door to half our light upon Maggie, just as it is she who opens it to half our light upon himself. . . . We see Charlotte also at first, and we see Adam Verver, let alone our seeing Fanny Assingham, and everyone and everything else, but as they are visible in the Prince's interest, so to speak—by which I mean of course in the interest of his being himself handed over to us. (*AN* 330)

Each volume, then, is presented primarily in the light of a specific "interest," pertaining to each of the two central reflectors. In volume 1, where the prince is the central focus, access to the consciousness of Fanny, Charlotte, and Adam serves primarily to reveal their respective relations with and attitudes toward him. Here, where both marriages are contracted[12] and the adulterous relationship between Charlotte and Amerigo is initiated, the Prince marvels at "the extraordinary substitute for perception" (1.333) blinkering Maggie; in volume 2, where Maggie becomes aware of her situation and of the complications engendered by her imperfect perception, she is accorded centrality and brought fully into play as a "compositional resource" (*AN* 329).

Thus, the switch to Maggie as a center of consciousness coincides with her awakening to consciousness; this is consistent with James's position that

the figures in any picture, the agents in any drama, are interesting only in proportion as they feel their respective situations; since the consciousness, on their part, of the complication exhibited forms for us their link of connexion with it. (*AN* 62)

In volume 2, Maggie becomes one of the "more deeply wondering . . . the really sentient" (*AN* 62). In her "exposed and entangled state" (*AN* 65) she grapples doggedly for understanding and control. This volume, then, is dominated by Maggie's "process of vision" as she is precariously launched on her "adventure of the imagination" (*AN* 351).

The incident near the end of the novel where Maggie takes the "right volume" of a three-part novel to Charlotte can be seen as emblematic of the structure of the novel. In presenting her with "the right volume" (2.308), the missing section of the three-part novel without which the work would be incomplete, Maggie can be seen as offering Charlotte her version of events: the volume devoted to the consciousness and interpretation of "The Princess." Her companion, however, merely "flung it down again" (2.317) as she is incapable of "reading it right," of understanding Maggie's point of view or attempting to see things her way; she has no interest in collating the different volumes or reconciling different interpretations. (As she explains to the prince, "I can't put my self into Maggie's skin" [1.311]).[13] Maggie explains that "I couldn't bear to think you should find yourself here without the beginning of your book. *This* is the beginning; you've got the wrong volume, and I've brought you out the right" (2.311). In a sense it is Maggie herself who is deprived of the "beginning" of the novel (volume 1), and who through the activity of the creative imagination attempts to reconstruct the section depicting "The Prince." She "put them [the two books] together and laid them down" (2.318), juxtaposing the two volumes that portray their complex relationships.

The reader is in an analogous situation. [S]he has only one volume depicting the point of view of the prince and Charlotte, as no direct access to the thoughts of the latter is afforded in volume 2—the reader has to rely on conjecture based on Maggie's perceptive observations and imaginings. (Maggie has direct access to only one half of the story—her own perception of the situation—but can make imaginative excursions into the experience of Charlotte and Amerigo; her imagination makes it possible for her to enter the experiential worlds of others.) The reader has access to both volumes and is enjoined to establish connections and points of comparison between them. In this way the reader can effect a reconciliation or balance between the divergent points of view, seeing each in the perspective established by the other and by securing reciprocal illumination extend his understanding. While one version is explicit, the other is implicit; thus while volume 2 is largely refracted through the consciousness of Maggie, the first volume—showing how things stand in the prince's book—is nevertheless persistently present in a qualifying capacity. Hence Maggie's personal perspective does not annul that of the prince and Charlotte, even though she does have the last word—or is accorded the last thought—in terms of the structure of the novel.

As in *The Portrait,* the change of perspective from authorial to figural is accompanied by—or implemented through—a shift from narrative report and psychonarration to more extended and complex passages of narrated monologue. However, a comparison with the mode of presentation in *The Portrait of a Lady* could again be illuminating here.

In *The Portrait,* extended passages of narrated monologue interspersed with psychonarration predominate in chapter 42 and recur intermittently, particularly in the latter half of the novel; in *The Golden Bowl,* the entire volume 2 is dominated by excursions into Maggie's consciousness, in which narrated monologue is the prevailing mode, with the narrator-dominated psychonarration less in evidence. Retrospective evocations where the characters "revert . . . in thought" to previous experience are used extensively, as in the first section of the novel, where the prince relives in imagination his relationship with the Ververs up to that point.

Analepses refracted through the consciousness of the characters (as opposed to those evoked by the narratorial voice) are more frequent and more extended than in *The Portrait,* where they are represented primarily by Isabel's retrospective musings by the fireside. Amerigo, Adam, and particularly Maggie are frequently involved in the "play" of "this backward speculation" (1.323). The first section of the novel is dominated by an extensive flashback recorded through Amerigo's consciousness, and he is to undertake many other such excursions. Later, for example, "It was, as I say, at Matcham . . . that it most befell him, oddly enough, to live over inwardly, for its wealth of special significance, this passage by which the event had been really a good deal determined" (1.327). We find that Adam, too, "could live over again . . . the long process of his introduction to all present interests" (1.149)—and does, for many pages. Charlotte also, when access is given to her consciousness, "was to remember . . . was inwardly to dwell on" various occurrences (1.289). It is for Maggie in particular, of course, that "Her best comprehension . . . was in her recall" (2.222). She undertakes the most complex and extended excursions into retropection, finding that "it was not till afterwards that she discriminated" (2.28) as to the significance of a specific event.

This technique of portraying an occurrence (an event, conversation, encounter, and so on) not immediately, as it occurs, but later, as it is recalled, confers further accretions of meaning in that an additional process of selection—imposed by the memory of the reflector—is at play. "Backward speculation" as a means of imposing or extracting meaning is given new impetus in this novel where analeptic excursions are so predominant.

Thus, the events of the novel are refracted far more consistently through the consciousness—and more specifically, through the *memory*—of the reflector. In the prince's perambulatory evocation of scenes with Maggie we have not merely the narrator "recording" the contents of the focalizer's mind or process of thought: the action is presented as passing through the additional filter of the focalizer's memory. What is registered is an indication of its significance to Amerigo, as the memory activates its own subjective screening mechanism.

The workings of the memory—what is retained and what is suppressed—provide an indication of the values, priorities, and criteria of the reflector. Of his prenuptial discussions with Maggie, Amerigo recalls and ruminates on what is most meaningful to him. As will emerge later, a significant contrast can be observed between his first portrayed response to Maggie in retrospective evocation of his conversations with her and the immediate rendering of his direct, sensuous response to Charlotte.

Scenes often slip imperceptibly from the past to the present, as in the first section of the novel, where description of the present occasion shifts subtly into what is "reverted to in thought." Fanny, too, is described as analyzing in "the snug laboratory of her afterthought," although her cognitive capers are usually confined to her discussions with Bob. By contrast, Maggie's struggle for understanding is enacted in her consciousness rather than in conversation; this emphasizes her essential aloneness in meeting the challenge of her "ordeal of consciousness."

Paul Armstrong has noted that "James's depiction of the present of reflection reduplicating the past of perception celebrates temporal distance as the enabling condition of self-consciousness."[14] This is certainly demonstrated in *The Portrait,* particularly in chapter 42, where it is with the wisdom of hindsight that Isabel can understand her present position. Maggie in *The Golden Bowl* also exemplifies the truth of this claim, which is supported by Kierkegaard's contention (cited earlier) that "life is lived forward and understood backward."

* * *

When examining the deployment of the three modes of representing consciousness in *The Golden Bowl,* one finds a significant difference between this and earlier works in the use of quoted monologue. Traditional quoted monologue is proportionately less well represented in *The Golden Bowl,* and of the dozen examples all occur in volume 2 and all represent the thoughts of Maggie Verver. Maggie thus has the monopoly of the quoted monologue mode. This is generally signaled by phrases such as "mutely reflected" (2.69), "she commented deep within" (2.52), "she groaned to herself" (2.80), or "she was saying to herself" as opposed to the formulation "he said"—with the implication "to himself"—which often accompanied quoted monologue in the earlier novels (for example, *Watch and Ward*).

Although Amerigo is the central focalizer in volume 1, his thoughts are never expressed in quoted monologue. Only one dubiously classifiable example of this mode occurs in this volume. At the Embassy ball, Charlotte confides to Fanny that Adam "did tell me that he wanted me just *because* I could be useful about her [Maggie] . . . . So you see I *am!*" This is followed by Fanny's unvoiced response, which, being tacitly directed at Charlotte, is not strictly quoted monologue:

> It was on Fanny Assingham's lips for the moment to reply that this was on the contrary what she saw least of all; she came in fact within an ace of saying: "You strike me as having quite failed to help his idea to work." (1.262)

Furthermore, the device of the quoted monologue takes on new permutations as it modulates toward imagined discourse, or what I have called
"imputed monologue": discourse ostensibly formulated in the consciousness of a specific character but in effect attributed to that character by
another (the reflector). (This feature of imagined/hypothetical, or "imputed" discourse, although also present in *The Wings,* becomes far more
prevalent in *The Golden Bowl.*)

An example of imputed monologue can be seen in the following extract
from a conversation between Maggie and Adam in which each tries to
conceal from the other an awareness of unforeseen complications in their
relations with Charlotte and Amerigo. In a shift from dialogue to representation of Maggie's consciousness, an "imputed monologue" is embedded in narrated monologue:

> So much was crowded into so short a space that she knew already she was
> keeping her head. She had kept it by the warning of his eyes; she shouldn't
> lose it again; she knew how and why, and if she had turned cold this was
> precisely what helped her. He had said to himself, "She'll break down and
> name Amerigo; she'll say it's to him she's sacrificing me; and it's by what
> that will give me—with so many other things too—that my suspicion will be
> clinched." (2.268)

Here the context (narrated monologue) makes it clear that it is Maggie
and not the narrator who has assigned this monologue to Adam. (Quoted
monologue is ascribed by the narrator to a specific character; here the
reflector virtually assumes the role of narrator by author-itatively attributing unvoiced reflections to another character.)

At times, however, ambiguity attends the attribution of such suppositious speeches and their designation. In some contexts, this hypothetical
discourse could be attributable to either the reflector or the narrator. On
Amerigo's return from Matcham, for example, the hypothetical/imputed
speech seems to represent what Maggie would like to imagine him hearing
her saying:

> It would have been most beautifully therefore in the name of the equilibrium,
> and in that of her joy at their feeling so exactly the same about it, that she might
> have spoken if she had permitted the truth on the subject of her behaviour to
> ring out. . . .
>   "'Why, why' have I made this evening such a point of our not all dining
> together? Well, because I've all day been so wanting you alone that I finally
> couldn't bear it, and that there didn't seem any great reason why I should try
> to. . . . After all I've scarcely to explain that I'm as much in love with you
> now as the first hour; except that there are some hours . . . that show me I'm
> even more so. They come of themselves—and ah they've been coming! After

all, after all—!" Some such words as those were what *didn't* ring out, yet it was as if even the unuttered sound had been quenched here in its own quaver. It was where utterance would have broken down by its very weight if he had let it get so far. Without that extremity, at the end of a moment, he had taken in what he needed to take—that his wife was *testifying,* that she adored and missed and desired him. (2.18–19)

Although this speech is in quotation marks, it is clearly not a transcription of Maggie's uttered words, but rather a rendering of the words she "might have spoken." But does the speech qualify as quoted monologue if it represents not words that Maggie has indeed formulated in her mind, but "some such words as these [that] *didn't* ring out"? Has the narrator formulated the words on her behalf or does the speech represent words that Maggie imagines the prince to have divined in her from her manner— that is, the "speech" is Amerigo's hypothetical interpretation of her thoughts? The discourse could be seen as the prince's quoted or imputed monologue, as "heard" in "the mind's ear," intuitively perceived and interpreted by Maggie.

The designation and attribution of these "speeches" is suffused with uncertainty. At times they could be interpreted as being speech which is "supposititious" as opposed to (or in addition to) "suppositious," embodying Maggie's wishful thinking in these projections of her imagination.

The phenomenon of "imputed monologue" could be linked to the increasing prevalence of mute or subliminal communication in the late novels. Like the conventional quoted monologues, these occur most frequently in volume 2 and are largely the preserve of Maggie herself.

The importance of "the unmistakeable language of a pair of eyes"[15] and "the element of the unuttered" (*GB* 289), of hearing or perceiving "in the mind's ear" (as opposed to the mind's eye) pervades all the late novels. Where Isabel is engaged in guessing "the unseen from the seen," Maggie is involved also in "guessing the unheard from the heard" or exploring the implications of the intuited. This process is adumbrated in *What Maisie Knew,* where the child learns to "translate" what is conveyed when it is at variance with what is overtly expressed.

"*Am* I to tell him?" the child went on. It was then that her companion addressed her in the unmistakeable language of a pair of eyes of deep dark grey. "I can't say No," they replied as distinctly as possible: "I can't say No, because I'm afraid of your mama, don't you see? Yet how can I say Yes after your papa has been so kind to me." (18)

Maggie is engaged in a comparable process of "translation," as she grapples with the discrepancies between what is expressed and what remains unexpressed—or what is expressed through verbal language on the one hand and "body language" on the other. A gnomic observation by the narrator highlights this process in *The Golden Bowl:* "It made her look for a moment as if she had actually pronounced that word of unpermitted presumption—so apt is the countenance, as with a finer consciousness than the tongue, to betray a sense of this particular lapse" (1.342). Here, paradoxically, "the countenance" is credited with giving more direct access to, or expression of, thought than "the tongue"—for those versed in "the art to find the mind's construction in the face."

A vivid example of the "translation" or transcription of what is conveyed by the countenance as opposed to the tongue can be found in Maggie's interpretation of Adam's smile in the scene where Maggie becomes aware of the "silken halter" linking him to Charlotte. Maggie responds to her father's "mute facial intimations"

> which his wife's presence didn't prevent his addressing his daughter. . . . They amounted perhaps only to a wordless, wordless smile, but the smile was the soft shake of the twisted silken rope, and Maggie's translation of it, held in her breast till she got well away, came out only, as if it might be overheard, when some door was closed behind her. "Yes, you see—I lead her now by the neck, I lead her to her doom." (2.287)

Here the facial expression ("wordless smile") is first invested with metaphoric import by being compared to a "twisted silken rope" with its connotations of genteel yet menacing compulsion, and then "translated" into imagined speech. There is no direct narratorial endorsement to guarantee that Maggie's "interpretation" is just, but the device of stylistic contagion suggests a conjunction of the perceptions of the narrator and reflector and reinforces the impression that the reader is to take Maggie's interpretation as author-itative—in all senses of the term.

As in *The Portrait*, the "absorbed mutual gaze" in *The Golden Bowl* often conveys more than can be communicated verbally. In a lull in a conversation between Fanny and Amerigo, "The unspoken had come up, and there was a crisis . . . during which they were reduced, for all interchange, to looking at each other on quite an inordinate scale." The "intensity of their communion" (1.33) does not find verbal expression. Fanny later registers a discrepancy between the prince's words and his real meaning: "Wasn't it simply what had been written in the Prince's own face *beneath* what he was saying?" (1.286). Fanny, too, is attempting to deploy "the art to find the mind's construction in the face" of her interlocutor.

Charlotte's reference to the vendor of the golden bowl as having a "way of saying nothing with his lips when he's all the while pressing you so with his face" (1.106) could also apply to Amerigo's later approach to

Maggie. The "element of the unuttered" precludes verbal expression. Maggie conjures up the words she would like to hear the prince utter to dispel her fears: "'Come away with me, somewhere, *you*'. . . . She waited for them, and there was a supreme instant when by the testimony of all the rest of him she seemed to feel them in his heart and on his lips; only they didn't sound . . ." (2.60). At the end of the novel their "mutual gaze" (rather than spoken utterance) consolidates the newly created bond between them and confirms the restoration of harmony: "each recording to the other's eyes that it was firm under their feet" (2.364).

As in the novels discussed earlier, we find in *The Golden Bowl* that **psychonarration** is eminently suited to rendering erotic experience, "an inner realm particularly in need of narrative mediation . . . with its simultaneous involvement of psyche and soma" (Cohn 49). The passionate embrace of Amerigo and Charlotte, evoked in vividly imagistic psychonarration, illustrates the use of this mode:

> They vowed it, gave it out and took it in, drawn, by their intensity, more closely together. Then of a sudden, through this tightened circle, as at the issue of a narrow strait into the sea beyond, everything broke up, broke down, gave way, melted and mingled. Their lips sought their lips, their pressure their response and their response their pressure; with a violence that had sighed itself the next moment to the longest and deepest of stillnesses they passionately sealed their pledge. (1.312)

Tumultuous passion is evoked through the image of tempestuous straits and seas where everything "broke down, gave way," suggesting a casting off of restraints and strictures. Although not as apocalyptic as D. H. Lawrence's images of seismic convulsions and electrifyingly fiery explosions, the image of seething waters does vividly convey the chaotic tumult of erotic passion.

Adam's hallucinatory vision in *The Golden Bowl* exemplifies the way in which purely imaginary perceptions are at times introduced by the same phrases that signal a character's perception of the world around him. In the context of the full evocation of his "vision," the repetition of the verb "he saw" underlines the paradox of mental vision.

> Light broke for him at last, indeed, quite as a consequence of the fear of breathing a chill upon this luxuriance of her [Maggie's] spiritual garden. As at a turn of his labyrinth he saw his issue, which opened out so wide, for the minute, that he held his breath with wonder. . . . This hallucination . . . was brief, but it lasted long enough to leave him gasping. (1.207)

Adam's revelatory hallucination—or quasi-epiphany—issues in his decision to marry Charlotte. In extracts such as this, psychonarration tends to be dissonant rather than consonant, suggesting an ironic distance between the reflector and the narrator. In volume 2, where emphasis is on the presentation of Maggie's consciousness, psychonarration tends to be consonant as the distance between reflector and narrator is lessened.

Narrated monologue, like psychonarration, gives access to the thoughts of most of the characters in volume 1 and Maggie's in volume 2. As the deployment of narrated monologue in the portrayal of the central characters will be examined in detail in the next chapter, I shall mention only some general features that come to the fore here; these include ironic effects, stylistic contagion, and the prevalence of the metaphoric mode.

First, the ironic dimension. The pervasive "dialectic between blindness and insight" which is an abiding feature in all James's novels, acquires greater complexity in the later novels, such as *The Golden Bowl,* as it is an inherent feature of the modes of presentation of consciousness.[16] The dialectic between blindness and insight is manifested in the interplay between what a character knows or acknowledges and what he or she does not know or suppresses. This discrepancy between the overt and the covert pervades the mode of narrated monologue: as seen in earlier works, narrated monologue is used to highlight these disparities between the acknowledged and the suppressed. This often takes the form of rationalization and self-deceit, as instantiated by the process whereby Adam persuades himself of the soundness of his scheme to marry Charlotte, and Amerigo later convinces himself that his renewed liaison with Charlotte is morally acceptable.

In *The Golden Bowl,* this process has added complexity in that the mode of narrated monologue foregrounds not only equivocation and the evasion of unpleasant truths but also the recasting or restructuring of those "truths" through a process of linguistic transmutation. In this often satirical portrayal of representatives of the "Wording Class," who have no vulgar obligations to earn a living in the conventional 9-to-5 routine, and are endowed with infinite leisure for the production of decorous euphemistic terminology to camouflage the reality of their activities, rationalization rises to new heights—or sinks to new depths. Charlotte and Amerigo, it will be seen, are particularly adept at this game. Concepts such as "decency," "trust," "good faith," [the] "sacred" are twisted out of shape and invested with new meanings. This procedure can be observed at play in the presentation of both speech and thought. In effect, "double-speak" takes on new permutations as it becomes "double-think."

In a sense, this process represents the obverse of the capacity of the creative imagination, as demonstrated in Maggie, to constitute or compose relevant "pictures" or images corresponding to and elucidating the situation the character is trying to understand.

The second significant feature is the high incidence of stylistic contagion, particularly in volume 2, where it is often impossible to distinguish narrated monologue from psychonarration and determine whether the voice is that of the reflector or the narrator. These features are discussed in context. The third feature, which will now be discussed in greater detail, is the prevalence of narrated monologue in the densely imagistic representation of consciousness.

The complex metaphorical mode used in *The Golden Bowl* has led to much critical controversy. Dorothea Krook objects to "the relentlessly sustained metaphors" (see above) of *The Golden Bowl* and Gabriel Pearson condemns the "increasing addiction to the alchemy of metaphor and the reticulation of reality in syntax."[17] The validity of these comments can be questioned; one should consider whether there are specific thematic and aesthetic rationales for James's use of what was disparagingly dismissed as "the alchemy of metaphor." Indeed, if alchemy entails the transubstantiation or metamorphosis of reality, this figure is ironically an apt one for evoking the power of metaphor to metamorphose or transform. The constitutive power of consciousness is reflected at least in part in its capacity to deploy metaphor creatively. The phrase "the reticulation of reality in syntax" also implies a process whose validity should not be summarily dismissed; a character's "reality," as is demonstrated in *The Golden Bowl,* is to a large extent a linguistic construct or a construct of consciousness.

The "imagistic density" of James's oeuvre[18] indubitably increased substantially in the late novels. What is more significant than the increased density, however, is the proportional distribution—the mode in which the imagery is incorporated. As mentioned earlier, the metaphoric mode in James's oeuvre shifts progressively from narratorial comment and dialogue in *Roderick Hudson,* to being deployed more frequently in psychonarration in *The Portrait* and in narrated monologue in *The Golden Bowl.* Thus, in the later novels it is more closely interfused with, or embedded in, the modes for representing consciousness, and particularly the mode of narrated monologue.

Furthermore, the connection between the effacement of the intrusive adjudicating narrator and the preponderance of imagery has not been fully appreciated by the above-mentioned critics. As previously mentioned, the imagistic mode in a sense "fills the gap" left by the absent narrator and is a valuable guide to the reader in his or her interpretation of the novel.

In James's oeuvre, different novels are characterized by specific iterative image patterns. Imagery in the later novels is drawn from a more varied field of experience. In *Roderick Hudson* and *The Portrait,* the major image clusters are drawn from nature (gardens, flowers, birds), art, and architecture, the sea (particularly suggesting exploration and discovery), the commercial world and the theater. In *The Golden Bowl,* these images recur but are supplemented by a new range of imagery drawn from, for example, the animal world (indicating a heightened awareness—usually attributed to Maggie—of predatory elements in human nature) and the circus (sometimes in conjunction with theater imagery).[19] The familiar light/dark dichotomy acquires new nuances when supplemented by that of the "white curtain" or concealing mist. A crucial iterative image that often recurs in the evocation of Maggie's consciousness is that associated with balance or equilibrium, which emphasizes her conception of the precarious nature of human relationships.

Although (as has been noted) a number of studies have been written on James's use of metaphor, none examines the role of metaphor in the representation of consciousness. Some surprisingly inept observations have been made, including the contention that

> Maggie Verver is said to "have" images of the mechanical sort but although the novel contains very many, James himself uses most of them and the remainder are distributed among the characters, with Maggie getting few or none. As a matter of fact, she uses few images of any sort.[20]

A more careful reading of the novel would reveal that Maggie uses a wider number and range of images than any other character in the novel. Short's misconception stems from his failure to differentiate between the use of images in the representation of speech and of thought. Maggie admittedly uses fewer images in dialogue than, say, Amerigo and Roderick Hudson, the eponymous hero of the first novel discussed, but in the representation of her thought, as opposed to her speech, the imagistic mode is very much in evidence. Imagery is, indeed, used extensively in the representation of the consciousness of all the central characters, and conceptualisation through metaphor comes to the fore even more tellingly in James's last completed novel.

Just as in *The Portrait,* where the reflector's process of vision is dramatized through recurrent clusters of imagery, so in *The Golden Bowl* the prime function of iterative imagery is to present the cognitive processes of the central characters. Images deployed in *The Golden Bowl,* however, are often more complex and can take on the dimensions of a metaphysical conceit, as in the extended image of the pagoda. Here the very elaboration of the conceit dramatizes the slow, tortuous nature of Maggie's struggle for comprehension. By contrast, a more concrete and immediate image depicts Adam's swift, instantaneous vision—"light broke for him" (1.207)—prompting him to marry Charlotte. The very instantaneous *coup de foudre* nature of the image suggests a state of autosuggestion and highlights the spurious nature of his ostensibly inspirational "idea." Various permutations of such light imagery—suggesting different forms of insight—are among the most prominent of the metaphors with a strong cognitive function, but the iterative images mentioned earlier all share to a greater or lesser extent in this process.

* * *

When considering the deployment of the various modes of representation of consciousness in the portrayal of the first of the central characters, Amerigo, we note that the depiction of his inner world is restricted to volume 1, "The Prince"; the reader is given only oblique access to his consciousness in volume 2. The portrayal of the prince in "his" volume is dominated by "backward speculation": the initial representation of the prince consists largely of a retrospective evocation of events and conversations leading up to this present state of his relations with Maggie. Extracts from conversations with Maggie are presented as conjured up in his memory which can be seen as acting as a supplementary "screen"— filtering out what is most significant to be recalled and dwelt on later in thought.

After the initial description of the London setting the narrator informs the reader that "at the moment we are concerned with him" (1.3) what is most significant in Amerigo's life is not what he is doing or perceiving around him but what he is recollecting. Emphasis is on his consciousness "on the occasion of which we thus represent him as catching the echoes from his own thoughts while he loitered" (1.10–11). The scenes depicted in this first section are presented not as conventional "scenes," as in punctual narration, but as retrospectively evoked through the consciousness of the reflector. It is the first of many passages in which the characters "revert to in thought" (1.191) or "live over inwardly" (1.327) significant experiences in their lives.

Although the focus is on Amerigo's consciousness, the physical setting in which his thoughts are recorded is significant. He is appropriately placed in the context of "Imperium," surrounded by "the loot of far-off victories" (1.3), exotic and valuable goods acquired by a rapacious materialistic society.[21] Although he himself, as Maggie informs him, has been acquired as a *morceau de musée* (1.12), a "representative precious object" of great historical and aesthetic value, Amerigo conceives of himself and his impending marriage in terms of the victor of a successfully concluded campaign: "Capture had crowned the pursuit—or success, as he would otherwise have put it, had rewarded virtue" (1.4). In a narrated monologue, he formulates the idea, "Well, he was *of* them now, of the rich peoples; he was on their side—if it wasn't the rather pleasanter way of putting it that they were on his" (1.18).

An indication of Amerigo's characteristic mode of thought and speech emerges clearly in these extracts and is further established in the early sections of the novel. His mode of thinking and perceiving is revealed in the way his discourse is often expressed in balanced antitheses, as in "capture/pursuit," "success/virtue," and "he was on their side . . . or they were on his." He recalls that in discussing the Verver's romanticism he had said to Maggie that "her father, though older and wiser, and a man into the bargain, was as bad—that is as good—as herself" (1.11). The use of antonymic pairs is again illustrated in his recollected observation to Maggie on the subject of the Ververs' "romantic disposition": "You see too much—that's what may sometimes make you difficulties. When you don't, at least," he had amended with a further thought, "see too little" (1.11). (Ironically, although Amerigo prides himself on his own discernment and believes that Maggie is "constitutionally inaccessible" to knowledge [1.334], he himself lacks insight into her character and initially "sees too little" of her real substance.)

The prince's conception of the difference between the European and the American sense of morality is expressed in terms of an antithesis between a "tortuous stone staircase . . . in some castle of our *quattrocento*" and the "'lightning elevator' in one of Mr. Verver's fifteen-storey buildings" (1.31). Amerigo explains to Fanny Assingham that "Your moral sense works by steam—it sends you up like a rocket. Ours is slow and steep and unlighted, with so many of the steps missing . . ." (1.31). These paired images can be seen as proleptic of developments in the novel where Amerigo demonstrates that, contrary to what his conduct might indicate to a superficial eye, he does have a developed moral sense; it is simply very different from that which he attributes to the Americans. Ironically, he underestimates Maggie's capacity to dissociate herself from the "lightning elevator" type of moral response; she is to demonstrate her capacity to eschew the lightning elevator reaction. She does not react with knee-jerk rocket-like rapidity to the disclosure of her husband's infidelity and indulge in the denunciation and rejection that would seem, in terms of the prince's image, to follow automatically. Maggie undertakes a tortuous route—one that is "slow and steep and unlighted," like Amerigo's "staircase" mode of ascent, but is ultimately successful in creating a new set of relations between them.[22]

Amerigo's penchant for euphemistic qualification or reformulation is demonstrated in his fairly innocuous substitution of "success had rewarded virtue" for "capture had crowned . . . pursuit" (1.4); this nevertheless foreshadows his later reformulation and radical subversion of traditionally sanctioned moral concepts when transforming his renewed liaison with Charlotte into a "sacred" trust. By coining new concepts to undermine the currency of those in general circulation, Amerigo can justify his own actions. Thus what would commonly be regarded as an adulterous liaison is transmuted into a bond that is "too beautiful," "too wonderful" (1.312), and redolent of the sacrosanct.

The prince's adoption of a high moral tone is matched by Charlotte who speaks of their new arrangement as compatible with "one's decency and one's honour and one's virtue. These things, henceforth . . . are my rule of life, the absolute little gods of my worship, the holy images set up on the wall" (1.318). The warped idealism in this conception of a highly egregious situation is echoed in Amerigo's correspondingly distorted idea, expressed in narrated monologue, of "that intimacy of which the sovereign law would be the vigilance of care, would be never rashly to forget and never consciously to wound" (1.325).

What Amerigo had appreciated from the outset in Charlotte as "a strange sense for tongues, with which she juggled as a conjuror at a show juggled with balls" (1.54) takes on new permutations as it is revealed to entail an ability (shared by Amerigo) to juggle with language itself—with the usual connotations and denotations of words. Through deft linguistic virtuosity words such as "decency," "trust" are drained of their accepted connotations and infused with new meanings that invariably veer toward the aesthetic register. The ease with which Amerigo can deploy linguistic maneuvring is, as we shall see, demonstrated in both speech and thought.

In reliving in imagination his prenuptial conversations with Maggie, Amerigo evinces a certain disquiet at the realization that Maggie's appreciation of him is based on his lineage, his family history—and the romantic associations of the name "Amerigo"—rather than on an appreciation or understanding of his individual self. Ironically, he had maintained that he himself, on the other hand, knew enough about the Ververs "never to be surprised," and had continued, as he recalls:

"It's you yourselves meanwhile . . . who really know nothing. There are two parts of me. . . . One is made up of the history, the doings, the marriages, the crimes, the follies, the boundless *bêtises* of other people . . . you've both of you wonderfully looked them in the face. But there's another part, very much smaller doubtless, which represents my single self, the unknown, unimportant—unimportant save to *you*—personal quality. About this you've found out nothing." (1.9)

Neither Maggie nor Amerigo can, of course, appreciate the full ironic import of her rejoinder (which, with its echo of Othello, is reminiscent of the ending of *Roderick Hudson*): "Luckily, my dear . . . for what would then become of the promised occupation of my future?"[23] And what Amerigo does not perceive is that he also has a blinkered view of Maggie, seeing her merely as a "cluster of signs," a representative of a particular highly desirable class and way of life that he wishes to espouse.

Indeed, through access to Amerigo's consciousness the reader is in a position to perceive that each of the prospective spouses has a limited understanding of the other outside of categories such as those of nationality, class, rank, and status. Each views the other less as an individual than as a "collection of attributes and powers" (*PL* 1.143) guaranteeing a desirable "envelope of circumstances" (*PL* 2.287) and is accorded appreciation on the same basis.

In his view of himself, Amerigo makes a distinction between vices of a "personal" and a "racial" origin. Where Maggie sees the glamour of his ancestral history, Amerigo is conscious of the vices it displays. Although in conversation with Fanny he avers that he has no "moral sense" (1.31) as Americans understand the term, his unvoiced reflections reveal that he is conscious of "dangers from within" (1.16) and is determined to withstand the assaults of "arrogance and greed" (1.16) to which his ancestors had so flamboyantly succumbed. An extended passage of psychonarration and narrated monologue evokes his meditations on this topic during his prenuptial perambulation in the first chapter. We find that

> Personally, he considered, he hadn't the vices in question—and that was so much to the good. His race, on the other hand, had had them handsomely enough, and he was somehow full of his race. Its presence in him was like the consciousness of some inexpungable scent in which his clothes, his whole person . . . might have been steeped as in some chemical bath. (1.16)

The "chemical bath" of Amerigo's ancestral tradition, then, threatens to counteract the effect of the "aromatic bath" in which he feels he is steeped by the Ververs. The image serves to highlight the question as to whether Amerigo will openly follow the family tradition, flout it entirely, or fall prey to his inherited traditions in a more insidious way—like the ancestral (and therefore of dubious celibacy) Pope, indulging in a "sanctified" quest for personal gain and self-gratification. When Fanny Assingham calls Amerigo "Machiavelli" (1.31), "the Prince" is obliquely placed in the context of the famous book bearing that title, a tome in which are expounded the Machiavellian "virtues" of opportunism, ruthlessness, and the cynical belief that the ends justify the means.

Access to Amerigo's consciousness, afforded through psychonarration and narrated monologue, allows the reader to perceive the quintessential male chauvinism in his attitude to Maggie, marriage, and women in general. Surrounded, in Bond Street, by opulent material objects in shop windows and "possibilities in faces" of pretty women on the street, he accords both a comparably appreciative scrutiny. Indications of previously indulged philandering propensities are hinted at in the observation that "the last idea that would *just now* have occurred to him in any connection was the idea of pursuit" (1.4; my emphasis). Amerigo has the conventional stereotypical view of the Italian *galantuomo*, seeing women primarily, in contemporary parlance, as "sex objects." (This is corroborated by Fanny's remark that Amerigo doesn't "really care for Charlotte," implying that the bond between them is primarily erotic.) This attitude is revealed through presentation of both his thought and his speech.

Virtually at the outset, access to Amerigo's thoughts in psychonarration confirms the more serious implications of arrogant condescension in his attitude to women:

> The Prince's notion of a recompense to women . . . was more or less to make love to them. . . . He liked in these days to mark them off, the women to whom he hadn't made love: it represented . . . a different stage of existence from the time at which he liked to mark off the women to whom he had. (1.21–22)

Even allowing for the more attenuated connotations of the term "make love" as used by James, it is clear that at this stage Amerigo has a very restricted range of possible responses to women. Balanced antitheses again characterize his mode of thought when he considers that "he had, after all, gained more from women than he had ever lost by them" (1.350). The same considerations of profit (to himself) animate his view of Charlotte in particular; he even relegates her to that generalized class—"the woman"—whose behavior "produced for the man that extraordinary mixture of pity and profit in which his relation with her, when he was not a mere brute, mainly consisted" (1.50). (While priding himself on his percipience and expressing a patronizing appreciation of her ability to "arrange appearances" [1.50], he ironically fails to perceive how Charlotte also "arranges" or manipulates him; firstly, during their expedition undertaken ostensibly to choose a gift for Maggie, and later when he is adroitly maneuvred into re-establishing their former liaison.) Like Densher in *The Wings*, Amerigo is prepared to remain passively aloof while "the woman" arranges appearances from which he is to benefit. This attitude is reminiscent too of Osmond, who welcomed a "prize" dropped into his lap by Madame Merle without his stir. Verbal echoes highlight the similarity between Osmond and Amerigo here in the prince's exculpatory rationalization which is dramatized through narrated monologue: "He hadn't struggled nor snatched; he was taking but what had been given him; the pearl dropped itself, with its exquisite quality and rarity, straight into his hand" (1.358).

We find, then, that the ironic dimension of psychonarration and narrated monologue in the portrayal of Amerigo's consciousness is pervasive, and frequently takes the form of rationalization, euphemism, or equivocation.

And so there is often a discrepancy between what is grasped by the reflector in his backward speculations and general meditations and what is perceived by the reader. This pervasive ironic dimension is often intensified by an element of ironic mimicry which foregrounds the disparity between the acknowledged and the suppressed—or the dialectic of blindness and insight. Stylistic contagion is exploited, as psychonarration sometimes blends imperceptibly into narrated monologue or incorporates vocabulary characteristic of the reflector rather than the narrator, creating a parodic effect. This is frequently evident in the presentation of Amerigo's thoughts on the eve of his marriage, even in a statement as ostensibly innocuous as the following: "If there was one thing in the world the young man, at this juncture clearly intended it was to be much more decent as a son-in-law than lots of fellows he could think of had shown themselves in that character" (1.5). The narrator's comment shifts into the idiom of the prince in the course of this sentence, with the parodic effect highlighting the oddity of his reasoning. The most important person to him in his newly acquired set of contractual relations is not his wife but his father-in-law. (The term "decency," as has been indicated, is to be problematic.) Indeed, at this stage in his relations with Maggie he exhibits careful and politic consideration for her rather than a spontaneously appreciative response to her personal qualities.

An illustration of how the subtle deployment of psychonarration and narrated monologue reveals these ironic disparities can be found in the following extract from Amerigo's thoughts at Matcham; the extract highlights the discrepancy between what he imagines is a course of action freely embarked upon and the reality of his manipulation by Charlotte.

He had taken it from her [Charlotte], as we have seen moreover, that Fanny Assingham didn't now matter—the "now" he had even himself supplied, as no more than fair to his sense of various earlier stages. . . . he had for the first time . . . a little disappointedly, got the impression of a certain failure, on the dear woman's part, of something he was aware of having always rather freely taken for granted in her. Of what exactly the failure consisted he would still perhaps have felt it a little harsh to try to say; and if she had in fact, as by Charlotte's observation, "broken down," the details of the collapse would be comparatively unimportant. They came to the same thing, all such collapses— the failure of courage, the failure of friendship, or the failure just simply of tact; for didn't any one of them by itself amount really to the failure of wit?— which was the last thing he had expected of her and which would be but another name for the triumph of stupidity. It had been Charlotte's remark that they were at last "beyond her"; whereas he had ever enjoyed believing that a certain easy imagination in her would keep up with him to the end. He shrank from affixing a label to Mrs. Assingham's want of faith. (1.313–14)

In this passage, the shift from psychonarration to narrated monologue highlights the dubious nature of the prince's contention that the reasons for Fanny's "collapse"—what the uninitiated or less linguistically adept might call her failure to condone an adulterous relationship—are unimportant. The prince evades examining Fanny's stance, as it is much more convenient to take refuge in a suspect generalization, the claim that "all such collapses" can be attributed to "the failure of courage . . . friendship . . . tact . . . or wit." The repetition of "failure" also underscores both the prince's belief in the "success" of his own interpretation of the situation and the contrast with "triumph" (the prince's thinking is again characterized by antonymic pairs). The use of the interrogative form—"didn't any of them by itself amount really to the failure of wit?" (as usual, an aesthetic rather than ethical category)—suggests the process by which the prince is trying to convince himself of the validity of his own interpretation. The oxymoronic "triumph of stupidity" is a label conveniently conjured up to facilitate the contemptuous dismissal of Fanny's objections to their liaison.

Although "he shrank from affixing a label to Mrs Assingham's want of faith," both he and Charlotte do in effect indulge in a strategy of affixing anodyne or reassuring labels to their activities as part of their policy of "treating" the Ververs. Language itself is used to swaddle Adam and Maggie in protective tenderness while their spouses indulge in a sanctified affair behind their coddled backs.

Ironically, the reader is in a position to recall a conversation with Charlotte in which these very terms "courage" and "wit" were used to influence Amerigo into accepting Charlotte's view of the situation. The reader is aware, as Amerigo is not, of the insidious influence of Charlotte's mode of reasoning. She demonstrates awesome semantic virtuosity in the way in which sanitized "labels" or euphemistic linguistic tags are affixed to legitimize or justify. During the visit which culminated in their passionate embrace, Charlotte had subtly maneuvred the prince into "seeing their way together": "It's not that you haven't my courage," Charlotte said, "but that you haven't, I rather think, my imagination. Unless indeed it should turn out after all . . . that you haven't even my intelligence" (1.301). Charlotte shrewdly uses the words "courage . . . imagination . . . intelligence" as a challenge to Amerigo to demonstrate, by seeing things her way, that he is indeed endowed with these qualities and can match her—in all senses of the term. As always, it is the aesthetic register which predominates in her mode of reasoning.

This passage provides a significant illustration of how glibly persuasive words used by Charlotte in conversation seep into Amerigo's consciousness and recur in narrated monologue as he convinces himself that he is adopting the "right view of their opportunity for happiness" (1.246). The distortion of moral concepts in self-justificatory rhetoric can be seen in the following narrated monologue, where Amerigo muses on the "rightness" of his relation with Charlotte:

> They had these identities of impulse—they had had them repeatedly before; and if such unarranged but unerring encounters gave the measure of the degree in which people were, in the common phrase, meant for each other, no union in the world had ever been more sweetened with rightness. (1.356)

The unfounded assumptions and sweeping claims expressed here emphasize the ironic use of the equivocal term "rightness," which in this context has decidedly blurred epistemological and moral contours. Their union is clearly not invested with conventional moral rightness; Amerigo, judging in accordance with "the touchstone of taste," a purely aesthetic criterion, assumes that if the perfection of form is adhered to, if they behave "beautifully" and the Ververs are protected from exposure to knowledge of the true situation, everything is "right."

The imagistic mode is used with telling effect in the depiction of Amerigo's consciousness. And among the many functions of imagery in the portrayal of Amerigo, one of the most significant is the cognitive. His attempts to understand the Ververs and the intricacies of his own position in relation to them are often couched in vivid imagery. In securing the wealthy Maggie Verver, Amerigo (whose name in itself has metaphorical overtones, suggesting the discovery, exploration, and perhaps appropriation of a New World) had indeed established himself, as Fanny put it, "*in* [the] port . . . of the Golden Isles" (1.27). Fanny, to whose good offices he is indebted for the successful arrangement of his marriage, is to satisfy his abiding need for a lodestar or "educative" consort (until Charlotte ousts her in this capacity and induces him to see things her way).

The sea imagery dramatizes this theme in both dialogue and representation of consciousness. In a conversation with Fanny, Amerigo explains, "I'm starting on a great voyage—across the unknown sea; my ship's all rigged and appointed . . . . But what seems the matter with me is that I can't sail alone. . . . I must keep your sail in sight for orientation" (1.26).

This image recalls the one used in both *Roderick* and *The Portrait* to suggest being launched on the exploratory voyage of life; here, it takes on more complex resonances in psychonarration when access is given to Amerigo's consciousness. An image from his childhood reading is recalled and the sea imagery becomes interfused with that of the obfuscatory "white curtain":

> He remembered to have read as a boy a wonderful tale by Allan Poe . . . the story of the shipwrecked Gordon Pym, who, drifting in a small boat further

toward the North Pole—or was it the South?—than any one had ever done, found at a given moment before him a thickness of white air that was like a dazzling curtain of light, concealing as darkness conceals, yet of the colour of milk or of snow. There were moments when he felt his own boat move upon some such mystery. The state of mind of his new friends, including Mrs. Assingham herself, had resemblances to a great white curtain. (1.22)

The parenthetical question "or was it the South?" indicates that the mode here shifts into narrated monologue, evoking the exploratory movement of Amerigo's mind as he grapples with the mystery of the composition of the American mind. He clearly finds it difficult to orientate himself when confronted with the "white curtain" of what he takes to be the New World mentality. To him, this "dazzling curtain of light" is an emanation of the hazy romantic imagination of the Americans in which their intentions, expectations, and very nature are shrouded. The prince wonders "what *was,* morally speaking, behind their veil" (1.24), but when he questions Fanny he finds that even she, ostensibly his guiding light, is enveloped, albeit to a lesser degree, in the obfuscating element; in his perception, her laugh "came out, for his fancy, from behind the white curtain" (1.26).

The image of the "white curtain" of nebulous American romanticism as perceived by Amerigo is associated with the related image of "exquisite colouring drops" depicting Maggie's "good faith." The sea imagery takes on different permutations here as "the waters in which he now floated" lose their connotations of danger and mystery as their reference is narrowed down to the comfortable circumference of an "aromatic bath" in which the prince feels he is luxuriating. In a passage of narrated monologue Amerigo conceives of the buoyant security of wealth as

the element that bore him up and into which Maggie scattered, on occasion, her exquisite colouring drops. They were of the colour—of what on earth? of what but the extraordinary American good faith? They were of the colour of her innocence, and yet at the same time of her imagination, with which their relation, his and these people's, was all suffused. (1.10)

In Amerigo's conception, these "exquisite colouring drops" are dispensed from "a gold-topped phial," again emphasizing that the Ververs' romanticism is an emanation of their opulent liquidity.

After Maggie's exposure to the golden bowl and its implications in volume 2, and her admonition to the prince to "Find out for yourself!" (2.203) what revelations had been afforded by this purchase, he is again depicted as grappling with an obfuscating medium: "He was walking ostensibly beside her [Maggie] but in fact given over, without a break, to the grey medium in which he helplessly groped" (2.281). The image here is refracted through Maggie's consciousness as it represents her perception of his condition. The "grey medium," contrasting with the "dazzling curtain," suggests the condition of bleak ignorance in which Amerigo is later steeped.

The complex of sea and ship imagery dramatizes issues involving exploration, discovery, or embarking on new experiences. It occurs in presentation of both thought and speech. At times it takes on more comical overtones. It is suffused with humor when it occurs in fairly lighthearted banter as in Fanny's awareness that "it had taken his father-in-law's great fortune . . . to surround him with an element in which . . . he could pecuniarily float" (1.268), and when Amerigo explains to Fanny that he and Charlotte are "in the same boat" (1.267), Mr. Verver's boat, which "is a good deal tied up at the dock, or anchored, if you like, out in the stream. I have to jump out from time to time to stretch my legs" (1.270). Charlotte, too, he explains, "has to take a header and splash about in the water" at times. Through the use of sea imagery in its more comical mode, the reader, with Fanny, is forewarned that "one of the harmless little plunges, off the deck, inevitable for each of us" (1.270) is bound to have more serious repercussions.

Although the images of the white curtain, silver mist, and gray medium often suggest impediments or challenges to insight—or degrees of purblindness?—light imagery in its more conventional forms often evokes moments of heightened insight. This complex of imagery occurs most frequently in depicting Maggie's moments of revelatory insight, but there are instances where Amerigo's sudden access of insight is also rendered in terms of light imagery. Immediately before Charlotte arrives in Portland Place on the memorable occasion that will terminate in their passionate embrace, Amerigo experiences what he takes to be a moment of visionary clarity that makes him more susceptible to Charlotte's charms. In an extended passage of introspection rendered through psychonarration and narrated monologue, Amerigo comes to the conclusion that he is merely a peripheral presence in the Verver household, and that Adam and Maggie share a "community of interest" from which he is excluded. He experiences a moment of revelatory lucidity in which he sees himself as a nonentity in their eyes and realizes that he is appreciated only as a contributor to the Ververs' lustrously opulent "shell." A series of observations rendered in psychonarration and narrated monologue culminate in the following insight:

> the series together resembled perhaps more than anything else those fine waves of clearness through which, for a watcher of the east, dawn at last trembles into rosy day. The illumination indeed was all for the mind, the prospect revealed by it a mere immensity of the world of thought. (1.294)

He is subsequently confronted with the appearance of Charlotte, whose advent at this moment seemed surely providential: "Charlotte Stant, at such an hour . . . Charlotte Stant turning up for him at the very climax of his special inner vision, was an apparition charged with a congruity at which he stared almost as if it had been a violence" (1.295).

What Amerigo "sees" so vividly is the possibility of a resumption of their former relationship. "His vision of alternatives . . . [to his present situation] opened out" (1.297), and in a related visual image he "sees" a pictorial presentation of palpable renewal: "The sense of the past revived for him . . . it made that other time somehow meet the future close, interlocking with it, before his watching eyes, as in a long embrace of arms and lips" (1.297–98). This visual image presented in psychonarration graphically anticipates the physical embrace with which their encounter is concluded.

Another significant cluster of images that frequently recurs in Amerigo's narrated monologues is the one involving references to monetary transactions. In *The Golden Bowl,* as in the earlier novels, commercial metaphors are often used to indicate the way in which characters regard or assess each other; these highlight the inversion of values obtaining in a society where human "worth" is expressed in materialistic terms.

The prince feels that his intrinsic personal worth (as opposed to his worth as a "personage") is not adequately acknowledged by the Ververs. He recreates in imagination an exchange with Maggie in which he claimed that his worth would be recognized only "if it were a question of parting with me. . . . My value would in that case be estimated." Maggie's rather glib reply, "Yes, if you mean that I'd pay rather than lose you" (1.13) ironically foreshadows the process of "payment" she has to endure—and the role of scapegoat she feels obliged to assume.

The monetary image is elaborated during Amerigo's meditative musings on the way the Ververs take his worth for granted as though he were a representative example of valuable articles in general circulation. In the following extract, the abstract formulation of the first sentence modulates into imagistic expression in narrated monologue:

What was singular was that it seemed not so much an expectation of anything in particular as a large bland blank assumption of merits almost beyond notation, of essential quality and value. It was as if he had been some old embossed coin, of a purity of gold no longer used, stamped with glorious arms, medieval, wonderful, of which the "worth" in mere modern change, sovereigns and half-crowns, would be great enough, but as to which, since there were finer ways of using it, such taking to pieces was superfluous. That was the image for the security in which it was open to him to rest; he was to constitute a possession, yet was to escape being reduced to his component parts. What would this mean but that practically he was never to be tried or tested? (1.23)

The image of the gold coin recalls the one used in *The Portrait* to describe Osmond, but here the image is used by the reflector, in narrated monologue, rather than by the narrator in the authorial mode. In a sense, of course, Amerigo is indeed to be tried or tested in the course of the novel.

Various analogies with commercial transactions also later crystallize Amerigo's perception of his position in the Verver household. Amerigo feels that his father-in-law, in keeping with his position as a good banker, values him primarily as a good investment, a speculation that has paid off and yielded handsome dividends (perhaps even the production of the Principino, a tangible extension of the Verver empire, could be seen as a form of capital growth).

Ironically, Amerigo himself is implicated in this mode of viewing others in materialistic and instrumentalizing terms. This is exemplified most vividly in the preponderance of monetary images, combined with comparisons drawn from the arts and the natural world, which pervade his appraisal of Charlotte at her first reappearance. As it is through Amerigo's perception rather than the narrator's description that Charlotte is depicted, his "exhibitory vision" of Charlotte sheds as much light on himself as on the woman he is observing. A combination of aesthetic, commercial, and mechanistic images animates what amounts to a sensuously indulgent inventory of her charms rendered in narrated perception:[24]

> But it was, strangely, as a cluster of possessions of his own that these things in Charlotte Stant now affected him; items in a full list, items recognised, each of them, as if, for the long interval, they had been "stored," wrapped up, numbered, put away in a cabinet . . . he took the relics out one by one. . . . He saw again that her thick hair was, vulgarly speaking, brown, but that there was a shade of tawny autumn leaf in it for "appreciation" . . . something that gave her at moments the sylvan head of a huntress. He saw the sleeves of her jacket drawn to her wrists, but he again made out the free arms within them to be of the completely rounded, the polished slimness that Florentine sculptors in the great time had loved. . . . He knew her narrow hands, he knew her long fingers and the shape and colour of her finger-nails, he knew her special beauty of movement and line when she turned her back, and the perfect working of all her main attachments, that of some wonderful finished instrument, something intently made for exhibition, for a prize. He knew above all the extraordinary fineness of her flexible waist, the stem of an expanded flower, which gave her a likeness also to some long loose silk purse, well filled with gold pieces, but having been passed empty through a finger-ring that held it together. It was as if, before she turned to him, he had weighed the whole thing in his open palm and even heard a little the chink of the metal. (1.46–47)

A striking feature of this passage is the controlled cumulative rhythm reinforced by the repetition of "he saw . . . he knew." The subdued erotic overtones in this appraisal by an obviously informed appraiser confirm the impression that the more specifically Elizabethan connotations of the verb "knew" are intended to be exploited. (Fanny later assures Bob that there wasn't time for Charlotte to have become the prince's mistress, but one feels that Bob's rather ribald rejoinder, "Does it take so much time?" [1.72] is probably closer to the mark. The prince is clearly intimately acquainted with Charlotte's physical attributes.)

The description of Charlotte as seen by Amerigo is also revealing in that the possibility of predatory proclivities underlying a charming surface are hinted at by the telling comparison, "the sylvan head of a huntress." Ironically, the prince, although formulating this comparison, does not perceive the subliminally registered truth that Charlotte is capable of ensnaring and manipulating him.

Thus, in a curious compound of the proprietorial, aesthetic, erotic, and utilitarian, Amerigo sees Charlotte successively in terms of a Florentine statue, an instrument (and here a feminist objection to the "sex object" implications in his appreciation of "the perfect working of all her main attachments" would be valid), a flower, and a silk purse. Personal profit, and more specifically sensual gratification, is often depicted in terms of clinking lucre; this image recurs during the sojourn at Matcham, for instance, when Amerigo again experiences "the chink of gold in his ear" (1.345) at the prospect of renewing an intimate relationship with Charlotte and sees the possibilities of his position in terms of "a bottomless bag of solid shining British sovereigns" (1.333). Before that, he had conceived of the bond linking them as the forging of a "mystic golden bridge" (2.325) between them.

As Amerigo and Maggie are the two most important reflectors in the novel, with Adam assuming the position of reflector in the seven chapters of book 2 of volume 1, comparatively little sustained access is given to the consciousness of Charlotte. Nevertheless, the reader is given significant if tantalizingly infrequent glimpses into her inner world.

The first important excursion into Charlotte's consciousness occurs when, after an ellipsis of a few years following her marriage to Adam, Charlotte is portrayed in all her splendor at the Embassy ball. As noted earlier, the shift in focalization is signalled by the opening sentence of book 3, chapter 1: "Charlotte, halfway up the 'monumental' staircase" (1.245). The narrator comments that "At the particular instant of our being again concerned with her," Charlotte is depicted "with a consciousness materially, with a confidence quite splendidly, enriched" (1.245). Through narrated perception we have access to her awareness that "She was herself in truth crowned, and it all hung together, melted together, in light and colour and sound" (1.246).

At this stage, Charlotte has just attained the recognition that, as she explains to Fanny, Adam's feeling for Maggie is "the greatest affection of which he is capable," and that being "placed" or "fixed as fast as a pin stuck, up to its head, in a cushion" in this anomalous situation where, as his wife, she is less important and necessary to his happiness than his daughter (1.261–62), she should be prepared to react accordingly.

The light imagery, which, as seen earlier, dramatizes Amerigo's comparable recognition, recurs here in Charlotte's narrated monologue as she recognizes "in the direction in which the light had dawned" (1.255) that her solution lay in "the direction of her greater freedom." Through this access to her consciousness we find that she is aware of "hovering and warning inward voices" but manages to dispel them in favor of adopting "the right view of her opportunity for happiness" (1.246). The term "right" is again fraught with ambiguity, as in this context it can be equated not with "correct" or morally sound but "expedient" or "opportunistic."

In book 3 chapter 4, after an interlude of conversation between Fanny and Amerigo in chapter 2, and an intense discussion between Fanny and Bob in chapter 3, the focus is again on Charlotte's consciousness for the first half of the chapter (1.288–91) before reverting to Amerigo. Psycho-narration in this section seems at times to be portraying the combined consciousness of Charlotte and Amerigo, thus emphasizing the shared "community of vision" they have attained (*AN* 299). The terms applied to Kate and Densher in the preface to *The Wings* seem applicable at times to Charlotte and Amerigo: "the associated consciousness of my two prime young persons . . . [becomes] a practical *fusion* of consciousness" (*AN* 299): "It appeared thus that they might enjoy together extraordinary freedom, the two friends, from the moment they should understand their position aright" (1.288). The term "aright" here is again ambiguous; no distinction is made by "the two friends" between what is "right" from the ethical point of view and what is right in terms of the "touchstone of taste."

The ironic statement that in Amerigo's view "the wonderful thing was that her sense of propriety had been, from the first, especially alive about it [their case]" further highlights Charlotte's failure to recognize that her sense of propriety and sense of morality are at variance. "Propriety" as Charlotte's criterion complements "taste" as Amerigo's; in this situation the reader can see, as Amerigo and Charlotte apparently choose not to, that propriety and taste can be radically out of kilter with morality.

According to Charlotte, the apportionment of blame is a self-evident affair:

"There has been plenty of 'doing', and there will doubtless be plenty still; but it's all theirs, every inch of it; it's all a matter of what they've done *to* us."

And she showed how the question had therefore been only of their taking everything as everything came, and all as quietly as might be. Nothing stranger surely had ever happened to a conscientious, a well-meaning, a perfectly passive pair: no more extraordinary decree had ever been launched against such victims than this of forcing them against their will into a relation of mutual close contact that they had done everything to avoid. (1.289)

The modulation from direct to indirect and then free indirect speech foregrounds the irony in Charlotte's asseverations. Her view is, of course, riddled with half-truths and suppression of established facts. Charlotte uses linguistic camouflage to disguise the fact that she was not coerced into marriage with Adam and its attendant proximity to the prince. Furthermore, the contention that they are "perfectly passive" is ironic in that, although Amerigo does display a culpable passivity or readiness to be manipulated, Charlotte herself has actively schemed and worked for the resumption of their liaison.

Access to Charlotte's consciousness after this reported speech reveals that she is aware of this distortion of facts in her account of their "fate." She recognizes, too, that the prince, although prepared to accept her version of events, is no mere dupe. Once again the full import of the exchange emerges in her "backward speculation" when she "reverts to it in thought," as the following passage of psychonarration and narrated monologue depicting her thoughts on this occasion reveals:

She was to remember not a little meanwhile the particular prolonged silent look with which the Prince had met her allusion to these primary efforts at escape. She was inwardly to dwell on the element of the unuttered that her tone had caused to play up into his irresistible eyes; and this because she considered with pride and joy that she had on the spot disposed of the doubt, the question, the challenge . . . that such a look could convey. He had been sufficiently off his guard to show some little wonder as to their having plotted so very hard against their destiny, and she knew well enough of course what in this connexion was at the bottom of his thought, and what would have sounded out more or less if he hadn't happily saved himself from words. (1.289–91)

Suppression of the truth by "saving oneself from words" or substituting others that conform more closely to one's desires is, as we have seen, a strategy frequently indulged in by Amerigo and Charlotte. In a continuation of this narrated monologue, Charlotte then produces an axiom concerning "all men" that is reminiscent of Amerigo's generalizations about women:

All men were brutes enough to catch when they might at such chances for dissent—for all the good it really did them; but the Prince's distinction was in being one of the few who could check himself before acting on the impulse. This, obviously, was what counted in a man as delicacy. If her friend had blurted or bungled he would have said, in his simplicity, "Did we do 'everything to avoid' it when we faced your remarkable marriage?" (1.290)

In Charlotte's book, honesty is equated with "blurting," "bungling," and "simplicity"; suppression of the truth is seen as proof of "delicacy."

An indication of the success with which Charlotte imposes her interpretation is given in a passage of narrated monologue featuring Amerigo's thoughts at the end of this chapter:

What had happened in short was that Charlotte and he had, by a single turn of the wrist of fate—"led up" to indeed, no doubt, by steps and stages that conscious computation had missed—been placed face to face in a freedom that extraordinarily partook of ideal perfection, since the magic web had spun itself without their toil, almost without their touch. (1.298)

The "steps and stages"—and stratagems—whereby Charlotte, undetected by the prince, has "led [him] up to" espousing her view of their "opportunity," are more easily detected by the reader. The pervasive ironic mode makes it unnecessary for an intrusive narrator to point out that the implicit disclaimer of personal responsibility is not endorsed by the narrator.

After this chapter, access to Charlotte's consciousness is largely oblique. Her views are expressed in dialogues with Amerigo and Fanny, in which her "independent, not to say original, interpretation of signs" (1.288) is often manifested. In volume 2, it is only through Maggie's projection of her thoughts that the reader has access to her state of mind.

The role of the *ficelles*, Fanny and Bob Assingham, is largely that of choric commentator, although Fanny, as primary *ficelle* and confidante to Maggie, and sponsor and matchmaker for both Amerigo and Charlotte, is intimately involved in the complex not-so-eternal quadrangle in which the four central characters are embroiled.[25] In contrast to Maggie's more reflective mode, Fanny's views are expressed most frequently in dialogue—as in the tortuous analytical sessions with Bob. Fanny's "unravelling, interpretative agonizings" prompt Kenneth Graham's observation that she "functions as a mode of knowing and coping as much as she does as a character."[26] Although direct access to her consciousness is limited, there are two important scenes in which Fanny functions, if only briefly, as focalizer. The first of these scenes is at the Embassy ball and the second is that depicting the smashing of the golden bowl. It seems to have escaped the attention of commentators on the novel that this scene represents a second significant departure (with the chapter featuring the

last collusive colloquy between Fanny and Bob) from the declared strategy of using Maggie as sole reflector in volume 2.

At the Embassy ball access is given to Fanny's consciousness to reveal
her unspoken response to what Charlotte and Amerigo are conveying
concerning their new conception of their relationship. One important feature of Fanny's experience, conveyed in narrated monologue, is shared
to a greater or lesser extent by each of the central characters: "She was
embarrassed by the difference between what she took in and what she
could say, what she felt and what she could show" (1.267).

Fanny opts for willful blindness, refusing to discuss or recognize the
right—or even the existence—of Amerigo and Charlotte's stated intention to make the most of "a certain decent freedom" afforded by Maggie
and Adam's neglect of their respective spouses.

In an extended passage of psychonarration the monetary image used
earlier by Amerigo to convey his concept of his "worth" recurs to express
Fanny's conception of Amerigo as "inordinately valued, quoted, as they
said, in the stock-market, so high" (1.268). Fanny had considered that his
debt to Adam for providing him with an "element in which he could
pecuniarily float" would ensure that he had "on his conscience some sort
of return for services rendered" and would accordingly "behave beautifully" (1.268). Fanny does not allow for the manifest discrepancy between
their respective conceptions of "beautiful" behavior: to Amerigo, adher-
ence to the aesthetic criterion ensures that observing the right (that is,
"beautiful") form is all that is required. One could say that, in the terminology of *The Portrait,* what he would regard as the "magnificent form"
of the marriages would be regarded by Fanny as a "ghastly form."

Fanny's mode of analysis is vividly depicted in the following image
used in psychonarration:

> She found his eloquence precious; there wasn't a drop of it that she didn't in
> a manner catch, as it came, for immediate bottling, for future preservation.
> The crystal flask of her innermost attention really received it on the spot, and
> she had even already the vision of how, in the snug laboratory of her after-
> thought, she should be able chemically to analyse it. (1.271)

Whereas analyzing in "the snug [or in Maggie's case, anguished] laboratory of afterthought" is an activity all the central characters are engaged
in, Fanny's analysis usually takes the form of thinking aloud in her dialogues with Bob. She, too, responds to the "element of the unuttered"
(1.289) and attempts to decipher it. In conversation with Amerigo, for
instance,

> with the meeting of their eyes something as yet unnameable came out for her
> in his look, when something strange and subtle and at variance with his words,

something that *gave them away,* glimmered deep down, as an appeal, almost an incredible one, to her finer comprehension. What, inconceivably, was it like? Wasn't it, however gross such a rendering of anything so occult, fairly like a quintessential wink, a hint of the possibility of their *really* treating their subject—of course on some better occasion. (1.271)

In this extract the shift from psychonarration to narrated monologue is marked by the urgent questions through which Fanny attempts to grasp the meaning of what the prince, through subliminal communication and "the language of the eyes," is conveying to her.

The image of water (or, in the case of the "drops" of the prince's "eloquence," an unspecified fluid) recurs in more comical guise in a passage of psychonarration where the narrator coyly elucidates his own image:

> She felt like the horse of the adage, brought—and brought by her own fault—to the water, but strong, for the occasion, in the one fact that she couldn't be forced to drink. Invited, in other words, to understand, she held her breath for fear of showing she did, and this for the excellent reason that she was at last fairly afraid to. It was sharp for her, at the same time, that she was certain, in advance, of his remark; that she heard it before it had sounded, that she already tasted in fine the bitterness it would have for her special sensibility. (1.272)

This reluctance to accept the implications of what he is conveying—with the concomitant sense of self-blame—contrasts with her previous attitude, also expressed in terms of gastronomic inducements: at that stage, after listening to Charlotte's account of how Maggie and Adam preferred to spend their time with each other, leaving their respective spouses to their own devices, Fanny had seen the situation in terms of a banquet of cognitive possibilities:

> Fanny Assingham had at this moment the sense as of a large heaped dish presented to her intelligence and inviting it to a feast—so thick were the notes of intention in this remarkable speech. But she also felt that to plunge at random, to help herself too freely would . . . tend to jostle the ministering hand, confound the array and, more vulgarly speaking, make a mess. She picked out after consideration a solitary plum. "So placed that *you* have to arrange?"
>
> "Certainly I have to arrange."
>
> "And does [the Prince] arrange," Mrs Assingham asked, "to make up *his* arrears?" The question had risen to her lips—it was as if another morsel, on the dish, had tempted her. (1.259)

Later, in the carriage on the way home with Bob, Fanny's refusal to partake freely of the insights proffered by her erstwhile protégés is manifested. She steadfastly wards off uncomfortable recognitions: "The sense of seeing was strong in her, but she clutched at the comfort of not being sure of what she saw" (1.277).

Fanny's rather Byzantine cognitive contortions (expressed most frequently in dialogue with Bob and thus beyond the scope of this discussion) contrast forcibly with the blunt truth uttered by Bob: "What in the world did you ever suppose was going to happen? The man's in a position in which he has nothing in life to do" (1.278). In Bob's book, therefore, adultery would be one of the inherent occupational hazards of what I have dubbed the "Wording Class"—stemming from the sheer lack of alternative forms of productive activity.

In volume 2, it is through Fanny's perspective, and not Maggie's, that we experience the climactic scene of the smashing of the golden bowl. This shift of focus has not been noted by commentators on the novel; even a critic as perceptive as Nicola Bradbury has claimed that in "The Princess" volume, "Apart from one scene between the Assinghams . . . every perception and reaction is reached through the heroine, either directly or in her projections of the other characters."[27] On the contrary, it is Fanny who serves as focalizer for this crucial scene. And when Maggie requests her immediate attendance at Portland Place, it is Fanny's view of Maggie that is portrayed. On her arrival,

> The Princess, she noted, was completely dressed . . . and she presented herself, in the large clear room . . . as for the first time in her life rather "bedizened." Was it that she had put on too many things, overcharged herself with jewels, wore in particular more of them than usual, and bigger ones, in her hair? (2.151–52)

The shift from psychonarration to narrated monologue dramatizes Fanny's sense of wonderment; the portrayal of her consciousness then modulates back to psychonarration for her interpretation of Maggie's bedecked state and flushed cheeks:

> These . . . items of her aspect had promptly enough their own light for Mrs. Assingham, who made out by it that nothing more pathetic could be imagined than the refuge and disguise her agitation had instinctively asked of the arts of dress, multiplied to extravagance, almost to incoherence. (2.152).

Fanny intuitively realizes that Maggie's symbolic change of attire here is undertaken in response to a new emotional perspective. The reader recalls that to mark the significance of her reception of the prince alone, at Portland Place, on his return from Matcham, Maggie had "bedecked" herself in her newest frock, which was "even perhaps a little too stiff and too grand for a familiar and domestic frock" (2.12). Her new garb expresses the recognition that the "familiar and domestic" is inadequate in a situation where she is obliged to don all the worldly arts and artifices as aids in her struggle.

Fanny's access of insight concerning Maggie's intentions after the discovery of the golden bowl and its revelatory implications is rendered in terms of a visual perception: "She saw her—or she believed she saw her—look at her chance for straight denunciation, look at it and then pass it by" (2.162). Fanny accurately grasps Maggie's "lucid higher intention." The narrated monologue in which she reads Maggie's motives— "It was like a fresh sacrifice for a larger conquest"—then modulates into what I have called "imputed monologue" as Fanny interprets, or renders in verbal form, what she imagines Maggie is thinking and trying to convey to her subliminally:

> "Only see me through *now*, do it in the face of this and in spite of it, and I leave you a hand of which the freedom isn't to be said." The aggravation of fear—or call it apparently of knowledge—had jumped straight into its place as an aggravation above all for her father; the effect of this being but to quicken to passion her reasons for making his protectedness, or in other words the forms of his ignorance, still the law of her attitude and the key to her solution. She kept as tight hold of these reasons and these forms, in her confirmed horror, as the rider of a plunging horse grasps his seat with his knees and she might absolutely have been putting it to her guest that she believed she could stay on if they should only "meet" nothing more. (2.163)

Fanny, to whom, as she acknowledges to Bob, "the forms are two-thirds of conduct" (1.390), is to be only too willing to keep up the "forms" of her own ignorance, pretending that she suspects nothing untoward in the relationship between Amerigo and Charlotte.

Fanny's interpretation of the way she sees Maggie "look at her chance for straight denunciation, look at it and then pass it by" (2.162) is proleptic in that it alerts the reader to the possibility of Maggie rejecting "straight denunciation" of Charlotte and Amerigo as well—as she does in the crucial scene of the card game later. In resisting the temptation to apportion blame, Maggie is already demonstrating that she is to react more imaginatively instead of acting "with the blind resentment with which, in her place, ninety-nine women out of a hundred would act" (2.125). The path of vindictive retaliation is one that, as Fanny senses, Maggie is to abjure.

Fanny's response to the golden bowl, presented through narrated perception, also adds another dimension to the symbolism of the bowl whose significance lies less in its status as an emblematic object in itself than in the way it is perceived by the characters. Her first impression is that "it was inscrutable in its rather stupid elegance," then it "put on, under consideration, a sturdy, a conscious perversity; as a 'document' somehow, it was ugly, though it might have a decorative grace" (2.165). When considering it more closely, Fanny "found herself in fact eyeing it as if, by her dim solicitation, to draw its secret from it rather than suffer the imposition of Maggie's knowledge." She perceives it as "brave and firm and rich, with its bold deep hollow; and, without this queer torment about it, would . . . figure to her as an enviable ornament, a possession really desirable" (2.167).

However, upon discovering that the bowl is in fact not gold but gilded crystal, and not perfect but cracked, Fanny declares "Then your whole idea has a crack" and smashes the bowl dramatically to the floor. Throughout this scene, the focus is on Fanny's consciousness; with the dramatic appearance of the prince there is a shift of focus to Maggie and little further direct access is given to Fanny's consciousness. The device of using Fanny as focalizer in this scene serves to involve the reader in a sense of shared mystification as to exactly what Maggie knew.

Fanny's consort and fellow-*ficelle,* Bob, has a far more circumscribed role to play. And yet the extraordinary claim has been made that "James tells the story through the eyes of Colonel Assingham, rather than through his own."[28] This ludicrous statement could emanate only from a careless or cursory reading of the text. On the other hand, the fact that Bob does indeed function at times as focalizer seems to be ignored by critics of the novel who tend to see the Assinghams only as choric commentators.[29] Access to Bob's consciousness is of course limited and invariably occurs in association with the presentation of inside views of Fanny's consciousness, which are incorporated in their lengthy dialogues.

These dialogues between Fanny and Bob are described as "their old custom of divergent discussion, that intercourse by misunderstanding" (1.365). This description is reminiscent of Austin Warren's account of the mode of knowing that he called "dialectic":

> a cerebral process, pursued by two or more minds, in contrapuntal movement of thesis, antithesis, synthesis. The topic is attacked from without; the speakers circle round it. . . . There are mutual misunderstandings, false clues, shifts of position.[30]

Nevertheless, in spite of the frequency of "mutual misunderstanding," Bob does in effect display understanding and sympathy for Fanny in her tortuous grappling with the intricacies of the situation. Fanny attempts to plumb the depths, and Bob accompanies her, as far as possible, when she launches herself on her exploratory cognitive excursions. Imagistic representation with occasional comical overtones is used to depict these epistemological forays. So Bob shares her "consciousness of deep waters." This iterative image takes on almost baroque proportions in the following portrayal of Bob's perspective:

> He hadn't quitted for an hour, during her adventure, the shore of the mystic lake; he had on the contrary stationed himself where she could signal to him at need. Her need would have arisen if the planks of her bark had parted— *then* some sort of plunge would have become his immediate duty. His present position, clearly, was that of seeing her in the centre of her sheet of dark water, and of wondering if her actual mute gaze at him didn't perhaps mean that her planks *were* now parting. He held himself so ready that it was quite as if the inward man had pulled off coat and waistcoat. Before he had plunged, how-ever—that is before he had uttered a question—he saw, not without relief, that she was making for land. He watched her steadily paddle, always a little nearer, and at last he felt her boat bump. The bump was distinct, and in fact she stepped ashore. "We were all wrong. There's nothing." (1.366)

The bathetic outcome of the convoluted elaboration of the image under-lines the ludicrous nature of Fanny's obfuscatory cognitive contortions. So much intellectual effort—to produce nothing but a lie. The continu-ation of the image in what appears to be narrated monologue indicates that Bob is aware of his role as accomplice in this process of self-deception. Convincing herself (and Bob) that she was mistaken in her suspicions is to be Fanny's only conceivable salvation—or method of salving her conscience.

This complicated image thus depicts, in psychonarration, the proce-dure whereby Bob conceives of Fanny's elaborate mental processes. He observes the maneuvres Fanny deploys to convince herself (largely as a self-exculpatory exercise) that there is "nothing" untoward in the relation-ship between Amerigo and Charlotte. After a lengthy and convoluted discussion in which she deploys her linguistic virtuosity to persuade Bob that all is well, the water image recurs with the intrusive narrator again in evidence (as he had been to explain the labyrinthine water image) to comment on their achieved state of understanding. Having secured Bob's concurrence in her interpretation, Fanny lapses with Bob into the silence of achieved understanding:

> their silence . . . might have represented their sinking together, hand in hand for a time, into the mystic lake where he had begun, as we have hinted, by seeing her paddle alone—the beauty of it was that they now could really talk better than before, because the basis had at last once for all, defined itself. What was the basis, which Fanny absolutely exacted, but that Charlotte and the Prince must be saved—so far as consistently speaking of them as still safe might save them? It did save them somehow for Fanny's troubled mind—for that was the nature of the mind of women. He conveyed to her now, at all

events, by refusing her no gentleness, that he had sufficiently got the tip, and that the tip was all he had wanted. (1.378)

The gnomic generalization concerning the nature of the mind of women is embedded in narrated monologue and thus emanates from the consciousness of Bob rather than the narrator. Bob clearly sees through Fanny's transparent attempt to dispel all well-founded misgivings and cling to the illusion that "still speaking of them as safe might save them." Her capacity for lighting upon a conveniently innocuous term and investing it with far-reaching implications had previously been demonstrated in the way she pounced on Bob's term "rum": "That's all I claim," she seemed thankful for the word. "I don't say it's anything more—but it *is* distinctly rum" (1.374).

At the conclusion of this scene a brief shift to narrated monologue again gives access to Bob's thoughts, in the course of which he concludes reassuringly that "he had, when it came to the tight places of life . . . the most luminous of wives" (1.399). The iterative light imagery here again has ironic overtones in view of the display of obfuscatory rhetoric that Fanny has indulged in. When Bob follows her upstairs, "making out how all the clearness they had conquered was even for herself a relief—how at last the sense of the amplitude of her exposition sustained and floated her" (1.399), the convergence of light and sea imagery is charged with ambiguity as the reader perceives how willfully chosen blindness confers immunity from self-reproach. Ironically, the gastronomic image discussed earlier also reappears here, this time applying to Bob's desire to put another probing question and extract another juicy morsel of information: "He held her a minute longer—there was another plum in the pie" (1.399).

At the conclusion of the last scene between Fanny and Bob, at the end of volume 1, Fanny expresses her conviction that Maggie is at last "awake." It is with her awakening to consciousness of her situation that she assumes centrality in volume 2. Before we are given direct access to Maggie's consciousness, the effects of the change in her on her friend and confidante are revealed, in much the same way that in *The Portrait* the reader is first given Rosier and Ralph's impressions of Isabel before her inner world is revealed.

I shall now look more closely at the deployment of modes of representation of consciousness in the depiction of both Adam and Maggie. The presentation of the Ververs forms the subject of the following chapter.

6

The Golden Bowl: The Ververs

"Constitutionally inaccessible to knowledge"?

ADAM VERVER: "A RARE POWER OF PURCHASE"

THE first sustained access to Adam's inner world is given in volume 1, book 2, chapter 1: "Adam Verver, at Fawns . . . might have been observed . . . had there been a spectator in the field" (1.125) enjoying his solitude in the billiard room. In a rare assumption of shared experience linking narrator, reader, and character, we find "We share this world . . . for the hour, with Mr Verver." And in a comment surprisingly reminiscent of the observation concerning the desired response to Isabel in *The Portrait,* the narrator speaks of "investing him with an interest that makes our attention . . . tender indeed almost to compassion." (The difference, it gradually emerges, is that the narratorial voice exudes irony here.) This is followed by what appears to be a characterization of Adam in the authorial mode, a procedure abjured or sparingly used in the presentation of the other characters: "For it may immediately be mentioned that this amiable man bethought himself of his personal advantage, in general, only when it might appear to him that other advantages, those of other persons, had successfully put in their claim" (1.125–26). Later, with hindsight, the reader can see that once again this ostensibly direct characterization is tinged with irony: Adam's egotism takes far more subtle and insidious forms, as will be seen in the train of reasoning leading up to his decision to marry Charlotte—and his attitude to his providentially deceased first wife.

The presentation of Adam's consciousness modulates from apparently direct definition through psychonarration and narrated monologue. In the evocation of his past financial success, Adam's single-minded dedication to making his fortune is underscored by a parodic rhetorical question:

Variety of imagination—what is that but fatal in the world of affairs unless so disciplined as not to be distinguished from monotony? Mr Verver then, for a

190

fresh full period . . . had been inscrutably monotonous behind an iridescent cloud. (1.128)

In Adam, "variety of imagination" is essentially curtailed by his egotism. Although his aesthetic imagination is well developed, this is accompanied by atrophy of the sympathetic or vicarious imagination as he is incapable of seeing others save in terms of their usefulness to Maggie and himself. In spite of his ostensible generosity in considering the claims of his guests before allowing himself to indulge in a snatched "quarter of an hour of egotism," his claim to more than superficial amiability is suspect. The "iridescent cloud," his "native envelope," recalls the impenetrable "white curtain" registered by Amerigo, and suggests perhaps a deceptively nebulous softness concealing the steely resolution beneath.[1]

Just as book 1 opens with Amerigo in a state of contemplative solitude reviewing, or "reverting to in thought," his immediate past, so the first chapter of book 2 presents Adam in a state of "backward speculation." This is achieved through a series of analepses (flashbacks) which fluctuate from the authorial to the figural mode, with Adam's past being recalled by the narrator as much as by Adam himself.

In a summary evocation of the past twenty months, which is largely refracted through Adam's consciousness, the iterative architectural image occurs in psychonarration veering to narrated monologue to conjure up Adam's conception of his son-in-law:

At first, certainly, their decent little old-time union, Maggie's and his own, had resembled a good deal some pleasant public square, in the heart of an old city, into which a great Palladian church, say—something with a grand architectural front—had suddenly been dropped. (1.135)

In reliving in imagination the impact made by his presence, Adam concedes with satisfaction that the potential for inconvenient disruption of the pleasant commerce of their lives had not, however, materialized:

no violence of accommodation, in retrospect, emerged. The Palladian church was always there, but the piazza took care of itself . . . the Prince, for his father-in-law, while remaining solidly a feature ceased to be at all ominously a block. (1.135–36)

The architectural image here vividly presents Adam's mode of thought and demonstrates how Adam conceives of Amerigo in purely aesthetic terms in which accent is laid on his imposing appearance and social cachet—"grand architectural front": he provides an appropriate backdrop which, while enhancing the tone of the piazza, does not impede or obstruct its established modus vivendi. (Adam, of course, fails to grasp the implications of this image.)

This conception, rendered metaphorically, is the counterpart of Amerigo's realization that he has been relegated to a position of peripheral impotence in their domestic arrangements. Socially, he has provided Maggie with the luster of a romantic backdrop and historically imposing connections; biologically he has fulfilled his role in furnishing her with an heir (an essential component of any dynasty), but the intensity of the shared intimacy between father and daughter remains unimpaired.

We find that the capacity to use euphemistic terms to ensure the smooth operation of one's schemes is exemplified in Adam as much as in Amerigo and Charlotte. Thus, he appreciates his son-in-law being devoid of "angularity":

> He clung to that description [not "angular"] of his daughter's husband as he often did to terms and phrases, in the human, the social connexion, that he had found for himself: it was his way to have times of using these constantly, as if they had just then lighted the world, or his own path in it, for him. (1.136)

Later, in a comparable feat of linguistic engineering, Adam fabricates the right terms to "light his path" toward proposing to Charlotte with full justification of his motives. In both instances his "producing . . . that right good word" which "figured for him clearly as a final idea, a conception of the last vividness" (1.137) is invested with the quasi-epiphanic. The analogy conjured up in his mind between the prince and a Palladian church is further elaborated (in psychonarration) as he explores the qualities usually associated with "the sharp corners and hard edges, all the stony pointedness . . . of [a] spreading Palladian church"; these include the potential for rigid assertiveness or an adamantine intractability, qualities which the prince fortunately does not display. What Adam appreciates in his son-in-law is the contact with "practically yielding lines and curved surfaces" (1.137), a pliancy that he expresses in the concept "round" as opposed to "abominably square." What Adam does not conceive of is the possibility of a Palladian facade and ostensibly accommodating structure housing features that express resistance or dissent, not in overt opposition but in more subtle and imperceptible forms.

An ominous hint of underlying ruthlessness in Adam (the steely heart behind the soft "iridescent cloud") appears in his complacent appreciation of the prince's "smoothness . . . yielding lines." It is not clear whether the observation "Oh, if he had been angular!—who could say what might then have happened?" is rendered in narrated monologue or free indirect speech, but either way there is a hint of sinister menace in this bland statement. The implication is that Amerigo would have had his edges smartly—albeit subtly—rounded off, just as Charlotte is later to be chastened through the smooth operation of the "silken halter."

This impression is later corroborated when he tells Charlotte, in reply to her query as to Amerigo's possible reaction to their marriage plans, "I'm afraid . . . [then] he'll just have to accept from us whatever his wife accepts; and accept it . . . just because she does. That . . . will have to do for him" (1.232).

Adam's other, complementary conception of Amerigo is that of "a pure and perfect crystal" (1:138). Once again it is the perfection of form and finish that is suggested by this image. Adam is to discover, however, that Amerigo is not as transparent as the crystal image might lead him suppose; other facets of the "crystal" are to be revealed later. Amerigo's response to Adam's image is indeed proleptic: "I believe that they [crystals] sometimes have cracks and flaws" (1.139). Adam, who prides himself on being a connoisseur, does not consider the possibility that his perfect specimen might have hidden flaws.

Having been afforded this access to Adam's inner world, the reader sees a new relevance in Amerigo's being placed, in the opening passage of the novel, amid the spoils of Empire and concrete embodiments of the acquisitive urge of Imperium. He himself is subjected to the same acquisitive urge as epitomized in Adam.

In a rare direct intrusive comment, the narrator deflects attention from consideration of the ramifications of Amerigo's reply and the notion of his "good taste" to point out that "It is his [Adam's] relation to such aspects, however, that now most concerns us, and the bearing of his pleased view of this absence of friction on Amerigo's character as a representative precious object." Adam, like Amerigo himself, adheres to the "touchstone of taste" which had guided him in his assessment of the prince. Amerigo is placed in the context of all the other "representative precious object[s]" that had "for a number of years . . . so engaged all the faculties of his mind, that the instinct, the particular sharpened appetite of the collector, had fairly served as a basis for his acceptance of the prince's suit" (1.140).[2]

In this section dealing with Adam's view of his past and present situation, there is a shift into a more extensive analeptic excursion for the account of Adam's first revelatory experience. Psychonarration is used here, as elsewhere, to render hallucinatory moments of insight in which his "vocation" is dramatically revealed to him.

Adam's moment of recognition of his "mission" is ironically placed in the perspective of Keats's Cortes: "His 'peak in Darien' was the sudden hour that had transformed his life, the hour of his perceiving . . . that a world was left him to conquer" (1.141). The ubiquitous and ambivalent light imagery again dramatizes this experience: when "the light, in his

mind, had so broken," Adam had pledged himself, with the fanatical dedication of the convert, "to rifle the Golden Isles." He recalls how he had
thus, "read into his career, in one single magnificent night, the immense
meaning it had waited for" (1.142). The modulation from psychonarration
to narrated monologue in the following extract highlights his arrogant
egoism:

> The thought was that of the affinity of Genius, or at least of Taste, with some-
> thing in himself. . . . He was equal somehow with the great seers, the invokers
> and encouragers of beauty—and he didn't after all perhaps dangle so far below
> the great producers and creators. (1.141)

His conception of his scheme for American City is presented in narrated
monologue that foregrounds the ironic resonances:

> It hadn't merely, his plan, all the sanctions of civilisation; it was positively
> civilisation condensed, concrete, consummate, set down by his hands as a
> house on a rock—a house from whose open doors and windows, open to
> grateful, to thirsty millions, the higher, the highest knowledge would shine out
> to bless the land. (1.145)

The mockingly alliterative "civilisation condensed, concrete, consummate" underscores the absurdity of his pretensions. And the parodic biblical overtones of "set down . . . as a house on a rock," designed to effect
"the release from the bondage of ugliness" (a variation on the Christian
release from the bondage of sin) stress the preposterously messianic nature of his scheme. Furthermore, just as historical religious crusades were
characterized by looting and plunder, so Adam's latter-day cultural cru-
sade has inherently sinister overtones.

In this flashback to Adam's discovery of his mission, when he "read
into his career, in one single magnificent night, the immense meaning it
had waited for" (1.142), it emerges that he had realized, with hindsight,
that his aesthetic sense had initially been stunted by his sentimental attachment to his wife. His sense of incredulity at his previous benighted
state is expressed in narrated monologue: "The futilities, the enormities,
the depravities, of decoration and ingenuity, that before his sense was
unsealed she had made him think lovely!" (1.143). This misdirection of
his aesthetic sense—or blunting of the touchstone of taste—seems to
appall him more than the tragedy of her early death. Her death indeed is
seen only in terms of its effect on his own development: "he even sometimes wondered what would have become of his intelligence . . . if his
wife's influence upon it hadn't been, in the strange scheme of things, so
promptly removed" (1.143). Adam seems to feel that the timeous removal
of this unfortunate impediment to his aesthetic development was in fact

providential, liberating him for a higher realm. A series of questions in narrated monologue highlights the egotism that has been so studiously if ironically disavowed in the first part of this chapter. "Would she have led him altogether, attached as he was to her, into the wilderness of mere mistakes? Would she have prevented him from ever scaling his vertiginous Peak?" (1.143). His attachment to her is seen in retrospect as a millstone round his neck, an instance of youthful folly that would have hampered his subsequent dedication to the only valid touchstone, that of taste.

In view of all these considerations, the claim that "We are no more meant to disapprove of Adam Verver's tycoonery than we are of old Mr Touchett's banking" is clearly not valid.[3] It stems at least partly from the failure to distinguish the voice of the narrator from that of the reflector, and particularly from the thoughts expressed in narrated monologue.

The role of memory as a filtering mechanism has interesting implications in Adam's "backward speculation." As we have seen, his abiding memory of his wife is primarily that of a mere impediment to his development. His most vividly accessible memory, indeed, concerns his "road to Damascus" conversion. "The very finest spring that ever responded to his touch was always there to press—the memory of his freedom as dawning upon him, like a sunrise all pink and silver . . . some three years after his wife's death" (1.150). Adam "could live over again at almost any quiet moment the long process of his introduction to his present interests" (1.149).

In the amplification of the epiphany briefly referred to earlier, this experience is evoked in terms of the pervasive—and ambivalent—light imagery. In a narrated monologue Adam's idea of enjoying preferential supernatural sponsorship is conflated with that of revelatory insight. He believes that "A wiser hand than he at first knew had kept him hard at acquisition of one sort as a perfect preliminary to acquisition of another," and that "It was the strange scheme of things again: the years of darkness had been needed to render possible the years of light" (1.144). The device of narrated monologue highlights his perception of a teleological guiding hand in his destiny, nurturing him for his "mission."

The permutations of the light imagery again predominate in the evocation, largely through dissonant psychonarration, of the hallucinatory vision inspiring Adam to propose to Charlotte. He is moved primarily by a desire to secure Maggie's peace of mind:

Light broke for him at last, indeed, quite as a consequence of the fear of breathing a chill upon this luxuriance of her [Maggie's] spiritual garden. As at a turn of his labyrinth he saw his issue, which opened out so wide, for the minute, that he held his breath with wonder. He was afterwards to recall how just then the autumn night seemed to clear to a view in which the whole place, everything round him, the wide terrace . . . lay there as under some strange midnight sun. It all met him during these instants as a vast expanse of *discovery,* a world that looked, so lighted, extraordinarily new. . . . The hallucination, or whatever he might have called it, was brief, but it lasted long enough to leave him gasping. (1.207)

The illuminating perception giving Adam access to his solution or "remedy" (1.208) is described in terms reminiscent of his sudden accession of aesthetic illumination. The eerie hallucinatory quality of Adam's vision suggests an inversion of the value of light, which is usually associated with sudden illuminating insight. The world as lit up by Adam's light takes on a surrealistic quality and can be seen as an emanation of the falsifying imagination associated with the "white curtain." In this state of autosuggestion, the fulgent flash highlighting Charlotte as a "remedy" could be seen as a travesty of the *coup de foudre* that traditionally strikes the smitten lover. Adam is first and foremost a smitten father:

The sharp point to which all his light converged was that the whole call of his future to him as a father would be in his so managing that Maggie would less and less appear to herself to have forsaken him. And it not only wouldn't be decently humane, decently possible, not to make this relief easy to her—the idea shone upon him, more than that, as exciting, inspiring, uplifting. (1.207–08)

Here psychonarration modulates to narrated monologue in the second sentence, highlighting the repertoire of self-deceiving stratagems that Adam uses to convince himself of the transcendent rectitude of his "idea." The awkward succession of negatives and the ironic repetition of "decent" suggest the process of elaborate rationalization and reinforce the impression of slippery logic justifying his decision. The conventional connotations of the term "decent" are once again subverted here; his process of self-deception entails ignoring the *in*decency of treating Charlotte as a means to an end—that of securing his daughter's peace of mind.

Adam's reification of Charlotte is foregrounded by the way in which his proposal of marriage coincides with his purchase of a set of precious Damascene tiles. In each case

It was all at bottom in him, the aesthetic principle, planted where it could burn with a cold, still flame; where it fed almost wholly on the material directly involved, on the idea (followed by appropriation) of plastic beauty, of the thing visibly perfect in its kind. (1.197)

Like Osmond in *The Portrait,* Adam instrumentalizes his prospective wife by seeing her "in the chill of his egotism and in the light of her use"[4]

to himself and his daughter. Charlotte, "by becoming for him a domestic resource had become for him practically a new person" (1.201).

Access to Adam's inner world—and specifically to the images in terms of which he conceives of his "idea"—reveals that marriage, to him, is a magnificent form dedicated to the Ververs' interests. Proceeding with "the deliberation of a plan" (1.211) he envelopes his scheme in a romantic aura, and, like Osmond, endeavors to play the conventional role of romantic lover; he successfully deludes himself that he had always been captivated by her charms, even rising to admiration of "Her extraordinarily fine eyes, as it was his present theory that he had always thought them" (1.230). Here the sly innuendo points to his self-justificatory rationalization or pseudoromantic indulgence.

By being privy to Adam's conception of his marriage, the reader realizes that it is basically a marriage of convenience—but one where the desired convenience is primarily that of a third person, the daughter of the aspirant spouse. For Adam, of course, this is seen as justification, although his view of Maggie as essentially an extension of himself merely makes his attitude that of egoism at one remove—or egotism in a more rarefied form.

Ironically, Adam finds satisfaction in the rationality of his "majestic scheme" (1.210). In a narrated monologue, his thought on this topic is expressed in a series of balanced antitheses reminiscent of Amerigo's mode of deliberation: "He was acting—it kept coming back to that—not in the dark, but in the high golden morning; not in precipitation, flurry, fever, dangers these of the path of passion properly so called, but with the deliberation of a plan" (1.211).

The glow of the "high golden morning" is later linked to—or displaced by—the "red glow" (1.216) accompanying "the burning of his ships" (1.160). Adam seems somehow oblivious to the connotations of danger. Although he sees "the sacrifice of his vessels" (1.218) as irrevocable, he does not register the implicit sense of disaster. On the contrary, "the fine pink glow, projected forward, of his ships, behind him, definitely blazing and crackling—this quantity was to push him harder than any word of her own could warn him" (1.221). By a process of mental attrition, Adam gradually persuades Charlotte to see things his way, to "make Maggie right" (1.226). Ironically, this phrase recalls the authorial comment made after the apparently successful consummation of the marriage between Maggie and Amerigo, when Maggie and Adam discuss their fortunate state at Fawns: "mightn't the moment possibly count for them—or count at least for us while we watch them with their fate all before them—as the dawn of the discovery that it doesn't always meet *all* contingencies to be right?" (1.167).

Adam, of course, has no way of knowing that Charlotte, who is by no means a starry-eyed romantic, could be accused of a culpable complicity in going along with his idea of a marriage of convenience as a way of securing a more advantageous "state"—and permanent proximity to the prince.

In volume 2, access to Adam's consciousness is restricted to Maggie's projection of his thoughts, feelings, and attitudes. Maggie's consciousness assumes centrality in the second volume as she undergoes her "process of vision" and demonstrates conclusively the fallaciousness of the belief that she is "constitutionally inaccessible to knowledge."

MAGGIE VERVER: "IMAGINATION . . . RUFFLED"

In volume 1, the portrayal of Maggie is accomplished largely through "her suitor's and her husband's exhibitory vision of her" (*AN* 330) complemented by the "exhibitory" views of Adam, Charlotte, and the Assinghams. All are aware, to varying degrees, of the limitations of Maggie's romantic view of life, of her tendency to shy away from unpleasant knowledge and her seeming inability to acknowledge the existence of the darker recesses of human nature. Charlotte's view of Maggie as a "special case" irremediably steeped in ignorance and innocence is corroborated by Fanny when she tells Bob that "There are things that no-one could tell Maggie. . . . She wasn't born to know evil. She must never know it" (1.78). One is reminded of Little Bilham's words to Strether in *The Ambassadors:* "You're not a person to whom it's easy to tell things you don't want to know" (1.202). By the end of volume 1, Fanny has modified her view to express the conviction that "Her [Maggie's] sense will have to open . . . to what's called Evil—with a very big E. . . . To the harsh bewildering brush, the daily chilling breath of it" (1.384–85).

Fanny also provides a "scenario" of subsequent developments—anticipating Maggie's awakening to "Evil" and her "taking it all on herself" so as to protect her father and preserve the marriages; volume 2, where much of the action is refracted through Maggie's consciousness, represents a shift from Fanny's "scenario" to Maggie's "drama of consciousness."

In one of Amerigo's narrated monologues, we find that he too is profoundly frustrated by

the extraordinary substitute for perception that presided, in the bosom of his wife, at so contented a view of his conduct and course—a state of mind that was positively like a vicarious good conscience cultivated ingeniously on his behalf. (1.333).

Like Fanny and Charlotte, he is struck by the fact that "her imagination was clearly never ruffled by the sense of any anomaly" (1.334) in his "go[ing] about' at such a rate with such a person as Mrs. Verver in a state of childlike innocence, the state of our primitive parents before the Fall" (1.335). In volume 2, Maggie's imagination is at last "ruffled," and through access to her consciousness we can examine the forms in which this "ruffling" is expressed as she undergoes her "awakening." This is the central focus of the second volume.

One of the crucial questions in the portrayal of Maggie's awakening to consciousness is that concerning the extent of her insight. Does she attain complete understanding or is she still purblind with regard to Adam, refusing to acknowledge his defects, even to herself? Careful consideration of the terms (and specifically images) in which she conceives of him and his relations to others, particularly Charlotte, provides invaluable clues to the nature and extent of her insight.

As the ramifications of the ironic dimension of narrated monologue have been fully examined in the preceding discussion of the other characters, and as irony is interfused with greater subtlety and complexity here, rarely taking the more overt forms of rationalization and self-deceit, I shall concentrate here in my analysis of the portrayal of Maggie's consciousness on two other aspects: the phenomenon of "imagined discourse," and the imagistic mode in psychonarration and narrated monologue.

The composing power of consciousness or the creative imagination is manifested primarily in the capacity to "image" experience. However, another important aspect of the activity of the creative imagination is its capacity to project or construe the unvoiced discourse of an interlocutor. This feature—the ability to conjure up in imagination what I have called "imputed monologue" or "hypothetical discourse"—is another significant aspect of cognitive activity and complements that of imagistic representation. Before moving to an examination of imagistic representation I propose to look more closely at this phenomenon of imagined discourse and specifically "imputed monologue."

We note at the outset that an important contrast between the two volumes lies in the preponderance of imagined monologues or dialogues in volume 2 as opposed to the dramatically enacted dialogues in volume 1. These extended passages of imagined discourse abounding in volume 2 represent Maggie's endeavor to "get into the skin" of the other characters (*AN* 37). Unlike Charlotte, who admits to Amerigo that "I can't put myself into Maggie's skin—. . . It's not my fit. I shouldn't be able, as I see it, to breathe in it" (1.311), Maggie attempts to make imaginative excursions into the "skin," or more specifically the inner world, of others; this is achieved in part by "translating" or giving verbal formulation to their unexpressed thoughts.

This activity is reminiscent of James's own description of the endeavor of the creative artist; he writes of "the intensity of the creative effort to get into the skin of the creature, the act of personal possession of one being by another at its completest" (*AN* 37).[5] Cohn comments that "This espousal of a character by his narrator 'at its completest' is precisely what James attains in moments when he uses the narrated monologue" (115). By the same token, it could be said that imputed monologue or imagined discourse is the stylistic device which represents the most complete identification of the reflector with another character in the novel, by the most far-reaching kind of vicarious participation in their experience. The reflector could thus be seen as superseding the narrator through the device of imputed discourse as [s]he overcomes the "opacity" of other minds and attributes thoughts to them—an act that is traditionally the function of the narrator.

This activity is exemplified in Maggie; acting in fidelity to her belief that "One must always, whether or no, have some imagination of the states of others" (2.258), Maggie projects herself into the state of mind of others so that she can adopt their perspective. Her capacity to look "with Charlotte's grave eyes" (2.283), for example, is manifested in her ability to project or deduce Charlotte's thoughts, to think, vicariously, with her troubled mind.

The first significant instance of imagined discourse occurs on the prince's return from Matcham, when Maggie, departing from custom by awaiting his return at Portland Place, attempts to convey by mute communication what she cannot put into words (see earlier discussion of this passage). As there is initially no indication that this is not a passage of quoted monologue, it is only at the conclusion of this "discourse" that one discovers that it is not a direct quotation of her thoughts but an approximation rendered by the narrator: "Some such words as those were what didn't ring out" (2.18).

In other instances, it is more unambiguously Maggie herself who renders in verbal form an impression based on the "language of the eyes," gestures, facial expression or "body language." We find, for example,

> It was as if he might for a moment be going to say: "You needn't *pretend,* dearest, quite so hard, needn't think it necessary to care quite so much!"—it was as if he stood there before her with . . . some such intimate reassurance, on his lips. Her answer would have been all ready—that she wasn't in the least pretending. (2.27)

Here Amerigo's imagined speech or thought is counterpointed with Maggie's formulated but unvoiced speech.

Maggie's rendering, in imagination, of the "mute communication" of Charlotte is particularly poignant and takes on ever greater intensity in the course of the novel. During the scene where she follows Charlotte into the garden, with the purpose of further reinforcing the "saving lie" she has proffered Charlotte, she imagines the form that Charlotte's probable misinterpretation of her motives might take:

> the Princess had the vision of her particular alarm. "It's her [Maggie's] lie, it's her lie that has mortally disagreed with her; she can keep down no longer her rebellion at it, and she has come to retract it, to disown it and denounce it—to give me full in my face the truth instead." This for a concentrated instant Maggie felt her helplessly gasp—but only to let it bring home the indignity, the pity of her state. (2.310)

Through imputed monologue, as through imagistic representation, Maggie can enter imaginatively into the experience of Charlotte's anguished condition. In a protracted excursion into Maggie's consciousness (which is embedded in a dialogue with Fanny), the convergence of the two modes captures the intensity of Maggie's compassionate identification with Charlotte's suffering:[6]

> Behind the glass lurked the *whole* history of the relation she had so flattened her nose against it to penetrate—the glass Mrs. Verver might at this stage have been frantically tapping from within by way of supreme, irresistible entreaty. . . . She could thus have translated Mrs. Verver's tap against the glass, as I have called it, into fifty forms; could perhaps have translated it most into the form of a reminder that would pierce deep. "You don't know what it is to have been loved and broken with. You haven't been broken with, because in *your* relation what can there have been, worth speaking of, to break? Ours was everything that a relation could be, filled to the brim with the wine of consciousness." (2.329)

Here Maggie's projection of Charlotte's thought indicates that she is subconsciously registering what her conscious mind is reluctant to recognize. Maggie ascribes to Charlotte views which in fact reflect her own growing awareness of the initial poverty of her relation with her husband. In projecting onto Charlotte this mordant criticism of the relationship between herself and Amerigo, imputing this consciousness to her rival (and, ironically, echoing Fanny's assertion that she and Amerigo had never really known each other), Maggie evinces a new clarity of insight.[7]

Through projections of the creative imagination, attempts are made to penetrate the soundproof "glass," but there is no objective criterion in terms of which to ascertain the accuracy of these projections—no narratorial corroboration of the reflector's insights. The narrator "records"

Maggie's "translation"—one of many possibilities, and perhaps invested with no more validity than any other.

The device of hypothetical or imagined discourse is deployed in Maggie's relations with Adam and Amerigo as well as Charlotte. With Adam, it sometimes takes the form of a protracted imaginary dialogue, as in book 2, 73–74. This extract presents a particularly complex patterning of the various modes. In this scene Maggie's narrated monologue modulates into imagined speech (imputed to Adam): "as if he had said to her, in default of her breaking silence first: 'Everything is remarkably pleasant, isn't it?—but *where* for it after all, are we?'" This is followed by a shift back to narrated monologue for Maggie's consciousness that "The equilibrium, the precious condition, lasted in spite of rearrangement" (2.73). Later, we have Maggie's (instead of Adam's) unuttered speech: "she would have been all ready to say to him, "Yes, this is by every appearance the best time we've had yet; but don't you see, all the same, how they must be working together for it?" (2.73–74). In a narrated monologue that incorporates imagined speeches emanating from both herself and Adam, Maggie then wonders

> For how could she say as much as that without saying a great deal more? without saying "They'll do everything in the world that suits us, save only one thing—prescribe a line for us that would make them separate." How could she so much as imagine herself even faintly murmuring that without putting into his mouth the very words that would have made her quail? "Separate, my dear? Do you want them to separate? Then you want *us* to—you and me? For how can the one separation take place without the other?" That was the question that in spirit she had heard him ask. (2.74)

Near the end of the novel, Maggie's translation of Adam's "mute facial intimations" when observing Charlotte acting as *cicerone* are complemented by her interpretation of Fanny's "mute appeal" (2.291): "'You understand, don't you, that if she didn't do this there would be no knowing what she might do?' This light Mrs. Assingham richly launched" (2.291). Maggie's response to Charlotte's penitential activity is very different from the attitude of vindictive triumph suggested by her translation of the imaginary discourse which she ascribes to Adam: "yes, you see, I lead her now by her neck" (2.287). It is impossible to verify whether what Maggie hears "in the mind's ear" is also detected by Adam. At times it seems to be indicated that he does share her compassionate anguish:

> The high voice went on; its quaver was doubtless for conscious ears only, but there were verily thirty seconds during which it sounded, for our young woman, like the shriek of a soul in pain. . . . Maggie felt herself the next thing turn with a start to her father. "Can't she be stopped? Hasn't she done it *enough*?"—

some such question as that she let herself ask him to suppose in her. Then it was that, half across the gallery . . . he struck her as confessing, with strange tears in his own eyes, to sharp identity of emotion. "Poor thing, poor thing"— it reached straight—"*isn't* she, for one's credit, on the swagger?" After which, as held thus together they had still another strained moment, the shame, the pity, the better knowledge, the smothered protest, the divined anguish even, so overcame him that, blushing to his eyes, he turned short away. (2.292)

According to Maggie's interpretation, Adam does share her "conscious ears" and can discern "in the mind's ear" the unvoiced pain Charlotte is expressing. But as the interpretation of Adam's emotion—"shame, pity . . . protest . . . anguish"—is that of the reflector rather than the narrator, it is difficult to establish with any certainty what his emotions are. It has been suggested that "her need to believe that Adam is both in control yet capable of genuine sympathy has caused her to exaggerate his commiseration with his wife."[8]

The device of imagined discourse is most in evidence in the portrayal of Maggie's endeavors to fathom the depths of both her father's and her husband's understanding. When it is initially unsignaled, it enhances the ambiguity as to what exactly is expressed and what is left unvoiced, as in the following extract:

From hour to hour she fairly expected some sign of his [Amerigo's] having decided on a jump. "Ah yes, it *has* been as you think; I've strayed away, I've fancied myself free, given myself in other quantities, with larger generosities, because I thought you were different—different from what I now see. But it was only, only because I didn't know—and you must admit that you gave me scarce reason enough. Reason enough, I mean, to keep clear of my mistake; to which I confess, for which I'll do exquisite penance, which you can help me now, I too beautifully feel, to get completely over."

That was what, while she watched herself, she potentially heard him bring out. (2.141)

What this imagined discourse also "brings out" is Maggie's own acknowledgment of her culpability: those commentators who find Maggie implausibly good or impossibly blind could find indications in these hypothetical speeches that Maggie does indeed accept some share of the blame, even if ostensibly obliquely, by attributing insights such as the above to another. The reader, having had access to the prince's version in volume 1, is in a position to compare these insights with how things stand in the prince's book and can establish that her intuitive understanding is indeed close to the truth.

Imagined or potential discourse such as this marks stages in Maggie's cognitive progress, as she demonstrates that she is now becoming "accessible to knowledge" and capable of an accurate projection of Amerigo's feelings and motives.

In the scene depicting the aftermath of the smashing of the golden bowl, Maggie, far from gloating triumphantly over the prince and enjoying his discomfiture, desires to spare him the pain and humiliation of its incriminating disclosures. She turns away from him to avoid exposure to his distressed expression, and, unable to convey her sentiments verbally, hears "in her mind's ear" what she wants to communicate. This then is an unvoiced rather than an imagined speech, but cannot be classified as conventional quoted monologue as it is silently addressed to another.

> She wanted to say to him "Take it [time], take it, take all you need of it; arrange yourself so as to suffer least, or to be at any rate least distorted and disfigured. Only *see,* see that *I* see, and make up your mind on this new basis. (2.184)

In a more complex manifestation of this subliminal communication, Maggie attributes to the prince an awareness of what she is trying to convey; she invests him with her own ability to read between the lines or hear behind the spoken words:

> "Yes, look, look," she seemed to see him hear her say even while her sounded words were other—"look, look, both at the truth that still survives in that smashed evidence [of the golden bowl] and at the even more remarkable appearance that I'm not such a fool as you supposed me. Look at the possibility that since I *am* different there may still be something in it for you—if you're capable of working with me to get that out." . . . And her uttered words meanwhile were different enough from those he might have inserted between the lines of her already-spoken. (2.187–88)

What Maggie imagines—and hopes—the prince is hearing in his "mind's ear," or inserting between her spoken words, is at variance with what is verbally asserted. Her "uttered words" concern themselves only with the factual account of the purchase of the bowl and the subsequent disclosures vouchsafed by the shopkeeper. As this projected discourse is embedded in a passage of narrated monologue, it is clear that "she seemed" implies that she seemed to herself rather than to the narrator.[9]

This imagined speech complements that quoted above (2.141): in the latter, the prince's thoughts are formulated on his behalf by Maggie; in the second extract, she credits him with being able to sound her own thoughts, which are generated in response to his (as projected by her). What Dorrit Cohn calls James's "Chinese box" effects (130) takes on new permutations in this complex interlinking network of communication which is achieved through an oblique interchange of consciousness and not through the uttered discourse of the characters.

The last significant imagined discourse between Maggie and Amerigo incorporates once again the notion of gauging from "the language of the eyes" what cannot be verbally communicated:

> she had imagined him positively proposing to her a temporary accommodation. It had been but the matter of something in the depths of the eyes he finally fixed upon her, and she had found in it . . . the tacitly-offered sketch of a working arrangement. "Leave me my reserve; don't question it—it's all I have, just now, don't you see? so that, if you'll make me the concession of leaving me alone with it for as long a time as I require I promise you something or other, grown under cover of it, even though I don't yet quite make out what, as a return for your patience." She had turned away from him with some such unspoken words as that in her ear, and indeed she had to represent to herself that she had spiritually heard them. (2.220–21)

The device of the imputed monologue, apart from functioning as a cognitive aid, appears here to be also a sophisticated self-defense mechanism—part of the strategy whereby Maggie attempts to preserve the equilibrium, the form, of the marriages. Maggie is in effect anticipating the prince's overt request to her later to "wait" (2.351) until the departure of Adam and Charlotte before he can offer her "a return for [her] patience." The image of "something grown" that Maggie imputes to Amerigo links up with the image of the flower conjured up later in a narrated monologue, where Maggie feels a sense of potentiality and promise in their altered relationship: "It was like hanging over a garden in the dark; nothing was to be made of the confusion of growing things, but one felt they were folded flowers" (2.295).

As is evident in this and many of the other extracts discussed above, imagined discourse works in conjunction with imagistic representation in facilitating the reflector's cognitive progress. This cognitive function of metaphor in the representation of Maggie's consciousness will be the focus of the last section of this discussion of *The Golden Bowl*.

IMAGISTIC REPRESENTATION IN THE PORTRAYAL OF MAGGIE'S CONSCIOUSNESS

Volume 2, "The Princess," opens with an elaborate psychoanalogy conjured up in Maggie's imagination; in an extended passage modulating from psychonarration to narrated monologue, Maggie conceives of her egregious situation in terms of an exotic pagoda erected in "the garden of her life" (2.3). The bizarre eidetic image of the pagoda represents the culmination of a series of earlier recognitions and perceptions, vague unformulated misgivings that are now embodied in more specific form.

A narratorial comment confirms that the image is conjured up by Maggie herself in narrated monologue rather than by the narrator in psychonarration:

> If this image . . . may represent our young woman's consciousness of a recent change in her life. . . . The pagoda in her blooming garden figured the arrangement—how other wise was it to be named?—by which . . . she had been able to marry without breaking, as she liked to put it, with her past. (2.4–5)

The question Maggie poses herself in narrated monologue reinforces the impression of her groping for understanding by the aid of both imagistic representation and the more logical processes of linguistic "naming." (Indeed, the acquisition of a more highly developed capacity for linguistic manipulation is an important aspect of Maggie's growing cognitive sophistication.)

By means of a flashback it is later revealed that in terms of this imagistic correlative of her situation, what Maggie sees as her first tentative tap on the surface of the pagoda corresponds to the first of the "small variations and mild manoeuvres" (2.9) she is to embark upon: her unprecedented decision to disrupt expectations by leaving her father in Eaton Square while she awaited her husband's arrival from Matcham at Portland Place. The faint response elicited to her "tap" represents Amerigo taking note of her change of attitude, of her awakening to new perceptions.

This first important recognition scene is comparable to Isabel's fireside vigil in *The Portrait* in that in each case the reflector "had a long pause before the fire during which she might have been fixing with intensity her projected vision" (2.23). In each case the protagonist is assailed by predominantly visual images that present her experience in quasi-pictorial form. This is achieved retrospectively, in "backward speculation": for Maggie,

> the whole passage was backwardly there, a great picture hung on the wall of her daily life. . . . It fell, for retrospect, into a succession of moments that were *watchable* still; almost in the manner of the different things done during a scene on the stage. (2.10–11)

The theater image is supplemented by that of a string of pearls: "Several of these moments stood out beyond the others, and those she could feel again most, count again like the firm pearls on a string" (2.11), she frequently returns to in imagination. The implication seems to be that her "later and more analytic consciousness" (2.20) constantly relives those moments in thought. It is suggested that unlike Isabel, who is depicted in the process of a specific retrospective evocation, Maggie returns repeatedly to these retrospectively evoked incidents.

This section abounds in images supplementing that of the pagoda which contribute to portraying Maggie's state of agitation. Whereas the pagoda is conjured up by Maggie herself, other comparisons are drawn by the narrator, as in, for example, "might I so far multiply my metaphors, I should compare her to the frightened but clinging young mother of an unlawful child" (2.7). This suggests that Maggie is slightly appalled at, yet protective of and determined to retain, this nascent new awareness.[10] At times it is unclear whether the image is Maggie's or the narrator's, as in "she tried to deal with herself, for a space, only as a silken-coated spaniel who has scrambled out of a pond and who rattles the water from his ears" (2.6–7). At first this appears to be an image introduced by the narrator but later seems to be Maggie's in the light of her self-protective assertion, in narrated monologue, that "she had not, so to speak, fallen in; she had had no accident, and had not got wet," and in a shift to psychonarration, "this at any rate was her pretension" (2.7).[11]

The imagistic density of this first chapter in volume 2 is considerably higher than in volume 1 and indeed foreshadows the generally greater preponderance of imagistic representation in "The Princess." Apart from the images already mentioned, those featuring most prominently in this chapter and forming part of an intricate network of iterative images include the following: imagery concerned with performance—drama and dancing; military, animal, architectural, sea and light imagery; images of a key, spring, cup, "family coach," flower, medallion, "silver tissue" and balance.

As it is impossible to explore all these images fully, I shall discuss only those metaphors that play the most important part in dramatizing Maggie's cognitive progress.

Metaphors of performance—for example, those associated with drama, dancing, and the circus—are among the most significant recurrent images. In the first recognition scene (dominated by the pagoda image), Maggie's decision to revert to more active participation in the Verver's social life is expressed in terms of an analogy with resuming activities such as "the proper playing of one's part" or participation in dancing: to her mind, "the case resembled in a manner that of her once-loved dancing, a matter of remembered steps that had grown vague from her ceasing to go to balls. She would go to balls again" (2.8). This image is amplified by the narrator: "She would have been easily to be figured for us at this occupation; dipping . . . into her rich collections and seeing her jewels again a little shyly but all unmistakably glow" (2.8). Amerigo, we recall, had also thought of Maggie in terms of her resemblance to "a little dancing-girl at rest" (2.322). Now, newly roused, she demonstrates a surprising range of virtuosity—to perform, her detractors would no doubt say, with a vengeance.

In learning to deploy with greater facility and expertise a whole gamut of social skills (including equivocation, prevarication, and what she calls "humbugging") Maggie is compared to various exponents of the performing arts. "Dancing" can be a public performance, as when Maggie is compared to "some panting dancer of a difficult step who had capered, before the footlights of an empty theatre, to a spectator lounging in a box" (2.222).

The theater imagery is often used in conjunction with a whole range of metaphors that suggest playing a specific role.

Maggie's role has many permutations as she changes from being a dancer to finding herself elevated to the position of leading lady:

> she felt not unlike some young woman of the theatre who, engaged for a minor part in the play and having mastered her cues with anxious effort, should find herself suddenly promoted to leading lady and expected to appear in every act of the five. (2.208)

This is a development of an image appearing earlier in psychonarration where Maggie "reminded herself of an actress who had been studying a part and rehearsing it, but who suddenly, on the stage, before the footlights, had begun to improvise, to speak lines not in the text" (2.33).

Adam's role has been established (by the narrator as opposed to by the character himself) in a telling complementary image:

> his position . . . [was that of] the back of the stage, of an almost visibly conscious want of affinity with the footlights. He would have figured less than anything the stage-manager or the author of the play, who must occupy the foreground; he might be at the best the financial "backer," watching his interests from the wing. (1.169–70)

This complex of imagery heightens the ambiguity of Adam's position in the novel. One is never sure whether as "financial backer" he leaves the management of the "scenario" entirely to Maggie, or whether he is indeed a form of deus ex machina, an *éminence grise* manipulating everything from the wings. The decision to "transport" Charlotte to America was obviously his own, although the scheme for their separation was first openly mooted by Maggie.

Maggie's dawning awareness of the complicity between Amerigo and Charlotte is also rendered in theatrical imagery. In a narrated monologue, she expresses her realization that Amerigo "was acting in short on a cue, the cue given him by observation" (2.39)—Maggie is only later to discover Charlotte's role in giving "cues." (The theater imagery is also prominent in the card scene that will be examined in detail later.)

The qualities suggested by the theater imagery are closely linked to those evoked by imagery drawn from the circus world. Thus, the mental agility and linguistic dexterity Maggie is increasingly obliged to develop is also expressed in terms of a comparison with the physical agility displayed by performers in the circus. At the dinner party for the Matcham set, Maggie, in a narrated monologue, considers that

> Fanny Assingham might really have been there . . . like one of the assistants in the ring at the circus, to keep up the pace of the sleek revolving animal on whose back the lady in short spangled skirts should brilliantly caper and posture. (2.71)[12]

In her acquisition of the flexibility, resilience, and supple sense of balance needed in her new role, Maggie is also depicted as an "overworked little trapezist girl" (2.302). In learning to deploy a more sophisticated repertoire of roles, and to apply what Fanny calls "painting," Maggie is in effect learning to don what in "The Beast in the Jungle" is referred to as "a mask painted with a social simper" (82). She is thus associated with Isabel Archer, who had learned to emulate Madame Merle in having recourse to wearing a mask; we recall, too, Eugenia (in *The Europeans*) who understood the advisability of being equipped with "a copious provision of the element of costume," which facilitates adaptability of manner.[13] Role playing, however, is not seen as synonymous with the meretricious and duplicitous. A consciously adopted role, Maggie discovers, can allow hitherto submerged aspects of the personality to assume useful prominence and can thus be a valuable means of self-discovery and self-preservation.

One of the significant aspects of role playing, Maggie finds, is the acquisition of linguistic virtuosity. Successful role playing demands not only flexibility of social manner and the use of costume as disguise, but it extends even further to the use of language itself as the most sophisticated form of camouflage. Linguistic dexterity is an important asset in the tangle of personal relationships making up the social jungle. Through her new awareness of discrepancies between appearance and reality, and between the overtly expressed and the suppressed, Maggie learns that she can, by dextrous linguistic manipulation, exploit this discrepancy to her own advantage. She develops the ability to create convenient fictions or sustaining illusions as a means of adapting to or trying to control a difficult situation. Maggie, like Isabel, when disabused of her illusion that one can judge by appearances, learns to manipulate appearances. By the same token, when she perceives the depths of deceit lurking behind seemingly sincere words, she learns to exploit the potential of language as a weapon for deliberate obfuscation. Maggie joins the ranks of the sophisticated ("lions") who appreciate the value of sophistry as a finely honed social weapon.

This idea is further developed through the **military imagery,** which forms another significant strand of iterative imagery deployed in the presentation of Maggie's cognitive development. In this first recognition scene, a military image suggests her awareness of the seriousness of the maneuvers she is now indulging in—that life is not to be seen merely as an entertaining game: "this was what was before her, that she was no longer playing with blunt and idle tools, with weapons that didn't cut. There passed across her vision ten times a day the gleam of a bare blade" (2.9). The military metaphors reinforce the idea of Maggie's gradually learning to deploy worldly weapons in her fight to preserve her marriage. "There were hours truly when the Princess saw herself as not unarmed for battle if battle might only take place without spectators" (2.106); she is described as having "taken the field" (2.35), being "under arms," (2.158), and as a "small erect commander of a siege" (2.214). She perceives her relations with Charlotte in terms of a military campaign, seeing her "mounting guard . . . seeing her always on the rampart . . . march to and fro" (2.143–44); in her confrontation with Charlotte in the garden, "it was like holding a parley with a possible adversary" (2.311).

Animal imagery too provides a good illustration of how a measure of the change taking place in Maggie is given through metaphor. In this recognition scene, predatory images, which usually cluster round Charlotte ("the sylvan head of a huntress" [1.46]; "the splendid shining supple creature was out of the cage, was at large" [2.239]) are now applied to Maggie. In a narrated monologue, she likens herself to "a timid tigress" in "her little crouching posture" (2.10). This image suggests that Maggie, though by nature ill-adjusted to jungle morality, is nevertheless learning to acquire the proclivities and strategies of the predatory as she responds to the imperative to save her marriage. The "timid tigress" grows in confidence and assurance of her strength as she learns to unsheathe her defensive and offensive powers.

Another recurrent animal image, that of the lamb, first occurs in Fanny's ironical description of Amerigo as "a domesticated lamb tied up with pink ribbon" (1.161). Maggie uses the same image when imagining what Adam is attempting to convey to her in an imputed speech: he seems, to her mind, to be "like some precious spotless exceptionally intelligent lamb [bleating] "Sacrifice me, my own love, do sacrifice me . . . !" (2.82–83). The idea of the inversion of roles is reinforced by the implicit analogy with the threatened sacrifice of the offspring by the parent (Isaac by Abraham) as Maggie asks herself "if it weren't thinkable, from the perfectly practical point of view, that she should simply sacrifice him" (2.82).

This in turn gives rise to the crucial image of the scapegoat, the "pharmakos," which is the role Maggie later sees herself as assuming. By encouraging Adam to go "into exile" with Charlotte, Maggie is in a sense to "sacrifice" him.

Maggie herself is by implication seen in terms of the image of the lamb in Fanny's pronouncement that "no imagination's so lively, once it's started, as that of really agitated lambs. Lions are nothing to them, for lions are sophisticated, are *blasés,* are brought up from the start to prowling and mauling" (2.128). Maggie, as a "really agitated lamb," demonstrates her "lively imagination" both in her method of coming to grips with the epistemological and ethical problems inherent in her situation and in the strategies she devises for coping.

In a further elaboration of the animal metaphor, Maggie conceives of both Charlotte and Amerigo as being in different ways "caged." Charlotte is imprisoned in the cage of ignorance forged by Amerigo and Maggie's refusal to enlighten her as to the extent of their own knowledge. Charlotte is increasingly tormented by her lack of knowledge, "cabin'd, cribb'd, confin'd, bound in / To saucy doubts and fears,"[14] as she is incarcerated in "the cage [of] the deluded condition" (2.229).

For Maggie, Amerigo, too, "struck her as caged" (2.338) during his time of voluntary sequestration from her. She perceives that his is a state of penitential confinement; in a narrated monologue she expresses the view that "There was a difference . . . between his captivity and Charlotte's—the difference, as it might be, of his lurking there by his own act and his own choice" (2.338); Maggie sees that Amerigo's "captivity" is a temporary self-imposed expiatory state undertaken in preparation for his later reestablishment of his relationship with her on a different basis.

Variations on the **architectural imagery** also occur in this recognition scene and recur throughout the novel. By contrast with the metaphor of the stately pagoda at the beginning of this scene, the image depicting Maggie's awareness of her previous instinctive postponement of analysis of her situation is one of apparently trivial domestic mismanagement or inefficiency: the image of a higgledy-piggledy lumber-room. Her procrastination or suppression of recognitions is depicted in terms of tossing awkward objects into a kind of mental storeroom:

> her accumulations of the unanswered . . . were *there* . . . they were like a roomful of confused objects, never as yet "sorted," which for some time now she had been passing and re-passing, along the corridor of her life. . . . So it

was that she was getting things out of the way. . . . What she should never know about Charlotte's thought—she tossed *that* in. (2.14–15)[15]

When Maggie does at last undertake the mental spring cleaning involved in sorting out "the accumulations of the unanswered" she subjects these unanswered questions to searching scrutiny. The image of domestic bustle reappears in a new guise to dramatize this process:

> Ah when she began to recover piece by piece the process became lively; she might have been picking small shining diamonds out of the sweepings of her ordered house. She bent, in this pursuit, over her dust-bin; she challenged to the last grain the refuse of her innocent economy. (2.42)

In her process of "recover[ing], piece by piece" her stored away questions and impressions, she lights upon a telling perception that she had temporarily thrust aside, that of the expression of embarrassment on Amerigo's face on his return from Matcham. His reassuring reception had subsequently disposed of her misgivings, but, in a variation of the architectural image (again in its more domestic mode): "the prime impression had remained, in the manner of a spying servant, on the other side of the barred threshold; a witness availing himself in time of the lightest pretext to re-enter" (2.43). Analysis of this prior impression now aids Maggie in her discovery of the complicity between Amerigo and Charlotte.

The architectural image takes on more menacing overtones in Maggie's realization, in a narrated monologue, that

> They had built her in with their purpose—which was why, above her, a vault seemed more heavily to arch; so that she sat there in the solid chamber of her helplessness as in a bath of benevolence artfully prepared for her, over the brim of which she could but just manage to see by stretching her neck. (2.43–44)

This image of claustrophobic confinement and curtailed liberty is a development of an earlier perception: "it now arched over the Princess's head like a vault of bold span that important communication between them [Amerigo and Charlotte] couldn't have failed of being immediate" (2.42).

The realization of the complicity between Amerigo and Charlotte and her concomitant exclusion takes on new permutations in Maggie's image of the "bath of benevolence" with its connotations of being immersed in a soothing, protective, all-enveloping but stifling medium. This image succinctly conveys Maggie's feeling that she is being treated as a special case—if not positively moronic, at least suffering a degree of mental retardation and thus in need of benevolent protection (for her own good).

In a continuation of her narrated monologue, the architectural image is used in conjunction with that of the cage to reinforce her sense of entrapment: "She had flapped her little wings as a symbol of desired flight, not merely as a plea for a more gilded cage and an extra allowance of lumps of sugar" (2.44).

Maggie's image of the "bath of benevolence" contrasts with the sea imagery with its connotations of freedom of movement and possibilities of exploring an unlimited expanse; it also recalls the prince's image of luxuriating (rather than being confined) in the Ververs' aureate aromatic bath. Later, near the end of the novel, Maggie conceives of the situation in which they are all embroiled in terms recalling both the image of the bath and architectural imagery, used now in conjunction with that of the circus. She sees that the Verver party at Fawns is taking refuge in the "forms" of harmonious sociability and preserving appearances:

> Maggie grew to think again of this large element of "company" as of a kind of renewed water-supply for the tank in which, like a party of panting goldfish, they kept afloat. . . . They learned fairly to live in the perfunctory; . . . it took on finally the likeness of some spacious chamber in a haunted house, a great overarched and overglazed rotunda where gaiety might reign, but the doors of which opened into sinister circular passages. . . . here they closed numerous doors carefully behind them—all save the door that connected the place, as by a straight tented corridor, with the outer world, and, encouraging thus the irruption of society, imitated the aperture through which the bedizened performers of the circus are poured into the ring. (2.288–89)

Maggie's growing awareness of the precarious nature of human relationships and the relatively small area of conquered security in which one can live and move and have one's being is conveyed in this complex of imagery. She perceives that they are all enclosed together, under the protection of "the perfunctory," suppressing acknowledgment of the darker depths of their relations: instead of enjoying the intimacy of their domestic circle, as before, they rely on fresh supplies of "company" to dilute the intensity and provide lubrication for their potentially abrasive proximity.[16]

Permutations of the architectural imagery illustrate the many facets of Maggie's cognitive activity, which ranges from vividly imagistic representation of her situation in elaborate psychoanalogies (the pagoda, for example) to meticulous analysis of domestic "debris" to pick up clues.

Threats to her cognitive progress are at times conveyed through sea imagery, which, as we've seen, is also used, usually in psychonarration, to evoke subliminal areas of experience such as erotic passion. Like the light imagery, the sea imagery is often charged with ambiguity.

The **sea imagery** often conveys Maggie's experience of the warm reassurance generated by Amerigo's displays of physical passion. On Amerigo's return from Matcham, her initial misgivings are dispelled by his "holding out his arms" and "It was for hours and hours later on as if she had somehow been lifted aloft, were floated and carried on some warm high tide beneath which stumbling blocks had sunk out of sight" (2.24–25). Here the water imagery obliquely links Amerigo's conduct to the "treatment" associated with "the bath of benevolence," a policy designed to allay her suspicions.

When analyzing, in retrospect, the scene of Amerigo's return, Maggie realizes that her initial suspicions had been stifled by the experience of passion and the "plenitude of his presence" (2.42): "the warmly-washing wave had travelled far up the strand. She had subsequently lived . . . under the dizzying smothering welter—positively in submarine depths where everything came to her through walls of emerald and mother-of-pearl" (2.43).

Maggie gradually becomes conscious of the threat posed by Amerigo's "sovereign personal power" (2.139), his ability to reduce her to "passive pulp" as he uses his sexual magnetism as a substitute for more exacting modes of communication: "the act operated with him *instead* of the words he hadn't uttered—operated in his view as probably better than any words, as always better in fact at any time than anything" (2.29). Maggie's process of attaining insight is under threat; her intuitively registered doubts are subtly deflected as she feels herself "held . . . and as she could but too intimately feel, exquisitely solicited . . . she was in his exerted grasp." This is clearly a form of sexual manipulation:

> what her husband's grasp really meant . . . was that she *should* give it up: it was exactly for this that he had resorted to unfailing magic. He *knew how* to resort to it. . . . To this [capitulation] every throb of her consciousness prompted her—every throb, that is, but one, the throb of her deeper need to know where she "really" was. (2.56–57)

Maggie clings courageously to her need to "know where she was going. Knowledge, knowledge, was a fascination as well as a fear" (2.140).

Paradoxically, the sea image recurs to portray the sudden access of insight with which Maggie becomes aware of Amerigo and Charlotte's complicity. In a narrated monologue she expresses her realization that "Ah! Amerigo and Charlotte were arranged together, but she—to confine the matter only to herself—was arranged apart," and then the sea imagery is incorporated in the shift to psychonarration: "It rushed over her, the full sense of all this, with quite another rush from that of the breaking wave of ten days before" (2.45). Here, the image of the sea as representing in this context the overwhelming onrush of insight displaces the sea of erotic passion.

Maggie also experiences knowledge in the form of a rushing torrent when she achieves an access of insight into her father's motives for marrying Charlotte: she feels the impact of "the confounding, the over-whelming wave of the knowledge of his reason. 'He did it for *me,* he did it for me'" (2.81). She then feels "the wonderments involved in these recognitions flash at her with their customary effect of making her blink" as though to clear her vision.

As illustrated in this extract, insights are often conveyed through a conjunction of different images; in this instance, metaphors concerning the sea and light. The pervasive **light imagery** often evokes the notion of insight—real or spurious. For example, a short while after her fireside vigil, when Maggie has had the opportunity to observe Amerigo and Charlotte together, she attains new insight, which is corroborated by the revived memory of Amerigo's expression on his return from Matcham:

> [this] prompted in Maggie a final reflexion, a reflexion out of the heart of which a light flashed for her like a great flower grown in a night. As soon as this light had spread a little it produced in some quarters a surprising distinctness. . . . The word for it, the word that flashed the light, was that they were *treating* her, that they were proceeding with her . . . by a plan that was the exact counterpart of her own. (2.41)

As in the case of Adam, Amerigo, and Charlotte, the "word" is invested here with revelatory power, but in Maggie's case the insight yielded seems to be genuine rather than spurious.

During her fireside vigil, when Maggie is pondering the implications of her situation, she is described as "one for whom a strong light has sud-denly broken" as she responds to the implications of her image of the "family coach." Maggie "found in this image a repeated challenge" (2.23–24) which precipitates new insight. In a passage of narrated monologue and psychonarration, Maggie, in retracing events leading up to the pres-ent situation, finds that retrospective illumination now enables her to see her father's marriage in a new light. She perceives with new clarity that she and Adam have shamelessly exploited Charlotte and Amerigo, using them both as a "domestic resource" and being content to have them "living always in harness" (2.22). This colloquialism is invested with fresh force as it sparks off an important train of imagery in Maggie's mind:

> what perhaps most came out in the light of these concatenations was that it had been for all the world as if Charlotte had been "had in," as the servants always said of extra help, because they had thus suffered it to be pointed out to them that if their family coach lumbered and stuck the fault was in its lacking its complement of wheels. Having but three, as they might say, it had wanted another, and what had Charlotte done from the first but begin to act . . . ever

so smoothly and beautifully, as a fourth? . . . She might have been watching the family coach pass and noting that somehow Amerigo and Charlotte were pulling it while she and her father . . . were seated inside together . . . so that the exertion was all with the others. (2.23–24)

This elaborate psychoanalogy is comparable with that of the pagoda in that through imagistic representation both the present situation and Maggie's response to it (a tap on the surface of the pagoda, a jump from the coach) are figured:

> Maggie found in this image a repeated challenge; again and yet again she paused before the fire: after which, each time, in the manner of one for whom a strong light has suddenly broken, she gave herself to livelier movement. She had seen herself at last, in the picture she was studying, suddenly jump from the coach. (2.24)

In this vivid pictorial image Maggie represents to herself that she "had taken a decision" (2.24). In her "projected vision," her jump from the family coach represents her dissociating herself from their present way of "going about" and instead taking independent action. The insight attained when "the strong light had suddenly broken" is clarified when the "jump" is rendered in more concrete terms. Her plan of action, which "consisted of the light that, suddenly breaking into her restless reverie, had marked the climax of that vigil" (2.25), entails greater participation and a realignment with Amerigo.

Later, having reestablished a "community of interest" with Amerigo, Maggie perceives, in a narrated monologue, that "They were together thus, he and she . . . whereas Charlotte, though rising there radiantly before her, was really off in some darkness of space that would steep her in solitude" (2.250). This image takes on even more harrowing overtones in a later narrated monologue inserted in a conversation between Maggie and Adam:

> *There* was his idea, the clearness of which for an instant almost dazzled her. It was a blur of light, in the midst of which she saw Charlotte like some object marked by contrast in blackness, saw her waver in the field of vision, saw her removed, transported, doomed. (2.271)

Maggie's conception of Adam's "idea" evinces deep compassion for Charlotte. The imagery here, and the repetition of "she saw," provide an ironic parallel with the hallucinatory vision with which Adam had initially conceived of—and justified—his "idea" of using Charlotte as a "remedy." His new "idea" is to ship her off as she has proved to be a liability rather than a solution.

In another complex of imagery, which includes both the light and the **flower image,** Maggie is depicted as "plucking [her plan] in the garden of thought, as if it had been some full-blown flower that she could present to him on the spot. Well, it was the flower of participation" (2.26). Later, the realization that Amerigo and Charlotte were "treating" her is also evoked in terms of this combination of light and flower imagery, as it comes in the form of "a reflection out of the heart of which a light flashed for her like a great flower grown in a night" (2.41). This "flower" has the effect of annulling or blighting her proffered "flower of participation." The image recalls, ironically, Amerigo's experience at Matcham where "the exquisite day bloomed there like a large fragrant flower that he had only to gather. But it was to Charlotte he wished to make the offering" (1.355).

In the scene where Maggie offers Charlotte her saving fiction—the assurance that she "accused her [Charlotte] of nothing," which later even includes Maggie's taking the blame herself for any problems in Charlotte's marriage—a narrated monologue expresses her view that "she had kept in tune with the right, and something, certainly, something that might be like a rare flower snatched from an impossible ledge, would, and possibly soon, come of it for her" (2.250). The image here recalls the elusive flower (symbolizing happiness) that Roderick attempts to snatch from the "impossible ledge" of the Coliseum for Christina, and that Rowland plucks from the alpine ledge for Mary. What was physically enacted in James's early novel, *Roderick Hudson*—a physical effort to snatch a real flower from a dangerous ledge—is transposed to the symbolic plane in his last completed novel. In a modulation of this image in the last scene of the novel, Maggie is to be rewarded with the "golden fruit" (2.367) of her endeavors.

Maggie's "process of vision," like Isabel's, is accomplished partly through a gradual accretion of insights and partly through a succession of more clearly demarcated recognition scenes. One of the other significant recognition scenes is that of the card game at Matcham which Maggie observes. Here she is exposed successively to the onslaughts of temptation (the temptation to succumb to "the straight vindictive view, the rights of resentment" [2.236] and "sound out their doom in a single sentence" [2.233]) and then to the "assault" of Charlotte herself.

The fusion of the literal and the figurative in this scene has great dramatic impact, as the iterative image of the card game, reinforcing the idea of life as a battlefield where tactical ability is a determinant factor, takes on new force. Maggie has been conscious for some time that, as experienced in a narrated monologue,

> there was a card she could play, but there was only one, and to play it would be to end the game. She felt herself—as at the small green table, between

the tall old silver candlesticks and the neatly arranged counters—her father's playmate and partner; and what it constantly came back to, in her mind, was that for her to ask a question, to raise a doubt, to reflect in any degree on the play of the others, would be to break the charm. (2.34)

Now that Maggie's suspicions have been confirmed by the disclosures afforded by the golden bowl, the temptation to play the trump card must be even more insistent. Maggie's prime motive for desisting had been established in a narrated monologue before the purchase of the bowl:

That hideous card [revealing her suspicions to her father] she might in mere logic play—being by this time . . . intimately familiar with all the fingered pasteboard in her pack. But she could play it only on the forbidden issue of sacrificing him. (2.107)

Now, moving from the realm of the figurative to the literal, Maggie finds herself observing a real card game in which the others are participants. She is no longer depicted as Adam's "playmate and partner"—indeed, Adam has scant respect for her "cardmanship," her ability to hold her own when engaged in the game. His own skill is that of the "high adept" (2.233), just as behind his poker-faced exterior he is a "high adept" at the tactical strategies of life. Maggie is to demonstrate that her mode of understanding and moral action, informed as it is by the sympathetic imagination rather than shrewd intelligence, transcends that of the card-sharp mentality.

Various strands of imagery converge in this climactic scene. In the theater imagery, Maggie is initially depicted as a "tired actress who has the good fortune to be 'off', while her mates are on" (2.231), but when she moves out on to the terrace and sees the scene framed in the lit window, psychonarration shifts to narrated monologue as she sees that her companions "might have been figures rehearsing some play of which she herself was the author" (2.235). Maggie recognizes the power and responsibility inhering in her new role; no longer a mere participant, she is responsible for the future scenario of their lives. This perception is analogous to her feeling that she might be conceived of as "holding them in her hand" as they hold their cards and she held the pieces of the shattered golden bowl. The potentiality for reconstruction or for destructive dénouement is hers. She looks into the drawing room

lighted also, but empty now, and seeming to speak the more in its own voice of all the possibilities she controlled. Spacious and splendid, like a stage again awaiting a drama, it was a scene she might people, by the press of her spring, either with serenities and decencies and dignities, or with terrors and shames and ruins, things as ugly as those formless fragments of her golden bowl she was trying so hard to pick up. (2.236)

In this extract narrated perception modulates into narrated monologue to render her interpretation, which is animated by imagery drawn from the theater in conjunction with that of the "spring."

The nature of this crucial recognition scene makes it reminiscent both of Maggie's earlier fireside vigil and of Isabel's "motionlessly seeing" during her midnight meditation. Conceiving of a situation in a visual image, rendering it as a picture or a scene, frames it for more searching scrutiny than would be possible by merely balancing abstract concepts. The greater involvement of the imagination makes possible access to a more profound level of understanding.[17]

It is while watching her companions ostensibly absorbed in their innocuous pursuit that Maggie is assailed by the temptation to give way to the urge for denunciation and revenge. Maggie successfully withstands the irruption of this destructive impulse to "sound out their doom in a single sentence"; she "faced that blinding light and felt it turn to blackness" (2.233–34). Here the "blinding light" of the illuminating flash of recognition of her power to avenge herself turns to the blackness of futility as Maggie rejects "the straight vindictive view, the rights of resentment" (2.236).

As she moves on to the terrace, she carries with her the impression of the appeal emanating from "the four pairs of eyes," the appeal which Maggie interprets as a plea to assume the burden of "the whole complexity of their peril" (2.234). As Fanny had predicted, she assumes the responsibility to "charge herself with it as the scapegoat of old, of whom she had once seen a terrible picture, had been charged with the sins of the people and had gone forth into the desert to sink under his burden and die" (2.234).[18]

Although Charlotte can also be seen later as enacting the role of scapegoat (or rather, of having the role thrust upon her) as she is "doomed" to go forth into the "desert" of America, the reader is presumably meant to feel that it is largely in expiation of her own sins that she goes. Maggie, on the other hand, sees herself as assuming the burden of the sins of them all, as subsuming her own "sins" under those of the others.

The temptation depicted here as a "blinding light" is soon after rendered, retrospectively, in terms associating it more closely with the primitive passions. The animal imagery reinforces this. In Maggie's narrated monologue as she moves out of the lighted room into the darkness of the terrace, she feels that "the air was heavy and still . . . she . . . could get away, in the outer darkness, from that provocation of opportunity which had assaulted her, within[,] on her sofa, as a beast might have leaped at her throat" (2.235). The subtly ambiguous phrasing here suggests that "the assault . . . within" took place not only literally within the house and within the complex of relations in which Maggie is involved, but also—most devastatingly—"within" herself. Maggie, like Amerigo, has to withstand the assault of "dangers from within" (1.16). (The suppression of the comma after "within" in the New York Edition blurs the ambiguity here.)[19] Having abjured the temptation of denunciation and revenge, Maggie's recognition of her motives for doing so are rendered in the imagistic mode, with visual images predominating:

> it was as if the recognition had of itself arrested her—she saw as in a picture, with the temptation she had fled from quite distinct, why it was she had been able to give herself from the first so little to the vulgar heat of her wrong. . . . [she had rejected] a range of feelings which for many women would have meant so much, but which for *her* husband's wife, for her father's daughter, figured nothing nearer to experience than a wild eastern caravan, looming into view with crude colours in the sun, fierce pipes in the air, high spears against the sky, all a thrill, a natural joy to mingle with, but turning off short before it reached her and plunging into other defiles. (2.236–37)

Here it is difficult to determine if and when psychonarration modulates into narrated monologue. The emphasis on "*her* husband's wife" seems to suggest that Maggie's own thought is being reflected or that it represents at least an instance of stylistic contagion. Either way, imagistic representation helps to clarify Maggie's reasons for not succumbing to what she sees as the lure of "the wild eastern caravan," which contrasts with the tame domestic familiarity of the "family coach." She feels constrained to conduct herself in a manner befitting the dignity of "her husband's wife . . . her father's daughter," and the reader notes that her gradually developing new priorities are reflected in the order in which she mentions these two vital connections or restraining obligations. Maggie's initial motive, that of protecting her father from knowledge, has been displaced by her desire to preserve rather than to rend the complex fabric of their connection. (There are, in any case, indications that Maggie intuitively realizes that his knowledge probably matches hers.)

Maggie's revelatory encounter with evil is another recognition couched in vividly imagistic terms. It was presaged by Fanny when she told Bob that Maggie's "sense will have to open. . . . To what's called Evil—with a very big E" (1.385). However, it is rendered here as an encounter with a concrete presence rather than an abstract entity "with a very big E."

> the horror of finding evil seated all at its ease where she had only dreamed of good; the horror of the thing hideously *behind,* behind so much trusted, so much pretended, nobleness, cleverness, tenderness. It was the first sharp falsity she had known in her life, to touch at all, or be touched by; it had met her like some bad-faced stranger surprised in one of the thick-carpeted corridors of a house of quiet on a Sunday afternoon. (2.234)

Fanny had spoken of "the harsh, bewildering brush, the daily chilling breath" of contact with evil (1.385). Here evil is imaged as a sinister presence insidiously pervading the intimacy of tranquil domesticity, "seated, all at its ease" at the dinner table—or the card table. When caught off guard, its presence is manifested as that of a "bad-faced stranger" lurking behind trusted faces in the warm security of the home.[20]

The animal imagery takes on new resonances when, having withstood "the provocation of opportunity which had assaulted her . . . as a beast might have leaped at her throat," Maggie is subsequently obliged to confront Charlotte, who is implicated in the same kind of "assault" by being compared to "a splendid shining supple creature . . . out of the cage [and] at large" (2.239). Maggie feels the effect of Charlotte's presence as that of "having been thrown on her back . . . her helpless face staring up" (2.242). Nevertheless, Maggie manages to go through with the role she has assumed. She dexterously deploys language as a form of camouflage as she deals in assumed ignorance, verbal evasions, and half-truths, creating "saving lies" and proving that she has become as proficient as Charlotte in manipulating one of the most powerful weapons of the worldly. She even tries to compose her features into the appropriate "blank blurred surface" (2.247), which is commensurate with her former "blurred absent eyes" (1.187), but finds it difficult to prevent her eyes from revealing a meaning that contradicts her spoken words.

Because the reader is restricted to Maggie's consciousness, it is difficult to determine to what degree Charlotte is taken in by Maggie's performance and to what extent she simply finds it expedient to "believe" Maggie's proffered version of events in which she, Charlotte, is exculpated.

In the course of her "process of vision," Maggie attains insight into Charlotte, Amerigo, and Adam. Whereas at first she sees only Amerigo's "public" self and has to learn to understand his private, personal self, in her relations with Adam the opposite process obtains. The light imagery animates the portrayal of her acquisition of new insight into his character: "she saw him during these moments in a light of recognition which . . . had never been so intense and so almost admonitory" (2.273). Adam is seen by his daughter in a new capacity as a "personage," "above and beyond his being her perfect little father." She sees him now as a highly competent, managing, "public" character who has the capacity to succeed in maintaining his marriage as he has succeeded in all his other enterprises—in part, perhaps, through his "rare power of purchase."

By the end of the novel, Maggie has demonstrated her capacity for independent thought and action. Just as she no longer relies on Adam for guidance, so she resists more elevated forms of tutelage as represented by Father Mitchell's offer of assistance. Her attitude is expressed in terms of the cup image. Earlier, the cup image was deployed to depict the possibilities of happiness and passionate fulfillment, as at Matcham where "it passed between them [Amerigo and Charlotte] that their cup was full; which cup their very eyes, holding it fast, carried and steadied and began, as they tasted it, to praise" (1.356). The image recurs here with different connotations. Maggie, in an imagined discourse, had attributed to Charlotte the concept of a cup "filled to the brim with the wine of consciousness" (2.329), an image whose biblical resonances ("my cup runneth over") link it with that portraying the combined consciousness of Charlotte and Amerigo at Matcham. (Associations with the traditional "loving cup" and, proleptically, with the cup of Christ's betrayal, could also be pertinent here.) The image now takes on new permutations as Maggie conceives of herself in a narrated monologue as "carrying in her weak, stiffened hand a glass filled to the brim, as to which she had recorded a vow that no drop should overflow. She feared the very breath of a better wisdom, the jostle of the higher light, of heavenly help itself" (2.298). Maggie, in demonstrating that she is indeed eminently "accessible to knowledge," is determined to bear the cup of knowledge without interference and to shun external sources of insight (albeit beneficent and comforting) which entail diminished responsibility. In rejecting all external luminaries Maggie displays her aspiration to do her best according to her own lights, relying only on her own "heroic lucidity."

It is no doubt James's careful preservation of ambiguity that has fostered debate on the nature and extent of Maggie's "heroic lucidity"—and the forms of expression it takes. Two extremes are posited in a study entitled "Maggie Verver: Neither Saint nor Witch."[21] A fair number of critics, succumbing to the temptation of easy oversimplification, do indeed tend to categorize Maggie as either saint or witch. Early proponents of the view that Maggie is a "saintly" embodiment of "innocence outraged" (2.237) and that Charlotte is guilty of villainous treachery include, for example, R. P. Blackmur, Jacques Barzun, and Quentin Anderson.[22] Dorothea Krook and Frederick Crews emphasize the "redemptive" nature of Maggie's love and the importance of Christian imagery conveying this idea.[23]

Also among early critics—in the opposing camp—it is held that "Maggie is an all but unmitigated tyrant. . . . Life terrifies this Machiavellian creature not at all. She manipulates it to her purposes."[24] This view is supported in essence by, inter alia, Maxwell Geismar, Jean Kimball, Leavis, and Matthiessen.[25] Indeed, Geismar has averred that Maggie is representative of all Jamesian characters, who have

> a limited range of emotions. . . . [They are] without the capacity for love, fearful even of friendship as another trap of the human spirit . . . controlled

only by the yearnings and demands of an immaculate egotism which eschewed all the ordinary solaces, rewards and supports of human existence.[26]

The claim has even been made that the liaison between Charlotte and Amerigo is merely a figment of Maggie's over-active imagination and that "Outside of Maggie's suspicions and accusations, there is no proof that either Charlotte or the Prince have lied about anything."[27] The exponent of this ingenious theory, John Clair, supports the view, attributed to Jean Kimball, that "the illicit alliance is entirely fictive and that Charlotte Stant is the innocent victim of Maggie Verver's viciousness."[28]

A more careful reading of the novel would refute this view of Maggie, and due consideration given to the contents of Maggie's consciousness would confirm that she is indeed capable of a spectrum of emotions ranging from love, friendship, and compassion to jealousy and a "selfish" determination to promote her own possibilities for happiness while inflicting the minimum of pain on others; in effect, being "neither saint nor witch" makes her a more plausible character.[29]

More recent critics, responding from a post-Freudian, post-structuralist perspective and with different assumptions about the nature of fiction and unitary character, tend to avoid dichotomies such as that of saint/witch, noting instead the complexity of a character who is herself aware that "there was honestly an awful mixture in things" (2.292). According to Donna Przybylowicz, James does not perceive the individual as "an integrated ego ideal" but rather as "prone to ambivalence and self-division." She argues that James deliberately dismantles the "totalising tendencies and binary oppositions underlying nineteenth-century realistic fiction."[30]

Irrespective of one's theoretical framework, interpretation of Maggie's character and motives is dependent on the crucial recognition of the difference between a specific image emanating from the narrator or being generated in the imagination of the character concerned; as Donald Mull observes,

The cruelty of Charlotte's predicament has been seen as the crowning touch in the case for the Ververs' villainy; and surely James—or should we say Maggie?—takes great pains to insure that we shall not miss the extent of Mrs Verver's suffering. For it is Maggie, after all, who is the measure of Charlotte's pain, as in the image of the invisible leash with which she figures Adam's power to control Charlotte. F.O. Mathiessen's [sic] comment that "James's neglect of the cruelty in such a cord, silken though it be, is nothing short of obscene," certainly goes far astray. Maggie totally realises the cruelty of the figure, for the figure is of her own making.[31]

It is clear that the judicious application of Cohn's categories (psycho-narration and narrated monologue) could contribute to a clarification of these issues and obviate misreadings such as that evinced in William MacNaughton's claim that "One notes that this halter image is introduced by the narrator, who discerns the new element of somewhat sinister control exercised subtly but unmistakably by Adam."[32] On the contrary, the image is indeed conjured up by Maggie herself and thus marks an important stage in her cognitive development—her ability to view her father with a more critical eye.

A certain degree of critical dissension is inevitable, however, as the presentation of Maggie is indubitably fraught with equivocality. As I have indicated, ambivalence is most evident in Maggie's relations with Adam at the conclusion of the novel. Although Maggie is clearly aware of Adam's latent sadism (revealed in the silken halter image), the reader is unsure whether Maggie condemns him sufficiently or even allows her "lucidity" fully to illuminate his defects. What does seem indisputable is that in the course of the novel she manages largely to dissociate herself from his point of view. When, in the parting scene, Adam and Maggie survey the "picture" comprising all the "important pieces" in their lives, it seems clear that although "their eyes moved together" over the scene, the convergence of vision between them is now merely superficial or "perfunctory":

> Their eyes moved together from piece to piece, taking in the whole nobleness—quite as if for him to measure the wisdom of old ideas. The two noble persons seated in conversation and at tea fell thus into the splendid effect and the general harmony: Mrs Verver and the Prince fairly "placed" themselves, however unwittingly, as high expressions of the kind of human furniture required, aesthetically, by such a scene. The fusion of their presence with the decorative elements, their contribution to the triumph of selection, was complete and admirable; though to a lingering view, a view more penetrating than the occasion really demanded, they also might have figured as concrete attestations of a rare power of purchase. There was much indeed in the tone in which Adam Verver spoke again, and who shall say where his thought stopped? "*Le compte y est.* You've got some good things." (2.360)

Because Maggie's "telescope has gained in range," as she formulated it in a narrated monologue (2.207), she now sees further than Adam; it is subtly conveyed that, although ostensibly acquiescing in her father's view, Maggie really dissociates herself from it. This divergence between the perspectives of Maggie and Adam is highlighted by the interpolated phrase, "to a lingering view, a view more penetrating than the occasion really demanded," which implies a bifocal or binary vision and holds the preceding and succeeding sections of the sentence in an interpretative suspension. Thus, when confronted with the view that the prince and Charlotte "might have figured as concrete attestations of a rare power of purchase," the reader realizes that this is so in Adam's eyes and that Maggie is probably aware of it. She has the insight to perceive that their respective "sposi" represent for Adam "the triumph of selection" and a "rare power of purchase," but that the occasion, which dictated the necessity to preserve "the splendid effect and the general harmony" at all costs, could not stand up to "a more penetrating view": "the occasion, socially and psychologically, *also* demands the turning of a blind eye."[33] A pose of "bandaged eyes" and blurred vision (2.182) is thus adopted to avoid probing beneath the surface of achieved harmony and "so complete a conquest of appearances" (2.233).[34]

The impression of Adam's abiding aestheticism—from the sterility of which Maggie has dissociated herself—is confirmed by what follows the reference to a "rare power of purchase": "There was much indeed in the tone in which Adam Verver spoke again, and who shall say where his thought stopped? '*Le compte y est.* You've got some good things'" (2.360).

The parenthetical question "who shall say where his thought stopped?" could arouse the response "not the narrator, certainly!" No narratorial guidance is afforded to enlighten one as to Adam's feelings or thoughts. The reader is restricted to Maggie's interpretation.

Maggie's reply, "Ah, don't they look well?" is ambiguous on several counts. "They" presumably refers to the amassed "good things" on display, but in the context the term embraces their respective spouses (and specifically, Adam's view of them) who are accorded the same appreciative scrutiny and who attest to "the triumph of selection" on the same level. (This impression is confirmed by talk during the parting scene of the emptiness of a house "with half of its best things removed" [2.362].) The implication could also be that so long as they (Charlotte and Amerigo) "look" well, their real feelings don't matter; the preservation of appearances has been maintained. The ironic term "human furniture" reinforces the idea that these "representative precious objects" (1.140), too, can be restored, repolished when their luster becomes unaesthetically tarnished, and rearranged in new configurations to preserve the harmonious appearance of the refurbished domestic sanctum.

The serenely harmonious "picture" viewed here indeed seems to vindicate Maggie's decision (dramatized during the card-playing scene where she and Charlotte "side by side . . . fixed this picture of quiet harmonies" [2.243–44]) to eschew exposure and revenge—"terrors and shames and ruins, things as ugly as those formless fragments of the golden bowl" (2.236)—and preserve the "serenities and dignities and decencies." The verbal echoes also recall Maggie's intention to make "her care for

[Adam's] serenity, or at any rate for the firm outer shell of his dignity, all marvellous enamel, her paramount law" (2.202–03).

The imagery here alerts us to the fact that in preserving intact the "magnificent form" of the marriages, Maggie is acting in accordance with her aspiration to realize what is represented by "the golden bowl as it *was* to have been . . . the bowl without the crack" (2.216–17). This suggests perhaps the vestigial romanticism (imaged by the "white curtain" earlier) of a grail-like quest for impossible perfection. The illusory nature of the quest is underscored by the resonances of both Blake's "Can wisdom be kept in a silver rod / Or love in a golden bowl?" and the allusion to the passage in Ecclesiastes suggesting "mortality and evanescent perfection[35]—"the silver cord be[ing] loosed, or the golden bowl be[ing] broken." It has also been noted that "the fact that the bowl is a flawed crystal, and the repeated allusions to the perfect simplicity of crystal elsewhere . . . may very well have an allusion to the well-known symbolism of [the] great love legend" of Tristan, "whose praise of love's crystalline simplicity James very likely had in view."[36] (The conceit of the flawed crystal representing Amerigo is also pertinent here.)[37]

According to another recent critic, "Maggie Verver restores harmony and balance to her world by putting back together a dialogic relation with her husband, which ultimately becomes a triumphant feminine 'utterance'."[38] Maggie's "methodology" is furthermore "held to be in accord with the tenets of post-structuralist feminism since her revisions disrupt the masculine referentiality of Book I by privileging the pluralising nature of the feminine Other in Book II. The feminine . . . subverts referentiality, for it is plural and open."[39] Indeed, in revising the script written for her by the prince, whose identity and responses are determined by his imposing family traditions, Maggie reveals a talent for imaginative improvization which is vividly suggested by her image of herself as a "settler or . . . trader in a new country" (*GB* 517). Whereas the prince "had a place . . . something made for him beforehand by innumerable facts, facts largely of the sort known as historical, made by ancestors, examples, traditions, habits" (*GB* 516), Maggie has only an improvized "post" of the kind associated with her pioneering forbears exploring new geographical frontiers. Maggie's creative rewriting of their subsequent story does indeed evince the "plurality" and "openness" of what is held to be the characteristically feminine utterance. Being devoid of the constricting trappings of tradition—and conventional responses—is advantageous to Maggie when faced with the challenge to refashion their lives or revise the script dictated by the patriarchal tradition.

Maggie could also be seen as motivated primarily by the more practical and worldly consideration that the preservation of the form of the marriages is necessary to foster restitution of their substance. "Restitution and new growth will be possible only if feelings are harnessed into shapes, into the articulate elisions of mannered behaviour, mannered language"[40]—"a brilliant surface—to begin with, at least" (2.216), as Fanny put it.

Maggie's residual romanticism and her shying away from "a view more penetrating" could be seen as being in accordance with the view that "Human kind / Cannot bear very much reality."[41] Initiated into as much knowledge as she is capable of "bearing," Maggie finds it imperative to part not only on "Charlotte's 'value'" (2.365) but on Adam's, to retain the "saving illusion" without which their precariously balanced equilibrium would totter. Just as she has vouchsafed to Charlotte her "saving lie" (thus enabling her to preserve her brazen facade), so she needs to cling to hers.

Maggie's construction of saving fictions casts the pejorative comment concerning "the reticulation of reality in syntax," cited earlier, in a new light. Language does shape experience; the constitutive consciousness in a sense forges one's reality. It could be said that *The Golden Bowl* highlights "one of the primary illusions by which we all live: that our private images of others (and even of ourselves) are true." Indeed, *The Golden Bowl* "undermines the notion that there is some objective criterion by which we may determine whose vision has more validity. . . . It shows us that all constructs are corrupted."[42]

Ironically, this reliance on a "saving lie" (or suppressed truth?) links Maggie with Charlotte's own admission to Amerigo that "for things I mayn't want to know I promise you shall find me stupid" (1.363). Maggie has demonstrated that she was erroneously classified as "constitutionally inaccessible to knowledge"; but just as Charlotte opts for selective inaccessibility to knowledge by refusing to recognize anything detrimental to her own interests, so Maggie is reluctant to acknowledge flaws in Adam which could damage her faith in him. Perhaps Fanny's observation that "Stupidity pushed to a certain point *is,* you know, immorality" (1.88) is apposite here.

An ironic tension between the trivialities that are expressed and the truths that are stifled pervades this parting scene. In a narrated monologue, Maggie perceives, without overtly acknowledging it, "how impossible such a passage would have been, how it would have torn them to pieces, if they had so much as suffered its suppressed relations to peep out of their eyes" (2.362).

In accordance with the structuring principle of the novel, access is given only to Maggie's consciousness in the last scene. Amerigo's feelings must be gauged from his words, facial expression, gestures, and Maggie's response to them. In the representation of Maggie's consciousness, the metaphoric mode is manifested in a convergence of various recurrent strands of imagery. In a narrated monologue, Maggie conceives of her "reward" in terms of the "golden fruit" or "money-bags" to be presented to her on the successful coming to fruition of her plan—or, as the more cynical would say, the triumphant conclusion of her strategy. In a narrated monologue, light imagery—"a sudden blinding light"—in conjunction with that of gamesmanship or gambling dramatizes her insight that the form her "reward" is to take is still uncertain: "She had thrown the dice, but his hand was over the cast" (2.367).

Amerigo's response is a demonstration of unstinting devotion and commitment expressed in his tenderly solicitous gesture—"his whole act enclosing her" and his declaration "I see nothing but you." No longer dependent on Fanny or Charlotte, Amerigo, in response to Maggie's exhortation to "Find out for yourself!" (2.203) has indeed seen for himself and now understands and appreciates Maggie's real worth—measured not merely in monetary terms. Maggie is intensely moved: "And the truth of it had, with this force . . . so strangely lighted his eyes that, as for pity and dread of them, she buried her own in his breast" (2.369).

It has been suggested that "Maggie buries her head in the Prince's breast . . . in knowledge that she has had to become a predator and he her prey."[43] Furthermore, according to Blackmur, "Maggie 'pities' the Prince because she knows that this moment marks his final subjugation to her moral tyranny."[44] By implication, Amerigo is thus seen as having exchanged his "pink ribbon" if not for a silken halter at least for "the steel hoop of an intimacy" (2.141).

A different emphasis, which seems to be reinforced by the understanding afforded the reader through being given access to Maggie's inner world, is given by Krook's statement that "the pity and the dread in the last lines may surely be taken to refer to . . . the confession and repentance implied in his 'I see nothing but you'" ("no longer Charlotte but only you, Maggie").[45] Maggie has certainly superseded Charlotte in Amerigo's affections (the cliché "having eyes only for her" takes on new relevance here), and his "touchstone of taste" has been largely discredited, but his espousal (literally and figuratively) of a new form of moral consciousness is surely not to be equated so simplistically with "subjugation to moral tyranny." The cynic would probably agree with Bob Assingham that in their world "life [is], for far the greater part, a matter of pecuniary arrangement" (1.67), but it seems evident that Maggie's securing Amerigo's allegiance represents more than "a rare power of purchase." Maggie and Amerigo should probably be regarded henceforth as "seeing their way together" (2.30)—as Charlotte and Amerigo had done previously.[46] Maggie could well echo the words spoken by Kate Croy to Merton Densher at the conclusion of *The Wings of the Dove:* "We shall never be again as we were"; but whereas Kate's realization is an expression of despair at their blighted prospects of happiness, the relationship between Amerigo and Maggie, undergoing a comparably drastic transformation, is suffused with hope and promise. In each case the perhaps culpably passive consort has changed his allegiance from the woman subscribing to a code of opportunism and expediency to the one representing a finer moral consciousness.

Maggie represents a new departure for the Jamesian protagonist—she does not emulate earlier disillusioned innocents like Isabel, Catherine Sloper, Milly Theale, and Fleda Vetch by opting for resignation or renunciation. Nevertheless, one of the questions besetting some readers seems to be whether Maggie's is a Pyrrhic victory, whether she sacrifices her moral integrity in "stooping to conquer" and using the weapons of the worldly; the implication in James's last completed novel seems to be, however, that the world cannot be evaded and must be fought with its own weapons. In *The Golden Bowl* compromise appears finally to be accepted as a viable alternative to the renunciation or stoical resignation espoused by more inveterately idealistic heroines such as Isabel, who feels impelled to return to her sterile marriage.[47] The reader is thus probably meant to condone Maggie's resorting to "humbugging" and other distortions of the truth that are conventionally regarded as morally reprehensible.[48] As Pearson opines, "The lie in James is sanctified by what it salvages and the disaster it postpones."[49] One could say that the purpose for which Maggie perpetrates her "humbugging" transforms it into a form of hallowed hypocrisy. To venture a variation on Blake's aphorism that "A Truth that's told with bad intent / Beats all the lies you can invent,"[50] one could say that "A Lie that's told with good intent / Beats all the Truths you can't invent." Harmonious relationships are in some cases as dependent on a "salvaging lie" as on a "saving truth" (2.255). Maggie thus attains the insight that, paradoxically, lying can in certain circumstances be seen as a creative and life-enhancing activity. As a representative of "civilized" society, Maggie would seem to illustrate the view that "Civilized society needs fiction, as well as legislation, to make its veiled intersubjective worlds intelligible."[51] This would accord with James's own observation that "there are decencies that in the name of the general self-respect we must take for granted, there's a kind of rudimentary intellectual honour to which we must, in the interest of civilization, at least pretend" (*AN* 222).

As we have seen, the reader has little direct narratorial guidance on these and other fundamental issues of interpretation. Like the prince, the reader is enjoined to "find out for [her]/himself!," and probably finds, like Charlotte on receiving the prince's telegram, that "the message had remained ambiguous; she had read it in more lights than one" (1.290), or that, as in Maggie's experience, "the intention remained . . . subject to varieties of interpretation" (2.345).[52] The reader has to rely on insights gleaned through exposure to the inner world of the characters; here the subtle deployment in the representation of consciousness of devices such as a complex imagistic mode and hypothetical discourse offer significant guidelines.

Conclusion

In the preceding chapters, I have explored the process of constituting consciousness in James and endeavored to elucidate crucial facets of the narrative techniques James deployed in the representation of fictional consciousness. In so doing, I hope to have shown that identifying the various literary modes used in the representation of consciousness can contribute clarity and precision to the discussion of central thematic and stylistic issues in James's novels. Using Cohn's typology, it has been possible to make significant discoveries concerning aspects of James's narrative strategies. This study has also moved beyond Cohn's theoretical framework, demonstrating that certain adjustments are necessary when applying this paradigm to James's novels.

We have seen that representative novels from the early, middle, and late phases illustrate the increasing tendency to refract the action of the novel through the consciousness of the central reflectors, a modulation that is reflected in the increasing predominance of the mode of narrated monologue (free indirect discourse). This movement corresponds to the shift from a more "realist" mode in *Roderick* to a symbolist mode in *The Golden Bowl*. The latter represents the culmination of the process adumbrated in the other late novels of embodying "external reality" in the consciousness of the reflectors or the figural medium. Thus, *The Golden Bowl* can be seen as representing the final working out of James's narrative positions. In his last completed novel James most fully implements his conception of the novel's primary focus—"for its subject, magnificently, it has the whole human consciousness."

In the course of this study I have also reexamined (and exposed as problematic) certain positions held by earlier theorists, such as Stanzel. In examining the distribution and deployment of inner views of James's characters, for example, it was possible to refute Stanzel's claim that interiorization necessarily creates sympathy. We saw that, just as vouchsafing an inside view of Osmond demonstrably fails to enlist sympathy for him (and indeed, is not calculated to do so), so, too, in *The Golden Bowl* inner views of characters such as Charlotte, Adam, and Amerigo tend to alienate rather than enlist the reader's sympathy.[1]

Using a more sharply defined taxonomy also makes it possible to replace potentially misleading statements such as "James allows himself to be displaced in the compositional process by Maggie"[2] with more accurate formulations conveying the recognition that the displacement of the *narrator* (rather than the *author*) by the reflector is implicit in the increasing predominance of the figural mode. This is implemented in the later novels through the displacement of the narrator-dominated psychonarration by narrated monologue, in which the reflector's voice generally enjoys ascendency, although the narrator's voice is still implicit in a qualifying capacity. In the terminology of Ian Watt, the narrator's presence is evident in his capacity as "the implied external categoriser of [the character's] action"[3] or, to adapt this observation to give it a more specifically Jamesian application, "the implied external categoriser of the reflector's inner world or consciousness."

At times commentators smudge the even more fundamental distinction between the reflector and the narrator, as in the claim that "Rowland [the reflector in *Roderick*] is a kind of narrator who causally intervenes in the events he recounts."[4] As we have seen, the reflector in the novel reflects, and reflects on, events in the novel but by definition never *narrates*. Misleading observations such as these could be obviated through a sure grasp of categories for representation of consciousness and the concomitant distinction between the narrating and the experiencing consciousness in the novel.

In my discussion of the conflicting interpretations of *The Golden Bowl,* I demonstrated that here, too, misinterpretations often stem from the failure to distinguish the voice of the narrator from that of the reflector, thus illustrating the necessity for distinguishing between psychonarration and narrated monologue. A striking example of how an inadequate understanding of modes of representation of thought and speech can lead to erroneous deductions is found in a recent claim that Maggie is in effect a closet masochist. According to commentators proceeding from a psychoanalytical approach, the following passage exposes disturbing facets of masochism in Maggie's psyche. Maggie, it is claimed, "indulges in masochistic fantasies, figuring herself as the abused woman in a mimetic triangle of desire."[5] (I shall desist from exploring the implications of "mimetic triangle of desire"; presumably it is more ephemeral than the conventional eternal triangle?)

> One of the most comfortable things between the husband and the wife meanwhile . . . was that she never admired him so much, or so found him heartbreakingly handsome, clever, irresistible, in the very degree in which he had originally and fatally dawned upon her, as when she saw other women reduced to the same passive pulp that had then begun, once for all, to constitute *her* substance. . . . even should he some day get drunk and beat her, the spectacle of him with hated rivals would, no matter after what extremity, always, for the

sovereign charm of it, charm of it in itself and as the exhibition of him that most deeply moved her, suffice to bring her round. (*GB* 138–39)

According to Stevens, "The passage implies a savage sexuality lurking beneath civilized ('comfortable') form. . . . Maggie occupies with peculiar force [these] clichés of femininity (a 'passive pulp') desirous of violence and abuse), which she opposes to, in fact sees engendered by, a hackneyed image of masculinity—violent, 'heart-breakingly handsome, clever, irresistible.' "[6]

Seen in context, however, it is clear that the above is not a fantasy conjured up in Maggie's imagination, but rather a flamboyantly hyperbolic compliment to her husband's sexual charm expressed in playful banter between Maggie and the prince. The commentator has failed to recognize that the mode of representation here is free indirect *speech* rather than free indirect *thought*. Although one acknowledges that "In the Prince, James examines the code of machismo,"[7] there seems to be a radical confusion here between "machismo" and "masochism." (Or perhaps being seduced by machismo necessarily makes one a masochist?) James's sometimes oblique or understated humor is often unappreciated by his readers, particularly if they take things literally, and here Maggie's extravagant oblique compliment to her husband's charismatic presence is certainly not meant to be taken literally—either by the prince himself or by the reader. There is a vast difference between thinking such thoughts privately, to oneself, without even an iota of irony, and bandying them about with playful irony in amatory persiflage. This is all obvious from the context. The fact that this extract reflects free indirect speech rather than thought emerges even more clearly further on where we read that Maggie "to add to the joke . . . told her father." The suspect putative desire to be subjected to physical abuse is obviously no such thing; Maggie is merely playing around, verbally, with hyperbolic possibilities as a way of conveying her intense appreciation of her husband's charms.

It is essential, then, that when determining which mode is being used in a particular passage of discourse, one should consider the extract in context. Thus, one could avoid not only wildly off-target barbs such as the above, but also misapplication of Cohn's terminology, as evinced in the following rare example of criticism making use of her model: a recent critic claims, when discussing the pagoda image in *The Golden Bowl*, that "the analogy is the narrator's and not Maggie's. . . . The figure is an example of what Dorrit Cohn calls 'psychonarration.' "[8] As I have shown in the exploration of this image in the context of the whole section in which it occurs, the image is Maggie's own, as is illustrated where it appears in narrated monologue.

Exploring modes of representation of consciousness has also led to clearer understanding of the nature of the ambiguity inherent in figural narration. Thus, we can contribute more finely nuanced discriminations to Ruth Yeazell's perception that James's use of free indirect discourse (narrated monologue)

> creates a world where the boundaries between unconscious suspicion and cer-
> tain knowledge, between pretence and reality, are continually shifting—a world
> in which the power of language to transform facts and even to create them
> seems matched only by the stubborn resistance of the facts themselves.[9]

This is instantiated with particular force in *The Golden Bowl*, where the mode of narrated monologue foregrounds not only equivocation and the evasion of unpleasant truths but also the recasting of those "truths" through a process of linguistic transmutation. So we find the prince, at Matcham, immediately prior to the consummation of his renewed liaison with Charlotte, thinking

> It had all been just in order that his—well, what on earth should he call it but
> his freedom?—should at present be as perfect and rounded and lustrous as
> some huge precious pearl. He hadn't struggled nor snatched; he was taking
> but what had been given him. (1.358)

Maggie's spouse has indeed an egregious conception of "freedom."

In the course of the novel, other concepts such as "[the] sacred," "good faith," and "decency" are distorted and invested with new meanings. A radical subversion of conventional moral concepts is illustrated in Amerigo's transformation of his renewed liaison with Charlotte into a "sacred trust." The capacity to use euphemistic terms to ensure the smooth operation of one's schemes is exemplified in Adam as well as in Amerigo and Charlotte. Maggie too discovers "the power of language to transform facts"; she learns to deploy linguistic engineering in the course of the novel and dexterously uses language as a form of camouflage—and of saving creativity—in the later scenes.

We have seen that the ambiguity inherent in figural narration is more prevalent in *The Golden Bowl* than in the earlier novels: whereas in *Roderick* one finds a reversion to the didactic mechanism of the adjudicating narratorial voice when moral issues are at play, *The Golden Bowl* is devoid of such intrusive authorial guidance. The ambiguity arising from the abdication of the narrator as "cognitive cicerone"[10] is reinforced by the absence of a reliable subsidiary commentator or "touchstone" such as Ralph Touchett in *The Portrait*.

Another significant (and concomitant) shift that has emerged here concerns the narratorial stance in James's novels. The nature and function of that metaphorical persona, the narrator, undergoes a crucial change in the course of James's oeuvre. The stance of biographer or historian objectively presenting "facts" about his characters is gradually abandoned. In the later novels, the narrator as historian is largely superseded by the more evanescent "hypothetical observer." The reader is restricted to the perspective of the characters and no longer shares the cognitive privilege of the narrator. The frequent allusions made by the narrator of *The Golden Bowl* to a hypothetical observer serve to imply that the narrator is simply a marginally more cognitively advantaged version of the reader.

Furthermore, the narratorial stance in later novels is fraught with uncertainty. Gnomic utterances, for example, are not as straightforward in *The Golden Bowl* as in the earlier novels, and are not necessarily to be taken at face value. Thus, the narratorial comment describing Maggie as "More and more magnificent now in her blameless egoism" (2.145) converts irony into ambiguity. This applies also to various other ostensibly honorific epithets such as "wonderful," which in the context of the novel are often problematic terms, as they cast an ironic light on seemingly sympathetic narratorial observations. Thus, the narrator's gnomic utterance concerning Adam, "Amiability, of a truth, is an aid to success; it has even been known to be the principle of large accumulations" (1.128), infuses the concept of "amiability" with suspect connotations implying that the quality (as embodied in Adam) is of dubious merit.[11]

At times the narrator himself seems to be participating in an ironic game of "naming of parts" or at least ostensibly experiencing the difficulties of naming:

> Deep at the heart of that roused unrest in our young man which we have had to content ourselves with calling his irritation—deep in the bosom of this falsity of position glowed the red spark of his inextinguishable sense of a higher and braver propriety. (1.334)

The latter section of this quotation is colored by what one could call "lexical contagion" or lexical ventriloquism (perhaps a more appropriate term than "stylistic contagion" in contexts such as these) as the voice is unmistakably that of the narrator, but he seems to be echoing, with parodic intent, the formulation of the character himself.

A further significant feature to emerge from this study is the recognition of discrepancies between James's theoretical perspective, as formulated in his prefaces, and his novelistic practice. This too is an aspect of James's narrative practice that does not appear to have been examined by previous commentators. (Constraints of space have limited further exploration of this issue here.) Since drafting this work, I have come across a paper by David B. McWhirter, published in a recent edition of *The Henry James Review,* in which he touches on this issue—without, however, examining it fully. McWhirter argues that while the prefaces have often been treated as "authorised" interpretations, "they are in fact notoriously problematic, and sometimes plainly inaccurate, in relation to the texts which they discuss."[12] However, McWhirter does not examine the discrepancies between James's theoretical perspective and novelistic practice that are noted, albeit cursorily, in my study. He is instead preoccupied with the gap between the prefaces as statements of aesthetic practice, and the novels they introduce, in which sociopolitical realities not present in the prefaces become significant.[13] McWhirter's emphasis thus differs from that of Cohn, which underplays the issue of the reader's cultural formation.

Another recent critical study, William R. Goetz's *Henry James and the Darkest Abyss of Romance,* notes that the prefaces "use the novelistic techniques of a first-person narrator, invented dialogue and figurative language, and thus take the form of literary narrative rather than metacriticism."[14] The implication here is: why should one expect authorially "placed" statements to be more reliable than fiction? An apt response would surely be: simply because the author classifies them as prefaces. That is, they must have a different logical status from the fiction they "precede" (logically, if not chronologically; James's prefaces are, of course, retrospectively conceived prefatorial observations). Thus, in this instance we can evade or at least merely skirt the slippery issue of the parameters of the fictional world.

In *Roderick* and *The Portrait,* I have shown that the principle of using a central reflector is not implemented with the degree of consistency that remarks in the relevant prefaces would lead one to expect. In *The Golden Bowl,* multiple focalization is used, whereas the preface creates expectations that the organizing principle would be that of dual focalization. Furthermore, the multiple focalization is only partly figural; although there are multiple figural perspectives, the authorial mode is still sporadically manifested in narratorial mediation, albeit muted.

I have noted that the change of perspective from authorial or quasi-figural to more fully figural narration is accompanied by—or implemented through—a shift from narrator's report or psychonarration to more extended and complex passages of narrated monologue. In *The Portrait,* extended passages of narrated monologue interspersed with psychonarration predominate in the evocation of Isabel's retrospective midnight vigil (chapter 42) and recur intermittently, particularly in the latter section of the novel; in *The Golden Bowl,* the entire volume 2 is dominated by excursions into Maggie's consciousness in which narrated monologue is the prevailing mode.

Indeed, analeptic excursions (in the figural as opposed to the authorial mode) constitute an increasingly major proportion of the action of the late novels. The events of the novel are refracted far more consistently through the consciousness—and specifically, through the memory—of the reflector, and "backward speculation" as a means of extracting or imposing meaning acquires new impetus.

I have thus emphasized the significant shift in the incidence and deployment of Cohn's three modes for the representation of consciousness: the tendency in the later novels is for narrated monologue rather than psychonarration to be the dominant mode. Also noteworthy is the high incidence of stylistic contagion, especially in volume 2 of *The Golden Bowl,* where it is often impossible to distinguish narrated monologue from psychonarration and determine whether the voice is that of the reflector or the narrator. (This device clearly contributes to the ambiguity in the novel).

Furthermore, conventional quoted monologue is proportionately less prevalent in the later than the earlier novels. A significant development here—which appears to have largely eluded critical comment—is the emergence of a mode of discourse not adequately catered for in the current taxonomy, a mode of discourse for which I have coined the neologism "imputed monologue." In *The Golden Bowl,* particularly, we have seen how traditional quoted monologue takes on these new permutations as it modulates toward imagined, hypothetical, or imputed discourse: discourse ostensibly formulated in the consciousness of a specific character but in effect attributed to that character by another character (the reflector) rather than by the narrator.

Subsequent to the drafting of the chapter on *The Golden Bowl,* an article investigating this device came to my attention. In the article, "Hypothetical Discourse as Ficelle in *The Golden Bowl,*"[15] Arlene Young defines hypothetical discourse as "dialogues or monologues which are presented as quoted speech on the page, though not in fact (or fiction) ever verbalised" (383). In fact—and in James's fiction—these "speeches" are by definition verbalized, if not articulated, but not by the character to whom they are attributed: they are verbalized by the figural medium or reflector.

Furthermore, the concept of "hypothetical discourse as *ficelle*" is problematic: although *ficelle* is not necessarily synonymous with confidante, it does have inescapably anthropomorphic connotations. Hypothetical or imputed discourse can more usefully be regarded as a supplementary or ancilliary mode in the representation of consciousness, or, in some instances, a variation of quoted monologue.

Arlene Young rightly queries the claim made by Carren Kaston that "imagined speech [is] an 'instrument' used by Maggie to discharge her suppressed emotions,"[16] but her reservations concern the restriction of this device to Maggie's consciousness rather than the restriction of its function to that of emotional discharge. She observes that "hypothetical discourse has an important place not only in the development of Maggie but also in the development of all the major characters in the novel"[17] but does not explore the cognitive as opposed to the emotive function of the device. As I demonstrated in chapter 6, the cognitive function of imputed monologue or hypothetical discourse is of paramount importance.

In a recent study, the term "interior dialogue" is used to designate a comparable device: "the depiction of a private thought process by means of a discussion or debate between a number of clearly distinguishable voices."[18] Drawing on examples of this procedure in *Jane Eyre,* Hawthorn illustrates his contention that "the mature adult—especially the literate and educated adult—reverts to a dialogic form of thinking when presented with problems which cannot be discussed publicly" (89). It would seem that "interior dialogue" could have similarities with the kind of hypothetical discourse in *The Golden Bowl* in which Maggie not only imputes "monologues" to other characters but also projects imaginary dialogues, for example between herself and Adam, in which suppressed feelings are communicated.

However, a major difference between the device of "interior dialogue" as illustrated by Hawthorn and that deployed in *The Golden Bowl* is that in *Jane Eyre* the contending voices represent different aspects of her own consciousness (for example, passion vs. conscience) or various voices in the community, voices whose injunctions are often at variance with personal inclinations. As Hawthorn notes,

> The educated person will possess something like a "cast" of characters or voices which have their origins outside the individual, in ordinary social intercourse, but which will have fused with inner experience and will compose a means whereby the drama of one's own inner life can be acted out. Such a person will be able to recruit *social* forces to solve *personal* problems through a simulated social discussion rendered possible by the "verbal importation" of other people. (91)

In *The Golden Bowl,* on the other hand, the "verbal importation" is not that of voices representing the interests of society—voices "created from public attitudes, ideologies, institutions" (91–92)—but that of specific individuals whose shifting relations to herself Maggie is striving to comprehend and control. Nevertheless, the cognitive force of this projected or hypothetical discourse is in each case a primary function; it provides the means whereby the characters concerned attain understanding and independent selfhood: "We learn a self by, among other things, internalizing the behaviour, the opinions, and, importantly, the language of others."[19]

I have interpreted the device of imputed monologue as embodying what W. B. Yeats calls, in "The Autumn of the Body," the "communion of mind with mind in thought and without [uttered] words." However, as is invariably the case in James's late works, it is possible to view the device from a different angle. These unspoken utterances in the minds of others, which are formulated by Maggie, can be seen not as Maggie's sympathetic, intuitive awareness of what others are thinking, but instead as a form of pernicious control. According to a recent study, Sharon Cameron's *Thinking in Henry James* (referred to in the introduction), expressing another's thoughts can be tantamount to determining his or her meanings—designating or literally dictating meaning on his or her behalf. Thus, Maggie, in learning to think for herself, learns also to think for others—in particular, for Amerigo; this facilitates the imposition of her own solution to the problem created by their entangled relationships: she can redistribute the elements and extricate Amerigo from what becomes a not-so-eternal quadrangle of marital entanglements and secure him, finally, for herself.

In this reading, the deployment of the device of imaginary discourse or imputed monologue thus becomes yet another manifestation of what Mark Seltzer has called Maggie's "imperialism of sympathy and care" or "domestic colonialism."[20] And then one has to ask to what extent Maggie's projection of the contents of Charlotte's consciousness ultimately determines or "fixes" that consciousness so that by the end of the novel Charlotte is "placed" far more subtly and securely than by mere social position or family dynamics. We recall that after her marriage to Adam, she describes herself to Fanny as being "fixed—fixed as fast as a pin stuck up to its head in a cushion. I'm placed—I can't imagine anyone *more* placed. There I *am!*" (*GB* 1.256). Charlotte sees herself as "fixed" or "placed" by the expectations of the Ververs, fulfilling the role into which they have cast her. By the end of the novel, then, is this "fixing" superseded by the more subtle psychological form of "fixing" entailed in having the contents of her consciousness conjured up not by the narrator but by her archrival, Maggie? Is Maggie demonstrating here the maleficent, rather than beneficent, power of the constituting consciousness? Maggie feels her way into Charlotte's thought "as a hand into a glove"; by insinuating herself into Charlotte's mind is she in fact hand in glove with her creator, extending an insidious form of control over the scapegoat who needs to be expelled from the coterie in order to preserve the "ghastly form" of the marriages?[21] Of course, my inference here does not necessarily represent the logical conclusion of Cameron's position. Although a compelling case might be made for such a reading, it does not square either with James's views on the "high and helpful . . . civic use of the imagination . . . a faculty for the fine employments of which in the interest of morality my esteem grows every hour I live" (*AN* 223) nor the pervasive essentially beneficent exercise of the sympathetic imagination in James. (The capacity of the imagination to participate vicariously and sympathetically in the experience of others, and the question of the creative restitution of the marriages, has been discussed in the preceding chapter.)

As we are restricted to Maggie's own consciousness in volume 2, we are not in a position to decide unequivocally whether Maggie's "reading" of the thoughts of others is indeed accurate. In effect, then, this imputed discourse can be seen as another—perhaps the most sophisticated and complex—narrative strategy reinforcing the ambiguity inherent in figural narration and most compellingly exemplified in *The Golden Bowl.*

Another crucial determinant of James's fiction to emerge from this study is the deployment of the imagistic mode in the representation of consciousness. Although it has been generally recognized that the "imagistic density" of James's oeuvre increased substantially in the late novels, the significance of the proportional distribution of the imagery—the mode in which the imagery is incorporated—does not seem to have been hitherto appreciated. I have shown that the metaphoric mode shifts progressively from narratorial comment and dialogue in *Roderick Hudson,* to being deployed more frequently in psychonarration and narrated monologue in *The Portrait,* and then predominantly in narrated monologue in *The Golden Bowl.* Thus, in the later novels the metaphoric mode is far more closely interfused with the modes for representing consciousness, and particularly that of narrated monologue.

I have furthermore attempted to establish the connection between the effacement of the intrusive adjudicating narratorial voice and the prevalence of a complex metaphorical mode. The imagistic mode in a sense "fills the gap" left by the absent (or absenting) narrator, and is an indispensable guide to the reader in interpreting the novel.

The nature and function of the complex patterns of imagery change in the course of James's oeuvre. An early work such as *Roderick* does use complex clusters of imagery, but it is only in the late novels that the significance of emblematic images (reminiscent of metaphysical conceits) that are conjured up in the figural consciousness is fully exploited. Thus a crucial emphasis in this study has been on the cognitive function of metaphors—their role in representing the world. *The Golden Bowl* most vividly illustrates this cognitive function of metaphor.

Implicit in this function is the constitutive power of the creative imagination. The way a character "images" reality is determined largely by the conceptions of the image-making faculty, the imagination. The function of the creative imagination is manifested in the way both the figural and the narrating consciousness use metaphor to define ideas and analyze situations in concrete terms. Conceiving of a situation in a visual image, rendering it as, for example, a picture, a scene, an exotic construction, or a mode of conveyance (the "family coach") frames it for more searching scrutiny than would be possible by merely balancing abstract concepts.

A comparison between James's management of the metaphoric mode in, respectively, *Roderick, The Portrait,* and *The Golden Bowl* has revealed a significant development in his method of presentation: whereas in the early novel the metaphoric mode occurs most frequently in dialogue, narratorial comment, and psychonarration, a progressive shift toward a greater imagistic density in narrated monologue has been discerned. I have demonstrated that the midnight vigil in *The Portrait,* which exemplifies the presentation of the reflector engaged in the process of "motionlessly seeing," foreshadows the more extensive use of this device in *The Golden Bowl* where it culminates in sustained explorations of the figural consciousness. Thus, the increasing "inwardness" in the presentation of consciousness entails a shift of the imagistic mode from passages of psychonarration to those (increasingly extensive) of narrated monologue.

This appropriation of the imagistic mode by the figural as opposed to the narrating consciousness reflects the increasing capacity of the central reflector to "think for herself" instead of having the cognitive process managed by the narrator on the character's behalf. As we have seen, the locus of the image indicates who is responsible for the generation or formulation of meaning. Increasingly it is the figural rather than the narrating consciousness that is empowered through being conceded control over the deployment of metaphor.

The constitutive power of consciousness or the creative imagination is manifested primarily in the capacity to "image" experience, but another important aspect of the activity of the creative imagination is its capacity to project the unvoiced discourse of an interlocutor. This ability to conjure up in the imagination "imputed monologue" or hypothetical discourse has been shown to be another significant and related aspect of cognitive activity and complements that of imagistic representation. Maggie's deployment of imagined or projected discourse marks stages in her cognitive progress as she demonstrates her increasing ability to project or enter into the feelings and experience of others. Thus, imagined discourse works in conjunction with imagistic representation in facilitating the reflector's cognitive progress.

Although Cohn's typology offers a fruitful approach to this topic,[22] some limitations have nevertheless emerged, and various critics have expressed reservations which echo those of McWhirter, mentioned earlier. For example, Paul Armstrong and Roy Pascal have drawn attention to an aspect largely ignored by Dorrit Cohn—or tacitly acknowledged as lying beyond the ambit of her study: that of the reader's response to the devices used for the representation of consciousness. In discussing style indirect libre (narrated monologue), for example, Pascal comments:

> what processes take place in the reader when he reads a passage of SIL, or a page in which it alternates with other forms? In what way, in what order, does he apprehend the double presence of character and narrator? Is it accurate to say that he momentarily slips into the skin of the character?. . . . These and other questions can only be answered by the examination of texts.[23]

One could counter this by pointing out that in Cohn's examination of selected texts, she does, in effect, implicitly address these issues without foregrounding them. However, Pascal's view is also supported by Paul Hernadi who observes that "a more profound kind of attention to the implied and actual readers of modern prose fiction would have strengthened the theoretical fiber of this circumspect study of texts."[24]

Paul Hernadi has furthermore queried Cohn's formulation "Narrative Modes for *Presenting* Consciousness in Fiction" (my emphasis), pointing out that the literary evocation of nonverbal phenomena (and consciousness includes the nonverbal "mind stuff") can only be *re*-presentation (diegesis) rather than direct presentation (mimesis). Another commentator, John Ellis, contends that Cohn's claim that "fiction alone among the major genres makes minds transparent" should be qualified: "Cohn does not discuss the obvious issues one would want discussed here—for example, how interior monologue differs in this respect from dramatic soliloquy or from certain kinds of lyric poetry" which would seem to perform a comparable function.[25] Perhaps in entitling her study "modes for presenting consciousness" as opposed to "*re*-presenting consciousness," Cohn does not fully take cognizance of the fact that narrative fiction as a genre adopts different conventions or strategies for re-presenting consciousness from those adopted with equal validity by the aforementioned genres. As John Auchard has demonstrated in his study *Silence in Henry James,*[26] even silence can, paradoxically, be effectively exploited as a means of representing the consciousness of a character. Different conventions are adopted by the different genres and the claim that any one genre has more validity or inherent "verisimulitude" should perhaps be queried. Ellis contends that Cohn "casually allows one characteristic opportunity in fiction to become the most important characteristic of fiction and even the defining characteristic of fiction."[27] Although this is a valid objection, it could certainly be claimed that as far as the (later) fiction of Henry James is concerned the presentation of consciousness is indeed a "defining characteristic."

Some critics feel that the phenomenon of narrated perception as opposed to narrated monologue has been inadequately analysed by Cohn. Brian McHale has noted that "Cohn's treatment of the border area between consciousness and perception could have profited from the consideration of two recent approaches which are, perhaps, complementary: first . . . the Genette model of focalisation" (Genette 1972), which was subsequently modified by Bal; and second, "Ann Banfield's study . . . of non-reflective consciousness."[28] However, I feel that although representation of perception, the zone where consciousness shades off into extramental description, has not been exhaustively examined by Cohn, it perhaps falls beyond the scope of her study; this does not in any event seriously impede the elucidation of James's oeuvre in the light of the insights afforded by her model.

The usefulness of Cohn's model in illuminating James's narrative strategies has, I hope, been sufficiently established. Although I would dispute Ellis's contention that Cohn's typology is "confusing and unconvincing,"[29] there is nevertheless an area in which I feel that further precision could be attained, and that commentators appear to have neglected: the concepts of dissonance and consonance, which establish modal differentiation (dissonant: authorial, narrator-dominated; consonant: figural, reflector-dominated) need further qualification or supplementation.

In *The Portrait,* for example, where a modal shift from dissonant to consonant narration was observed in the course of the novel, a different kind of consonance between narrator and reflector is apparent from the outset and persists throughout the novel. This consonance could be classified as empathetic or ethical and exists independently of the mode of narration. Similarly, although cognitive dissonance obtains between the narrator and the central reflector at the outset and is gradually dissolved in the course of the novel, this does not seem to affect the empathetic consonance. (Throughout, the narrator's attitude toward his protagonist, as he himself points out, is one of tender concern and understanding.)

A comparable phenomenon can be observed in *The Golden Bowl.* In volume 1, modal consonance obtains when Adam or Amerigo function as figural medium, but cognitive and ethical dissonance prevails in these sections as there is no identification between the perspective (in the widest sense of the term) of the narrator and that of the reflector. Volume 2 is dominated by figural narration reinforced by empathetic and ethical consonance. This is in evidence even before Maggie is enlightened as to the true state of affairs—particularly that of Charlotte and Amerigo—thus attaining greater cognitive consonance with the narrator. Because of the potential confusion or lack of clarity in differentiating between modal consonance and ethical, empathetic, and cognitive consonance, the terminology here could be more finely honed.

One could argue that the narrating consciousness by its very nature and function has a cognitive advantage over the experiencing consciousness, and that no complete cognitive consonance is possible. Ethical or empathetic consonance is less problematic, as evidenced by the apparent identity (or identification) between the ethical perspective of the narrating and the figural consciousness in volume 2 of *The Golden Bowl*. This contrasts with the subtle, oblique manner in which the narrator, using devices such as irony, dissociates himself more conclusively from the assumptions of Adam, Charlotte, and Amerigo.

* * *

We have explored throughout this study the stylistic means whereby James's "central intention . . . to stress the primacy of the receptive and transformative consciousness"[30] is implemented. I hope that this exploration of the process of constituting consciousness in Henry James will at least stimulate the reader's concurrence in Armstrong's claim that "the discoveries that James, Conrad and Ford make possible constitute a challenge to the reader to develop greater self-consciousness about the workings of consciousness in representation and interpretation."[31] Of course, no arsenal of critical terms can be completely definitive, but in view of the contribution made by Cohn's model in facilitating the clarification of hitherto unexplored aspects of James's technique in the presentation of consciousness in fiction, it is to be hoped that the insights conveyed—if not necessarily the terminology conveying them—will have an appreciable influence on future literary scholarship in this field.

James, in recounting significant experiences of his life in his autobiography, speaks of "milestones on the road of so much inward or apprehensive life."[32] In this study I have focused on milestones on the road of the inward life of representative Jamesian characters, as well as milestones in the evolution of James's own repertoire of narrative strategies for depicting such important landmarks. I hope that this study will, analogously, serve as another of the milestones (or, more modestly perhaps, stepping stones) affording further perspectives to the "passionate pilgrim" on the path of exploration of the Jamesian oeuvre. This path can at times be a rather tortuous one; James, that master of obliquity, indirection, and ambiguity, who was appalled at the idea that he as author "could do anything so foul and abject as to *state!*" could never be accused of restricting his readers to the straight and narrow (or possibly primrose?) path of predictability. One proceeds, therefore, with the recognition of the impossibility of ever erecting that definitive milestone, or one marking the end of the road. This study represents, I hope, a convenient vantage point from which to survey both the terrain already explored and that still beckoning tantalizingly ahead.

Notes

Chapter 1. Introduction

1. William Shakespeare, *Macbeth,* I. iv. 12–13.

2. Henry James, *The Art of the Novel: Critical Prefaces,* introd. Richard P. Blackmur (1907; reprint New York: Charles Scribner's Sons, 1936), 66. Hereafter referred to parenthetically as *AN.*

3. "The Lesson of Balzac," 1905, in *The House of Fiction: Essays on the Novel,* ed. and introd. Leon Edel (1957; reprint London: Mercury Books, 1962), 77.

4. *Theory of Fiction,* ed. James E. Miller, Jr. (Lincoln: University of Nebraska Press, 1972), 321.

5. "Gustave Flaubert," 1902, in *Henry James: Selected Literary Criticism,* ed. Morris Shapira (Heineman: London, 1963), 235.

6. Ibid., 235.

7. Dorrit Cohn, *Transparent Minds: Narrative Modes for Presenting Consciousness in Fiction* (Princeton: Princeton University Press, 1978).

8. Sharon Cameron, *Thinking in Henry James* (Chicago: The University of Chicago Press, 1989), 22.

9. "The Art of Fiction" (1884; reprint in *The House of Fiction,* ed. and introd. Leon Edel, 1957; reprint London: Mercury Books, 1962), 29.

10. John E. Tilford, "James the Old Intruder," *Modern Fiction Studies* 4 (Summer 1958): 175–84.

11. Frederick C. Crews, *The Tragedy of Manners* (New Haven: Yale University Press, 1957), 81.

12. Many more recent critics have commented in passing or in depth on ambiguity in James. These include Sallie Sears, in *The Negative Imagination: Form and Perspective in the Novels of Henry James* (1968); Ruth B. Yeazell, *Language and Knowledge in the Late Novels of Henry James* (1976); J. A. Ward, "The Ambiguities of Henry James," *Sewanee Review* vol. 83 (1975); C. T. Samuels, *The Ambiguity of Henry James* (1971), Allon White, *The Uses of Obscurity: The Fiction of Early Modernism* (1982); and John Carlos Rowe, *The Theoretical Dimensions of Henry James* (1985). (Publication details in bibliography). According to White, the function of ambiguity has been imperfectly grasped; for example, the "New Critical" cherishing of ambiguity "failed to analyse the function of obscurity as a structure of meaning rather than a subtle multiplier of sense" (*The Uses of Obscurity: The Fiction of Early Modernism,* 18). Rowe notes that "James's ambiguity is not just that of the "literary symbol"; it is a more profound ambiguity that inheres in language" (65). Although these and other contemporary critics offer valuable insights into the nature of ambiguity as exploited by James, they do not explore the link between ambiguity and figural narration.

13. Studies on imagery in James's novels include, inter alia, Miriam Allott,

245

Symbol and Image in the Later Work of Henry James (1953); Holder-Barell, *The Development of Imagery and its Functional Significance in Henry James's Novels* (1959); Robert Gale, *The Caught Image: Figurative Language in the Fiction of Henry James* (London: Oxford University Press, 1964); and Austin Warren, "Henry James: Symbolic Imagery in the Later Novels" in *Rage for Order: Essays in Criticism* (1948). Matthiessen, in "The Painter's Brush and Varnish Bottle," the appendix to *Henry James: The Major Phase* (1944; reprint New York: Oxford University Press, 1970), has commented on "the growth from ideas to images" (158) resulting from James's revisions, and has noted that "one of his most recurrent types of revision [is] endowing his *dramatis personae* with characterizing images" (159). These works on imagery tend to be early studies grounded in a phenomenological approach; more recent criticism has developed different emphases.

14. Reprint in Vol. 1 of the *Complete Tales of Henry James,* ed. and introd. Leon Edel (London: Rupert Hart-Davis, 1963), 18.

15. Cohn, *Transparent Minds,* 7–8.

16. Jessie Chambers, in her memoir of D. H. Lawrence, published as E. T., *D. H. Lawrence: A Personal Record* (1935), 105. Quoted in David Gervais, *Flaubert and Henry James: A Study in Contrasts* (London: Macmillan, 1978), 45.

17. *The Inward Turn of the Novel* (Princeton: Princeton University Press, 1973) is the title of a study by Eric Kahler.

18. Henry Fielding, *The History of Tom Jones,* eds. Martin C. Battestin and Fredson Bowers (Oxford: Clarendon, 1983), 609.

19. Dorrit Cohn, *Transparent Minds,* 7.

20. Robert Scholes and Robert Kellogg, *The Nature of Narrative* (New York: Oxford University Press, 1966), 165. My discussion of this topic is based largely on this study.

21. Ibid., 171.

22. "Theaetetus," 189, E; "Sophist," 263, E. Cited by ibid., 180.

23. Ibid., 180. Cohn points out that this erroneous assumption is also manifested in studies that apply the model of the techniques for quoting spoken discourse to the techniques for presenting consciousness. She cites the example of Genette, who, in his *"Discours du Recit,"* "pairs spoken and silent discourse according to degrees of 'narrative distance,' arriving at a threefold division between the poles of pure narration (diegesis) and pure imitation (mimesis)." *Figures III* (Paris, 1972, 191–93; cited by Cohn, 10.

24. Cohn, *Transparent Minds,* 11.

25. Malcolm McKenzie, "On the Presentation of Speech and Thought in Narrative Fiction," *Theoria* (1986–87): 37.

26. Scholes and Kellogg, *Nature of Narrative,* 198.

27. Paul de Man has recently produced a substantially new translation.

28. "Gustave Flaubert," 1902, 235.

29. Scholes and Kellogg, *Nature of Narrative,* 268.

30. *Henry James: Selected Literary Criticism,* ed. Morris Shapira (London: Heinemann, 1964), 138.

31. "The Lesson of Balzac" (1905), in *The House of Fiction,* 70.

32. Stephen Ullman, *Style in the French Novel* (Oxford: Blackwell, 1964), 119.

33. Ibid.

34. Ibid., 120.

35. Letter to Georges Sand, 15–16 December 1866; *Correspondence 5* (Paris, 1929), 257; in Cohn, 113–14; Cohn's emphasis.

36. Cohn, *Transparent Minds*, 114.

37. Ullman, *Style in the French Novel*, 118.

38. Ibid., 101.

39. Ibid., 106.

40. Ibid., 118.

41. "Gustave Flaubert," 1902, 238.

42. *Middlemarch* (1871–72; reprint London: Oxford University Press, 1950), 225.

43. See Scholes and Kellogg for further discussion of this point.

44. "Gustave Flaubert," 1902, 222.

45. Ibid., 232.

46. Ibid., 222.

47. Ibid., 231.

48. Cohn, *Transparent Minds*, 136.

49. Dominick LaCapra, *"Madame Bovary" on Trial* (Ithaca: Cornell University Press, 1982) 145.

50. Pascal, *The Dual Voice*, 104.

51. *Madame Bovary* (Paris: Flammarion, 1986) 3, 6, 357; my translation.

52. LaCapra, *Madame Bovary*, 143.

53. Philip Grover, *Henry James and the French Novel: A Study in Inspiration* (London: Paul Elek, 1973), 91.

54. "Gustave Flaubert," 1893, 153.

55. "A Propos du 'style' de Flaubert," *Nouvelle Revue Francaise* 14, no. 1 (1920): 72–90, cited by Ullman, 94 (my translation).

56. *The Novel in France* (Harmondsworth: Penguin, 1962), 291.

57. Cited in Turnell, 279.

58. *The Novel in France*, 279.

59. LaCapra, "Madame Bovary," 120.

60. Paul Armstrong, *The Challenge of Bewilderment: Understanding and Representation in James, Conrad and Ford* (Ithaca: Cornell University Press, 1987), 19.

61. Dorothea Krook, *The Ordeal of Consciousness in Henry James* (Cambridge: Cambridge University Press, 1962).

62. *The Challenge of Bewilderment: Understanding and Representation in James, Conrad and Ford* (Ithaca: Cornell University Press, 1987), 2.

63. William Blake, letter to Dr Trusler, *The Complete Writings of William Blake* (London: Oxford University Press, 1966), 79.

64. *Natural History*, trans. H. Rackham, XI, 146. Quoted by E. H. Gombrich, *Art and Illusion: A Study in the Psychology of Pictorial Representation* (1959; reprint London: Phaidon Press, 1962), 12.

65. F. O. Matthiessen, *Henry James: The Major Phase* (1944; reprint New York: Oxford University Press, 1970), 31–32.

66. Gombrich, *Art and Illusion: a Study in the Psychology of Pictorial Representation* (London: Phaidon Press, 1959; reprint 1962), 86.

67. Ibid., 89.

68. Other functions of metaphor that could be profitably explored in James's work but that fall beyond the scope of this study would include (apart from the general thematic function of heightening the significance of a passage and emphasizing a structurally important action, situation, or gesture): the use of imagery for characterization, for foreshadowing future events (proleptic imagery), and rendering concrete what is abstract. Some of these functions are implicit in

the present focus: the way a character attains understanding through imagery would include rendering concrete what is abstract, and imagery used to evoke the way in which people conceive of each other would encompass the role of imagery in characterization.

69. Peter Garrett, *Scene and Symbol from George Eliot to James Joyce: Studies in Changing Fictional Mode* (New Haven: Yale University Press, 1969), 107.

70. Dorrit Cohn, "The Encirclement of Narrative: On Franz Stanzel's' *Theorie des Erzahlens*," *Poetics Today* 2, 3–4 (1981): 157.

71. Indeed, James, as critic no less than as novelist, made a significant contribution to the development of narrative poetics in the first decade of this century. Not only was the problem of point of view largely ignored in literary criticism before the advent of James, but he also formulated or brought to the fore terms such as scene and summary, drama and picture, foreshortening, center of consciousness, reflector, and *ficelle*. These are still central concepts in contemporary narrative theory but only those such as focalization that have a direct bearing on this study will be further explored here.

72. John E. Tilford, "James the Old Intruder," *Modern Fiction Studies* 4 (Summer 1958): 175–64.

73. *The Dual Voice: Free Indirect Speech and its Functioning in the Nineteenth-Century European Novel* (Manchester: Manchester University Press, 1977), 99.

74. Preeminent among these theorists would be, for example, Stanzel and Genette, who contributed the notions of figural and authorial novel, and focalization, respectively.

75. Franz K. Stanzel, *Narrative Situations in the Novel,* trans. James P. Pusack (Bloomington: Indiana University Press, 1971), 99.

76. For further discussion see inter alia Norman Friedman, "Point of View in Fiction," *PMLA*, 70 (1955); reprint in Philip Sevick, ed., *The Theory of the Novel* (New York: The Free Press, 1967), 113; and Wiesenfarth, *Henry James and the Dramatic Analogy*. According to Wiesenfarth,

> The peculiar problem that James faced in dramatizing the novel was to create in a form controlled by a narrator and committed to action in the past—even if 'the only interval between its occurring and the reader hearing about it is that occupied by the narrator's voice telling it'—the qualities of intensity, objectivity and economy peculiar to a dramatic form uncontrolled by a narrator and committed to action and dialogue in the present. (*Henry James and the Dramatic Analogy,* 14)

Wiesenfarth, discussing in the early sixties the techniques used by James to create the sense of dramatic present, does not take into account what is probably the most important factor in the technique used to create this sense of immediacy—the use of free indirect style/discourse. Wiesenfarth's observation is a good example of the limitations of certain earlier commentators and illustrates the need for undertaking further exploration of this field—equipped with more finely honed critical categories.

77. Stanzel first drew attention to this phenomenon in *Narrative Situations,* 258.

78. Stanzel, *A Theory of Narrative,* trans. Charlotte Goedsche (Cambridge: Cambridge University Press, 1984), 128–29.

79. Ibid., 178.

80. Stanzel distinguishes between the internal perspective of figural narration, where the reflector-character is within the fictional world, and the external per-

spective of authorial narration, where the story is told by an omniscient narrator who is not part of the fictional world. His concept of "perspective" was replaced by Genette and other theorists by the term "focalization." Genette's terminology differs somewhat from Stanzel's in that he speaks of nonfocalized narrative (narrative with zero focalization), narrative with external focalization, and narrative with internal focalization. Nonfocalized narrative has an omniscient author, that with external focalization has a "hero [who] performs in front of us without our ever being allowed to know his thoughts or feelings" (for example, Hemingway's "The Killers"), and narrative with internal focalization is written from the point of view of a character in the novel. According to Genette, there are three types of narrative with internal focalization: fixed, as in *The Ambassadors,* where everything is filtered through the consciousness of the central character, Strether; variable, as in *Madame Bovary,* where first Charles, then Emma, then Charles again, act as focalizer; and multiple, as in epistolary novels, where the same event may be related many times according to the point of view of various letter-writing characters (189–90).

81. Although Genette's distinctions between fixed, variable, and multiple focalization contribute a greater measure of precision in discussion of narrative perspective, a certain ambiguity or lack of clarity still needs to be dispelled. The concept of "fixed" focalization, for instance, is applied to novels as diverse as *What Maisie Knew* and *The Ambassadors.* Although focalization in the two novels is "fixed" in the sense that the protagonist in each case is theoretically the sole focalizer (in practice, the primary focalizer), the two differ profoundly in that in *What Maisie Knew* an initial cognitive dissonance between narrator and protagonist is gradually superseded by consonance: disparity between the immature and ignorant Maisie and the knowing narrator decreases in the course of the novel. To obviate confusion and increase precision here, perhaps the term "fixed" focalization should be replaced by something like "single" or "unitary" focalization. If, however, we retain Stanzel's term "figural," within unitary focalization the mode could be either "fixed," as in *The Ambassadors,* or fluid and sliding, as in *Maisie.* Furthermore, the term "multiple" could surely serve for both novels with several focalizers, like *Madame Bovary* and *The Wings of the Dove* ("variable" focalization), as well as for "epistolary novels where the same event may be related many times according to the point of view of various letter-writing characters." Since the determining factor is the focalizer rather than the focalized object or event, it is the number of characters reflecting or reflecting on a specific event or events that is important, not whether they reflect on the same event or several. To preclude all ambiguity, it might be preferable to adopt Cohn's term "multi-figural" for these novels.

82. Genette's "non-focalized narrative," with omniscient narration, would be the mode dominated by Stanzel's "teller-character" who narrates, records, informs, quotes witnesses and sources, refers to his own narration, addresses the reader, comments on the story, anticipates the outcome of an action, or recapitulates what happened before the story opens (*Theory of Narrative,* 144). The potential ambiguity or lack of clarity here in Stanzel's classification as "teller-characters," narrators who are as diverse as the teller of *Tom Jones* and *Vanity Fair* on the one hand, and *David Copperfield* and *Moll Flanders* on the other, is dispelled when he later qualifies his initial taxonomy by employing the term "authorial teller," rather than "teller-character," for the first group. It is unfortunate that he tends to revert to "teller-character" in subsequent discussion. Cohn points out that Genette has also found it necessary to review Stanzel's terminology here,

"for where Stanzel views a relative difference (and thus a sliding scale) between the "I" of a David Copperfield and the "I" of a Fielding, Genette establishes an absolute barrier between "two very different situations which grammar renders identical." ("The Encirclement of Narrative," 165)

Cohn welcomes Stanzel's introduction of "a new conceptual creature, the reflector, at the mimetic pole of his typological circle" (171). This is regarded as

> a salutary move, if only because it should put a stop once and for all to the sloppy habit of calling the protagonists of figural novels (Stephen of *The Portrait* . . . or Strether) the "narrators" of their stories. For the Jamesian term reflector, as his name indicates far more precisely than James' more popular term "centre of consciousness" or even Stanzel's rather ghostly term "figural medium," is a fictional character who reflects (registers) and reflects (mediates) [*sic*; meditates?] *on* the fictional events, but who (by definition) "never 'narrates'." (171)

In contrast to Stanzel's teller-character, a reflector-character such as Strether, Stephen Dedalus, or Emma Bovary never narrates in the sense of verbalizing his or her perceptions, thoughts, and feelings, since he or she does not attempt to communicate these to the reader. This produces the illusion in the reader that [s]he obtains an unmediated and direct view of the fictional world, seeing it with the eyes of the reflector-character. Thus, the main function of a reflector-character such as Strether is to reflect, that is, to register or mirror in his consciousness what is happening in the world outside or inside himself, and to reflect on the fictional events. Stanzel also stresses the point that while the concepts "reflector-character" and "teller-character" can refer to the first as well as to the third person, the concept "figural narrative situation" is applicable only to the third-person form (145).

83. Geoffrey N. Leech and Michael H. Short, *Style in Fiction: A Linguistic Introduction to English Fictional Prose* (London: Longmans, 1981), 350.

84. LaCapra, *Madame Bovary on Trial,* 126.

85. Turnell, *The Novel in France,* 272.

86. Grover, *Henry James and the French Novel,* 76.

87. Observations made on this subject are also sometimes contradictory; for instance, Grover avers that "Of first importance in a comparison of Flaubert's and Henry James's techniques is the way Flaubert intermingles his description with the states of mind of his characters" (75), and subsequently contends that "James carried the intermingling of character and place to much greater lengths than did Flaubert . . . in *The Wings of the Dove*" (82).

88. Philip Grover, *Henry James and the French Novel,* 88.

CHAPTER 2. THE REPRESENTATION OF CONSCIOUSNESS IN FICTION: DORRIT COHN'S MODEL

1. For example, Stanzel and Genette. Other influential studies both preceding and following the publication of Cohn's work include those of Roy Pascal (1962, and particularly *The Dual Voice: Free Indirect Speech and its Functioning in the Nineteenth Century European Novel* (1977), Ann Banfield (1973, 1978, 1981), Bronzwaer (1970), Hernadi (1971, 1972), McHale (1978), and Norman Page (1972, 1973). See Shlomith Rimmon-Kenan, in *Narrative Fiction: Contemporary Poetics* (London: Methuen, 1983), 110. Norman Page's *Speech in the English Novel* (1988)

predictably concentrates on the presentation of speech rather than thought, although some aspects of what he establishes with reference to speech representation could apply to the presentation of thought. Characters are individualized substantially through their speech, with individual modes of expression; in examining the novels of James one could consider whether comparably significant differences or idiosyncrasies in ideolect or mind-set can be discerned. Studies produced by Chatman (*Story and Discourse: Narrative Structure in Fiction and Film* (1978) and Leech and Short (*Style in Fiction: A Linguistic Introduction to English Fictional Prose,* 1981) also offer detailed exposition of speech and thought presentation.

2. The second half of *Transparent Minds* deals with first-person narration; as the texts selected for discussion here are all novels written in the third person, no space has been allotted to an elucidation of this section.

3. Cohn points out that the study of techniques for rendering consciousness has thus far concentrated virtually exclusively on third-person narrative texts, to the exclusion of first-person texts. This is a serious omission, as "retrospection into a consciousness . . . is no less important a component of first-person novels than inspection of a consciousness is in third-person novels" (14). As the same basic types of presentation are involved, the same terms can be used, "modified by prefixes to signal the modified relationship of the narrator to the subject of his narration." Thus psychonarration in a first-person text will be "self-narration," and monologues in that context can be either "self-quoted" or "self-narrated." (Cohn justifies the retention of the terms first-person and third-person as opposed to Genette's corresponding terms "homodiegetic" and "heterodiegetic" on the grounds that the unfamiliarity of these terms does not compensate for the small gain in precision.)

The bipartite division of Cohn's study into third- and first-person narrative forms stems from the recognition of profound differences between the two forms, differences that she states have been underestimated by recent structuralist studies. Genette, for example, does not take sufficient cognizance of differences of person (voice) in his account of focalization (point of view) (273). An important aspect of this difference involves the altered relationship between the narrator and his protagonist when that protagonist is his own past self. The narration of inner events is much more strongly affected by this change of person than the narration of outer events, as past thought must now be presented as remembered by the self, not only as expressed by the self (15).

4. Thackeray, *Vanity Fair* (1848; reprint London: Blackie, n.d.), 34.

5. This could be illustrated through examining a recurrent motif in novels by Dickens and James: that of the lone female figure engaged in a meditative fireside vigil. In *Hard Times,* Louisa Bounderby's fireside vigils dramatize her sense of isolation and futility, but little access is given to her private thoughts: her disillusionment and cynicism are revealed in narratorial comment or in direct dialogue with her mother. In *The Portrait,* by contrast, direct and sustained access to Isabel's consciousness is rendered in a comparable scene (chapter 42).

6. See discussion of Flaubert and James in the previous chapter for amplification—and qualification—of this point.

7. These terms (authorial/figural, dissonant/consonant) correspond to a whole series of polarities designated by recent critics: vision *par derrière*—vision *avec* (Pouillon, Todorov), telling—showing (Booth), nonfocalized—focalized (Genette).

8. Cohn notes that this retrospective evocation is in fact "a narrated fantasy

within a narrated memory," and points out that such "Chinese-box effects" occur frequently in James's narrated monologues (130).

9. Leech and Short, *Style in Fiction*, 340.

10. Chatman, *Story and Discourse: Narrative Structure in Fiction and Film* (Ithaca: Cornell University Press, 1978), 206.

11. Malcolm McKenzie, "On the Presentation of Speech and Thought in Narrative Fiction," *Theoria* (1986–87): 44.

12. Rimmon-Kenan, *The Concept of Ambiguity: The Example of James* (1977); Samuels, *The Ambiguity of Henry James* (1971); Edmund Wilson, "The Ambiguity of Henry James," in *The Triple Thinkers* (1952; reprint Harmondsworth: Penguin, 1962). See chapter 1 for discussion on ambiguity.

13. *Pride and Prejudice* (1813: reprint London: Oxford University Press), 200–203.

14. Ortega y Gasset, *The Dehumanization of Art,* 33; cited by Cohn, *Transparent Minds,* 9.

15. "Henry James," in *The Question of Henry James: A Collection of Critical Essays,* ed. F. W. Dupee (New York: Holt and Co, 1973), 258.

16. "The Artist," in *A Backward Glance,* 1934; reprint in *Critics on Henry James,* ed. J. Don Vann (Florida: University of Miami Press, 1972), 52.

17. "Greville Fane," in *The Complete Tales of Henry James* (1891–1892), ed. Leon Edel (London: Rupert Hart-Davis, 1963), 8, 434.

18. This is explored more fully by Viola Hopkins in "Visual Art Devices and Parallels in James," in *Henry James: Modern Judgements* ed. Tony Tanner, 96–98 (London: Macmillan, 1968).

19. In *Watch and Ward,* for instance, Roger dreams of Nora while ill, and in *Roderick Hudson,* one could cite Rowland's dreams about Mary Garland and his vision of Roderick's "fall":

> His idea persisted; it clung to him like a sturdy beggar. The sense of the matter, roughly expressed, was this. If Roderick was really going, as he himself had phrased it, to 'fizzle out', one might help him on the way—one might smooth the *descensus Averni.* For forty-eight hours there swam before Rowland's eyes a vision of Roderick, graceful and beautiful as he passed, plunging like a diver into a misty gulf. The gulf was destruction, annihilation, death. (251)

20. *The Modern Psychological Novel* (New York, 1955), 55. Cited by Cohn, *Transparent Minds,* 56.

21. See Scholes and Kellogg, *The Nature of Narrative,* on the use of monologue in earlier fictional forms: epic and romance (177–90; 284–89).

22. Stanzel, *Narrative Situations in the Novel,* 100.

23. This is foregrounded in Roy Pascal's concept of a "dual voice," which highlights the bifocality of this mode. Cohn emphasizes a "two-in-one" effect rather than duality.

24. See note 1 of this chapter for discussion of important critical contributions to this topic. The emphasis of some theorists, such as Ann Banfield, is more strictly linguistic than literary. (There is, of course, no clear-cut distinction between the two; they represent differently weighted approaches to texts). An innovation suggested by the latter is the introduction of the term "subject-of-consciousness" to replace point of view or center of consciousness, "because, in spite of its awkwardness, it is a +human noun, while neither of the other two terms have this feature" ("Narrative Style and the Grammar of Direct and Indirect Speech," *Foundations of Language* 10 (1973): 30). However, I feel that the use-

fulness of this emendation could be disputed, as the term "subject-of-consciousness" could lead to increased ambiguity if "subject" is taken with its grammatical rather than its psychological connotations. More usefully, Banfield draws attention to features such as the fact that "in free indirect style third-person pronouns that refer to the subject-of-consciousness will behave like first-person pronouns" (32). She also comments on "the unusually frequent use of pronouns in the free indirect style," pointing out that as this style does not represent communication, it is natural that "the subject-of-consciousness should not always identify the referents of his pronouns by name or description, since he knows these facts" (32–33).

25. Pascal, *The Dual Voice*, 8, 11.

26. Ibid., 17.

27. Ibid., 1.

28. Pascal acknowledges Dorrit Cohn's amended typology but furnishes reasons for his preference for the term "free indirect speech" as opposed to "narrated monologue," while indicating that "the term 'speech' in these contexts refers not to actual spoken language, but to a mode of discourse" (32). For Pascal, then, "free indirect speech" seems to include free indirect thought; hence the term "free indirect discourse" would surely obviate ambiguity here.

29. Leech and Short, *Style in Fiction*.

30. In 1955, in his *Narrative Situations in the Novel*, Stanzel discussed *erlebte Rede* as a characteristic feature of the figural novel. Todorov and Genette, inter alia, have related it to their central categories of mode, aspect and voice, but have not as yet explored it fully. Genette, in *Figures III* (1972), accorded only a single paragraph to style indirect libre, which he regarded as a "variant" of indirect discourse (291). Cohn notes that "in view of the importance both these critics give to the relationship between narration and discourse, it is surprising that they never studied the technique where the borderline between these two language fields becomes effaced" (291).

31. As Leech and Short observe, free indirect speech, as opposed to free indirect thought, was used fairly extensively by Fielding (332).

32. Chatman points out that other terms suggested for narrated monologue are, inter alia, "substitutionary speech," "independent form of indirect discourse," "represented speech," "narrative mimicry," and "monologue interior indirect" (*Story and Discourse*, 203). Cohn, however, advances persuasive arguments to justify the adoption of the term "narrated monologue." In approving of the term, Chatman notes that "narrated" accounts for the indirect features—third person and prior tense—while "monologue" conveys the sense of hearing the very words of the character (203).

33. Leech and Short, *Style in Fiction*, 344.

34. R. J. Lethcoe, "Narrated Speech and Consciousness," 205. Quoted by Cohn, 134. Chatman also distinguishes between free indirect thought and free indirect perception or "substitutionary perception"—a phrase used by Bernard Fehr, in "Substitutionary Narration and Description: A Chapter in Stylistics," *Von Englands geistigen Bestanden* (Frauenfeld, 1944), 264–78. (*Story and Discourse*, 204.)

35. Cohn sets out these points in tabular form: the diagrammatic presentation of the relationship between these techniques and levels of consciousness illustrates the point that "The more direct the technique, the more evidently verbal the activity of the mind, and therefore the more clearly conscious the mind that is exposed" (139). See below.

Diagram 1.

Ucs ——————————————————————————————— Cs
       psycho-   narrated   quoted
      narration   monologue   monologue

Diagram 2.

	Ucs	Cs
psychonarration		————————————
narrated monologue		————————————
quoted monologue		————————————

CHAPTER 3. QUASI-FIGURAL NARRATION: *RODERICK HUDSON*

1. Hereafter referred to as *Roderick,* in keeping with James's own practice in his prefaces. Page references are to the Penguin Classics edition, 1986, which is a reprint of the 1878 text (James's revision of the origin serial version published in the *Atlantic Monthly* (January to December 1875). As the novel was revised extensively for the New York Edition, the original text of James's "first" novel was selected in this instance. Comparisons between the two versions are mentioned when relevant.

2. A term given currency by Ora Segal's critical work, *The Lucid Reflector* (New Haven: Yale University Press, 1969). In his preface to *The Wings of the Dove,* James refers to "a supplementary reflector, that of the lucid . . . spirit" (*AN* 305).

3. Stanzel cites James's Strether in *The Ambassadors* as being one of the earliest representatives of figural narration; he fails to take cognizance of the earlier *Roderick.*

4. *The Craft of Fiction* (1921; reprint London: Jonathan Cape, 1932), 199.

5. Space constraints make it impossible to comment in detail on significant emendations in the New York Edition. Some of these will be indicated in the endnotes to this chapter. The general tendency toward a greater infusion of imagery in the later works can be seen in this example.

6. This comment is omitted from the New York Edition, and in the following sentence psychonarration shifts into narrated monologue in the revised version: the original "It often seemed to Rowland that he had too decidedly forfeited his freedom, and that there was something grotesque in a man of his age being put into a corner" becomes "It often struck him that he had too abjectly forfeited his freedom. Wasn't it grotesque, at his age, to be put into a corner for punishment?" (NYE 447). In this version Rowland evinces a greater degree of self-excoriation which is foregrounded by the substitution of "abjectly" for "decidedly" and the addition of "for punishment" after "into a corner" to stress not only entrapment but punition of the kind customarily inflicted on transgressing juveniles.

7. This reading seems to be supported by the revision in the New York Edition where "cried Rowland to himself" is replaced with "her companion admirably mused"—"admirably" suggesting that Rowland is taking no credit for her transformation. The rest of this passage also undergoes extensive revision in the later edition. Whereas in the original the quoted monologue is followed by "When he said to Mary Garland that he wished he might see her ten years hence, he was paying mentally an equal compliment to circumstance and to the girl herself," in the amended version we have, with narrated monologue replacing the narratorial report: "She would develop, evidently, right and left, and to the top of her capacity; and he would have been at the bottom of it all. But that was where he would remain, essentially and obscurely; all taken for granted, merely for granted, as a good cellar, with its dusky supporting vaults, is taken for granted in a sound house" (NYE 344).

In the original, only "circumstance" and "the girl herself" are credited with responsibility for the transformation; in the revised text, with the introduction of narrated monologue, Rowland's awareness of his own unacknowledged contribution is recorded with a hint of petulant resentment. The repetition in "all taken for granted, merely taken for granted," with the tinge of bitter incredulity in "merely," heightens this effect. Once again the introduction of a more imagistic mode makes the presentation of Rowland's consciousness more vividly dramatic.

8. The theater imagery in the above extract forms part of a network of such images contributing to the presentation of some of the central issues of the novel. Related images recur frequently in psychonarration and narrated monologue, less frequently in direct speech. In describing Christina, Rowland declares to Madame Grandoni that "the girl is so deucedly dramatic . . . that I don't know what *coup de théâtre* she may have in store for us" (285), and in a letter to Cecilia: "She is an actress, she couldn't forego doing the thing dramatically, and it was the dramatic touch that made it fatal. . . . she desired to have the curtain drop on an attitude." (239). His first impression of Christina—"Rowland received an impression that for reasons of her own she was playing a part" (147)—takes on darker resonances when Rowland realizes that she has been coerced into marrying Prince Casamassima: "The dark little drama of which he had caught a glimpse had played itself out" (317). Theater imagery also dramatizes Rowland's insight into his friend's character in the revised New York Edition, presented here in narrated monologue: "Of his never thinking of others save as they figured in his own drama ["game" in the original version] this extraordinary insensibility to the injurious effects of his eloquence was a capital example" (NYE 429). Rowland views himself essentially as stage manager rather than hero of the play, with the vivid presences of Roderick and Christina as those of the center stage (ironically, both are subject to powerful influences behind the scenes).

9. The tendency toward a greater infusion of imagery in the later works is again exemplified in the revised version of this extract in the New York Edition; "to live in Rome" becomes "to live in the lap of the incomparable sorceress," and the following sentence becomes the more tortuously complex "but he sometimes wondered whether this were not a questionable gain in case of one's not being prepared to ask no more of consciousness than they [presumably the senses and the imagination] could give" (NYE 172). Perhaps the amended version prepares the way more effectively for the introduction of (or assertion of) the claims of "his conscience" (complementing the senses and the imagination as components of consciousness) further on. The alteration of "His customary tolerance of circumstances" to "His growing submission to the mere insidious actual" seems

more clearly to capture the specific nature of Rowland's "temptation," especially in view of the implicit departure from his initial stance of one who was incapable of response to "the simple, sensuous, confident relish of pleasure." The personification of Rome in the New York Edition is extended when the abstract formulation "the mere insidious actual" is followed by "which resembled somehow the presence of an extravagant, flattering visitor, questionably sincere" (NYE 172); this adds a new dimension to the quality of Rowland's captivation—it is presented as a form of seduction, of being led away from the straight and narrow and along a morally suspect primrose path.

10. In the New York Edition the terms "conscience" and "heart" are further elaborated by the addition of "that indispensable aid to completeness, a feeling heart" (NYE 220), which links with the discussion of the notion of "completeness" in both editions. Rowland says of himself at the beginning of the novel, "I sometimes think that I am a man of genius, half finished. The genius has been left out, the faculty of expression is wanting; but the need for expression remains" (53). In identifying and encouraging the development of Roderick's genius, Rowland in a sense attains a feeling of "completeness." Singleton comments on Roderick's "beautiful completeness" as an artist—"Complete, that's what he is" (171). Roderick himself responds to Christina's jibe that he is "weak" by claiming that "I am not weak. I am incomplete perhaps" (214)—presumably as a man rather than as an artist. In a later letter to Cecilia, Rowland confirms this diagnosis: "The poor fellow is incomplete" (237), associating this incompleteness with a lack of moral sense.

11. In the revised New York Edition the less abstract reformulation of the last sentence serves to highlight the paradox in Cecilia's observation and restrict the range of possible interpretations in the narrator's comment to one specific meaning: "His cousin Cecilia had once told him that he was too credulous to have a right to be kind. She put the case with too little favour, or too much, as the reader chooses; it is certain at least that he gave others, as a general thing, the benefit of any doubt, reserving for himself the detriment"(NYE 226–27).

12. The introduction of a more densely imagistic mode of expression in the New York Edition also vividly dramatizes the gap in understanding between them. In the original we have:

> "You are the best man in the world," he said, "and I am a vile brute. Only," he added in a moment, "*you don't understand me!*" And he looked at him with eyes of such pure expressiveness that one might have said (and Rowland did almost say to himself) that it was the fault of one's own grossness if one failed to read to the bottom of that beautiful soul.
> Rowland smiled sadly. "What is it now? Explain." (191)

In the revised version, a variation on the recurrent sea imagery—but reminiscent now of comparably complex images in *The Golden Bowl*—is introduced; in contrast to the narrative technique in the later novel, however, the image here is presented in the narrator's voice rather than being refracted through the consciousness of the figural mind. (In *The Golden Bowl* these imagistic representations are more prevalent in narrated monologue, as emanations of the experiencing rather than the narrating consciousness).

> And he looked at him out of such bottomless depths as might have formed the element of a shining merman who should be trying, comparatively near shore, to signal to a ruminating ox.

Rowland's own face was now a confession of his probably being indeed too heavy to float in such waters. (NYE 223)

Here the last sentence again seems to represent the narrator's interpretation of Rowland's expression rather than Rowland's own awareness.

13. Some significant emendations in the New York Edition of *Roderick* give greater precision to some of the effects created in this extract. The possible ambiguity in "It was a flirtation without the benefits of a flirtation" is dispelled by the addition of "for Roderick." Similarly, greater precision is attained by the addition of the word "right" after "She did everything but advise him" (NYE 48). (Ironically, Roderick, as Rowland is yet to discover, has no penchant for being advised "right"; Rowland's later declaration that he is to "preach [restraint] to my protégé . . . by example as well as by precept" (81) is doomed to dramatic failure.) The impression of naiveté in Rowland's view that "She was too old to let him fall in love with her" becomes one of arrogance or well-meaning prissiness in setting himself up as a moral arbiter in determining that "She was too old to make it quite exemplary she should let him [Roderick] fall in love with her." The change from "her inclination was to keep him young" to "it was her perversity to keep him notoriously fresh" is also indicative of a more condemnatory attitude on Rowland's part towards Cecilia (as this is narrated monologue rather than narrator's comment). The narrator's stance toward his protagonist becomes proportionately more critical, as is indicated in the change from "So Rowland reflected" to "So at least Rowland reflected" (NYE 48), indicating a greater measure of ironic detachment on the narrator's part.

14. The New York Edition presents Rowland in a more critical light: "By the wiser," he *sententiously* added" (NYE 140), emphasizing the difference between the two on all essential moral issues. At a later stage Rowland is obliged to re-examine all these assumptions: "Do what he would, Rowland could not think of Roderick's theory of unlimited experimentation, especially as applied in the case under discussion, as anything but a pernicious illusion" (192).

15. In the New York Edition the last sentence is replaced with a narratorial generalization—"It is of the very nature of such impressions, however, to show a total never represented by the mere sum of their constituent parts" (NYE 313)— that appeals to accepted wisdom for authentication rather than relying on the authority of illustrious literary precedents to elicit the reader's concurrence. An element of the metafictional seems to be lurking here: a blurring of boundaries between statements in the empirical author's preface on the one hand and the narrator's fictive world on the other. (This phenomenon was discussed in Chapter 1.)

16. Sheila Teahan, *The Rhetorical Logic of Henry James* (Baton Rouge: Louisiana State University Press, 1995), 78–79.

17. Philip Sicker, *Love and the Quest for Identity in the Fiction of Henry James* (Princeton: Princeton University Press, 1980), 45.

18. In the New York Edition this image acquires rather melodramatic overtones: "The question struck him as a flash intenser than when the jaws of the night opened to the whiteness of a thousand teeth" (NYE 517). On the other hand, this image, with its possible reference to an all-engulfing leviathan, is perhaps calculated to link with that of a tempestuous sea which follows: "But before he could answer the tempest was in possession and the rain, about them, like the sound of the deeps about a ship's side." The fusion of the literal and metaphoric references to the disastrous wreck of Roderick's career is thus proleptic, foreshadowing the discovery of Roderick's drenched body lying "as if the billows of the

ocean had flung him upon the strand" (386). At the conclusion of the novel, the revised version again deploys the imagistic mode of psychonarration more fully to portray Rowland's sense of arid desolation. In the original edition, we find an echo of *Othello* in the statement that "Now that all was over Rowland understood how exclusively, for two years, Roderick had filled his life. His occupation was gone" (387). In the New York Edition the theater imagery recurs, appropriately, to portray Rowland's state of mind: "Now that all was over Rowland understood how up to the brim, for two years, his personal world had been filled. It looked to him at present as void and blank and sinister as a theatre bankrupt and closed" (NYE 526).

19. *Notes of a Son and Brother* (1914); reprinted in *Henry James: Autobiography*, ed. and introd. Frederick W. Dupee (London: W. H. Allen, 1956), 292.

CHAPTER 4. FROM AUTHORIAL TO FIGURAL: *THE PORTRAIT OF A LADY*

1. F. O. Matthiessen and Kenneth Murdock, eds., *The Notebooks of Henry James* (New York: Oxford University Press, 1947), 19.

2. Peter Buitenhuis, *The Grasping Imagination: The American Writings of Henry James* (Toronto: University of Toronto Press, 1970) 111–12.

3. Stanzel, *Narrative Situations in the Novel,* 258.

4. Ora Segal, *The Lucid Reflector: The Observer in Henry James' Fiction* (New Haven and London: Yale University Press, 1969), 34.

5. *The Finer Grain* is the title of a volume of short stories by James.

6. Martha Collins, "The Narrator, the Satellites and Isabel Archer: Point of View in *The Portrait of a Lady,*" *Studies in the Novel* 8 (1976): 146.

7. "Metaphor in *The Portrait*" (1957; reprint in *Henry James: Washington Square and The Portrait of a Lady: A Casebook,* ed. Alan Shelston (London: Macmillan, 1984), 26. James's use of architectural imagery has been explored by many critics. Interesting comments have been made by, for example, Tony Tanner in "The Fearful Self: Henry James's *The Portrait of a Lady,*" *Critical Quarterly* 7 (Autumn 1965): 205–19. David Galloway comments specifically on Isabel's preference, revealed here, for a dimly lit refuge. He notes that "Isabel has always sought the shadows. Mrs Touchett first meets her in the dimly-lighted library in Albany . . . Isabel seals herself off from the world, never opening the bolted door that leads to the street." (*Henry James: The Portrait of a Lady* (London: Edward Arnold, 1967), 31–32.

8. The same cluster of imagery is used in direct discourse by Henrietta, who expresses her concern about Isabel to Ralph by claiming that "Isabel is changing every day; she's drifting away—right out to sea" (1. 70). Ralph himself is described as "drift[ing] about the house like a rudderless vessel in a rocky stream" (2. 61) when feeling powerless to deflect her from her decision to marry Osmond.

9. *The Notebooks of Henry James,* ed. F. O. Mathiessen and Kenneth B. Murdock, 15.

10. Cohn, *Transparent Minds,* 33.

11. Stanzel, *A Theory of Narrative,* 128–29.

12. Krook, *The Ordeal of Consciousness in Henry James* (Cambridge: Cambridge University Press, 1962), 54.

13. Dorothea Krook, in *The Ordeal of Consciousness,* has examined this aspect of the novel in depth.

14. Osmond often dispenses glib aphorisms, telling Isabel, for example, that "A woman's natural mission is to be where she's most appreciated" (1. 380); here again a woman is seen as essentially passive, a recipient rather than initiator of appreciation. A slight modification of this "truism" would produce a more apt expression of Osmond's real position: that a woman's "natural" or most desirable mission is to be where her value, particularly that measured in monetary terms, can appreciate—to the credit and benefit of the woman's appreciator!

15. Michael Bell, *The Context of English Literature 1900–1930* (London: Methuen, 1980), 65. As Cohn has noted, the use of the past tense does not detract from the sense of immediacy, as in such portrayals one has the illusion of participating in a present process. (Narrated monologue, Cohn points out, adopts the temporal orientation of the figural consciousness; (127.)

16. Henry James, "The Art of Fiction," in *The House of Fiction,* 32.

17. Cited by Bernard Bergonzi, in *The Situation of the Novel* (1970; reprint Harmondsworth: Penguin, 1972), 34.

18. The procedure whereby "life is . . . understood backward" is exemplified also in, inter alia, *The Wings of the Dove, The Ambassadors* (Strether's "backward picture" in the Luxembourg Gardens) and *The Golden Bowl,* where this device will be explored more fully.

19. *The Bostonians* (1886; reprint Harmondsworth: Penguin, 1977), 355.

20. Cohn notes the inadequacy of Gordon Taylor's account of the method used for rendering Isabel's thoughts in this chapter: "although still cast in the third person, [it is] divested of most authorial trappings," and the "third-person intrusions approximate convincingly, though they fail to reproduce exactly, the links in her own train of thought." *The Passages of Thought: Psychological Representation in the American Novel 1870–1900* (New York, 1969), 64, 70.

21. "Rhapsody on a Windy Night," 2. 23–24.

22. Peter Garrett, *Scene and Symbol from George Eliot to James Joyce: Studies in Changing Fictional Mode* (New Haven: Yale University Press, 1969), 107.

23. Austen Warren, "Henry James: Symbolic Imagery in the Later Novels," *Rage for Order: Essays in Criticism* (Chicago: University of Chicago Press, 1948), 148–49.

24. Peter Garrett, *Scene and Symbol,* 107.

25. C. T. Samuels, *The Ambiguity of Henry James* (Urbana: University of Illinois Press, 1971), 100.

26. Paul Armstrong, *The Challenge of Bewilderment,* 6.

27. James, *Notes of a Son and Brother,* 292.

28. "A London Life," in vol. 7 of *The Complete Tales of Henry James,* ed. Leon Edel (London: Rupert Hart-Davis, 1963), 88.

29. Matthiessen and Murdock, *Notebooks,* 18.

CHAPTER 5. DUAL OR MULTIPLE FOCALIZATION: *THE GOLDEN BOWL*

1. *Middlemarch* (1872; reprint London: Oxford University Press, 1950), 225.

2. David Seed, "The Narrator in Henry James's Criticism," *Philological Quarterly* 60, no. 4 (Fall 1981): 515.

3. Percy Lubbock, *The Craft of Fiction* (1921, reprint London: Jonathan Cape, 1932), 258.

4. James anticipated the emphasis given by exponents of reader response

(such as Iser) on the participatory role of the reader in the "construction" of the text. He maintained that "In every novel the work is divided between the writer and the reader. . . . When [the writer] makes [the reader] interested, then the reader does quite half the labour." ("The Novels of George Eliot," in *Theory of Fiction: Henry James,* ed. James E. Miller Jr.), 321.

5. Seed, "The Narrator in Henry James's Criticism," 514.

6. Jonathan Culler, *Structuralist Poetics: Structuralism, Linguistics and the Study of Literature* (Ithaca: Cornell University Press, 1975; reprint 1980), 197.

7. "The Art of Fiction," 27.

8. Graham, *Indirections of the Novel: James, Conrad and Forster* (Cambridge University Press, 1988), 8.

9. Gabriel Pearson, "The Novel to End All Novels: *The Golden Bowl,"* in *The Air of Reality: New Essays on Henry James,* ed. John Goode (London: Methuen, 1972).

10. Krook, *The Ordeal of Consciousness,* 25.

11. This recurrent pattern is also exemplified in *The Wings.* In the preface, James states that Kate is the reflector in the section set in Venice: "She is turned on largely at Venice" (*AN* 301); however, only limited access to her mind is given in Venice, as Milly and then Densher function as reflectors in this section of the novel.

12. The original title, "The Marriages," reveals the crucial significance of these relationships.

13. Priscilla L. Walton points out that critics such as John Carlos Rowe, Leo Bersani, and Mark Seltzer all perceive Maggie as a textual reviser and suggest that book 2, written from her perspective, manifests her revision of book 1. She avers that "These male critics, however, display a disturbing tendency to denigrate Maggie and to minimalize her artistic process; they perceive her revisions as circumscriptive and dangerous." ("'A mistress of shades': Maggie as Reviser in *The Golden Bowl," The Henry James Review* 13 (1991–20): 43.) The question of Maggie's creative/destructive "revisions" is discussed further at the end of this chapter.

14. Armstrong, *The Challenge of Bewilderment,* 267.

15. *What Maisie Knew* (1897), in vol. 11 of *The Novels and Tales of Henry James,* rev. ed. (1908; reprint New York: Charles Scribner's Sons, 1936), 18.

16. Armstrong, *The Challenge of Bewilderment,* 19.

17. Pearson, "The Novel to End all Novels," 314.

18. Robert L. Gale, *The Caught Image: Figurative Language in the Fiction of Henry James* (University of North Carolina Press, 1977), 6.

19. This range of experience is adumbrated in *The Ambassadors* with Strether's perception, in Gloriani's garden, that "There was something in the great world covertly tigerish, which came to him across the lawn and in the charming air as a waft from the jungle" (1. 219); the implication is that the social world is governed by "survival of the fittest" jungle morality.

20. R. W. Short, "Henry James's World of Images," *Publications of Modern Language Association of America* 68 (1953): 946.

21. For a perceptive analysis of the implications of "Imperium," and specifically the Verver version of this phenomenon, see Michiel Heyns, *Expulsion and the Nineteenth-Century Novel: The Scapegoat in English Realist Fiction* (Oxford: Clarendon Press, 1994).

22. Maggie's strategy contrasts forcibly with that of the eponymous heroine of "Madame de Mauves" in a comparable situation. When confronted with the fact

of her husband's infidelity and subsequent repentance, Madame de Mauves adopts an unflinchingly unforgiving attitude, with disastrous consequences.

23. The situation recalls that in *Middlemarch,* where, according to George Eliot's authorial comment, "a man may be . . . belauded, envied, ridiculed, counted upon as a tool and fallen in love with, or at least selected as a future husband, and yet remain virtually unknown—known merely as a cluster of signs for his neighbour's false suppositions." (*Middlemarch* [1871–72; reprint London: Oxford University Press, 1959], 148.)

24. See chapter 2 for an account of narrated perception.

25. For more detailed discussion of the role of the Assinghams, see inter alia Lawrence B. Holland, *The Expense of Vision: Essays on the Craft of Henry James* (Princeton: Princeton University Press, 1964); Ora Segal, *The Lucid Reflector;* and Ruth Yeazell, *Language and Knowledge in the Late Novels of Henry James.*

26. Graham, *Indirections of the Novel,* 75.

27. Nicola Bradbury, *Henry James: The Later Novels* (Oxford: Clarendon Press, 1979), 194.

28. Eileen H. Watts, *"The Golden Bowl:* A Theory of Metaphor," *Modern Language Studies* 13, no. 4 (Fall 1983): 170.

29. See, for example, Ora Segal, *The Lucid Reflector,* 193–210; Sister Corona Sharp, *The Confidante in Henry James* (Notre Dame, Ind.: University of Notre Dame Press, 1963).

30. Warren, "Henry James: Symbolic Imagery in the Later Novels," 145.

CHAPTER 6. *THE GOLDEN BOWL:* THE VERVERS

1. In view of Adam's instrumentalizing of both Charlotte and Amerigo, whose "value" in terms of both aesthetic and utilitarian criteria is carefully calculated before he appropriates them, I find it difficult to accept the claim that "'the application of the same measure of value to such different pieces of property as old Persian carpets, say, and new human acquisitions' is not entirely sinister." (Merle Williams, *Henry James and the Philosophical Novel* [Cambridge: Cambridge University Press, 1993], 193).

2. Adam's approach is reminiscent of that of Mrs. Gareth in *The Spoils of Poynton,* in whom the "ruling passion [that of the collector] had despoiled her of her humanity." *The Novels and Tales of Henry James* (1897; reprint in vol. 10 of the New York edition, New York: Charles Scribner's Sons, 1937), 37.

3. Gabriel Pearson, "The Novel to End All Novels: *The Golden Bowl,"* in *The Air of Reality: New Essays on Henry James,* ed. John Goode (London: Methuen, 1972), 339.

4. "The Beast in the Jungle" (1903; rev. ed. 1909; reprint in vol. 17 of the New York Edition of *The Novels and Tales of Henry James* (New York: Charles Scribner's Sons, 1937), 126.

5. According to Dorrit Cohn, this "is probably the most direct allusion to the sexual act in [James's] entire *oeuvre*" (114). I feel, however, that this is too literal an interpretation of James's comment.

6. For some readers, on the contrary, in such scenes "Maggie . . . is not empathising with Charlotte's suffering. Indeed, she needs to see Charlotte so reduced." Beth Sharon Ash, "Narcissism and the Gilded Image: A Psychoanalytical Reading of *The Golden Bowl,"* *The Henry James Review* 15, no. 1

(Winter 1994), 78. Commentators on *The Golden Bowl* tend to fall into pro-Verver and anti–Verver camps; their bias is often determined by their decision as to whether a specific observation or image—such as that of the "silken halter"—should be attributed to the reflector or the narrating agency. Further discussion of this point follows.

7. The image culminating in Maggie's "translation" of her intuitive perception of what lay behind "the glass" recalls a comparable evocation of an impenetrable yet seemingly transparent barrier between the questing self and the object of knowledge in *What Maisie Knew*. For Maisie, "the sharpened sense of spectatorship . . . gave her often the odd air of being present at her history in as separate a manner as if she could only get at experience by flattening her nose against a pane of glass" (107). In Maisie's case, it is the ignorance and inexperience of youth, of not being fully "in the picture," which imposes a barrier to understanding. For Maggie, it is simply an inherent aspect of subjectivity, of being restricted, as regards others, to "spectatorship," which entails a concomitant awareness of the barriers to understanding imposed by being confined to one's own consciousness.

8. William R. MacNaughton, *Henry James: The Later Novels* (Ontario: Twayne Publishers, 1987), 118.

9. According to Arlene Young, "the tag ["she seemed to see him hear her say"] indicates that Maggie is the object being interpreted, not the subject doing the interpreting" and that "the words appear to be the narrator's formulation of Maggie's assessment of Amerigo's silent response to her." "Hypothetical Discourse in *The Golden Bowl*," *American Literature* 61, no. 3 (October 1989): 393. On the contrary, as I have suggested, the context, and specifically the recognition that the extract is embedded in a passage of narrated monologue, indicates that Maggie is indeed doing the interpreting.

10. A comparable image occurs in "The Beast in the Jungle," where Marcher is deprived of "the lost stuff of consciousness, [which] became for him as a strayed or stolen child to an unappeasable father" (117).

11. Statements such as "The fiction of the spaniel's tumble into the pond is both Maggie's and James's" (Williams, 194) seem to me singularly unhelpful. Any image used by Maggie is, of course, James's; the necessary distinction to be made here is that between images conjured up by the reflector, Maggie, and the narrator—hence the greater precision afforded by terms such as narrated monologue/free indirect discourse and psychonarration. This extract is also analyzed by Ruth Bernard Yeazell in *Language and Knowledge in the Late Novels of Henry James*.

12. James had read and commented on the novels of Dickens, and one could speculate as to whether Dickens's identification of the circus with the suppleness and vitality of the imaginative life in a novel such as *Hard Times* might have influenced James's choice of image here. He was probably also familiar with George Seurat's painting "Le Cirque" (1891), which is virtually a visual embodiment of this image.

13. *The Europeans* (1878; reprint in *Washington Square and The Europeans*, New York: Dell, 1963), 52.

14. *Macbeth*, 3. 4. 24.

15. Maggie's proleptic observation—"Yes, it was one of the things she should go down to her grave without having known—how Charlotte . . . *really* thought her stepmother looked" (307)—which is expressed in narrated monologue, makes an interesting comparison with a comparable proleptic comment in *The Ambassa-*

dors. When Strether is pressed by Maria Gostrey to divulge the identity of the object manufactured at Woollett, the narrator comments "But it may even now frankly be mentioned that he in the sequel never was to tell her" (1. 61). In the latter novel, the proleptic comment emanates from the narrator; here, in *The Golden Bowl,* it proceeds from the reflector, in narrated monologue. The reader feels that it has the same authority—that Maggie will indeed never know what Charlotte feels about her—that is another indication of the way in which the narrator's insights have been superseded by those of the reflector.

16. This image recalls Maisie's experience of the mysterious insecurity and hidden menace of life: "Everything had something behind it: life was like a long, long corridor with rows of closed doors. She had learned that at these doors it was wise not to knock" (*What Maisie Knew,* 33–34).

17. This is also evident in *The Ambassadors* where, in the riverside scene, Strether, "a man of imagination," experiences his situation in strongly visual or pictorial terms and acquires new insight, also undergoing a modification of earlier assumptions.

18. In his autobiography, James recalls seeing the picture "The Scapegoat" by Holman Hunt in 1858. He describes it as "so charged with the awful that I was glad I saw it in company" (*A Small Boy and Others,* 178–79).

19. This intense awareness of a latent "other self," "shadow" personality, or *doppelgänger* that would revel in the unleashing of the more destructive passions such as vengeance, "the rages of jealousy, the protests of passion" (2. 236) links Maggie with characters such as Spencer Brydon in "The Jolly Corner," one of several Jamesian characters who are brought to recognition of the darker aspects of their personality.

20. In "The Jolly Corner" (1906) the portrayal is not in metaphysical but in concrete physical terms. Whereas evil is experienced by Maggie as being "like some bad-faced stranger," Spencer Brydon, in his "house of quiet" on the Jolly Corner, confronts this "bad-faced stranger" in the flesh and recognizes a distorted version of his own features in the stranger's face. The stranger is an embodiment of less desirable proclivities in his own nature.

21. Walter Wright, in *Henry James: Modern Judgements,* ed. Tony Tanner (Bristol: Macmillan, 1968.)

22. See Blackmur's introduction to *The Golden Bowl;* Barzun's "Henry James, Melodramatist," in *The Question of Henry James,* ed. F. W. Dupee (London: Allen Wingate, 1947); and Anderson, *The American Henry James,* 281–346.

23. Krook, *The Ordeal of Consciousness;* Crews, *The Tragedy of Manners* (New Haven: Yale University Press, 1957).

24. Joseph J. Firebaugh, "The Ververs," *Essays in Criticism* 4 (October 1954): 401, 404.

25. Maxwell Geismar, *Henry James and the Jacobites* (Boston: Houghton Mifflin, 1963), 329; Jean Kimball, "Henry James's Last Portrait of a Lady: Charlotte Stant in *The Golden Bowl,*" *American Literature* 28, no. 4 (January 1957): 449–68; F. R. Leavis, *The Great Tradition* (1948; reprint, London: Chatto and Windus, 1955), 159; F. O. Matthiessen, *The Major Phase,* 1944; reprint 1970, 100.

26. Geismar, *Henry James and his Cult* (London: Chatto and Windus, 1964), 7.

27. John Clair, *The Ironic Dimension in the Fiction of Henry James* (Pittsburgh: Duquesne University Press, 1965), 100.

28. Ibid., 80.

29. The view that Maggie is "neither saint nor witch" is implicit in the observations of critics such as Oscar Cargill, *The Novels of Henry James* (New York:

Macmillan, 1961); and Sallie Sears, *The Negative Imagination: Form and Perspective in the Novels of Henry James* (Ithaca: Cornell University Press, 1968). Sears highlights the paradoxical nature of Maggie's position in her contention that "Maggie's consciousness is the consciousness of the martyr and saint, in which personal sacrifice is the paradoxical measure of personal triumph" (219–20).

30. Donna Przybylowicz, *Desire and Repression: The Dialectic of Self and Other in the Late Works of Henry James* (Alabama: University of Alabama Press, 1986), 18.

31. Donald Mull, *Henry James's "Sublime Economy": Money as Symbolic Center in the Fiction* (Wesleyan University Press, Middleton, 1973), 159–60; Matthiessen, *Henry James: The Major Phase*, 100.

32. MacNaughton, *Henry James: The Later Novels*, 117–18.

33. Kenneth Graham, *Indirections of the Novel: James, Conrad and Forster* (Cambridge University Press, 1988; reprint, 1989), 8.

34. My interpretation differs therefore from that of critics who maintain that James chooses to valorize Maggie's dutiful obedience to her father's patriarchal power by never raising questions about it or, more radically expressed, that "Maggie has been clitoridectomised." (Priscilla L. Walton, "'A Mistress of Shades': Maggie as Reviser *in The Golden Bowl*," (*The Henry James Review* 13 (1992): 151.) Although she does not, for the reasons mentioned above, express overt disobedience, her acquiescence in her father's patriarchal power is more apparent than real.

35. MacNaughton, *Henry James: The Later Novels*, 102.

36. Martha Craven Nussbaum, "Flawed Crystals: James's *The Golden Bowl* and Literature as Moral Philosophy," *New Literary History* 15 (1983): 49, 30.

37. The symbolism of the golden bowl has generated a great range of interpretations, including the problematic contention that "The bowl is not a phallic symbol, unlike the ornate pagoda image. . . . it is decidedly maternal." (Lynda S. Boren, *Eurydice Reclaimed: Language, Gender and Voice in Henry James* [Ann Arbor: U.M.I. Research Press, 1989], 86.) This is an irresponsibly simplistic reduction of the complex symbols of pagoda and bowl, but is marginally preferable to the comment concerning "the psychic position represented by the idealized anal body, the golden bowl." (Beth Sharon Ash, "Narcissism and the Gilded Image: A Psycho-analytic reading of *The Golden Bowl*," 84.) This astoundingly crass comment exemplifies the way in which a reductively psychoanalytical approach can lead one—literally and figuratively—into a cul-de-sac!

38. Boren, *Eurydice Reclaimed*, 86.

39. Priscilla L. Walton, "'A mistress of shades': Maggie as Reviser in *The Golden Bowl*," *The Henry James Review* 13 (1991–92): 144.

40. Graham, *Indirections of the Novel: James, Conrad and Forster*, 77.

41. T. S. Eliot, "Burnt Norton." 144–45, in *Collected Poems 1909–1935* (London: Farber and Faber, 1959), 186.

42. Phyllis van Slyck, "An innate preference for the represented subject": Portraiture and Knowledge in *The Golden Bowl*," *The Henry James Review* 15, no. 2 (Spring 1994): 186.

43. Gabriel Pearson, "The Novel to End All Novels: *The Golden Bowl*," 351.

44. Cited by Dorothea Krook, 323.

45. Krook, *The Ordeal of Consciousness*, 318. The verbal echo of Aristotle's terms "pity and fear" has been explored by Marianna Torgovnick, who observes that the verbal echo is appropriate "given the somewhat incestuous relationship

of Maggie and her father, and that of Charlotte and Amerigo." Maggie realizes that "to pursue the revelation of incest (like Oedipus) is disastrous; to avoid positive knowledge (like Maggie) is morally ambiguous, but emotionally sound." It is appropriate, then, that Maggie should bury her eyes rather than blinding them as Oedipus does. (*Closure in the Novel* [Princeton: Princeton University Press, 1981], 151.)

46. There are widely divergent readings of this final scene. According to the interpretation of Beth Ash, Amerigo's declaration does not signify "the reality of love at last" but rather his return to her as "self-interested worshipper, the husband with grandiose hopes of his own." Their marriage is seen as "a spectacle and a simulacrum, a perpetual theater for the denial of disillusionment." ("Narcissism and the Gilded Image: A Psycho-analytic Reading of *The Golden Bowl*," 87.) Marianna Torgovnick, in *Closure in the Novel,* provides both an illuminating discussion of the implications and ambiguities of this final scene and a comprehensive assessment of current critical comment.

47. According to Nussbaum, commenting on the moral dimension of Maggie's change, "Beginning to *live* is, for her, beginning to see that meaningful commitment to a love in the world can require the sacrifice of one's own moral purity. . . . Her love . . . must live on cunning and treachery; it requires the breaking of moral rules . . . (*GB* 134)." Cited by Phyllis van Slyck, in "An innate preference for the represented subject": Portraiture and Knowledge in *The Golden Bowl*," *The Henry James Review* 15, no. 2 (Spring 1994): 188.

48. Merle Williams notes that "Marius Bewley is disturbed by the manner in which James seems to blur the distinctions, and to invert the relations, between truth and falsehood, appearance and reality." (*Henry James and the Philosophical Novel,* 204.) Here again insufficient account is taken of the crucial difference between author, narrator and reflector character. Strategies adopted by the characters to manipulate or mislead others are not invariably endorsed by the narrator or the author.

49. Pearson, "The Novel to End All Novels: *The Golden Bowl*," 302.

50. Blake, "Auguries of Innocence", 1. 53–54 in *The Poetical Works of William Blake* (London: Oxford University Press, 1958), 172.

51. Richard Freadman, *Eliot, James and the Fictional Self: A Study in Character and Narration* (London: Macmillan, 1986), 176.

52. As Priscilla L. Walton puts it, "Maggie's text is open to different interpretations because she does not insist on her meanings as the only meanings. Indeed, this would be an abrogation of her polysemous project" ("'A mistress of shades': Maggie as Reviser in *The Golden Bowl*," 150). See also, inter alia, *The Henry James Review* 15, no. 2 (Spring 1994): 188 for further discussion of the ending.

Conclusion

1. Stanzel's claim that James's Strether in *The Ambassadors* is one of the earliest representatives of figural narration is also questionable, as he fails to take cognizance of James's earlier novel, *Roderick Hudson.*

2. David M. Craig, "The Indeterminacy of the End: Maggie Verver and the Limits of Imagination," *The Henry James Review* (Winter 1982): 134. A more recent critic, Beth Sharon Ash, somewhat surprisingly makes a comparably fuzzy observation: "the blurring between *novelist* and character effected by the later style dangerously strips the *novelist* of the freedom to transcend the limits of the

character he has chosen as his "perceiver" (my emphasis). "Narcissism and the Gilded Image: A Psycho-analytic Reading of *The Golden Bowl*," 82. Here the first reference to the "novelist" should be replaced by the term "narrator"; furthermore, as indicated earlier, the novelist in effect uses means other than the narratorial voice to convey his conception of his "perceiver," predominant among these indicators being the subtle deployment of the imagistic mode. Lack of clarity on this distinction can generate accusations of a "narratorial lapse" in scenes such as that where Maggie interprets Charlotte's "tap against the glass" (*GB* 521) (Ash, 83.)

3. "The First Paragraph of *The Ambassadors*," in *Henry James: Modern Judgements,* ed. Tony Tanner (London: Macmillan, 1968), 289.

4. Sheila Teahan, *The Rhetorical Logic of Henry James* (Baton Rouge: Louisiana State University Press), 79.

5. Hugh Stevens, "Sexuality and the Aesthetic in *The Golden Bowl*," *The Henry James Review* 14, no. 1 (Winter 1993): 63.

6. Ibid., 59.

7. Ibid., 59.

8. Meili Steele, "The Drama of Reference in James's *The Golden Bowl*," *Novel* (Fall 1987): 81.

9. Ruth Yeazell, *Language and Knowledge in the Late Novels of Henry James* (Chicago: University of Chicago Press, 1976), 3.

10. Maria Gostrey's term for her function in *The Ambassadors.*

11. It is surprising, therefore, that a commentator as perceptive as Merle Williams could regard Adam with such an indulgent eye, investing him with "a touching modesty" when Adam "concludes that it would be impermissible to consider marriage merely for his own sake, but that the project is justified by the intended influence on Maggie's domestic happiness" (*Henry James and the Philosophical Novel*, 192). Verver's putative "touching modesty" and ostensible "amiability" are clearly adopted as a means to many reprehensible ends. Indeed, his marriage to Charlotte exemplifies his intrumentalizing view of others. His is not, admittedly, the conventional "marriage of convenience," as it is not primarily for his own convenience but for that of his daughter that he undertakes this venture into matrimony; but then Maggie is seen largely as an adjunct of himself.

12. David B. McWhirter, "(Re)Presenting Henry James: Authority and Intertextuality in the New York Edition," Selected Papers on Henry James, *The Henry James Review* 12, no. 2 (Spring 1991): 139.

13. This emphasis is clearly evinced in the statement that "the privileged status of the prefaces as 'pure' aesthetic document needs to be reexamined in light of the ways in which surrounding social and cultural discourses (including historically determined political, class, and gender assumptions) are necessarily woven into James's text" (Ibid., 139).

14. Susan Elizabeth Gunter, in book reviews, *The Henry James Review* 12, no. 2 (Spring 1991): 191.

15. *American Literature* 61, no. 3 (October 1989): 382–97.

16. *Imagination and Desire in the Novels of Henry James* (New Brunswick: Rutgers University Press, 1984), 140.

17. "Hypothetical Discourse as Ficelle in *The Golden Bowl*," 383.

18. Jeremy Hawthorn, "Formal and Social Issues in the Study of Interior Dialogue: The Case of *Jane Eyre*," in *Narrative: From Malory to Motion Pictures*, ed. Jeremy Hawthorn (London: Edward Arnold, 1985), 87.

19. Ibid., 91.

20. Mark Seltzer, *Henry James and the Art of Power* (Ithaca: Cornell University Press, 1984), 72.

21. Michiel Heyns presents a cogent analysis of this issue in *Expulsion and the Nineteenth-Century Novel: The Scapegoat in English Realist Fiction* (Oxford: Clarendon Press, 1994).

22. This view is endorsed by a number of influential critics. Paul Hernadi has praised Cohn's *Transparent Minds* for its "commendably simple typology" (book review, *Comparative Literature* 32 (1980): 208), Brian McHale for "the clarity and definition . . . brought to hitherto nebulous areas of our poetics of prose" ("Islands in the Stream of Consciousness; Dorrit Cohn's *Transparent Minds*," *Poetics Today* 2, no. 2 [1981]: 87); and H. Foltiner for being "a definitive treatise on a special sector of narrative technique" (review, *Modern Language Review* 76 [1981]: 645.)

23. Pascal, *The Dual Voice,* 21.

24. Hernadi, *Comparative Literature* 32 (1980): 209.

25. Book review, *The Journal of English and Germanic Philology* 80 (1981): 309.

26. John Auchard, *Silence in Henry James: The Heritage of Symbolism and Decadence* (University Park and London: The Pennsylvania State University Press, 1986).

27. John Ellis, Book review, *The Journal of English and Germanic Philology* 80 (1981): 309.

28. Brian MacHale, "Islands in the Stream of Consciousness": Dorrit Cohn's *Transparent Minds*," *Poetics Today,* 2, no. 2 (1981): 187.

29. Ellis, Review of *Transparent Minds,* 309.

30. Tony Tanner, *Henry James and the Art of Nonfiction* (Athens: University of Georgia Press, 1995), 34.

31. Armstrong, *The Challenge of Bewilderment,* 25; quoted by Richard Swartz, in "Bewilderment and Obscurity: A Review-Essay," *The Henry James Review* 12, no. 3 (Fall 1991): 276.

32. *Notes of a Son and Brother,* 292.

Bibliography

Primary Texts

Austen, Jane. *Pride and Prejudice*. 1813. Reprint, London: Oxford University Press, 1964.

Blake, William. Letter to Dr Trusler. *The Complete Writings of William Blake*. London: Oxford University Press, 1966.

Eliot, George. *Middlemarch*. 1872. Reprint, London: Oxford University Press, 1950.

Fielding, Henry. *The History of Tom Jones A Foundling*. Edited by Martin C. Battestin and Fredson Bowers. Oxford: Clarendon Press, 1983.

James, Henry.

Fiction

————, *The Ambassadors*. 1903. Rev. ed. 1909; Reprinted as Vols. XXI and XXII of the New York Edition of *The Novels and Tales of Henry James*. New York: Charles Scribner's Sons, 1937.

————, *The Awkward Age*. 1899. Rev. ed. 1908; reprinted in Vol. IX of the New York Edition of *The Novels and Tales of Henry James*. New York: Charles Scribner's Sons, 1936.

————, "The Beast in the Jungle." 1903. Rev. ed. 1909; reprinted in Vol. XVII of the New York Edition of *The Novels and Tales of Henry James*. New York: Charles Scribner's Sons, 1937.

————, *The Bostonians*. 1886. Reprint, Harmondsworth: Penguin, 1977.

————, *The Europeans*. 1878. Reprinted in *Washington Square and The Europeans*. Edited and with an introduction by R. P. Blackmur. New York: Dell, 1959.

————, *The Golden Bowl*. 1904. Rev. ed. 1909; reprinted as Vols. XXIII and XXIV of the New York Edition of *The Novels and Tales of Henry James*. New York: Charles Scribner's Sons, 1937.

————, "Greville Fane." 1983. Reprinted in Vol. VIII of *The Complete Tales of Henry James*. Edited and with an introduction by Leon Edel. London: Rupert Hart-Davis, 1963.

————, "The Jolly Corner." 1906. Reprinted in Vol. XVII of The New York Edition of *The Novels and Tales of Henry James*. New York: Charles Scribner's Sons, 1937.

————, "A London Life." 1889. Reprinted in Vol. VII of *The Complete Tales of Henry James*. Edited and with an introduction by Leon Edel. London: Rupert Hart-Davis, 1963.

————, "Madame de Mauves." 1879. Rev. ed. 1908; reprinted in Vol. XII of the

268

New York Edition of *The Novels and Tales of Henry James*. New York: Charles Scribner's Sons, 1936.

————, *Notes of a Son and Brother*. 1914. Reprinted in *Henry James: Autobiography*. Edited and with an introduction by Frederick W. Dupee. London: W. H. Allen, 1956.

————, *The Portrait of a Lady*. 1881. Rev. ed. 1909; reprinted as Vols. III and IV of the New York Edition of *The Novels and Tales of Henry James*. New York: Charles Scribner's Sons, 1936.

————, "The Spoils of Poynton." 1897. Reprinted in Vol. X of the New York Edition of *The Novels and Tales of Henry James*. New York: Charles Scribner's Sons, 1936.

————, *Roderick Hudson*. 1876. Reprint, Harmondsworth: Penguin, 1986. Rev. ed. 1908; reprinted in Vol. I of the New York Edition of *The Novels and Tales of Henry James*. New York: Charles Scribner's Sons, 1935.

————, "A Tragedy of Error." 1864. Reprinted in Vol. I of *The Complete Tales of Henry James*. Edited and with an introduction by Leon Edel. London: Rupert Hart-Davis, 1963.

————, *Washington Square*. 1880. Reprint, Harmondsworth: Penguin, 1987.

————, *Watch and Ward*. 1871. Reprint, London: Rupert Hart-Davis, 1960.

————, *What Maisie Knew*. 1897. Rev. ed. 1908; reprinted in Vol. XI of the New York Edition of *The Novels and Tales of Henry James*. New York: Charles Scribner's Sons, 1937.

————, *The Wings of the Dove*. 1902. Rev. ed. 1909; reprinted as Vols. XIX and XX of the New York Edition of *The Novels and Tales of Henry James*. New York: Charles Scribner's Sons, 1937.

Critical Studies

James, Henry. "The Art of Fiction." 1884. Reprinted in *The House of Fiction*. Edited and with an introduction by Leon Edel, 1957. Reprinted, London: Mercury Books, 1962.

————, *The Art of the Novel: Critical Prefaces*. Introduction by Richard P. Blackmur. 1970. Reprinted, New York: Charles Scribner's Sons, 1936.

————, "The Future of the Novel." 1899. Reprinted in *The House of Fiction: Essays on the Novel by Henry James*. Edited with an introduction by Leon Edel, 1957. Reprinted, London: Mercury Books, 1962.

————, "Gustave Flaubert." 1893. Reprinted in *Henry James: Selected Literary Criticism*. Edited by Morris Shapira. London: Heinemann, 1964.

————, "Gustave Flaubert." 1902. Reprinted in *Henry James: Selected Literary Criticism*. Edited by Morris Shapira. London: Heineman, 1994.

————, *The House of Fiction: Essays on the Novel*. Edited and with an introduction by Leon Edel, 1957. Reprinted, London: Mercury Books, 1962.

————, "The Lesson of Balzac." 1905. Reprinted in *The House of Fiction: Essays on the Novel by Henry James*. Edited and with an introduction by Leon Edel, 1957. Reprinted, London: Mercury Books, 1962.

————, *The Notebooks of Henry James*. Edited by F. O. Matthiessen and Kenneth B. Murdock. 1947. Reprint, Chicago: University of Chicago Press, 1981.

————, "The Novels of George Eliot." 1866. Reprinted in *Theory of Fiction:*

Henry James. Edited by James E. Miller, Jr. Lincoln: University of Nebraska Press, 1972.

————, *Theory of Fiction*. Edited by James E. Miller, Jr. Lincoln: University of Nebraska Press, 1972.

Joyce, James. *A Portrait of the Artist as a Young Man*. 1916. Reprinted, Harmondsworth: Penguin, 1972.

Thackeray, William. *Vanity Fair*. 1848. Reprinted, London: Blackie and Son, n.d.

SECONDARY SOURCES

Monographs

Anderson, Quentin. *The American Henry James*. London: John Calder, 1958.

Armstrong, Paul. *The Challenge of Bewilderment: Understanding and Representation in James, Conrad and Ford*. Ithaca: Cornell University Press, 1987.

Auchard, John. *Silence in Henry James: The Heritage of Symbolism and Decadence*. University Park and London: The Pennsylvania State University Press, 1986.

Barzun, Jacques. "Henry James, Melodramatist." In *The Question of Henry James: A Collection of Critical Essays*. Edited by F. W. Dupee. London: Allen Wingate, 1947.

Bell, Michael. *The Context of English Literature 1900–1930*. London: Methuen, 1980.

Bergonzi, Bernard. *The Situation of the Novel*. 1970. Reprint, Harmondsworth: Penguin, 1972.

Booth, Wayne C. *The Rhetoric of Fiction*. 1961. Reprint, Chicago: Chicago University Press, 1983.

Boren, Lynda S. *Eurydice Reclaimed: Language, Gender and Voice in Henry James*. Ann Arbor: U.M.I. Research Press, 1989.

Bradbury, Nicola. *Henry James: The Later Novels*. Oxford University Press, 1979.

Buitenhuis, Peter. *The Grasping Imagination: The American Writings of Henry James*. Toronto: University of Toronto Press, 1970.

Cameron, Sharon. *Thinking in Henry James*. Chicago: Chicago University Press, 1989.

Cargill, Oscar. *The Novels of Henry James*. New York: Macmillan, 1961.

Chase, Richard. "Metaphor in *The Portrait*." Reprinted in *Henry James: Washington Square and The Portrait of a Lady*. Edited by Alan Shelston. London: Macmillan, 1984.

Chatman, Seymour. *Story and Discourse: Narrative Structure in Fiction and Film*. Ithaca: Cornell University Press, 1978.

Clair, John. *The Ironic Dimension in the Fiction of Henry James*. Pittsburgh, Pa: Duquesne University Press, 1965.

Cohn, Dorrit. *Transparent Minds: Narrative Modes for Presenting Consciousness in Fiction*. Princeton: Princeton University Press, 1978.

Crews, Frederick C. *The Tragedy of Manners: Moral Drama in the Later Novels of Henry James.* New Haven: Yale University Press, 1957.

Culler, Jonathan. *Structuralist Poetics: Structuralism, Linguistics and the Study of Literature.* Ithaca: Cornell University Press, 1980.

Dupee, Frederick W. *The Question of Henry James: a Collection of Critical Essays.* London: Allen Wingate, 1947.

Fowler, Roger. *Linguistics and the Novel.* London: Methuen, 1977.

Freadman, Richard. *Eliot, James and the Fictional Self: a Study in Character and Narration.* London: Macmillan, 1986.

Friedman, Norman. "Point of View in Fiction." *The Theory of the Novel.* Edited by Philip Stevick. New York: The Free Press, 1967.

Gale, Robert. *The Caught Image: Figurative Language in the Fiction of Henry James.* Norwood Editions: University of North Carolina Press, 1977.

Galloway, David. *Henry James: "The Portrait of a Lady."* London: Edward Arnold, 1967.

Garrett, Peter K. *Scene and Symbol from George Eliot to James Joyce: Studies in a Changing Fictional Mode.* New Haven: Yale University Press, 1969.

Geismar, Maxwell. *Henry James and the Jacobites.* Boston: 1943. Reprinted as *Henry James and his Cult.* London: Chatto & Windus, 1964.

Genette, Gerard. *Narrative Discourse: An Essay in Method.* Translated by Jane E. Levin. Ithaca: Cornell University Press, 1980. Trans. of *"Distours du Recit",* in *Figures III.* Paris: Seuil, 1922.

Gervais, David. *Flaubert and Henry James: A Study in Contrasts.* London: Macmillan, 1978.

Gide, André. "Henry James." In *The Question of Henry James: A Collection of Critical Essays.* Edited by F. W. Dupee. London: Allen Wingate, 1947.

Gombrich, E. H. *Art and Illusion: A Study in the Psychology of Pictorial Representation.* 1959. Reprint, London: Phaidon Press, 1962.

Goode, John, ed. *The Air of Reality: New Essays on Henry James.* London: Methuen, 1972.

Graham, Kenneth. *Indirections of the Novel: James, Conrad and Forster.* Cambridge: Cambridge University Press, 1988.

Grover, Philip. *Henry James and the French Novel: A Study in Inspiration.* London: Paul Elek, 1973.

Hawthorn, Jeremy. "Formal and Social Issues in the Study of Interior Dialogue: the Case of Jane Eyre." In *Narrative: From Malory to Motion Pictures.* Edited by Jeremy Hawthorn. London: Edward Arnold, 1985.

Heyns, Michiel. *Expulsion and the Nineteenth-Century Novel: The Scapegoat in English Realist Fiction.* Oxford: Clarendon Press, 1994.

Holland, Lawrence B. *The Expense of Vision: Essays on the Craft of Henry James.* Princeton, N.J.: Princeton University Press, 1964.

Kahler, Erich. *The Inward Turn of the Novel.* Princeton: Princeton University Press, 1973.

Kaston, Carren. *Imagination and Desire in the Novels of Henry James.* New Brunswick: Rutgers University Press, 1984.

Krook, Dorothea. *The Ordeal of Consciousness in Henry James.* Cambridge: Cambridge University Press, 1962.

LaCapra, Dominick. *"Madame Bovary" on Trial.* Ithaca: Cornell University Press, 1982.

Leavis, F. R. *The Great Tradition: George Eliot, Henry James, Joseph Conrad.* 1948. Reprint, Harmondsworth, Penguin, 1962.

Leech, Geoffrey N. and Michael H. Short. *Style in Fiction: a Linguistic Introduction to English Fictional Prose.* London: Longmans, 1981.

Lubbock, Percy. *The Craft of Fiction.* London: Jonathan Cape, 1921.

MacNaughton, William R. *Henry James: The Later Novels.* Ontario: Twayne Publishers, 1987.

Matthiessen, F. O. *Henry James: The Major Phase.* 1944. Reprint, New York: Oxford University Press, 1990.

————, and Kenneth B. Murdock, eds. *The Notebooks of Henry James.* 1947. Reprint, Chicago: University of Chicago Press, 1981.

Miller, James E. Jr., *Henry James: Theory of Fiction.* Lincoln: University of Nebraska Press, 1972.

Mull, Donald. *Henry James's "Sublime Economy": Money as Symbolic Centre in the Fiction.* Middleton: Wesleyan University Press, 1973.

Page, Norman. *Speech in the English Novel.* London: Macmillan, 1988.

Pascal, Roy. *The Dual Voice: Free Indirect Speech and its Functioning in the Nineteenth-Century European Novel.* Manchester: Manchester University Press, 1977.

Pearson, Gabriel. "The Novel to End All Novels: *The Golden Bowl.*" In *The Air of Reality: New Essays on Henry James.* Edited by John Goode. London: Methuen, 1972.

Przybylowicz, Donna. *Desire and Repression: The Dialectic of Self and Other in the Late Work of Henry James.* Alabama: University of Alabama Press, 1986.

Rimmon-Kenan, Shlomith. *Narrative Fiction: Contemporary Poetics.* London: Methuen, 1983.

Rowe, John Carlos. *The Theoretical Dimensions of Henry James.* London: Methuen, 1985.

Samuels, Charles Thomas. *The Ambiguity of Henry James.* Urbana: University of Illinois Press, 1971.

Scholes, Robert, and Robert Kellogg. *The Nature of Narrative.* New York: Oxford University Press, 1966.

Sears, Sallie. *The Negative Imagination: Form and Perspective in the Novels of Henry James.* Ithaca: Cornell University Press, 1968.

Segal, Ora. *The Lucid Reflector: The Observer in Henry James's Fiction.* New Haven: Yale University Press, 1969.

Seltzer, Mark. *Henry James and the Art of Power.* Ithaca: Cornell University Press, 1984.

Sharp, Sister Corona. *The Confidante in Henry James.* Notre Dame, Ind: University of Notre Dame Press, 1963.

Shelston, Alan, ed. *Henry James: Washington Square and The Portrait of a Lady.* London: Macmillan, 1984.

Stanzel, Franz K. *Narrative Situations in the Novel.* Translated by James P. Pusack. Bloomington: Indiana University Press, 1971.

————, *A Theory of Narrative*. Translated by Charlotte Goedsche. Cambridge: Cambridge University Press, 1984.

Tanner, Tony, ed. *Modern Judgements: Henry James*. London: Macmillan, 1968.

————, *Henry James and the Art of Nonfiction*. Athens: University of Georgia Press, 1995.

Taylor, Gordon O. *The Passages of Thought: Psychological Representation in the American Novel 1890–1900*. New York: Oxford University Press, 1969.

Teahan, Sheila. *The Rhetorical Logic of Henry James*. Baton Rouge: Louisiana University Press, 1995.

Torgovnick, Marianna. *Closure in the Novel*. Princeton: Princeton University Press, 1981.

Turnell, Martin. *The Novel in France*. 1950. Reprint, Harmondsworth: Penguin, 1962.

Ullman, Stephen. *Style in the French Novel*. Oxford: Blackwell, 1964.

Warren, Austen. "Henry James: Symbolic Imagery in the Later Novels." In *Rage for Order: Essays in Criticism*. Chicago: University of Chicago Press, 1948.

Wharton, Edith. "The Artist." In *A Backward Glance*. New York: Appleton-Century, 1934. Reprinted in *Critics on Henry James,* edited by J. Don Vann. Florida: University of Miami Press, 1972.

White, Allon. *The Uses of Obscurity: The Fiction of Early Modernism*. London: Routledge and Kegan Paul, 1981.

Wiesenfarth, Joseph. *Henry James and the Dramatic Analogy: a Study of the Major Novels of the Middle Period*. New York: Fordham University Press, 1963.

Williams, Merle. *Henry James and the Philosophical Novel*. Cambridge: Cambridge University Press, 1993.

Wright, Walter. "Maggie Verver: Neither Saint nor Witch." In *Modern Judgements: Henry James*. Edited by Tony Tanner. London: Macmillan, 1968.

Yeazell, Ruth Bernard. *Language and Knowledge in the Late Novels of Henry James*. Chicago: University of Chicago Press, 1976.

Journal

Ash, Beth Sharon. "Narcissism and the Gilded Image: A Psychoanalytic Reading of *The Golden Bowl*." *The Henry James Review* 15.1 (Winter 1994): 55–90.

Banfield, Ann. "Narrative Style and the Grammar of Direct and Indirect Speech." *Foundations of Language* 10 (1973): 1–39.

Cohn, Dorrit. "The Encirclement of Narrative: on Franz Stanzel's *Theorie des Erzahlens*." *Poetics Today* 2.2 (1981): 157–82.

Collins, Martha. "The Narrator, the Satellites and Isabel Archer: Point of View in *The Portrait of a Lady*." *Studies in the Novel* 8 (1976): 142–57.

Craig, David M. "The Indeterminacy of the End: Maggie Verver and the Limits of Imagination." *The Henry James Review* 3.2 (Winter, 1982): 133–44.

Ellis, John. Review of *Transparent Minds*. *The Journal of English and Germanic Philology* 80.2 (1981): 308–11.

Firebaugh, Joseph J. "The Ververs." *Essays in Criticism* IV (Oct. 1954): 400–410.

Foltiner, H. Review of *Transparent Minds*. *Modern Language Review* 76 (1981): 645–46.

Gunter, Susan. Review of William R. Goetz, *Henry James and the Darkest Abyss of Romance*. *The Henry James Review* 12.2 (Spring 1991): 188–90.

Hernadi, Paul. Review of *Transparent Minds*. *Comparative Literature* 32.2 (1980): 207–9.

Kimball, Jean. "Henry James's Last Portrait of a Lady: Charlotte Stant in *The Golden Bowl*." *American LIterature* 28.4 (Jan. 1957): 449–68.

McHale, Brian. "Islands in the Stream of Consciousness: Dorrit Cohn's *Transparent Minds*." *Poetics Today* 2.2 (1981): 183–91.

McKenzie, Malcolm. "On the Presentation of Speech and Thought in Narrative Fiction." *Theoria* (1986–7): 37–47.

McWhirter, David B. "(Re)Presenting Henry James: Authority and Intertextuality in the New York Edition." Selected Papers on Henry James. *The Henry James Review* 12.2 (Spring 1991): 137–41.

Nussbaum, Martha Craven. "Flawed Crystals: James's *The Golden Bowl* and Literature as Moral Philosophy." *New Literary History* 15 (1983): 25–50.

Seed, David. "The Narrator in Henry James's Criticism." *Philological Quarterly* 60.4 (Fall 1981): 501–18.

Short, R. W. "Henry James's World of Images." *Publications of the Modern Language Association of America* 68 (1953): 941–60.

Steele, Meili. "The Drama of Reference in James's *The Golden Bowl*." *Novel* (Fall 1987): 73–88.

Stevens, Hugh. "Sexuality and the Aesthetic in *The Golden Bowl*." *The Henry James Review* 14.1 (Winter 1993): 55–70.

Swartz, Richard. "Bewilderment and Obscurity: a Review-Essay." *The Henry James Review* 12.3 (Fall 1991): 276–81.

Tilford, John E. "James the Old Intruder." *Modern Fiction Studies* IV (Summer 1958): 175–84.

Torsney, Cheryl B. "Specula[riza]tion in *The Golden Bowl*." *The Henry James Review* 12.2 (Spring 1991): 141–45.

Van Slyck, Phyllis. "'An innate preference for the represented subject': Portraiture and Knowledge in *The Golden Bowl*." *The Henry James Review* 15. 2 (Spring 1994): 179–89.

Walton, Patricia L. "'A mistress of shades': Maggie as Reviser in *The Golden Bowl*." *The Henry James Review* 13 (1991–2): 143–53.

Ward, J. A. "The Ambiguities of Henry James." *Sewanee Review* 83 (1975): 39–60.

Watts, Eileen H. "*The Golden Bowl:* A Theory of Metaphor." *Modern Language Studies* 13 (Fall 1983): 169–76.

Young, Arlene. "Hypothetical Discourse as *Ficelle* in *The Golden Bowl*." *American Literature* 61.3 (October 1989): 382–97.

Index